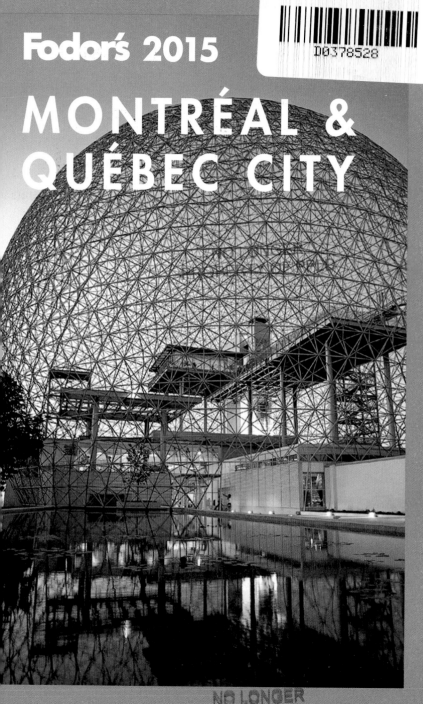

Fodor's 2015

MONTRÉAL &
QUÉBEC CITY

D0378528

WELCOME TO MONTRÉAL AND QUÉBEC CITY

France's old-world charm lives on in Montréal and Québec City, two enchanting Canadian cities with rich pasts. Their French heritage is ever-present, from the language to wonderful food to pockets of cobblestoned streets. Cosmopolitan Montréal rocks with lively cultural and shopping scenes; smaller Québec City is jam-packed with history. Visits are lovely year-round: summer brings festivals galore; spring and fall are perfect for city strolls and countryside jaunts; and winter, despite the cold, heats up with Winter Carnival, hot chocolate, and snow sports.

TOP REASONS TO GO

★ **French food:** *Haute* to hearty—including *poutine*, fries with cheese curds and gravy.

★ **Shopping:** Fashion-forward local designers, top-notch cold-weather wear, Inuit art.

★ **Festivals:** From Winter Carnival to Jazz Fest, Quebecers throw great parties all year.

★ **History:** Museums, monuments, and ancient fortifications bring the past to life.

★ **Hockey:** Tickets for Habs games are hard to get, but catch a game on TV at a local bar.

★ **Fun in the snow:** Winter brings ice-skating, tobogganing, skiing, and snowshoeing.

Fodor's MONTRÉAL & QUÉBEC CITY 2015

Publisher: Amanda D'Acierno, *Senior Vice President*

Editorial: Arabella Bowen, *Editor in Chief*; Linda Cabasin, *Editorial Director*

Design: Tina Malaney, *Associate Art Director*; Chie Ushio, *Senior Designer*; Ann McBride, *Production Designer*

Photography: Jennifer Arnow, *Senior Photo Editor*; Jennifer Romains, *Photo Researcher*

Production: Linda Schmidt, *Managing Editor*; Evangelos Vasilakis, *Associate Managing Editor*; Angela L. McLean, *Senior Production Manager*

Maps: Rebecca Baer, *Senior Map Editor*; David Lindroth, Mark Stroud (Moon Street Cartography), *Cartographers*

Sales: Jacqueline Lebow, *Sales Director*

Marketing & Publicity: Heather Dalton, *Marketing Director*; Katherine Punia, *Publicity Director*

Business & Operations: Susan Livingston, *Vice President, Strategic Business Planning*; Sue Daulton, *Vice President, Operations*

Fodors.com: Megan Bell, *Executive Director, Revenue & Business Development*; Yasmin Marinaro, *Senior Director, Marketing & Partnerships*

Writers: Chris Barry, Rémy Charest, Marcella DeVincenzo, Joanne Latimer, Vanessa Muri, Mayssam Samaha

Lead Editor: Kristan Schiller
Contributing Editor: John Rambow
Production Editor: Elyse Rozelle

ISBN 978-0-8041-4287-8

ISSN 1525–5867

All details in this book are based on information supplied to us at press time. Always confirm information when it matters, especially if you're making a detour to visit a specific place. Fodor's expressly disclaims any liability, loss, or risk, personal or otherwise, that is incurred as a consequence of the use of any of the contents of this book.

SPECIAL SALES

This book is available at special discounts for bulk purchases for sales promotions or premiums. For more information, e-mail specialmarkets@penguinrandomhouse.com

PRINTED IN THE UNITED STATES OF AMERICA

10 9 8 7 6 5 4 3 2 1

CONTENTS

1 EXPERIENCE MONTRÉAL AND
QUÉBEC CITY 9
Montréal and Québec City Today . . .10
What's Where 12
Montréal and Québec City
Top Attractions. 14
Montréal and Québec City
Top Experiences 16
Montréal and Québec City
Like a Local. 18
Montréal and Québec City
With Kids 20
Free and Almost Free
Things to Do 21
Great Itineraries 22
Montréal and Québec City's
Best Festivals 24
A Food-Lover's Tour of Montréal . . .26
How to Speak French Canadian . . .28

2 EXPLORING MONTRÉAL 29
Welcome to Montréal 30
Planning. 34
Old Montréal (Vieux-Montréal)
and the Lachine Canal 36
Downtown and Chinatown 47
The Latin Quarter and
the Village 57
The Plateau, Outremont, Mile End,
and Little Italy 60
Parc du Mont-Royal. 66
Côte-des-Neiges. 70
Hochelaga-Maisonneuve. 74
The Islands 80

3 NIGHTLIFE 85
Planning. 87
Nightlife Reviews 87

4 THE PERFORMING ARTS 101

Planning. 102
Performing Arts Reviews 103

5 SHOPPING 111
Planning. 112
Montréal Shop Reviews 114

6 SPORTS AND
THE OUTDOORS 131

7 WHERE TO EAT 141
Best Bets for Montréal Dining . . .143
Eat like a Local 144
Montréal Dining Planner. 146
Montréal Restaurant Reviews. . . .146

8 WHERE TO STAY 177
Planning. 178
Montréal Hotel Reviews 180
Best Bets for Montréal Lodging . .181

9 SIDE TRIPS FROM
MONTRÉAL 193
Welcome to Side Trips
from Montréal 194
The Laurentians 197
The Outaouais 209
The Eastern Townships. 215

10 QUÉBEC CITY 231
Welcome to Québec City 232
A Walk Through Québec City's
History. 234
Québec City Planner 237
Upper Town 238
Lower Town. 253
Outside the Old City 260
Where to Eat. 264
Best Bets for Québec City
Dining 266
Where to Stay 275

CONTENTS

Best Bets for Québec City
Lodging 278
Nightlife and Performing Arts 284
Sports and Outdoor Activities . . . 287
Shopping 293

11 SIDE TRIPS FROM
QUÉBEC CITY 297
Welcome to Side Trips from
Québec City 298
Côte-de-Beaupré 302
Île d'Orléans 308
Charlevoix 315

FRENCH VOCABULARY 325
Menu Guide 331

TRAVEL SMART MONTRÉAL
AND QUÉBEC CITY 335

INDEX 349

ABOUT OUR WRITERS 367

The Laurentians and
the Outaouais 199
The Eastern Townships 217
Upper Town (Haute-Ville) 240
The Fortifications 244
Lower Town (Basse-Ville) 255
Outside the Old City 261
Where to Eat and Stay
in Québec City 276–277
Côte de Beaupré and
Île d'Orléans 304
Charlevoix 316
Montréal métro 368

MAPS

Old Montréal 39
Downtown and Chinatown 48
The Underground City 54
Latin Quarter and the Village 58
The Plateau, Mile End,
Little Italy, & Outremont 61
Parc du Mont-Royal and Environs . . 68
Côte-des-Neiges 71
Hochelaga-Maisonneuve 75
Olympic Park and
Botanical Gardens 78
The Islands 81
Montréal Nightlife 88
Montréal Shopping 113
Where to Eat in Montréal . . . 148–149
Where to Stay in Montréal . . 182–183

ABOUT
THIS GUIDE

Fodor's Recommendations

Everything in this guide is worth doing—we don't cover what isn't—but exceptional sights, hotels, and restaurants are recognized with additional accolades. **Fodor's**Choice ★ indicates our top recommendations; and **Best Bets** call attention to notable hotels and restaurants in various categories. Care to nominate a new place? Visit Fodors.com/contact-us.

Trip Costs

We list prices wherever possible to help you budget well. Hotel and restaurant price categories from **$** to **$$$$** are noted alongside each recommendation. For hotels, we include the lowest cost of a standard double room in high season. For restaurants, we cite the average price of a main course at dinner or, if dinner isn't served, at lunch. For attractions, we always list adult admission fees; discounts are usually available for children, students, and senior citizens.

Hotels

Our local writers vet every hotel to recommend the best overnights in each price category, from budget to expensive. Unless otherwise specified, you can expect private bath, phone, and TV in your room. For expanded hotel reviews, facilities, and deals visit Fodors.com.

Top Picks
★ **Fodor's**Choice

Listings
⊠ Address
⊠ Branch address
☎ Telephone
🖷 Fax
⊕ Website
✉ E-mail
🎟 Admission fee
🕐 Open/closed times
Ⓜ Subway
✛ Directions or Map coordinates

Hotels &
Restaurants
🏨 Hotel
🛏 Number of rooms
🍴 Meal plans
✕ Restaurant
🍷 Reservations
👔 Dress code
💳 No credit cards
$ Price

Other
⇨ See also
☞ Take note
🏌 Golf facilities

Restaurants

Unless we state otherwise, restaurants are open for lunch and dinner daily. We mention dress code only when there's a specific requirement and reservations only when they're essential or not accepted. To make restaurant reservations, visit Fodors.com.

Credit Cards

The hotels and restaurants in this guide typically accept credit cards. If not, we'll say so.

EUGENE FODOR

Hungarian-born Eugene Fodor (1905–91) began his travel career as an interpreter on a French cruise ship. The experience inspired him to write *On the Continent* (1936), the first guidebook to receive annual updates and discuss a country's way of life as well as its sights. Fodor later joined the U.S. Army and worked for the OSS in World War II. After the war, he kept up his intelligence work while expanding his guidebook series. During the Cold War, many guides were written by fellow agents who understood the value of insider information. Today's guides continue Fodor's legacy by providing travelers with timely coverage, insider tips, and cultural context.

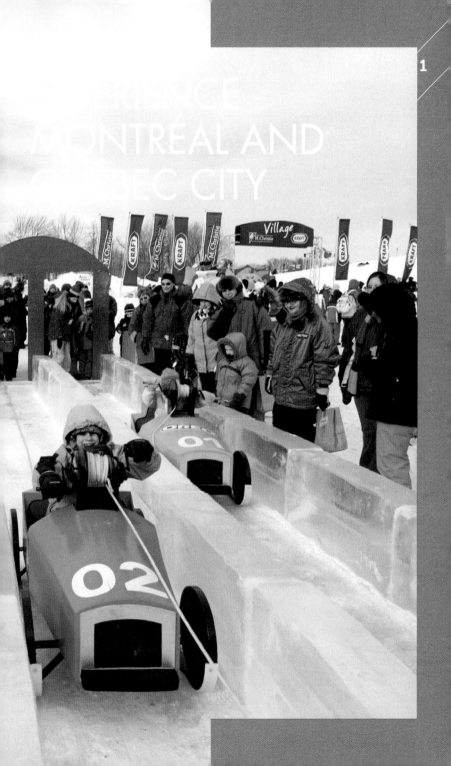

1

EXPERIENCE
MONTRÉAL AND
QUÉBEC CITY

MONTRÉAL AND QUÉBEC CITY TODAY

Ask Quebecers what they think of their city, and they'll rattle off tons of things to improve: potholes, bureaucratic corruption, construction strikes, parking meters, and the list goes on. Then ask them if they would move anywhere else in the world, and the answer is always a confident no. Any indication that the cold weather is gone and Quebecers will head to an outdoor terrace.

Locals in both Québec City and Montréal enjoy their city in the summer, with after-work drinks, picnics on the weekends, volleyball in the many parks, and with impromptu rendezvous outdoors. One of the most important rules here is to absorb as much sunlight as possible before the snow plows arrive to roar down the streets yet again. The European feel makes locals proud to call Québec their home—and it's a vibe that remains active, as exiles from France and Italy make their way to this province to find work in their native languages.

There's Music in the Air

With the massive success of home-grown band, Arcade Fire, international record labels are paying more and more attention to the city. The emerging Montréal music scene is comparable to Seattle's Indie music explosion of the 1990s. Bands such as the Sam Roberts Band, Half Moon Run, and Chromeo are making Montréal concert halls the place to be.

Political Progress

Quebecers went to the polling stations in April 2014 and the result surprised not just locals but all Canadians, when the incumbent separatist party, the Parti-Québécois, lost by a majority vote to the Liberal Party. With the Liberals now in power, talk of provincial separation has ceased, discussions about the controversial Charter of Values have been shelved, and the "Pastagate" nonsense—in which the French-language police, responsible for the preservation of the language, wanted to ban the word "pasta" from an Italian restaurant menu—has ended.

On the municipal level, Montréal's new mayor, Denis Coderre is a young, hip, charismatic politician who loves hockey and his city with equal zeal. He saved the bankrupted Bixi bike-share scheme, hates graffiti, and promises to make Montréal a top tourist destination in North America. Things are looking good.

WHAT WE'RE TALKING ABOUT

Food Trucks are here to stay! The 2013 pilot project was such a huge success that the city decided to keep it going, and there are now 40 official food trucks in 14 fixed locations. We're not talking hot dog carts here; the Montréal food trucks represent the excellences of the city's great culinary landscape, with pulled-pork sandwiches, gourmet grilled cheese, oysters, dim sum, and other artisanal treats. You can check them out in one location on the first Friday of every month (May through October) when they all congregate at the Olympic Stadium Park. Come hungry.

Locals and visitors who love fast cars and loud engines,

The Arts Make a Splash

Things are looking up in Montréal's Downtown arts district, the Quartier des Spectacles, as it continues to expand and grow. It's also the only place in the world with year-round artistic projections on the building facades and windows. Enjoy the views, but watch your step—water fountains shoot up beneath many of its concrete walkways.

As for Québec City, it's emerging as a premier stop for summer concerts and festivals. On the Plains of Abraham, outdoor performances accommodate more than 250,000 spectators, and people come from all over to watch under the stars. Past performers such as Madonna, Celine Dion, Paul McCartney, and Rush have helped put Québec City on the entertainment map, and in 2014, Journey and Lady Gaga entertained fans.

Sports Fans in High Places

Montréal's soccer team, The Impact, began competing in Major League Soccer in 2012. After that the fan base increased—and adding the popular (and hunky) Italian heavyweights such as Marco De Vaio and Argentinian midfielder Ignacio Piatti probably didn't hurt with bringing in some new fans, either.

Not wanting to feel left out, Québec City's mayor, Regis Labeaume, has decided that one of his priorities will be getting an NHL team back in town. He's building a C$400-million stadium, scheduled to be ready by the fall of 2015, but there's no team yet: "if you build it, they will come" seems to be the thinking.

Pedal Power

Montréal has come a long way since its 2009 introduction of Bixi, the bike-rental scheme that has since expanded to New York City, London, Chicago, and many other cities. Using the system, you pay to take a bicycle from a rental station and then leave it at a station near your destination. Every year more bike paths are added to city streets (there are at least 500 km [300 miles] of them now), much to the chagrin of some drivers. In 2014 came with the announcement that Bixi had gone bankrupt, but after some discussions, the new Montréal mayor, Denis Coderre, stepped in and said the city would take over ownership for at least one year. Much remains to be seen for the future, but many think the city will continue to keep it going. Fans of the scheme have their fingers crossed.

and are ready to party for a whole weekend, will be happy to hear that the Grand Prix of Montréal got renewed for another 10 years. Earplugs not included.

People are also talking about what's going on underground. With the extension of the subway line complete to the north of the island, the focus now is eastbound, with the Blue Line set to extend as far as Anjou. There are also plans for the Yellow Line to extend to Longueuil, and the Orange Line to reach Bois-Franc. It's believed the additional stops will be completed by the early 2020s.

WHAT'S WHERE

1 Montréal. Both Montréal and the island on which it stands take their name from Mont-Royal, a stubby plug of tree-covered igneous rock that rises high above the surrounding cityscape. This is a bustling, multiethnic city of neighborhoods, from the historic Old City to the hip Plateau.

2 The Laurentians. The Laurentians (les Laurentides) encompass thousands of miles of forests, mountains, and lakes, but for many people the draw is Mont-Tremblant and its world-class ski slopes. At just 1½ hours' drive from Montréal, the area has also become a favorite weekend golf destination.

3 The Eastern Townships. Called les Cantons de l'Est in French, the Eastern Townships region has quaint architecture and rolling hills that might remind you of New England. Atop imposing Mont-Mégantic, you're 3,150 feet closer to the heavens. Far from city lights, the sky here is ideal for stargazing.

4 The Outaouais. Bordering the Ottawa River, the Outaouais is known for its many lakes, majestic views, hiking trails, and interesting wildlife, as well as the imposing Château Montebello, often called the world's largest log cabin.

5 Québec City. The capital of the province of Québec is the most French city in North America. Québec's Old City (Vieux Québec) is split into two tiers, separated by steep rock against which are more than 25 *escaliers* (staircases) and a funicular. The surrounding cluster of small, low-rise neighborhoods each have their own charm and flavor.

6 Île d'Orléans. Famed for its wine and cider as well as its strawberry crop and other local produce, the Île d'Orléans is often called the "Garden of Québec." Made up of six small villages, this charming island has several bed-and-breakfasts and fabulous farm stands.

7 Côte de Beaupré. The coast hugged by the St. Lawrence River embraces the thundering Montmorency Falls and the impressive Ste-Anne-de-Beaupré shrine. It leads to Mont-Sainte-Anne, famous for its skiing, golfing, and mountain biking.

8 Charlevoix. The big bang of an ancient meteor created picturesque valleys, cliffs, and mountains that brush the St. Lawrence River. This Canadian Switzerland has inspired painters, poets, and musicians for generations.

Mont-Tremblant

THE LAURENTIANS

La Saint-P

2

TO OUTAOUAIS **4**

Berthierville **40**

15 St Jérôme **25**

Le Gardeur

Saint-Josep de-So

Boisbriand

Douv

Oka

20

Montréal **1**

Beloe

Candia

Mercier

Salaberry-de-Valleyfield MONTÉRÉGIE

Ibervil

CANADA

UNITED STATE

NEW YORK

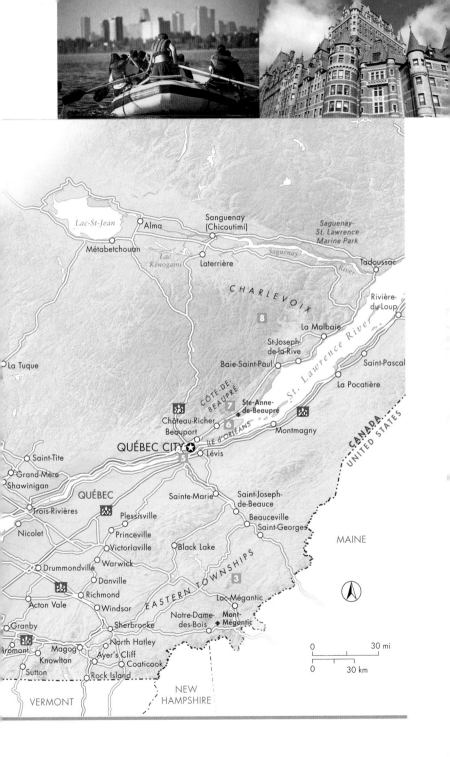

Lac-St-Jean
Alma
Sanguenay (Chicoutimi)
Saguenay-St. Lawrence Marine Park
Métabetchouan
Lac Kénogami
Laterrière
Saguenay River
Tadoussac
CHARLEVOIX
Rivière-du-Loup
8
La Malbaie
St-Joseph-de-la-Rive
La Tuque
Baie-Saint-Paul
Saint-Pascal
St. Lawrence River
CÔTE-DE-BEAUPRÉ
7 Ste-Anne-de-Beaupré
La Pocatière
73
Château-Richer
6
Beauport
ÎLE d'ORLÉANS
20
Montmagny
QUÉBEC CITY
Lévis
CANADA
UNITED STATES
Saint-Tite
35
Grand-Mère
Shawinigan
QUÉBEC
Sainte-Marie
Saint-Joseph-de-Beauce
Trois-Rivières
20
Plessisville
Beauceville
Saint-Georges
MAINE
Nicolet
Princeville
Victoriaville
Black Lake
Warwick
Drummondville
Danville
3
55
Richmond
Acton Vale
Windsor
EASTERN TOWNSHIPS
Lac-Mégantic
Granby
Sherbrooke
Notre-Dame-des-Bois
Mont-Mégantic
10
North Hatley
Magog
Ayer's Cliff
Bromont
Knowlton
Coaticook
0   30 mi
Sutton
Rock Island
0   30 km
VERMONT
NEW HAMPSHIRE

MONTRÉAL AND QUÉBEC CITY TOP ATTRACTIONS

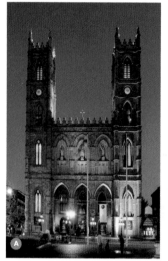

Basilique Notre-Dame-de-Montréal, Montréal

(A) Everything about Montréal's magnificent Roman Catholic basilica is grand, from the 228-foot twin steeples to the 7,000-pipe organ in the loft. The thousands of stars spattered across the vaulted blue ceiling are 24-carat gold and were painstakingly applied by hand. To experience a bit of heavenly pomp and hear the choir sing and the organ roar, consider attending the 11 am Mass on Sunday.

Parc du Mont-Royal, Montréal

(B) The modest mountain that gives Montréal its name is at the center of a 500-acre park with wooded trails, a trio of chalets, and splendid views from the city's highest point. City-weary people flirt here in spring, picnic in summer, enjoy the colors of autumn, and skate in winter.

Mont-Tremblant, Side Trips from Montréal

(C) This towering peak of the Laurentian Mountains, northwest of Montréal, has become one of North America's finest ski resorts, with 650 acres of skiable terrain, state-of-the-art snowmaking and lift equipment, first-class lodging, and an on-slope village of shops and restaurants.

Musée des Beaux-Arts de Montréal, Montréal

(D) One of Canada's oldest museums has an exceptional collection of Canadian art, from portrayals of pioneer life by Paul Kane to dazzling abstractions by Paul-Émile Borduas, all housed in a former church. The permanent collection features works by such world masters as Rembrandt, Renoir, and Picasso.

The Old Port, Montréal

In Montréal's Old Port, centuries-old warehouses now house art galleries, ice-cream parlors, and other attractions. It's

one of the city's most popular parks: a place to cycle, stroll, or take a jet-boat ride on the Lachine Rapids.

La Citadelle, Québec City

(E) The fascinating star-shaped fortress on Québec City's Cap Diamant is the largest fortified base in North America still occupied by troops. Built in the 1800s to protect the city from an American invasion that never came, La Citadelle is currently home to Canada's Royal 22nd Regiment. Every summer morning at 10 am, the regiment turns out in scarlet tunics and bearskin caps for the changing of the guard.

Fairmont Le Château Frontenac, Québec City

(F) The most photographed sight in Québec City, the Fairmont Le Château Frontenac towers above 18th- and 19th-century houses, which are now shops and bistros. At the hotel's base is Terrasse Dufferin, a wide boardwalk with sweeping views of the St. Lawrence River and the Laurentian Mountains.

Tadoussac, Side Trips from Québec City

This old trading post north of Québec City, situated at the confluence of the St. Lawrence and Saguenay rivers, is now a major whale-watching destination. You may see minke, finback, and even blue whales, but more commonly the southernmost colony of beluga whales. Watch them from shore, or sign up for a cruise to get a closer look.

Plains of Abraham, Québec City

It's a peaceful city park now, full of winding walking paths and bicycle trails, and a favorite in winter of Québec City's cross-country skiers. But on September 13, 1759, it was anything but peaceful, when British troops defeated the French in a half-hour and changed North American history forever.

MONTRÉAL AND QUÉBEC CITY TOP EXPERIENCES

À la Française

Steeped in the traditions and the language of its mother country, Québec has a distinctly Continental flavor. Where else in North America can you relax on the terrace at a bistro, sipping a café au lait while listening to everyone around you debate politics or popular culture in French?

Québec is a little like the European country next door, the France you can drive to in less than a day from many parts of the United States. It's different from anything just south, or north, or east, or west of its borders. The people who reside in this relatively laid-back part of the world—French, English, and newcomers from around the world—share an approach to life that is uniquely Quebecois. Locals are warm, intriguing, and gracious hosts. From the magnificent architecture of the grand basilicas to the trendy terraces lining the hipper enclaves of Montréal's Plateau district, the French face of Québec is omnipresent, and one of the most charming elements of this destination.

You can immerse yourself in French culture at several venues. The plays of such prominent Quebecois writers as Michel Tremblay command the stages of French-language theaters, including the Théâtre du Nouveau Monde and the historic Monument-National. The stately Grande Bibliothèque Nationale du Québec is home to more than a million books in French and English, with special collections for children and visually challenged readers. The Université de Montréal houses 18 libraries and several world-renowned research centers. With 60,000 students and a sprawling campus, it's one of the top universities in the French-speaking world.

Savor French and Local Cuisine

The Quebecois take their food very seriously. Traveling through most cities and towns you won't have to look too hard to find a restaurant serving traditional French fare and regional specialties. Many restaurants serve *cuisine du terroir* (food of the region) using ingredients like lamb, veal, bison, caribou, and foie gras. These temples of gastronomy create artful dishes, usually with a contemporary flair. But not everything in Québec is *haute*. A far cry from fine dining is the time-honored and much-cherished *casse croûte* (snack bar), where you can chow down on comfort foods like steamies or toasties (hot dogs) and chicken sandwiches with gravy. Every visitor has to sample *poutine*, a heap of french fries topped with gravy and melted cheese curds. And your best bet for a quick lunch might be a simple ham-and-cheese baguette from a great *boulangerie* (bakery).

Québec is one of the largest maple syrup producers in the world, so a visit to a traditional *cabane à sucre* (sugar shack) is a ritual that comes every spring with the maple syrup harvest. There's no better way to sample the province's wares than by stopping by one of these rural establishments for a home-cooked meal that may include pea soup, baked beans, eggs with ham, and deep-fried pork rinds called *les oreilles de Crisse* (Christ's ears), a slightly irreverent nod to the region's Catholic upbringing.

That said, the region's food also goes way beyond French, especially in Montréal. The city's long-established Jewish community has contributed bagels and smoked-meat sandwiches. The city also enjoys a world-beat of national treasures like Arabic shish kebab, Chinese dim sum,

Spanish tapas, Vietnamese spring rolls, and Lebanese tabbouleh.

Romp in the Snow

Ice-skating, cross-country skiing, tobogganing—the Quebecois embrace winter with enthusiasm. It's the best way to cope with the weather, since from mid-December until mid-April the province is covered in snow and often bitterly cold.

With much of the landscape blanketed in the white stuff for months at a time, it's not surprising that Québec has taken great pains to nurture its reputation as one of the top winter vacation destinations in North America. Fans of winter sports can revel in the thrilling adventures of dog sledding, ice fishing, and kite skiing on frozen lakes. You don't have to worry about staying warm because outfitters provide weatherproof gear. Globe-Trotter Aventure Canada Tours (☎ *888/598–7688* ⊕ *www.aventurecanada.com*) is one operator that organizes excursions lasting from a few hours to a full week.

The mountain-filled province has about 75 ski resorts. Skiers and snowboarders can enjoy a day on the slopes for C$40–C$60 a day at Mont-Blanc in the Laurentians, Owl's Head and Mont-Sutton in the Eastern Townships, Le Massif in Charlevoix, and Mont-Sainte-Anne near Québec City. Mont-Tremblant, northwest of Montréal, is pricier, but it's Eastern Canada's largest ski area, with a stylish slope-side village, five-star lodgings, and the fancy Casino de Mont Tremblant. Try night skiing at Mont-Saint-Sauveur (northwest of Montréal), Ski Bromont (Eastern Townships), or Mont-Sainte-Anne. The snow takes on a luminescent glow under the lights and the stars provide a little extra sparkle.

For a tamer ride, hop aboard one of the classic horse-drawn sleighs that glide through the streets of Montréal or Québec City.

Shop for Fur and Crafts

People have traveled to Canada to seek out furs ever since the early 1600s. The fur industry still generates about C$800 million annually and employs about 60,000 trappers and 5,000 fur farmers, manufacturers, craftspeople, and retailers. Mink, fox, and chinchilla are the most commonly farmed fur-bearing animals in Canada. Trappers in the wild, many of them First Nations Canadians, also supply beaver, raccoon, muskrat, otter, bear, seal, and wolf pelts. In Montréal, the best bargains are found in shops near rue Bleury and boulevard de Maisonneuve. However, most furriers have moved north to 9250 rue Parc in the rue Chabanel fashion district. Harricana on rue Atwater is an atelier for unique, stylish accessories like backpacks and boas made from recycled furs. In Québec City, try Richard Robitaille Fourrures in the Old City. You can pick up a toasty fur hat for about C$100 or splurge on a glamorous mink coat for around C$5,000.

Arguably, it was the fur trade that allowed many of Canada's First Nations peoples to live according to the traditions of their ancestors, which explains why Canada has such a rich heritage of native crafts. Québec's best-known crafts are wood carving, weaving, pine cabinetry, leather and bead work, and canoe making. For guaranteed authenticity, look for the Canadian government's igloo symbol on crafts and the Beautifully Canadian logo on furs.

MONTRÉAL AND QUÉBEC CITY LIKE A LOCAL

Visiting Montréal and Québec City is like stumbling upon a little corner of Europe in North America. Soak up the rich French culture by sampling local cuisine, meet up with a friend at a sidewalk terrace café and watch people go by, or finding yourself in the midst of some fabulous all-night party.

Try Some Poutine

The legend is that sometime in 1957 a customer walked into Le Café Idéal in the village of Warwick and asked owner Fernand Lachance to add a handful of cheese curds to his order of *frites-sauce* (fries and gravy). Lachance served the result while muttering "Quelle poutine!"—roughly translated as "What a mess!"

And so was born what has become Québec's favorite fast food. Poutine is everywhere, even at McDonald's. But it's no longer just hot french fries topped with cheese curds and a ladleful of thick brown gravy, as dozens of high- and lowbrow variations have sprung up.

Top chefs, for instance, use duck gravy instead of the usual gelatinous brown sauce, or blue cheese instead of curds. Martin Picard at Montréal's Au Pied de Cochon drew rave reviews for his foie gras poutine, and Chuck Hughes of Montréal's Garde-Manger won TV's *Iron Chef* competition with lobster poutine.

Enjoy Hockey Night

What soccer is to Brazilians and baseball is to Americans, hockey is to the Quebecois. It's not a game, it's a religion, and its winter-long rites are celebrated in hundreds of arenas across the province.

On weekend mornings, bleary-eyed parents hunker down in the stands watching their children practice. At 10 pm the beer-sponsored leagues take over the ice—men and women with full-time jobs strap on the skates and pads just for the fun of it.

If you can afford the scalpers' ticket prices (or if you have a friend with connections), catch a Montréal Canadiens game at the Centre Bell. The province's only National Hockey League team hasn't won a Stanley Cup since 1993, but a night watching the Habs—as they're known locally—is an experience to savor.

Attend a Cinq-à-sept

If someone invites you to what sounds like a "sank-a-sett," it has nothing to do with swimming or tennis. It's a *cinq-à-sept*, a cocktail party that's supposed to happen between 5 and 7 pm but that rarely starts before 6 pm and usually ends around 8 or 8:30 pm.

The true 5-à-7 isn't to be confused with a raucous 2-for-1 happy hour. The *cinq-à-sept is* a more refined affair, where conversation is at least as important as the drinks. Neither should it be confused with the tradition of the same name in France—where it was (and maybe, for some, still is) the after-work hours when businessmen would visit their mistresses!

One of the essential skills you should master before attending your first 5-à-7 is the two-cheek kiss. The secret to perfecting this Continental-style greeting is capturing the middle ground between the air kiss and the passionate enthusiastic smack of long-separated lovers. A light cheek brush, something that expresses delight, is just about right.

Embrace the Outdoors

Quebecers are crazy about the great outdoors, no matter what time of year. Cycling trails crisscross Montréal and Québec City, making good use of canal routes, former railroad track beds, and even major Downtown streets. One of

the most popular outings is a ride along a section of La Route Verte, a 5,000-km (3,100-mile) network of bike trails. **Fitz and Follwell Co.** (☎ 514/754–3691 ⊕ *www.fitzandfollwell.com*) arranges tours through Montréal that include hot chocolate, fresh bagels, and a lunch of poutine.

In winter, why try to avoid the weather when it's better to join the frosty fun? In Montréal, try ice-skating in Parc Lafontaine and cross-country skiing, snowshoeing, and snow tubing on Mont-Royal. In Québec City there's ice-skating at Place d'Youville, cross-country skiing on the Plains of Abraham, and tobogganing near the Château Frontenac.

Soak in a Nordic Spa

Quebecers have pioneered the concept of Nordic spas in America. Based on a 1,000-year-old Viking tradition, a Nordic spa sojourn consists of alternating between soaking in outdoor hot tubs, baking in saunas, and plunging into icy waters. Add a Turkish steam bath and a Swedish massage and you're cooked.

Also known as thermo-therapy, the experience is gently invigorating yet totally relaxing. Clad in swimsuits, spa-goers dash from a hot whirlpool into an icy pond, then heat up again in a sweltering steam bath and chill out under a cold waterfall. You'll be hot, cold, and hot again, for hours, marinating in the aromas of eucalyptus and pine or the fresh mountain air. It's especially fun in winter, when snow banks surround the whirlpools. The pioneer of Québec's Nordic spas is the Polar Bear's Club, which opened about 25 years ago in the Laurentians. Now, with approximately 40 Nordic spas in the province, this watery adventure is *de rigueur* after sports, shopping, or a stressful day. Expect to pay C$45 to C$55 for

the experience, including robe, towel, and locker. Massages and other treatments are extra. *See Chapter 10, Québec City, for more information on Nordic Spas*

Drink Some Beer

Not so long ago, a pint of Ex (Molson's Export Ale) or a tin of Blue (Labatt's Pilsner) were the staples of sports bars, taverns, and brasseries. Things have changed in the Canadian beer world, as microbreweries have entered the beer scene. Their products have taken their place alongside the best beers from Belgium, England, Germany, and, yes, the United States. In Québec, brewers tend to choose apocalyptic labels like Maudite (Damned) and La Fin du Monde (End of the World).

Linger at Sidewalk Cafés

There's something about surviving the harsh winters—which Québec winters still unquestionably are—that makes it particularly sweet to spend long summer evenings sipping drinks under the open sky. Alfresco dining blooms as early as May, when it still can be quite chilly, especially at night. But when locals have been cooped up indoors for months, a few buds on the trees or a few crocuses in the garden are enough to lure diners outside to sidewalk tables with colorful umbrellas or awnings. These *terrasses* are perfect for watching the passing parade of people.

MONTRÉAL AND QUÉBEC CITY WITH KIDS

There's no shortage of fantastic activities in Montréal and Québec City for kids. Here's a sampling of what the little ones might enjoy during a visit.

Montréal

Montréal's popular rent-a-bicycle **Bixi** system is a great way for families to see the city. The expanding network of car-free cycling paths now meanders around Parc du Mont-Royal and through Old Montréal, across Parc Jean-Drapeau on Île Notre-Dame, and along the Lachine Canal.

Kids who've had their fill of churches and museums can expend some pent-up energy at the adjacent **Old Port,** which has boats to pedal, a clock tower to climb, and a maze. There's also a new waterfront beach, but alas, no swimming is allowed.

For culturally adventurous youngsters, there are outdoor dance and theater presentations at **Parc Lafontaine.** Kids can also explore the mysteries of bonsai trees and Chinese gardens at the **Jardin Botanique** and drop into the on-site **Insectarium** to see the world's largest collection of bugs.

On hot summer days, spend some time at the Quartier des Spectacles, where the large fountains spread along the street will provide some fun and surely cool off your kids. You may even see some adults jumping in too.

Québec City

Ice-cream stands, street performers, and (in winter) a thrilling toboggan run make **Terrasse Dufferin** as entertaining for children as for adults, as do the **Plains of Abraham's** open spaces.

Place Royale in the Lower Town brings the 17th and 18th centuries to life for even the youngest children.

La Citadelle's changing-of-the-guard ceremony, complete with the Royal 22e Régiment's mascot, Batisse the Goat, has lots of kid appeal. The hands-on exhibits at the **Musée de la Civilisation** and the 19th-century jail cells preserved in the **Musée de Québec** are both must-see attractions.

And for a little animal fun, polar bears, seals, and walruses are the stars of the city's **Aquarium du Québec.**

Side Trips from Montréal and Québec City

In the Laurentians, the gentle rides of the **Au Pays des Merveilles** and the **Village du Père Noël** (Santa's Village) are perfect for younger children. There are plenty of thrills at the **Water Parks** at Mont-St-Sauveur in the Laurentians and Bromont in the Eastern Townships.

Montmorency Falls, on the Côte de Beaupré, aren't as grand as Niagara, but they're higher, and crossing the suspension bridge above the spectacular chutes of water is a thrill. Farther along the St. Lawrence coast in **Tadoussac** you can take a boat ride for an up-close encounter with whales (be careful not to get saltwater in your camera or phone).

FREE AND ALMOST FREE THINGS TO DO

There might be no such thing as a free lunch in Montréal or Québec City, but plenty of other things are free, or nearly so.

Art

Admission to the permanent collections of Montréal's Musée des Beaux-Arts (⊕ *www.mbam.qc.ca*) and Québec City's Musée National des Beaux-Arts (⊕ *www.mnba.qc.ca*) is always free. The Musée d'Art Contemporain (⊕ *www.macm.org*) is free on Wednesday nights. Every summer the city of Montréal mounts an outdoor exhibit of art or photographs on the sidewalks of avenue McGill College between rues Ste-Catherine and Sherbrooke.

Concerts

Montréal's Christ Church Cathedral (⊠ *635 rue Ste-Catherine Ouest* ☎ *514/843–6577*), a magnificent neo-Gothic treasure, and Oratoire St-Joseph (⊠ *3800 Chemin Queen-Mary* ☎ *514/733–8211*) offer free organ recitals on Sunday afternoons at 3 pm throughout the year. And Les Petits Chanteurs du Mont-Royal, one of the finest boys' choirs in North America, sings the 11 am mass at the Oratoire every Sunday from March to December 24. They also perform several free concerts through the year.

Montréal's Festival Internationale de Jazz every June and Québec City's Festival d'Été in July have dozens of free, open-air concerts. These huge happenings bring thousands, and tens of thousands, of revelers to the streets.

Fireworks

From mid-June through July, the sky comes alive with light and color on most Wednesday and Saturday evenings when fireworks teams from around the world compete in the spectacular L'International des Feux Loto-Québec. You can pay for a seat at La Ronde amusement park or join thousands of Montrealers in the Old Port, on the Jacques Cartier Bridge, and in Parc Champlain on the South Shore and watch for free.

Politics

Political junkies can join free guided tours of North America's only French-speaking legislature, the Assemblée Nationale du Québec (☎ *418/643–7239*). The parliamentary debates are on Tuesday to Thursday from August to November and February to May.

Science

McGill University's Redpath Museum (⊠ *859 rue Sherbrooke Ouest* ☎ *514/398–4086*) houses an eclectic collection of dinosaur skeletons, seashells, fossils, minerals, Egyptian mummies, and Stone Age tools in a beautiful 19th-century building. Watch for free lectures.

Sightseeing

For one of the best views of Québec City, take the C$3.25 ferry (⊠ *10 rue des Traversiers* ☎ *418/643–8420*) for a mini-cruise across the St. Lawrence River to Lévis and back. Or for C$2.25, ride the Funiculaire du Vieux-Québec (⊠ *16 rue Petit-Champlain* ☎ *418/692–1132*), the sharply vertical railway that creaks along the cliff from Lower Town to Upper Town.

GREAT ITINERARIES

Montréal and Québec City are perfect for long weekend trips, although if you'd like to see both areas, you could easily spend a week.

Essential Montréal in a Day

Start with a stroll to the peak of Mont-Royal, the city's most enduring natural symbol. Afterward, wander south on avenue du Parc and through McGill University's leafy campus to Downtown. The Musée des Beaux-Arts de Montréal, on rue Sherbrooke, was once the bastion of the Anglo-Canadian establishment, and is worth a visit.

For a Francophone perspective, head from Mont-Royal (the mountain) along rue Mont-Royal (the street) to rue St-Denis, home to funky boutiques and a boisterous strip of bars near the Université du Québec à Montréal.

In the late afternoon head down to Old Montréal, and pop into the Basilique Notre-Dame-de-Montréal before getting in some nightlife, as in the summer months the Old City is one of the most popular places to party. There are dozens of restaurants to choose from, as well as clubs and bars.

Day Trips and Overnights from Montréal

If you have only a couple of days for a visit and you need to concentrate on one area, the Laurentians are a good choice. Less than an hour's drive from Downtown Montréal, this resort area has recreational options (depending on the season) that include golf, hiking, and superb skiing, both Alpine and cross-country.

Pick a resort town to stay in and use that as a base for visiting some of the surrounding towns. Each town has its own style and appeal: St-Sauveur-des-Monts is lively, Morin Heights is tranquil, and

Ste-Adèle is a center of gastronomy. Mont-Tremblant, a sophisticated ski and golf resort, is worth a trip, particularly for the picturesque gondola ride to the summit.

You can combine a taste of the Eastern Townships with a two-day visit to the Laurentians. After an overnight stay in the Laurentians, head back south of Montréal to the Townships, which extend to the east along the border with New England. Overnight in Granby or Bromont: Granby has a zoo, and Bromont is known for golf, skiing, and its water park.

The next day, you can shop in pretty Knowlton (look for signs to Lac Brome) and explore regional history in such towns as Valcourt. Spend a night or two in the appealing resort town of Magog, along Lac Memphrémagog, or in the quieter North Hatley, on Lac Massawippi. You'll have good dining in either. Save some time for outdoor activities, whether it's golfing, skiing, biking, or hiking.

Essential Québec City in a Day

It's inspiring to start your day in Québec's Lower Town, the earliest site of French civilization in North America. Stroll along the narrow streets of the Quartier Petit-Champlain, visit the Maison Chevalier, and browse the craft stores and boutiques. From there, head to Place Royale, making a stop at the Église Notre-Dame-des-Victoires, and continue on to Terrasse Dufferin. In the afternoon, when the crowds thin out, check out the Musée National des Beaux-Arts du Québec or the Musée Canadien de l'Histoire.

Catch a gorgeous sunset from the Plains of Abraham—site of the battle that ended France's colonial dreams in North America and marked the beginning of British rule in Canada—before dining anywhere

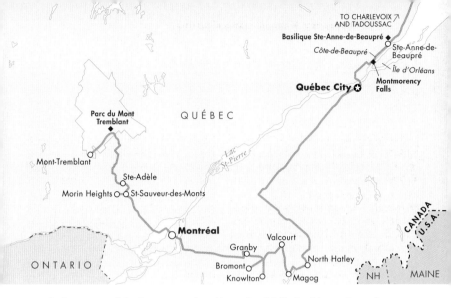

on rue St-Jean, one of the best streets in the city for restaurants and nightlife.

Day Trips and Overnights from Québec City

If you want to get out of Québec City for a day or two, take a 20-minute drive to Île d'Orléans, a picturesque island called the "garden of Québec." In summer, you can explore this idyllic island's boutiques, galleries, and food stands, then dine in a vineyard at Panache Mobile. Stay over in a cozy B&B, or continue on Route 138 northeast to Côte de Beaupré. Here you can visit the impressive Montmorency Falls and the ornate shrine at Ste-Anne-de-Beaupré. Don't miss the classic Québec cuisine of roast goose, tourtière, and sugar pie at historic Auberge Baker on Côte-de-Beaupré.

Another option is to take the Train du Massif de Charlevoix, which departs from the spectacular Parc de la Chute-Montmorency outside Québec City. It follows the St. Lawrence shore and the dramatic mountainous landscapes of Charlevoix. You'll visit the artistic community of Baie St-Paul, the impressive mountain Le Massif, and the cliff-top village of La Malbaie. You can do the rail trip in one day or stay overnight at the castlelike Fairmont Le Manoir Richelieu.

From La Malbaie, it's an hour by car to Tadoussac, at the confluence of the Saguenay and St. Lawrence rivers, where you can hop on a boat for a whale-watching excursion.

Montréal and Québec City over a Long Weekend

Looking for an ideal four-day getaway? It's possible to see the best of both cities without feeling rushed. Here's one expedient itinerary: Fly into Montréal's Trudeau International Airport on a Thursday evening, take a cab to your downtown hotel, put down your bags, and head out to grab a bite at a late-night bistro like L'Express. Spend Friday seeing the city's top sites, hit Old Montréal in the evening for dinner and nightlife, and enjoy a leisurely brunch on Saturday morning.

Rent a car from one of the many downtown rental agencies, then pack up and drive north to Québec City, which takes about three hours. Check into a B&B or boutique hotel in the Old City and spend the rest of the day exploring sites there. Spend Sunday morning in the Old City and dedicate the afternoon to the Fortifications, or take a day trip to the Côte-de-Beaupré or Île d'Orléans. On Monday, fly out of Québec City's Jean Lesage International Airport.

MONTRÉAL AND QUÉBEC CITY'S BEST FESTIVALS

January and February

Carnaval de Québec (*Québec Winter Carnival*). The biggest winter carnival in the world takes place on the Plains of Abraham over three weekends from the end of January to mid-February, with winter sports competitions, ice-sculpture contests, and parades. With its Bonhomme snowman mascot, the festival has been running for 60 years, and doesn't show any signs of slowing down. ⊠ *Plains of Abraham, Québec City, Québec* ☎ *866/422–7628* ⊕ *www.carnaval.qc.ca.*

Fête des Neiges de Montréal. Over four weekends from mid-January to mid-February, Montréal celebrates its winter festival at Parc Jean Drapeau across the Port from Old Montréal. Hockey games, tubing, skiing, dog sledding, and a Himalayan zip line are perfect activities to enjoy in the cold winter weather, but don't forget your toque. ⊠ *Montréal, Québec* ☎ *514/872–6120* ⊕ *www. parcjeandrapeau.com/events/fete-des-neiges-de-montreal* Ⓜ *Jean-Drapeau.*

Montréal en Lumière (*Montréal Highlights*). This festival brightens the bleak days of February with fabulous food and cultural activities. Leading chefs from around the world give demonstrations and take over the kitchens of top restaurants for special dinners. "Nuit Blanche," held on the last Saturday of this festival, lets you explore the city until the wee hours of the morning. ☎ *514/288–9955, 855/864–3737* ⊕ *www.montrealenlumiere.com.*

June

Fringe Festival. Open to playwrights, acting troupes, dancers, comics, and musicians, the Fringe Festival, during the first three weeks of June, is run on a lottery system to determine which performers get on stage. What you experience might be traditional, offbeat, or downright risqué, but you'll be sure to have a great time. ☎ *514/849–3378* ⊕ *www.montreal fringe.ca.*

Les FrancoFolies de Montréal. Such major Québecois stars as Isabelle Boulay, Paul Piché, and Nicola Ciccone play to packed concert halls, while lesser-known artists play free outdoor concerts during this mid-June festival celebrating the art of French songwriting. More than 1,000 musicians, many from France, Belgium, Senegal, and Haiti, perform rock, hip-hop, jazz, funk, and Latin. ☎ *514/876–8989, 855/372–6267* ⊕ *www.francofolies.com.*

Mondiale de la Bière. In Montréal, for five days every June, this beer festival transforms the exhibition hall of Palais de Congrès into a giant indoor beer garden serving some 600 ales, lagers, and ciders from nearly 100 microbreweries from Québec and around the world. Admission is free, tasting coupons are $1 each. ☎ *514/722–9640* ⊕ *www. festivalmondialbiere.qc.ca.*

July

Festival d'Été de Québec (*Québec City Summer Festival*). This exuberant 11-day music extravaganza in Québec City features rock, folk, hip-hop, and world-beat music. The main concerts rock nightly with ten indoor and outdoor stages in early July in or near Old Québec, including one on the Plains of Abraham. ☎ *418/529–5200, 888/992–5200* ⊕ *www. infofestival.com.*

Festival International de Jazz de Montréal (*Montréal International Jazz Festival*). This major event attracts more than 1,000 musicians for more than 400 concerts held over a period of nearly two weeks from the end of June through the beginning of July. Past stars have included B.B King,

Ella Fitzgerald, Lauryn Hill, Wynton Marsalis, Chick Corea, Dave Brubeck, and Canada's most famed singer-pianist, Diana Krall. ☎ *514/871–1881, 855/299–3378* ⊕ *www.montrealjazzfest.com*

Festival OFF. A sidekick of the Festival d'Été International de Québec, this event takes to the stage in July at the same time as its big brother. Most of the shows are free and take place in offbeat spaces such as in front of Église St-Jean-Baptiste, Bar Le Sacrilège, and the Musée de l'Amérique Française, just to name a few. ☎ *418/529–5200, 888/992–5200* ⊕ *www.quebecoff.org.*

Juste pour Rire (*Just for Laughs*). Montréal's world-famous comedy festival hosts international comics, in French and English, from the second through third weeks of July. There are tons of shows to watch, from big concert halls to quaint bars. Walk around the Quartier des Spectacles during the festival and giggle your way from one outdoor act to another. ☎ *514/845–2322* ⊕ *www.hahaha.com.*

L'International des Feux Loto-Québec (*International Fireworks Competition*). Join the thousands heading to Montréal's Jacques Cartier Bridge or the Old Port to watch the free fireworks show most Wednesday and Saturday nights in late June and July. The launch site for this high-in-the-sky show, set off by competing international teams, is La Ronde, on Île Ste-Hélène. ☎ *514/397–2000* ⊕ *www.montrealfeux.com.*

August

Festival International des Films du Monde (*World Film Festival*). For several days in Montréal every August, this festival presents about 400 films from all over the world, including feature films, documentaries, shorts, animation, and student productions. During the festival, Cinema Under the Stars, in the Quartier des Spectacles, screens foreign films outdoors. Go early to grab a seat or bring your own blanket. ☎ *514/848–3883* ⊕ *www.ffm-montreal.org.*

Fêtes de la Nouvelle France (*New France Festival*). During this five-day festival, in early to mid-August, Québec City's centuries-old heritage comes alive. The streets of Lower Town are transported back in time, and events range from an old-time farmers' market to games and music—all done in period costume. ☎ *418/694–3311, 866/391–3383* ⊕ *www. nouvellefrance.qc.ca.*

St-Jean-sur-Richelieu's Hot-Air Balloon Festival. This colorful airborne event, the largest gathering of hot-air balloons in Canada, takes flight about 25 minutes drive southeast of Montréal. The balloons are so vivid and plentiful that you can sometimes see them from downtown. ☎ *450/347–9555* ⊕ *www.montgolfieres.com.*

October

Black and Blue Festival. Organized by the Bad Boy Club Montréal, this festival started more than 20 years ago as a gay community fundraiser for AIDS charities. It has grown to be a gay and gay-friendly week (in mid-October) of intense partying, featuring soirées like the Leather Ball, the Military Ball, and the Black and Blue Ball. ☎ *514/875–7026* ⊕ *www.bbcm.org.*

Festival of Colors. Farmers' markets, arts-and-crafts fairs, and weekend hikes are part of this festival, which celebrates the fall throughout Québec. If you head to a ski resort you can get a bird's-eye view of the splendid and vibrant red, orange, and yellow foliage from the chairlifts. ✉ *Québec.*

A FOOD-LOVER'S TOUR OF MONTRÉAL

Many Montrealers are true gourmets, or at least enthusiastic food-lovers. And, indeed, the city has thousands of restaurants, markets, and food boutiques catering to just about every conceivable taste, from Middle Eastern shish kebab to Portuguese barbecue to Tonkinese soup. Most menus are posted outside, so you can stroll around a neighborhood and leisurely choose whichever sounds most tantalizing.

Downtown

While you can't go wrong starting the day with a bowl of steaming café au lait at **Café Myriade** in Downtown, for something a little different head over to Chinatown for a dim sum breakfast at the neighborhood institution, **Maison Kam Fung.**

The Plateau

Fortified with filling dumpling dough, walk up through the streets of the Latin Quarter on rue St-Denis and you'll hit Square St-Louis.

Turn west, then north on boulevard St-Laurent and browse through dozens of ethnic food shops and delis, inhaling the aromas from the Caribbean, the Middle East, Asia, and Eastern Europe. If that reanimates your appetite, stop at the iconic **Schwartz's Delicatessen** and split one of the world's best smoked-meat sandwiches, served piled high on rye (it's best slathered with spicy deli mustard), with your walking companion.

Next, work up an appetite for lunch with a walk. Head east along avenue Duluth and take a stroll through Parc Lafontaine. There are two options for a bite to eat: exit the park on the southwest corner to rue Rachel and turn left for La Banquise, one of Montréal's top poutine spots (so popular you may have to wait in line to get in); or go northwest on rue de la Roche until you reach avenue Mont-Royal, a spirited stretch of terrasses, tattoo parlors, and thrift shops. Stop for a bagel sandwich on a hot and sweet Montréal-style bagel at **St-Viateur Bagel & Café.** In summer, stop for some ice cream at **Le Glacier Bilboquet,** on avenue Laurier Est.

Little Italy

Time to cheat. Hop on the métro at Laurier station and head north to the Jean-Talon stop for an afternoon visit to one of Canada's best markets, **Marché Jean-Talon.** You can spend hours browsing fish, sausage, and cheese shops and sampling everything from smoked buffalo to seasonal produce like heirloom tomatoes.

There's no leaving this area without stopping for dinner, so stroll over to boulevard St-Laurent and find a place to eat in Pétite-Italie (Little Italy). Two restaurants to try are **Inferno** and **Bottega Pizzeria.** Finish with a bracing espresso at **Café Italia,** where neighborhood men huddle around the TV to watch soccer.

From here, it's an easy walk back to the Jean-Talon métro stop for a ride back to Old Montréal or Downtown.

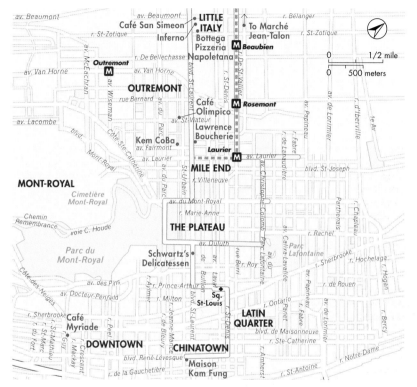

Highlights	A fat smoked meat sandwich at Schwartz's Delicatessen; walking around the Marché Jean-Talon tasting vendors' samples.
Where to Start	Chinatown, located in Downtown, at the ornately decorated red gate on St-Laurent off boulevard René-Lévesque.
Length	About 5.5 km (3.5 miles) walking, plus the métro from Laurier to Marché Jean-Talon on the Orange Line.
Where to End	Little Italy. From here, you can walk back to the Orange Line that runs through Downtown.
Best Time to Go	Busy summer Saturday (the crowds are half the entertainment).
Worst Time to Go	Dull winter Monday.
Editor's Choices	Walking up boulevard St-Laurent, peeking in the delis and offbeat boutiques; the colorful streets of the Plateau; the maple ice cream at Le Glacier Bilboquet.

HOW TO SPEAK FRENCH CANADIAN

Français, s'il vous plaît

Anytime you visit a foreign country, being familiar with the local language is only going to win you friends. Learning a few phrases, regardless of whether you pronounce them correctly, and the locals will appreciate it—if only for the novelty value. More than 80% of Quebecers claim French as their mother tongue, and while many Quebecois are bilingual or know at least a little English, plenty more don't, especially outside Downtown Montréal and the less touristy areas of the province. Rest assured that you will, at some point in your visit, come across more than a few unilingual Francophones.

As in France, accents and colloquialisms vary widely from region to region. Still, there are several commonly used, uniquely Quebecois words and expressions.

Everyday terms

For starters, Montréal's impressive subway system is known as *le Métro*. If you go around asking French Canadians where the closest subway station is you'll likely be greeted with a blank stare followed by a "*Je m'excuse, mais je ne parle pas l'anglais*" ("I'm sorry, but I don't speak any English"). Similarly, don't go looking for a "convenience store" when you need some last-minute item. Here, even Anglophones call them *dépanneurs*, or "*deps*" for short.

While here you'll probably spend a lot of time in *centre-ville* (Downtown) checking out splendid sights like the *Palais de Justice* (not a palace at all, but a courthouse). Except in order to do so you're likely going to need some *l'argent* (money), or better, *un peu de cash*, which is *franglais* (a curious yet distinct local hybrid of French and English) for "a bit of money." And where will you be getting that money? Nowhere if you start asking people for the closest ATM. In Québec a bank machine is called a *guichet* (the *gui* pronounced like guitar, the *chet* like "shea," as in the stadium). One last piece of friendly advice: Be careful with *je t'aime*, which means both "I like you" and "I love you." Getting that one wrong could potentially leave you in a pretty awkward position.

Dining out

Of course many things in Québec, like the menus in most restaurants, will be in both French and English, but you'll impress the waitstaff if you order a *steak-frites avec un verre de vin rouge* when you want steak with french fries and a glass of red wine. Later, when you ask for *la facture* (your bill) and your waiter inquires if you've enjoyed your meal, tell him it was *écúurant* (wonderful) and you'll likely see a big amused grin come over his face. It's the rare tourist who's in the know when it comes to Quebecois slang and/or colloquialisms, so locals will certainly be impressed if they hear you coming out with the occasional *mon char* (my car) when talking about your wheels or, *ma blonde* (girlfriend) when introducing somebody to your female significant other, who might just as easily be a brunette, by the way. Conversely, if you're talking about a boyfriend, *mon chum* is how the locals would say it.

Holy swear words

Almost all Quebecois swear words—aka *sacres*—come courtesy of the Catholic Church, so while the literal translation of words like *tabernac* (tabernacle) or *câlice* (chalice) might seem pretty tame or nonsensical in English, here they're the equivalent of the dreaded F-word, and definitely not meant to be used in polite company.

EXPLORING MONTRÉAL

WELCOME TO MONTRÉAL

TOP REASONS TO GO

★ **Browse public markets:** Amble through Marché Atwater, one of the city's oldest public markets, and the bustling Marché Jean-Talon, the largest open air market in North America.

★ **Check out the nightlife:** Enjoy famous nightlife spots that include rue Crescent, boulevard St-Laurent, and rue St-Denis, as well as Old Montréal and the Village, Montréal's gay epicenter.

★ **Get a dose of multiculturalism:** Explore ethnic neighborhoods and sample global cuisine.

★ **Celebrate Jazz Fest:** Montréal's biggest party, Jazz Fest, happens every year in late June and early July. Reserve early: hotels book up months in advance.

★ **Stroll Old Montréal:** Historic Vieux Montréal has cobblestone streets, a great waterfront, fine restaurants and bed-and-breakfasts, and the Old Port, which buzzes with nightlife.

1 Old Montréal (Vieux-Montréal). The oldest part of the city is known for historical buildings, horse-drawn carriages, street performers, and charming restaurants with terraces.

2 Downtown and Chinatown. You can shop with the masses on rue Ste-Catherine, take a quick walk over to Chinatown for lunch, and check out the museums' newest exhibitions.

3 The Latin Quarter and the Village. People watching is the order of the day in these two neighborhoods bordering the Downtown core. Have a drink at any number of the outdoor terraces lining rue St-Denis.

4 The Plateau, Mile End, Little Italy, and Outremont. Come to the cozy Plateau and bordering neighborhoods Mile End and Outremont for Sunday brunch, upscale boutiques, and art galleries.

5 Parc du Mont-Royal. Home of the mountain that gave Montréal its name, this is where city dwellers come for refuge—and for some of the city's best world cuisine in Côte-des-Neiges.

6 Hochelaga-Maisonneuve. Visit this corner of Montréal to see the site of the 1976 Olympics, explore the universe in the new planetarium, and take in its great parks and gardens.

7 The Islands. Île Ste-Hélène and Île Notre-Dame, which together make up Parc Jean-Drapeau, are now a vast playground in several ways—from La Ronde amusement park to Casino de Montréal to the Grand Prix's Formula 1 race track.

KEY

Ⓜ Métro Stations

Route Verte Bike Route

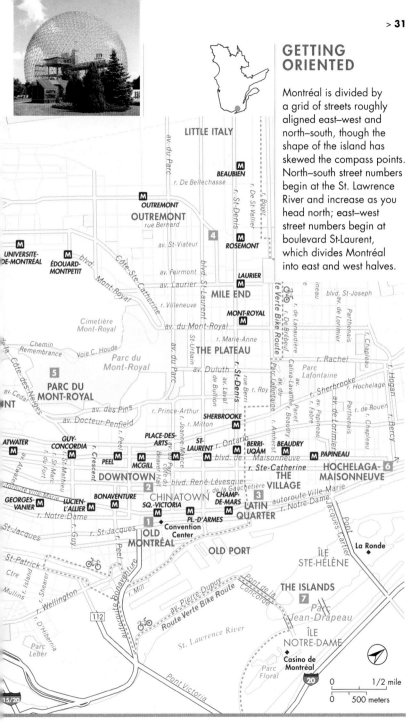

GETTING ORIENTED

Montréal is divided by a grid of streets roughly aligned east–west and north–south, though the shape of the island has skewed the compass points. North–south street numbers begin at the St. Lawrence River and increase as you head north; east–west street numbers begin at boulevard St-Laurent, which divides Montréal into east and west halves.

2

LITTLE ITALY

BEAUBIEN Ⓜ

av. du Parc

r. De Bellechasse

r. St-Vallier

r. De St-Vallier

r. St-Denis

r. Boyer

OUTREMONT Ⓜ

OUTREMONT
rue Bernard

4 ROSEMONT

UNIVERSITE-
DE-MONTRÉAL Ⓜ

ÉDOUARD-
MONTPETIT Ⓜ

av. St-Viateur

av. Fairmont

LAURIER Ⓜ

blvd. St-Laurent

av. Laurier

Côte-Ste-Catherine

MILE END

blvd. St-Joseph

MONT-ROYAL Ⓜ

blvd. av. de Lorimier

r. de Lanaudière

Route Verte Bike Route

r. De Brébeuf

r. Chapleau

Cimetière
Mont-Royal

r. Villeneuve

Mont-Royal

av. du Mont-Royal

r. Marie-Anne

THE PLATEAU

r. Rachel

Chemin
Remembrance

Voie C. Houde

Parc du
Mont-Royal

5

PARC DU
MONT-ROYAL

av. du Parc

av. Duluth

de Bullion

av. Laval

St-Urbain

r. Roy

rue Berri

r. St-Denis

Parc
Lafontaine

av. du Parc-Lafontaine

av. Papineau

av. Calixa-Lavallée, Panet

r. Sherbrooke

r. Hochelaga

r. Hogan

r. Bercy

av. des Pins

av. Docteur-Penfield

r. Prince-Arthur

r. Milton

av. Cedar

av. Cedar

la Côte-des-Neiges

NT

ATWATER Ⓜ

GUY-
CONCORDIA Ⓜ

r. Peel

r. Jeanne-Mance

PLACE-DES-
ARTS Ⓜ

ST-
LAURENT Ⓜ

r. Ontario

SHERBROOKE Ⓜ

BERRI-
UQÀM Ⓜ

BEAUDRY Ⓜ

r. Amherst

blvd. de
Maisonneuve

PAPINEAU Ⓜ

HOCHELAGA-
MAISONNEUVE 6

av. Atwater

r. St-Marc

r. du Fort

r. St-Mathieu

r. Crescent

PEEL Ⓜ

MCGILL Ⓜ

côte du Beaver Hall

DOWNTOWN

r. Ste-Catherine

av. Papineau

av. de Lorimier

Partenais

r. de Rouen

r. Chapleau

autoroute Ville-Marie

blvd. René-Lévesque

2

BONAVENTURE Ⓜ

CHINATOWN

SQ.-VICTORIA Ⓜ

r. de la Gauchetière

CHAMP-
DE-MARS Ⓜ

3

LATIN
QUARTER

THE
VILLAGE

autoroute Ville-Marie

r. Notre-Dame

Pont Jacques-Cartier

GEORGES-
VANIER Ⓜ

LUCIEN-
L'ALLIER Ⓜ

r. Notre-Dame

PL.-D'ARMES Ⓜ

St-Jacques

r. St-Jacques

r. Peel

Convention
Center

OLD
MONTRÉAL

La Ronde ◆

ÎLE
STE-HÉLÈNE

St-Patrick

r. Guy

autoroute Ville-Marie

r. St. Shearer

OLD PORT

THE ISLANDS

7

Parc
Jean-Drapeau

Ctre

r. Island

r. D'Hibernia

av. Bonaventure

r. Mill

av. Pierre-Dupuy

Pont de la Concorde

Mullins

r. Wellington

112

Route Verte Bike Route

St. Lawrence River

ÎLE
NOTRE-DAME

Parc
Leber

Parc
Floral

Casino de
Montréal ◆

20

0 _____ 1/2 mile

0 _____ 500 meters

15/20

Pont Victoria

Updated by
Marcella De
Vincenzo

Canada's most diverse metropolis, Montréal, is an island city that favors grace and elegance over order or even prosperity, a city where past and present intrude on each other daily. In some ways it resembles Vienna—well past its peak of power and glory, perhaps, yet still vibrant and beautiful.

But don't get the wrong idea. Montréal has always had a bit of an edge. During Prohibition, thirsty Americans headed north to the city on the St. Lawrence for booze, music, and a good time, and people still come for the same things. Summer festivals celebrate everything from comedy and French songs to beer and fireworks, and, of course, jazz. And on those rare weeks when there isn't a planned event, the party continues. Clubs and sidewalk cafés are abuzz from late afternoon to the early hours of the morning. And Montréal is a city that knows how to mix it up even when it's 20 below zero. Rue St-Denis is almost as lively on a Saturday night in January as it is in July, and the festival Montréal en Lumière, or Montréal Highlights, enlivens the dreary days of February with concerts, balls, and fine food.

Montréal takes its name from Parc du Mont-Royal, a stubby plug of tree-covered igneous rock that rises high above the surrounding cityscape. Although its height is unimpressive, "the Mountain" forms one of Canada's finest urban parks, and views from the Chalet du Mont-Royal in the Parc du Mont-Royal provide an excellent orientation to the city's layout and major landmarks.

Old Montréal holds museums, the municipal government, and the magnificent Basilique Notre-Dame-de-Montréal within its network of narrow, cobblestone streets. Although Montréal's *centre-ville*, or Downtown, bustles like many other major cities on the surface, it's active below street level as well, in the Underground City. Residential Plateau Mont-Royal and its surrounding trendy neighborhoods are abuzz with restaurants, nightclubs, art galleries, and cafés. The greener areas of town are composed of the Parc du Mont-Royal and the Jardin Botanique, where you can walk, bike, or take a horse-drawn carriage ride along miles of paths.

MONTRÉAL'S HISTORY

Montréal is the second-largest French-speaking city in the Western world, but it's not only Francophone culture that thrives here. About 14% of the 3.3 million people who call Montréal home claim English as their mother tongue.

The two cultures, however, are not as separate as they were. Chatter in the bars and bistros of rue St-Denis east of boulevard St-Laurent still tends to be French, and crowds in clubs and restaurants on rue Crescent in Downtown speak, argue, and court in English. But the lines have definitely blurred.

Both major linguistic groups have had to come to grips with no longer being the only players on the field. So-called *allophones*—people whose mother tongue is neither French nor English—make up fully 19% of the city's population.

The first European settlement on Montréal island was Ville-Marie, founded in 1642 by 54 pious men and women under the leadership of Paul de Chomedey, Sieur de Maison-neuve, and Jeanne Mance, a French noblewoman, who hoped to create a new Christian society.

But piety wasn't Ville-Marie's only raison d'être. The settlement's location near the convergence of the St. Lawrence and Ottawa rivers meant a lucrative trade in beaver pelts, as the fur was a staple of European hat fashion for nearly a century.

The French regime in Canada ended with the Seven Years' War—what Americans call the French and Indian War. The Treaty of Paris ceded all of New France to Britain in 1763. American troops under generals Richard Montgomery and Benedict Arnold occupied the city during their 1775–76 campaign to conquer Canada, but their efforts failed and the troops withdrew. Soon invaders of another kind—English and Scottish settlers, traders, and merchants—poured into Montréal. By 1832 the city became a leading colonial capital. But 1837 brought anti-British rebellions, and the unrest led to Canada's becoming a self-governing dominion in 1867.

The city's ports continued to bustle until the St. Lawrence Seaway opened in 1957, allowing ships to sail from the Atlantic to the Great Lakes without having to stop in Montréal to transfer cargo.

The opening of the métro in 1966 changed the way Montrealers lived, and the next year the city hosted the World's Fair. But the rise of Québec separatism in the late 1960s under the charismatic René Lévesque created political uncertainty, and many major businesses moved to Toronto. By the time Lévesque's separatist Parti Québécois won power in Québec in 1976—the same year the summer Olympics came to the city—Montréal was clearly No. 2.

Uncertainty continued through the 1980s and '90s, with the separatist Parti Québécois and the federal-ist Liberals alternating in power in Québec City. Since 1980 the city has endured two referenda on the future of Québec and Canada. In the most recent—the cliff-hanger of 1995—just 50.58% of Quebecois voted to remain part of Canada. Montréal bucked the separatist trend and voted nearly 70% against independence.

2

PLANNING

GETTING HERE AND AROUND

AIR TRAVEL

Montréal's Trudeau International Airport (also often referred to by its previous name, Dorval) is about 24 km (15 miles) west of the city center.

GROUND TRANSPOR-TATION The easiest way to get in is to take a cab for a fixed fare of C\$40 or a limousine for about C\$55, unless your hotel provides transportation. The cheapest way to get into town is the 747 express bus, a 24-hour shuttle service from the airport to the main bus terminal with stops at the Lionel-Groulx métro station and several additional stops near Downtown hotels. The fare is C\$10 one-way—with 24 hours of unlimited bus and métro travel included in the price. Plan on it taking about a half hour outside rush hour to get to Downtown from the airport. Another alternative is the 204 bus, with a one way fare of C\$3, taking you from the Dorval train terminal straight to the airport.

BICYCLE TRAVEL

An extensive network of bike paths and relatively flat terrain make Montréal ideal for bicycles. The Bixi (a contraction of "bicycle" and "taxi") system—with more than 3,000 sturdy aluminum-frame bikes at more than 300 credit-card operated stands throughout the city—makes two-wheel exploring easy. For just C\$7 you can take as many bike trips as you like over a 24-hour period, or for C\$15 you can extend that to 72 hours. Pay attention to the time, though: the system is designed for short hops; keep any one bike for more than 30 minutes, and you'll be charged extra.

CAR TRAVEL

If you're driving in to the city, take I–91 or I–89 from Vermont, I–87 from New York, and Autoroute 20 (also known as Autoroute Jean-Lesage) from Québec City.

Having a car in Downtown isn't ideal—garages are expensive and on-street parking can be a hassle. The city has a diligent tow-away and fine system for double-parking or sitting in no-stopping zones during rush hour, and ticket costs are steep. In residential neighborhoods, beware of alternate-side-of-the-street-parking rules and resident-only parking. In winter, street plows are ruthless in dealing with parked cars in their way. If they don't tow them, they'll bury them.

PUBLIC TRANSPORTATION

The Société de transport de Montréal (STM) operates both the métro (subway) and the bus system. The métro is clean and quiet (it runs on rubber tires), and will get you to most of the places you want to visit. For those few places that are more than a 15-minute walk from the nearest métro station, bus connections are available.

Métro hours on the Orange, Green, Blue, and Yellow lines are weekdays 5:30 am to 12:30 am and weekends 5:30 am to 12:30, 1, or 1:30 am (it varies by line). Trains run every three minutes or so on the most crowded lines—Orange and Green—at rush hours. The cash fare for a single ticket is C\$3. One- and three-day unlimited-use cards are also available for C\$10 and C\$18.

MONEY-SAVING TIPS

There are several good ways to save money during your trip. If you'll be visiting three or more of the city's museums, consider buying a museum pass. It's available for C$75 for three days, but the better deal is the C$80 pass, which also includes unlimited access to Montréal's transportation system, including the métro and buses.

Tourist passes also may be worth your while; one-day passes are C$10 and three-day passes are C$18. Weekly passes are C$24.50, but they're loaded electronically on a special Opus card that costs C$6.

Hitting the town earlier in the evening is a good way to save as well, by stopping into cafés and bars for food and drink specials offered during cinq-à-sept (5-to-7), Montréal's happy hour.

TAXI TRAVEL

Taxis in Montréal all run on the same rate: C$3.30 minimum and C$1.60 per kilometer (roughly ½ mile). They're usually easy to hail on the street, outside train stations, in shopping areas, and at major hotels. You can also call a dispatcher to send a driver to pick you up at no extra cost. A taxi is available if the white or orange plastic rooftop light is on.

⇨ *For more information on getting here and around, see Travel Smart.*

PLANNING YOUR TIME

Put Old Montréal and the Old Port at the top of your sightseeing list. Spend a full day walking around this area, head back to your hotel for a late-day break, and return for dinner. Aside from finding several of the city's top restaurants here, City Hall, Marché Bonsecours, and other charming buildings are illuminated at night. Also dedicate a full day to wandering around Downtown to visit museums, check out rue Ste-Catherine, and explore Chinatown. Visit the Latin Quarter and the area around McGill University—both have a busy student life, but shouldn't be dismissed as places where only under-20s frequent. Even if you're too tired to go out on the town, take a nighttime walk down rue Crescent or rue St-Denis for a taste of the city's *joie de vivre*.

For browsing, shopping, and dining out, explore Outremont, Mile End, the Plateau, and Westmount. For kid-friendly activities, check out Hochelaga-Maisonneuve and the Islands for the Biôdôme, La Ronde, and the Jardin Botanique.

And a city landmark not to miss is St. Joseph's Oratory, Canada's largest church. It's on the west end of the city, which makes it a little out of the tourist area, but it's worth the trip.

WHEN TO GO

To avoid crowds and below-freezing temperatures, Montréal's short spring, which typically starts in late April or early May but doesn't end until well into June, is ideal. Fall is gorgeous—and touristy—when the leaves change color, so expect traffic on weekends. Early September after Labor Day is another good time to visit.

OLD MONTRÉAL (VIEUX-MONTRÉAL) AND THE LACHINE CANAL

A walk through the cobblestone streets of Old Montréal is a lot more than a privileged stroll through history; it's also an encounter with a very lively present—especially in summer, when the restaurants and bistros spill out onto the sidewalks. Jugglers, musicians, and magicians jockey for performance space on the public squares and along the riverfront, and things get turned up a notch at the Old Port, one of the city's hottest spots for nightlife.

OLD MONTRÉAL (VIEUX-MONTRÉAL)

Old Montréal, which was once enclosed by thick stone walls, is the oldest part of the city. It runs roughly from the waterfront in the south to ruelle des Fortifications in the north and from rue McGill in the west to rue Berri in the east. The churches and chapels here stand as testament to the religious fervor that inspired the French settlers who landed here in 1642 to build a "Christian commonwealth" under the leadership of Paul de Chomedey, Sieur de Maisonneuve, and the indomitable Jeanne Mance. Stone warehouses and residences are reminders of how quickly the fur trade commercialized that lofty ideal and made the city one of the most prosperous in 18th-century Nouvelle France. And finally, the financial houses along rue St-Jacques, bristling with Victorian ornamentation, recall the days when Montrealers controlled virtually all the wealth of the young Dominion of Canada.

History and good looks aside, however, Old Montréal still works for a living. Stockbrokers and shipping companies continue to operate out of the old financial district. The city's largest newspaper, *La Presse,* has its offices here. Lawyers in black gowns hurry through the streets to plead cases at the Palais de Justice or the Cour d'Appel, the City Council meets in the Second Empire City Hall on rue Notre-Dame, and local shoppers hunt for deals in the bargain clothing stores just off rue McGill.

GETTING HERE AND AROUND

The easiest way to get from Downtown to Old Montréal is aboard Bus 515, a shuttle that provides a quick direct link to several sites in the Old City and Old Port. It runs from 7 am to midnight. You can also take the métro Orange line to the Place-d'Armes and Square-Victoria

stations, or you can walk, but the primary routes from Downtown go through some drab and somewhat seedy, although not especially dangerous, areas. If you want the exercise, it's better to rent a Bixi bicycle at a Downtown stand and drop it off at one in Old Montréal. Biking to Old Montréal is a breeze since it's all downhill, but the return trip to Downtown is a challenging workout.

Taxis can whisk you here from Downtown in about 10 minutes.

The best way to get around the Old City is on foot, but wear good shoes because the cobbles can be hard on the feet. A more romantic (and more costly) option is to hire a *calèche* from the stand on south side of Place-d'Armes for a horse-drawn tour of the district. Be aware that the city sets the fares—C$48 for 30 minutes and C$80 for an hour. You shouldn't be asked for more, though a small tip is always appreciated.

TIMING

Having enough time to see the sights, stroll around, and try some of the area's notable restaurants means dedicating at least one day. If it's your first time in the city and you're only here for an extended weekend, consider staying in one of Old Montréal's auberges or boutique hotels.

TOP ATTRACTIONS

Fodor'sChoice
★
Basilique Notre-Dame-de-Montréal (*Our Lady of Montréal Basilica*). Few churches in North America are as wow-inducing as Notre-Dame. Everything about the place, which opened in 1829, seems designed to make you gasp—from the 228-foot twin towers out front to the tens of thousands of 24-karat gold stars that stud the soaring blue ceiling.

Nothing in a city renowned for churches matches Notre-Dame for sheer grandeur—or noisemaking capacity: its 12-ton bass bell is the largest in North America, and its 7,000-pipe Casavant organ can make the walls tremble. The pulpit is a work of art in itself, with an intricately curving staircase and fierce figures of Ezekiel and Jeremiah crouching at its base. The whole place is so overwhelming it's easy to miss such lesser features as the stained-glass windows from Limoges and the side altars dedicated to St. Marguerite d'Youville, Canada's first native-born saint; St. Marguerite Bourgeoys, Canada's first schoolteacher; and a group of Sulpician priests martyred in Paris during the French Revolution.

For a peek at the magnificent baptistery, decorated with frescoes by Ozias Leduc, you'll have to tiptoe through the glassed-off prayer room in the northwest corner of the church. Every year dozens of brides march up the aisle of **Chapelle Notre-Dame-du-Sacré-Coeur** (Our Lady of the Sacred Heart Chapel), behind the main altar, to exchange vows with their grooms before a huge modern bronze sculpture that you either love or hate.

Notre-Dame is an active house of worship, so dress accordingly (i.e., no shorts or bare midriffs). The chapel can't be viewed weekdays during the 12:15 pm mass, and is often closed Saturday for weddings. ⊠ *110 rue Notre-Dame Ouest, Old Montréal, Montréal* ☎ *514/842–2925, 866/842–2925* ⊕ *www.basiliquenddm.org* ⊠ *Tours C$5, La Lumière Fut show C$10* ☉ *Weekdays 8–4:30, Sat. 8–4, Sun. 12:30–4; tours in French and English every 30 min* Ⓜ *Place-d'Armes.*

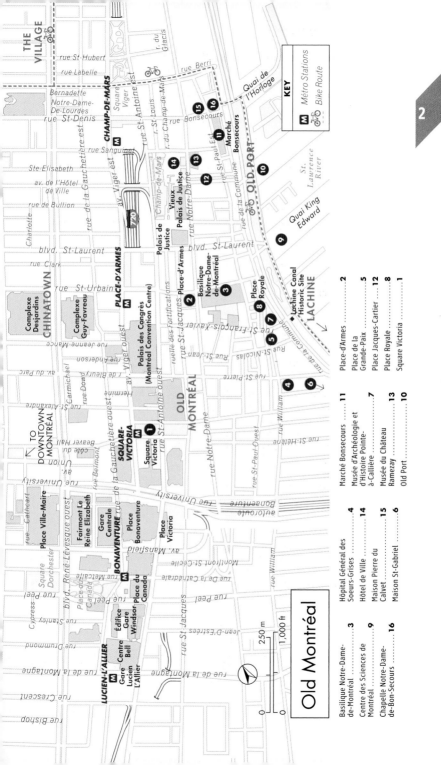

Old Montréal

Basilique Notre-Dame-
de-Montréal **3**

Centre des Sciences de
Montréal **9**

Chapelle Notre-Dame-
de-Bon-Secours **16**

Hôpital Général des
Soeurs-Grises **4**

Hôtel de Ville **14**

Maison Pierre du
Calvet **15**

Maison St-Gabriel **6**

Marché Bonsecours **11**

Musée d'Archéologie et
d'Histoire Pointe-
à-Callière **7**

Musée du Château
Ramezay **13**

Old Port **10**

Place-d'Armes **2**

Place de la
Grande-Paix **5**

Place Jacques-Cartier . . . **12**

Place Royale **8**

Square Victoria **1**

KEY

M Métro Stations
🚲 Bike Route

Chapelle Notre-Dame-de-Bon-Secours (*Our Lady of Perpetual Help Chapel*). Mariners have been popping into Notre-Dame-de-Bon-Secours for centuries to kneel before a little 17th-century statue of the Virgin Mary and pray for a safe passage—or give thanks for one. Often, they've expressed their gratitude by leaving votive lamps in the shape of small ships, many of which still hang from the barrel-vaulted ceiling. This is why most Montrealers call the chapel the Église des Matelots (the Sailors' Church), and why many people still stop by to say a prayer and light a candle before leaving on a long trip.

These days, the statue of Our Lady of Perpetual Help guards the remains of St. Marguerite Bourgeoys, who had the original chapel built in 1657 and is entombed in the side altar next to the east wall of the chapel. The current chapel dates from 1771; a renovation project in 1998 revealed some beautiful 18th-century murals that had been hidden under layers of paint.

The steep climb to the top of the steeple is worth the effort for the glorious view of the harbor, as is the equally steep climb down to the archaeological excavations under the chapel for a glimpse into the history of the chapel and the neighborhood. The dig is accessible through the adjacent **Musée Marguerite Bourgeoys,** which also has exhibits on the life of St. Marguerite and the daily lives of the colonists she served. The chapel is closed mid-January through February except for the 10:30 am mass on Sunday. ✉ *400 rue St-Paul Est, Old Montréal, Montréal* ☎ *514/282–8670* ⊕ *www.marguerite-bourgeoys.com* 🖼 *Museum C$10* ⊗ *May–mid-Oct., Tues.–Sun. 10–5:30; mid-Oct.–mid-Jan., Mar., and Apr., Tues.–Sun. 11–3:30* Ⓜ *Champ-de-Mars.*

Maison St-Gabriel. Thick stone walls, a steep roof, and mullioned windows mark the Maison St-Gabriel as one of Montréal's rare surviving 17th-century houses. But it's the interior and the furnishings that will sweep you back to the colonial days when St. Marguerite Bourgeoys and the religious order she founded used this house to train *les filles du roy* (king's daughters) in the niceties of home management. Les filles were young women without family or fortune but plenty of spunk who volunteered to cross the Atlantic in leaky boats to become the wives and mothers of New France. It wasn't an easy life, as the Maison's hard, narrow beds, primitive utensils, and drafty rooms attest—but it had its rewards, and the prize at the end was a respectable, settled life. St. Marguerite also had some state-of-the-art domestic equipment—the latest in looms and butter churns, labor-saving spit turners for roasting meat, and an ingenious granite sink with a drainage system that piped water straight out to the garden. Located on the little island of New France and deep in the working-class neighborhood of Pointe St-Charles, Maison St-Gabriel is off the beaten path, but it's well worth a 10-minute taxi ride from Old Montréal. ✉ *2146 pl. Dublin, Pointe-St-Charles, Montréal* ☎ *514/935–8136* ⊕ *www.maisonsaint-gabriel.qc.ca* 🖼 *C$10* ⊗ *June 23–early Sept., Tues.–Sun. 11–6 (hourly guided tours); early Sept.–Dec. 22 and Jan. 8–June 22, Tues.–Sun. 1–5* Ⓜ *Square-Victoria, then bus 61.*

OFF THE
BEATEN
PATH

Old Montréal has winding cobblestone streets, cafés with terraces for eating and drinking outside, and many of the city's top historical sites.

Fodor's Choice **Musée d'Archéologie et d'Histoire Pointe-à-Callière** (*Pointe-à-Callière*
★ *Archaeology and History Museum*). The modern glass building is impressive, and the audiovisual show is a breezy romp through Montréal's history from the Ice Age to the present, but the real reason to visit the city's most ambitious archaeological museum is to take the elevator ride down to the 17th century.

It's dark down there, and just a little creepy thanks to the 350-year-old tombstones teetering in the gloom, but it's worth the trip. This is a serious archaeological dig that takes you to the very foundations of the city. You begin on the banks of the long-vanished Rivière St-Pierre, where the first settlers built their homes and traded with the First Nations inhabitants. From there you climb up toward the present, past the stone foundations of an 18th-century tavern and a 19th-century insurance building. Along the way, filmed figures representing past inhabitants appear on ghostly screens to chat to you about their life and times. A more lighthearted exhibit explores life and love in multicultural Montréal. For a spectacular view of the Old Port, the St. Lawrence River, and the Islands, ride the elevator to the top of the tower, or stop for lunch in the museum's glass-fronted café. In summer there are re-creations of period fairs and festivals on the grounds near the museum.

By 2017, in time for Montréal's 375th anniversary, a major expansion of the museum, including new exhibits, will have been completed. ⊠ *350 pl. Royale, Old Montréal, Montréal* ☎ *514/872–9150* ⊕ *www. pacmuseum.qc.ca* 🖭 *C\$20* ⏲ *Tues.–Fri. 10–5, weekends 11–5 (also open Mon. 10–5, late June–late Aug.)* Ⓜ *Place-d'Armes.*

Musée du Château Ramezay. Claude de Ramezay, the city's 11th governor, was probably daydreaming of home when he built his Montréal residence, which is on UNESCO's list of "1001 historic sites you must see before you die." Its thick stone walls, dormer windows, and steeply pitched roof make it look like a little bit of 18th-century Normandy dropped into the middle of North America—although the round, squat tower is a 19th-century addition. The extravagant mahogany paneling in the Salon de Nantes was installed when Louis XV was still king of France. The British used the château as headquarters after their conquest in 1760, and so did the American commanders Richard Montgomery and Benedict Arnold. Benjamin Franklin, who came north in a failed attempt to persuade the Quebecois to join the American Revolution, stayed here during that winter adventure.

Most of the château's exhibits are a little staid—guns, uniforms, and documents on the main floor and tableaux depicting colonial life in the cellars—but they include some unexpected little eccentricities that make it worth the visit. One of its prized possessions is a bright-red automobile the De Dion-Bouton Company produced at the turn of the 20th century for the city's first motorist.

Head outside, through the back door, and you'll enter gardens full of 18th-century tranquillity. They are laid out just as formally as Mme. de Ramezay might have wished, with a *potager* for vegetables and a little *verger,* or orchard. You can sit on a bench in the sun, admire the flowers, and inhale the sage-scented air from the herb garden. ⊠ *280 rue Notre-Dame Est, Old Montréal, Montréal* ☎ *514/861–3708* ⊕ *www. chateauramezay.qc.ca* ⊠ *C\$10* ☉ *June–mid-Oct., daily 9:30–6; Oct.– May, Tues.–Sun. 10–4:30* Ⓜ *Champ-de-Mars.*

FAMILY **Old Port** (*Vieux Port*). Montréal's favorite waterfront park is your ideal gateway to the St. Lawrence River. Rent a pedal boat, take a ferry to **Île Ste-Hélène,** sign up for a dinner cruise, or, if you're really adventurous, ride a raft or a jet boat through the turbulent Lachine Rapids. If you're determined to stay ashore, however, there's still plenty to do, including street performances, sound-and-light shows, art displays, and exhibitions. Visiting warships from the Canadian navy and other countries often dock here and open their decks to the public. You can rent a bicycle or a pair of in-line skates at one of the shops along rue de la Commune and explore the waterfront at your leisure. If it's raining, the Centre des Sciences de Montréal on **King Edward Pier** will keep you dry and entertained, and if your lungs are in good shape you can climb the 192 steps to the top of the **Clock Tower** for a good view of the waterfront and the Islands; it was erected at the eastern end of the waterfront in memory of merchant mariners killed during World War I. You can, quite literally, lose the kids in **Shed 16's Labyrinthe,** a maze of alleys, surprises, and obstacles built inside an old waterfront warehouse. Every couple of years or so the **Cirque du Soleil** comes home to pitch its blue-and-yellow tent in the Old Port. But be warned: When the circus is in town, the tickets sell faster than water in a drought. ⊠ *Old Montréal, Montréal* ☎ *514/496–7678, 800/971–7678* ⊕ *www.quaysoftheoldport. com* Ⓜ *Place-d'Armes or Champ-de-Mars.*

FAMILY **Place Jacques-Cartier.** The cobbled square at the heart of Old Montréal is part carnival, part flower market, and part sheer fun. You can pause here to have your portrait painted or to buy an ice cream or to watch the street performers. If you have more time, try to get a table at one of the sidewalk cafés, order a beer or a glass of wine, and watch the passing parade. The 1809 monument honoring Lord Nelson's victory over Napoléon Bonaparte's French navy at Trafalgar angers some modern-day Québec nationalists. The campaign to raise money for it was led by the Sulpician priests, who were engaged in delicate land negotiations with the British government at the time and were eager to show what good subjects they were. ⊠ *Bordered by rues Notre-Dame Est and de la Commune, Old Montréal, Montréal* Ⓜ *Champ-de-Mars.*

WORTH NOTING

FAMILY **Centre des Sciences de Montréal.** You—or more likely, your kids—can design an energy-efficient bike, create a television news report, explore the impact that manufacturing one T-shirt has on the environment, find out what it's like to ride a unicycle 20 feet above the ground, create an animated film, or just watch an IMAX movie on a giant screen at Montréal's interactive science center. A recent addition, Clic! The Zone For Curious Young Minds, is a colorful and fun area for four- to seven-year-olds. Games, puzzles, and hands-on experiments make it an ideal place for rainy days or even fair ones. The center also has a bistro serving lights meals, a coffee and pastry shop, and a food court. ⊠ *Quai King Edward, Old Montréal, Montréal* ☎ *514/496–4724, 877/496–4724* ⊕ *www.centredessciencesdemontreal.com* ✉ *C$14.50, IMAX C$11.50, combined ticket C$21.50* ⊙ *Weekdays 9–4, weekends 10–5* Ⓜ *Place-d'Armes.*

Hôpital Général des Soeurs-Grises (*General Hospital of the Gray Nuns*). A few jagged stone walls are all that remain of Montréal's first general hospital. The ruins—which once formed the west wing and the transept of the chapel—have been preserved as a memorial to Canada's first native-born saint, Marguerite d'Youville (1701–71), who took over the hospital in 1747 and ran it until a fire destroyed the building in 1765. St. Marguerite's life was no walk in the park, as you'll find out if you visit the **Maison de Mère d'Youville** next door to the ruins. Marguerite started looking after the city's down-and-outs after the death of her abusive and disreputable husband. Amused that the widow of a whiskey trader should be helping the town drunks, locals took to calling Marguerite and her Soeurs de la Charité (Sisters of Charity) the Soeurs Grises (Grey Nuns), slang for "tipsy nuns." The Maison has some remarkable reminders of her life, such as the kitchen where she worked, with its enormous fireplace and stone sink. Call ahead for tours of the house. ⊠ *138 rue St-Pierre, Old Montréal, Montréal* ☎ *514/842–9411* ⊕ *www.sgm.qc.ca* ✉ *Free* ⊙ *By appointment only, weekdays 8–4* Ⓜ *Square-Victoria.*

Hôtel de Ville (*City Hall*). President Charles de Gaulle of France marked Canada's centennial celebrations in 1967 by standing on the central balcony of Montréal's ornate city hall on July 24 and shouting "*Vive le Québec libre*" ("Long live free Québec"), much to the delight of the separatist movement and to the horror of the federal government that

MONTRÉAL'S BEST WALKING TOURS

Circuit des Fantômes du Old Montréal (*Old Montréal Ghost Trail*). From mid-April to mid-November, you can join these walking tours through the old city, where a host of spirits are said to still roam the streets. Tours begin at 8:30 pm and the haunted journey lasts about 90 minutes. Reservations are required. ⊠ *360 rue St-François-Xavier, Old Montréal, Montréal* ☎ *514/844–4021, 800/363–4021* ⊕ *www.fantommontreal.com* ⌦ *C$22* Ⓜ *Place-d'Armes.*

Guidatour. You can walk through various historic, cultural, or architecturally diverse areas of the city with a costumed guide. Popular tours include Old Montréal, the Underground City, and the elite 19th-century neighborhood known as the Golden Square Mile. ⊠ *360 rue St-François-Xavier, Suite 400, Old Montréal, Montréal* ☎ *514/844–4021, 800/363–4021* ⊕ *www.guidatour.qc.ca* ⌦ *From C$14* ⊙ *Office: weekdays 9–5* Ⓜ *Place-d'Armes.*

Kaleidoscope. This company offers a wide selection of guided tours, from architecture to Montréal's Red Light district, and the city's many culturally diverse neighborhoods can be explored by foot, bike, or bus. ⊠ *Montréal* ☎ *514/990–1872* ⊕ *www.tourskaleidoscope.com* ⌦ *C$15–C$55.*

had invited him over in the first place. Perhaps he got carried away because he felt so at home: the Second Empire–style city hall, built in 1878, is modeled after the one in Tours, France. Free guided tours are available (reservations required). ⊠ *275 rue Notre-Dame Est, Old Montréal, Montréal* ☎ *514/872–0077* ⊕ *www.ville.montreal.qc.ca* ⌦ *Free* ⊙ *Weekdays 8–5* Ⓜ *Champ-de-Mars.*

Maison Pierre du Calvet. Merchant Pierre du Calvet was everything that British-ruled Montréal didn't like—a notorious republican, an admirer of Voltaire, a pal of Benjamin Franklin, and a fierce supporter of the American Revolution. But he was also prosperous enough in 1725 to build a fine residence with thick stone walls and multipane casement windows. His home now houses a restaurant and Pierre du Calvet AD 1725—a small, opulent bed-and-breakfast where you can enjoy the same hospitality Franklin did in the mid-18th century. ⊠ *405 rue Bonsecours, Old Montréal, Montréal* ☎ *514/282–1725, 866/544–1725* ⊕ *www.pierreducalvet.ca* Ⓜ *Champ-de-Mars.*

Marché Bonsecours (*Bonsecours Market*). You can't buy fruits and vegetables in the Marché Bonsecours anymore, but you can shop for local fashions and crafts in the row of upscale boutiques that fill its main hall, or lunch in one of several restaurants opening onto the Old Port or rue St-Paul. But the Marché is best admired from the outside. Built in the 1840s as the city's main market, it is possibly the most beautifully proportioned neoclassical building in Montréal, with its six cast-iron Doric columns and two rows of meticulously even sashed windows, all topped with a silvery dome. Perhaps the Marché was too elegant to be just a farmers' market. ⊠ *350 rue St-Paul Est, Old Montréal, Montréal* ☎ *514/872–7730* ⊕ *www.marchebonsecours.qc.ca* Ⓜ *Champ-de-Mars.*

Place-d'Armes. When Montréal was under attack, citizens and soldiers would rally at Place-d'Armes, but these days the only rallying is done by tourists, lunching office workers, calèche drivers, and flocks of voracious pigeons. The pigeons are particularly fond of the triumphant statue of Montréal's founder, Paul de Chomedey, with his lance upraised, perched above the fountain in the middle of the cobblestone square. Tunnels beneath the square protected the colonists from the winter weather and provided an escape route; unfortunately, they are too small and dangerous to visit. ⊠ *Bordered by rues Notre-Dame Ouest, St-Jacques, and St-Sulpice, Old Montréal, Montréal* Ⓜ *Place-d'Armes.*

Place de la Grande-Paix. If you're looking for peace and quiet, the narrow strip of grass and trees on Place d'Youville just east of Place Royale is an appropriate place to find it. It was here, after all, that the French signed a major peace treaty with dozens of aboriginal nations in 1702. It was also here that the first French colonists to settle in Montréal landed their four boats on May 17, 1642. An obelisk records the settlers' names. ⊠ *Between pl. d'Youville and rue William, Old Montréal, Montréal* Ⓜ *Place-d'Armes.*

Place Royale. The oldest public square in Montréal, dating to the 17th century, was a market during the French regime and later became a Victorian garden. ⊠ *Bordered by rues St-Paul Ouest and de la Commune, Old Montréal, Montréal* Ⓜ *Place-d'Armes.*

Square Victoria. The perfect Montréal mix: an 1872 statue of Queen Victoria on one side and an authentic Parisian métro entrance and a flower market to boot, on the other. Both are framed by a two-block stretch of trees, benches, and fountains that makes a great place to relax and admire the handsome 1920s business buildings on the east side. The art nouveau métro entrance, incidentally, was a gift from the French capital's transit commission. ⊠ *Rue du Square Victoria, between rues Viger and St-Jacques, Old Montréal, Montréal* Ⓜ *Square-Victoria.*

LACHINE

If you want to work up an appetite for lunch—or just get some exercise—rent a bike on rue de la Commune, in Old Montréal, and ride west along the 14-km (9-mile) Lachine Canal through what used to be Montréal's industrial heartland to the shores of Lac St-Louis. You could stop at the Marché Atwater to buy some cheese, bread, wine, and maybe a little pâté for a picnic in the lakefront park at the end of the trail. If paddling and pedaling sound too energetic, hop aboard an excursion boat and dine more formally in one of the century-old homes that line the waterfront in Lachine, the historic city borough at the western end of the canal that was once the staging point for the lucrative fur trade.

WORTH NOTING

FAMILY **Lachine Canal National Historic Site.** The canal is all about leisure—biking, rollerblading, strolls along the water and picnicking—but it wasn't always so. Built in 1825 to get boats and cargo around the treacherous Lachine Rapids, it quickly became a magnet for all sorts of industries. But when the St. Lawrence Seaway opened in 1959, allowing large cargo ships to sail straight from the Atlantic to the Great Lakes without stopping in Montréal, the canal closed to navigation and became an illicit dumping ground for old cars and the bodies of victims of underworld killings. The area around it degenerated into an industrial slum.

A federal agency rescued the place in 1978, planting lawns and trees along the old canal, transforming it into a long, thin park, or *parc linéaire*. The abandoned canneries, sugar refineries, and steelworks have since been converted into desirable residential and commercial condominiums. The bicycle path is the first link in the more than 97 km (60 miles) of bike trails that make up the **Pôle des Rapides** (*514/364–4490* ⊕ *www.poledesrapides.com*).

Two permanent exhibits at the **Lachine Canal Visitor Services Centre**, at the western end of the canal, explain its history and construction. The center also has a shop and lookout terrace. ⊠ *Lachine, Montréal* ☎ *514/283–6054* ⊕ *www.pc.gc.ca* ⊠ *Free* ⊘ *Path maintained Apr.–Nov.; open dawn–11 pm* Ⓜ *Angrignon, then bus 195.*

Fur Trade at Lachine National Historic Site. In the waterfront park at the end of the Lachine Canal, an 1803 stone warehouse has been converted into this museum, which commemorates the industry that dominated Canada's early history. ⊠ *1255 blvd. St-Joseph, Lachine, Montréal* ☎ *888/773–8888, 514/283–6054* ⊕ *www.pc.gc.ca* ⊠ *$3.90* ⊘ *June–Sept. 10–5.*

Lachine Canal Nautical Centre. You can rent anything from a one-person kayak to a 13-passenger Voyageur canoe here and paddle along the canal. Electric boat rentals are also available. It's about 3.5 km (2 miles) from Old Montréal. ⊠ *2985B rue St-Patrick, near Atwater Market, Lachine, Montréal* ☎ *877/935–2925, 514/842–1306* ⊕ *www.h2oadventures.ca* ⊘ *June–Aug., daily 9–9; May and Sept., weekdays 2–8, weekends 9–8.*

DOWNTOWN AND CHINATOWN

Rue Ste-Catherine—and the métro line that runs under it—is the main cord that binds together the disparate, sprawling neighborhoods that comprise Montréal's **Downtown,** or *centre-ville*, just north and west of Old Montréal.

DOWNTOWN

The heart of Downtown—with department stores, boutiques, bars, restaurants, strip clubs, amusement arcades, theaters, movie theaters, art galleries, bookstores, and even a few churches—runs from avenue Atwater to boulevard St-Denis. Ste-Catherine is also the main drag of the Quartier des Spectacles, which runs west to east from rue Bleury to rue St-Hubert. Inside this arts and entertainment district are the Place des Arts and several other cultural venues; it also serves as the Downtown home to most of Montréal's many summer festivals.

Walk even farther north on rue Crescent to the lower slopes of Mont-Royal and you come to what was once the most exclusive neighborhood in Canada—the **Golden Square Mile.** During the boom years of the mid-1800s, baronial homes covered the mountain north of rue Sherbrooke. Many are gone, replaced by high-rises or modern town houses, but there are still plenty of architectural treasures to admire, most of them now foreign consulates or university institutes.

And underneath it all—the entire Downtown area and then some—is Montréal's **Underground City,** a vast network of more or less anything you'd find on the street above.

GETTING HERE AND AROUND

Getting to and around Downtown is easy, thanks to the métro. There are several stations along boulevard de Maisonneuve, which is a block away from and runs parallel to rue Ste-Catherine. Many of them link directly to the **Underground City.** Note that if you're coming from Old Montréal you'll be walking uphill, and streets become steeper beyond Downtown toward the Plateau and Parc du Mont-Royal.

TOP ATTRACTIONS

Cathédrale Marie-Reine-du-Monde (*Mary Queen of the World Cathedral*). The best reason to visit this cathedral is that it's a quarter-scale replica of St. Peter's Basilica in Rome—complete with a magnificent

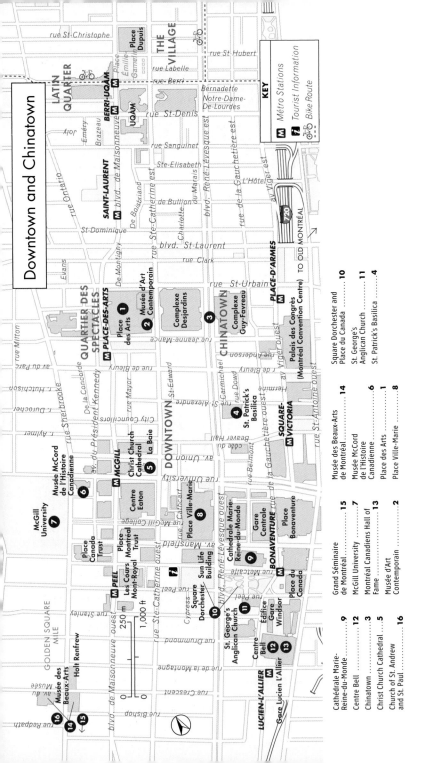

Downtown and Chinatown

THE VILLAGE

LATIN QUARTER

SAINT-LAURENT

QUARTIER DES SPECTACLES

DOWNTOWN

CHINATOWN

SQUARE-VICTORIA

GOLDEN SQUARE MILE

LUCIEN-L'ALLIER

TO OLD MONTRÉAL

KEY

Ⓜ Métro Stations

🛈 Tourist Information

⊙⊙⊙ Bike Route

Cathédrale Marie-Reine-du-Monde 9
Centre Bell 12
Chinatown 3
Christ Church Cathedral 5
Church of St. Andrew and St. Paul 16

Grand Séminaire de Montréal 15
McGill University 7
Montréal Canadiens Hall of Fame 13
Musée d'Art Contemporain 2

Musée des Beaux-Arts de Montréal 14
Musée McCord de l'Histoire Canadienne 6
Place des Arts 1
Place Ville-Marie 8

Square Dorchester and Place du Canada 10
St. George's Anglican Church 11
St. Patrick's Basilica 4

reproduction of Bernini's ornate baldachin (canopy) over the main altar and an ornately coffered ceiling. When Bishop Ignace Bourget (1799–1885) decided to build his cathedral in the heart of the city's Protestant-dominated commercial quarter, many fellow Catholics thought he was crazy. But the bishop was determined to assert the Church's authority—and its loyalty to Rome—in the British-ruled city. Bourget didn't live to see the cathedral dedicated in 1894, but his tomb holds place of honor among those of his successors in the burial chapel on the east side of the nave. ⊠ *1085 rue de la Cathédrale(enter through main doors on blvd. René-Lévesque), Downtown, Montréal* ☎ *514/866-1661* ⊕ *www.cathedralecatholiquedemontreal.org* ✉ *Free* ⊙ *Daily 7–6:15* Ⓜ *Bonaventure.*

Christ Church Cathedral. The seat of the Anglican (Episcopalian) bishop of Montréal offers downtown shoppers and strollers a respite from the hustle and bustle of rue Ste-Catherine, with free noontime concerts and organ recitals. Built in 1859, the cathedral is modeled on Snettisham Parish Church in Norfolk, England, with some distinctly Canadian touches. The steeple, for example, is made with aluminum plates molded to simulate stone, and inside, the Gothic arches are crowned with carvings of the types of foliage growing on Mont-Royal when the church was built. The stained-glass windows behind the main altar, installed in the early 1920s as a memorial to the dead of World War I, show scenes from the life of Christ. On the wall just above and to the left of the pulpit is the Coventry Cross; it's made of nails taken from the ruins of Britain's Coventry Cathedral, destroyed by German bombing in 1940. ⊠ *635 rue Ste-Catherine Ouest, Downtown, Montréal* ☎ *514/843-6577* ⊕ *www.montrealcathedral.ca* ✉ *Free* ⊙ *Daily 8–6* Ⓜ *McGill.*

Musée d'Art Contemporain (*Museum of Contemporary Art*). If you have a taste for pastoral landscapes and formal portraits, you might want to stick with the Musée des Beaux-Arts. But for a walk on the wild side of art, see what you can make of the jagged splashes of color that cover the canvases of the "Automatistes," as Québec's rebellious artists of the 1930s styled themselves. Their works form the core of this museum's collection of 5,000 pieces. One of the leaders of the movement, Jean-Paul Riopelle (1923–2002), often tossed his brushes and palette knives aside and just squeezed the paint directly on to the canvas—sometimes several tubes at a time. In 1948, Riopelle and his friends fired the first shot in Québec's Quiet Revolution by signing *Le Refus Global,* a manifesto that renounced the political and religious establishment of the day and revolutionized art in the province. The museum often has weekend programs and art workshops, some of which are geared toward children, and almost all are free. And for a little romance and music with your art, try the Vendredi Nocturnes (Nocturnal Fridays) with live music, bar service, and guided tours of the exhibits. Hours for guided tours vary.

With new government funding of C$18.9 million, the MAC will be expanding, doubling its exhibit space, adding an auditorium, and providing more educational activities. It's a welcome development for a museum that's been presenting art to Montréal for 50 years. ⊠ *185 rue*

The Musée des Beaux-Arts has one of Canada's largest permanent collections of Canadian art, as well as a gallery where you can buy paintings by local artists.

Ste-Catherine Ouest, Downtown, Montréal ☎ *514/847–6226* ⊕ *www. macm.org* ✉ *C$14, C$7 Wed. 5–9* ⊘ *Tues. 11–6, Wed.–Fri. 11–9, weekends 10–6* Ⓜ *Place des Arts.*

Musée des Beaux-Arts de Montréal (*Montréal Museum of Fine Arts*). Not surprisingly, Canada's oldest museum has one of the finest collections of Canadian art anywhere. The works of such luminaries as Paul Kane, the Group of Seven, Paul-Émile Borduas, and Marc-Aurèle Fortin are displayed here in a space built onto the back of the neoclassical Erskine and American United Church, one of the city's most historic Protestant churches. The nave has been preserved as a meeting place and exhibition hall and also displays the church's 18 Tiffany stained-glass windows, the biggest collection of Tiffany's work outside the United States. The rest of the gallery's permanent collection, which includes works by everyone from Rembrandt to Renoir, is housed in its two other pavilions: the neoclassical **Michal and Renata Hornstein Pavilion**, across rue de la Musée from the church, and the glittering, glass-fronted **Jean-Noël-Desmarais Pavilion**, across rue Sherbrooke. All three are linked by tunnels. The museum also includes the Musée des Arts Décoratifs, where you can see some fanciful bentwood furniture designed by Frank Gehry, a marvelous collection of 18th-century English porcelain, and 3,000—count 'em—Japanese snuff boxes collected by, of all people, Georges Clemenceau, France's prime minister during World War I. The museum also has a gift shop, a bookstore, a restaurant, a cafeteria, and a gallery where you can buy or even rent paintings by local artists. ✉ *1380 rue Sherbrooke Ouest, Downtown, Montréal* ☎ *514/285–2000* ⊕ *www. mmfa.qc.ca* ✉ *C$12 for ages 31 and up; special exhibitions C$20,*

C$10 Wed. after 5 ⊙ Tues.–Fri. 11–5 (also Wed. 5–9 for temporary exhibits only), weekends 10–5 Ⓜ Guy-Concordia.

Musée McCord de l'Histoire Canadienne (*McCord Museum of Canadian History*). David Ross McCord (1844–1930) was a wealthy pack rat with a passion for anything that had to do with Montréal and its history. His collection of paintings, costumes, toys, tools, drawings, and housewares provides a glimpse of what city life was like for all classes in the 19th century. If you're interested in the lifestyles of the elite, however, you'll love the photographs that William Notman (1826–91) took of the rich at play. One series portrays members of the posh Montréal Athletic Association posing in snowshoes on the slopes of Mont-Royal, all decked out in Hudson Bay coats and woolen hats. Each of the hundreds of portraits was shot individually in a studio and then painstakingly mounted on a picture of the snowy mountain to give the impression of a winter outing. There are guided tours (call for schedule), a reading room, a documentation center, a gift shop, a bookstore, and a café. ✉ *690 rue Sherbrooke Ouest, Downtown, Montréal* ☎ *514/398–7100* ⊕ *www.mccord-museum.qc.ca* 🎫 *C$14; free Wed. 5–9 ⊙ Tues.–Fri, 10–6 (to 9 Wed.), weekends 10–5 Ⓜ McGill.*

St. Patrick's Basilica. Built in 1847, this is one of the purest examples of the Gothic Revival style in Canada, with a high vaulted ceiling glowing with green and gold mosaics. The tall, slender columns are actually pine logs lashed together and decorated to look like marble, so that if you stand in one of the back corners and look toward the altar you really do feel as if you're peering at the sacred through a grove of trees. St. Pat's—as most of its parishioners call it—is to Montréal's Anglophone Catholics what the Basilique Notre-Dame is to their French-speaking brethren—the mother church and a monument to faith and courage. One of the joys of visiting the place is that you'll probably be the only tourist there, so you'll have plenty of time to check out the old pulpit and the huge lamp decorated with six 2-meter (6-foot) -tall angels hanging over the main altar. And if you're named after some relatively obscure saint like Scholastica or Aeden of Fleury, you can search for your namesake's portrait among the 170 painted panels on the walls of the nave.

For a solemn experience visit on the third Sunday of the month (September to to June) where the mass is sung completely in Latin. ✉ *454 blvd. René-Lévesque Ouest, Downtown, Montréal* ☎ *514/866–7379* ⊕ *www.stpatricksmtl.ca* 🎫 *Free ⊙ Sept.–June, daily 8:30–6, July and Aug., daily 9–5 Ⓜ Square-Victoria.*

The Underground City. Place Ville-Marie, the cruciform skyscraper designed by I. M. Pei, was the tallest structure in the city when it opened in 1962. Located in the heart of downtown, it signaled the beginning of Montréal's subterranean city. Montrealers were skeptical that anyone would want to shop or even walk around in the new "down" town, but more than four decades later they can't live without it.

About half a million people use the 32-km (20-mile) Underground City, or *la ville souterraine*, daily. The tunnels link 10 métro stations, 7 hotels, 200 restaurants, 1,700 boutiques, and 60 office buildings—not

DID YOU KNOW?

The Place des Arts is Montréal's Downtown meeting spot—especially when it's nice outside—with plenty of steps and fountains to sit on to take a break from sightseeing.

to mention movie theaters, concert halls, convention complexes, the Centre Bell, two universities, and a college. Those who live in one of more than 2,000 connected apartments can buy milk on a February day and never have to put on their coat. ⊠ *Downtown, Montréal.*

WORTH NOTING

Centre Bell. The Montréal Canadiens haven't won the Stanley Cup since 1993, and most of the team's fans can't remember the golden 1960s and '70s, when *Les Glorieux* virtually owned the trophy. The superstitious blame the team's fallen fortunes on its 1996 move from the hallowed Forum to the brown-brick Centre Bell arena. Still, Montréal is a hockey-mad city and the Habs, as locals call the team, are still demigods here, there are even university courses based on this superstar team. (When they celebrated their 100th season in 2009–10, the city changed the name of the strip of rue de la Gauchetière in front of the Centre Bell to Avenue des Canadiens-de-Montréal.) ⊠ *1260 av. des Canadiens-de-Montréal, Downtown, Montréal* ☎ *877/668–8269, 514/790–2525 for hockey tickets, 800/663–6786, 514/932–2582 for other events* ⊕ *www.centrebell.ca* Ⓜ *Bonaventure or Lucien-l'Allier.*

Church of St. Andrew and St. Paul. If you want to see the inside of Montréal's largest Presbyterian church—sometimes affectionately called the A&P—you'll have to call the secretary and make arrangements, or simply show up for Sunday services. Either way, it's worth the effort, if only to see the glorious stained-glass window of the risen Christ that dominates the sanctuary behind the white-stone communion table. It's a memorial to members of the Royal Highland Regiment of Canada (the Black Watch) who were killed in World War I. ⊠ *3415 rue Redpath(main entrance on rue Sherbrooke), Downtown, Montréal* ☎ *514/842–3431* ⊕ *www.standrewstpaul.com* ✉ *Free* ☉ *Sun. service at 11 am, other times by arrangement* Ⓜ *Guy-Concordia.*

Grand Séminaire de Montréal. Education goes way back at the Grand Séminaire. In the mid-1600s, St. Marguerite Bourgeoys used one of the two stone towers in the garden as a school for First Nations (Native American) girls while she and her nuns lived in the other. The 1840 seminary buildings behind the towers are now used by men studying for the priesthood. In summer there are free guided tours of the towers, the extensive gardens, and the college's beautiful Romanesque chapel. 2015 celebrates the seminary's 175th anniversary, with activities focusing on youth and multiculturalism. ⊠ *2065 rue Sherbrooke Ouest, Downtown, Montréal* ☎ *514/935–7775* ⊕ *www.gsdm.qc.ca* ✉ *By donation* ☉ *Guided tours June–Aug., Tues.–Fri. 1 and 3, Sat. 10 and 1* Ⓜ *Guy-Concordia.*

McGill University. Merchant and fur trader James McGill would probably be horrified to know that the university that he helped found in 1828 has developed an international reputation as one of North America's best party schools. The administration isn't too happy about it, either. But there's no real cause for alarm. McGill is still one of the two or three best English-language universities in Canada, and certainly one of the prettiest. Its campus is an island of grass and trees in a sea of traffic and skyscrapers. If you take the time to stroll up the drive that leads from the

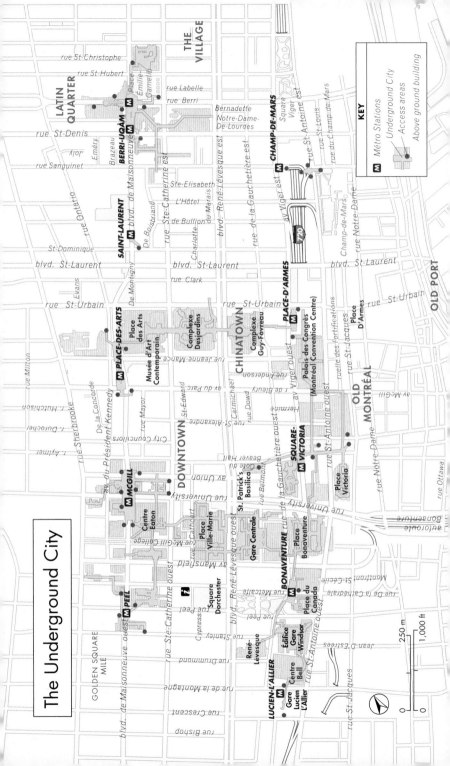

The Underground City

KEY

M Métro Stations

Underground City

Access areas

Above ground building

GOLDEN SQUARE MILE

LATIN QUARTER

THE VILLAGE

DOWNTOWN

CHINATOWN

OLD MONTRÉAL

OLD PORT

M BERRI-UQAM

M SAINT-LAURENT

M CHAMP-DE-MARS

M PLACE-DES-ARTS

M PLACE-D'ARMES

M McGILL

M SQUARE-VICTORIA

M PEEL

M BONAVENTURE

M LUCIEN-L'ALLIER

Place Émilie-Gamelin

Square Viger

Place des Arts

Musée d'Art Contemporain

Complexe Desjardins

Complexe Guy-Favreau

Palais des Congrès (Montréal Convention Centre)

Place D'Armes

Centre Eaton

St. Patrick's Basilica

Place Ville-Marie

Beaver Hall

Gare Centrale

Place Victoria

Square Dorchester

Place Bonaventure

Place du Canada

Édifice Gare Windsor

Gare Lucien L'Allier

Centre Bell

rue St-Christophe

rue St-Hubert

rue Labelle

rue Berri

Bernadette Notre-Dame-De-Lourdes

rue St-Denis

Emery

Brazeau

Joly

rue Sanguinet

blvd. de Maisonneuve est

rue Ste-Catherine est

Ste-Elisabeth

L'Hôtel

de Bullion

rue de Bordeaux

De Montigny

St-Dominique

blvd. St-Laurent

rue Clark

rue Ontario

rue St-Urbain

Evans

Ste-Elisabeth

du Marais

rue Charlotte

blvd. René-Lévesque est

rue de la Gauchetière est

av Viger est

rue St-Antoine est

rue St-Louis

rue du Champ-de-Mars

Square Viger

720

blvd. St-Laurent

Place D'Armes

rue St-Urbain

rue St-Jacques

ruelle des Fortifications

ruelle des Fortifications

rue Notre-Dame

av McGill

rue St-Urbain

rue St-Antoine ouest

rue de la Gauchetière ouest

rue St-Edward

av du Parc

rue Jeanne-Mance

rue St-Alexandre

rue Carmichael

av de Bleury

Hermine

rue Anderson

rue Dowd

Côte du Beaver Hall

av Union

rue University

rue Balmoral

rue Mansfield

rue Metcalfe

rue Peel

rue Stanley

rue Drummond

rue de la Montagne

rue Crescent

rue Bishop

rue Ste-Catherine ouest

rue Cathcart

rue De La Cathédrale

Montfort

St-Cécile

blvd. René-Lévesque ouest

rue Jean-D'Estrées

rue St-Jacques

Cypress

René-Lévesque

City Councillors

rue McGill College

rue Mayor

rue Sherbrooke

De la Concorde

av du Président-Kennedy

r. Durocher

r. Hutchison

r. Aylmer

blvd. de Maisonneuve ouest

rue Milton

autoroute Bonaventure

OLD MONTRÉAL

rue Ottawa

250 m

1,000 ft

0

0

Greek Revival Roddick Gates to the austere neoclassical Arts Building, keep an eye out to your right for the life-size statue of McGill himself, hurrying across campus clutching his tricorn hat. If you have an hour or so, drop into the temple-like **Redpath Museum of Natural History** to browse its eclectic collection of dinosaur bones, old coins, African art, and shrunken heads. ⊠ *859 rue Sherbrooke Ouest, Downtown, Montréal* ☎ *514/398–4455, 514/398–4094 tours, 514/398–4086 museum* ⊕ *www.mcgill.ca; www.mcgill.ca/redpath (for museum)* ☑ *Free* ☉ *Museum weekdays 9–5, Sun. 11–5* Ⓜ *McGill.*

Montréal Canadiens Hall of Fame. A visit to this 10,000-square-foot museum, devoted to Montréal's beloved hockey team, includes relics of the team's past and even visit a replica of the Habs' 1976–77 locker room. The Hall of Fame also organizes tours of the Centre Bell, complete with a visit to the alumni lounge, press gallery, and, depending on the schedule, the current dressing room. It's wise to call in advance to make sure tours will be operating: they're sometimes postponed on short notice. ⊠ *Centre Bell, 1909 av. des Canadiens-de-Montréal, Downtown, Montréal* ☎ *514/925–7777* ⊕ *hall.canadiens.com* ☑ *C$11; on game day with ticket C$6* ☉ *Tues.–Sat. 10–6, Sun. noon–5. On game days doors close 2 hrs before beginning of game* Ⓜ *Lucien-L'Allier or Bonaventure.*

Place des Arts. Montréal's primary performing-arts complex has been undergoing a major renaissance. The center's main lobby was completely refurbished in 2010 and a new 2,000-seat concert hall for the Orchestre Symphonique de Montréal opened on the northeast corner of the site in the fall of 2011, fulfilling a decades-old dream of Montréal music lovers. Place des Arts is also the centerpiece of the city's **Quartier des Spectacles**, a square kilometer dedicated to arts and culture, with performance halls, dance studios, broadcasting facilities, and recording studios. The huge plaza in front of the complex is a favorite gathering place for locals and visitors—especially during the Jazz Festival and Just For Laughs, when it's packed with free concerts and entertainment. ⊠ *175 rue Ste-Catherine Ouest, Downtown, Montréal* ☎ *514/842–2112 tickets, 514/285–4200 administration* ⊕ *www.pda.qc.ca* Ⓜ *Place des Arts.*

Place Ville-Marie. The cross-shape 1962 office tower was Montréal's first modern skyscraper; the mall complex underneath it was the first link in the Underground City. The wide expanse of the building's plaza, just upstairs from the mall, makes a good place to relax with coffee or a snack from the food court below. Benches, potted greenery, and fine views of Mont-Royal make it popular with walkers, tourists, and office workers. ⊠ *Bordered by blvd. René-Lévesque and rues Mansfield, Cathcart, and University, Downtown, Montréal* ☎ *514/866–6666* ⊕ *www.placevillemarie.com* Ⓜ *McGill or Bonaventure.*

Square Dorchester and Place du Canada. On sunny summer days you can join the office workers, store clerks, and downtown shoppers who gather in these two green squares in the center of the city to eat lunch under the trees and perhaps listen to an open-air concert. If there are no vacant benches or picnic tables, you can still find a place to sit on the steps at the base of the dramatic monument to the dead of the Boer War. Other statues honor Scottish poet Robert Burns (1759–96); Sir Wilfrid Laurier (1841–1919), Canada's first French-speaking prime minister; and Sir John A. Macdonald (1815–91), Canada's first prime minister.

With a C$9.2 million contribution from the city, Place du Canada is getting a face-lift, to include clearing old bones from the former Saint-Antoine Cemetery (closed in 1854), new planting of trees and flower gardens, and new lighting. Work is set to be completed by the end of 2015. ⊠ *Bordered by blvd. René-Lévesque and rues Peel, Metcalfe, and McTavish, Downtown, Montréal* Ⓜ *Bonaventure or Peel.*

St. George's Anglican Church. This is possibly the prettiest Anglican (Episcopalian) church in Montréal. Step into its dim, candle-scented interior and you'll feel you've been transported to some prosperous market town in East Anglia (England). The double hammer-beam roof, the rich stained-glass windows, and the Lady Chapel on the east side of the main altar all add to the effect. It certainly seems a world away from Centre Bell, the modern temple to professional hockey that's across the street. Several National Hockey League players and game announcers have been known to regularly drop in for a few minutes of quiet meditation before joining the action on the ice. ⊠ *1101 rue Stanley(main entrance on rue de la Gauchetière), Downtown, Montréal* ☎ *514/866–7113* ⊕ *www.st-georges.org* ▱ *Free* ☉ *Tues.–Fri. 9–4, weekends 9–3; Sun. services at 9 and 10:30 am* Ⓜ *Bonaventure.*

CHINATOWN

Sandwiched between Downtown and the Old City is bustling **Chinatown.** The center of the action is at the intersection of rue Clark and rue de la Gauchetière, where part of the street is closed to traffic. On weekends, especially in summer, it's particularly busy, crowded with tourists as well as residents shopping in the Asian markets for fresh produce, meat and fish, and health supplements.

Chinese immigrants first came to Montréal in large numbers after 1880, following the construction of the transcontinental railroad, and there's been a steady influx of peoples from Asia and Southeast Asia—including the Vietnamese—since then. Now the city's Chinatown covers about an 18-block area between boulevard René-Lévesque and avenue Viger to the north and south, and near rue de Bleury and avenue Hôtel de Ville on the west and east.

For an inexpensive breakfast or brunch, nothing is more satisfying than a few rounds of dim sum. Try Maison Kam Fung, at 1111 rue St-Urbain (*see the full listing for details*).

GETTING HERE AND AROUND

The best way to enter Chinatown is through the ornate gates on boulevard St-Laurent—Place d'Armes is the closest métro station—then head for the hub at rue de la Gauchetière at the intersection of rue Clark.

THE LATIN QUARTER AND THE VILLAGE

Both the Latin Quarter and what's often known as the Gay Village have a steady energy during the day, busy with students heading to class and sitting hunched over laptops in cafés. Both neighborhoods get more fun in the evening, though, and generally the later, the better.

THE LATIN QUARTER

The **Latin Quarter** (Quartier Latin), just south of the Plateau, has been a center of student life since the 18th century, when Université de Montréal students gave the area its name (courses were given in Latin), and today it continues to infuse the city with youthful energy. When night falls, its streets are filled with multinational hordes—young and not so young, rich and poor, established and still studying.

The Université de Québec à Montréal (UQAM) spreads across the district, along with theaters, restaurants and bars, bookstores, and movie theaters. Some area businesses cater to a young clientele and their penchant for the loud and flashy, but the quarter is also home to some of the city's trendiest restaurants and nightspots. In summer, the streets of the Latin Quarter are busy with summer festival events, such as the Just for Laughs Festival in July.

GETTING HERE AND AROUND
The Latin Quarter is concentrated on boulevard de Maisonneuve and rue St-Denis. The busy Berri-UQAM métro station is the closest.

WORTH NOTING
Chapelle Notre-Dame-de-Lourdes (*Our Lady of Lourdes Chapel*). Artist and architect Napoléon Bourassa called his work here *l'oeuvre de mes amours*, or a labor of love—and it shows. He designed the little Byzantine-style building himself and set about decorating it with the exuberance of an eight-year-old making a Mother's Day card. He covered the walls with murals and encrusted the altar and pillars with gilt and ornamental carving. It's not Montréal's biggest monument to the Virgin Mary, but it's the most unabashedly sentimental. ⊠ *430 rue Ste-Catherine Est, Latin Quarter, Montréal* ☎ *514/845–8278* ⊕ *www. cndlm.org* ✆ *Free* ⊙ *Weekdays 11–6, Sat. 10:30–6:30, Sun. 9–6:30* Ⓜ *Berri-UQAM.*

Chapelle
Notre-Dame-
de-Lourdes **2**

Square St-Louis ..**1**

Square St-Louis. The bourgeois families who built their homes around the fountain and trees here in the late 1870s would probably be dismayed to see the kind of people who congregate in their little park today. It's difficult to walk through the place without dodging a skateboarder or a panhandler. But they're generally a friendly bunch, and the square is still worth a visit just to see the elegant and colorful Second Empire–style homes that surround it. ⊠ *Bordered by av. Laval and rue St-Denis between rue Sherbrooke Est and av. des Pins Est, Latin Quarter, Montréal* Ⓜ *Sherbrooke.*

THE VILLAGE

Often called the **Gay Village**, this area is the center of one of the most vibrant gay communities in the world, widely supported by residents of this proudly liberal, open-minded city. In recent years the municipal, federal, and provincial governments have taken it upon themselves to promote the Village and Montréal's gay-friendly climate as a reason for tourists to visit, but its restaurants, antiques shops (on rue Amherst), and bars make it a popular destination for visitors of all persuasions. The lively strip of rue Ste-Catherine running east of the Latin Quarter is the backbone of the Village.

Seeing the Oratoire St-Joseph illuminated at night, it's easy to understand how this has become a point of pilgrimage.

In late July, the Village's Pride Parade, widely considered the biggest and most outrageous party of the year, attracts more than a million people.

GETTING HERE AND AROUND
The Village centers on the Beaudry métro station, which has its entrance adorned with rainbow pillars. Its borders are considered rue Ste-Catherine Est from Amherst to de Lorimier, and on the north–south axis from René-Lévesque to Sherbrooke.

THE PLATEAU, OUTREMONT, MILE END, AND LITTLE ITALY

Heading north and east of Downtown and the McGill campus will lead you to some of the most vibrant neighborhoods of Montréal, with a mix of ethnic communities, students, and young professionals. There aren't many traditional types of tourist attractions, but this is where you'll find exciting new restaurants, boutiques, and galleries are popping up, alongside long-established residential neighborhoods.

THE PLATEAU MONT-ROYAL

Plateau Mont-Royal—or simply the **Plateau** as it's more commonly called these days—is still home to a strong Portuguese community, but much of the housing originally built for factory workers has been bought and renovated by professionals, artists, performers, and academics eager to find a place to live close to all the action. The Plateau is always bustling, even in the dead of winter, but on sunny summer weekends it's packed with Montrealers who come here to shop, dine, and observe each other.

Many of the older residences in the Plateau and the nearby neighborhoods have the graceful wrought-iron balconies and twisting staircases that are typical of Montréal. The stairs and balconies, treacherous in winter, are often full of families and couples gossiping, picnicking, and partying come summer. If Montrealers tell you they spend the summer in Balconville, they mean they don't have the money or the time to leave town and won't get any farther than their balconies.

GETTING HERE AND AROUND

The Plateau's most convenient métro station is Mont-Royal on the Orange Line. It's a large district, but relatively flat and easy to walk around. If you want to cover more ground without resorting to a taxi, there are several Bixi bicycle stands in the area, and plenty of bike lanes.

TOP ATTRACTIONS

Boulevard St-Laurent. A walk along this section of the boulevard St-Laurent is like a walk through Montréal's cultural history. The shops and restaurants, synagogues and churches that line the 10-block stretch north of rue Sherbrooke reflect the various waves of immigrants that

Avenue
Bernard **5**

Boulevard
St-Laurent **3**

Chiesa della
Madonna
della Difesa **7**

Église de la
Visitation
de la
Bienheureuse
Vierge Marie **8**

Marché
Jean-Talon **6**

Musée des
Hospitalières de
l'Hôtel-Dieu **2**

Parc Lafontaine ..**4**

Rue
Prince-Arthur **1**

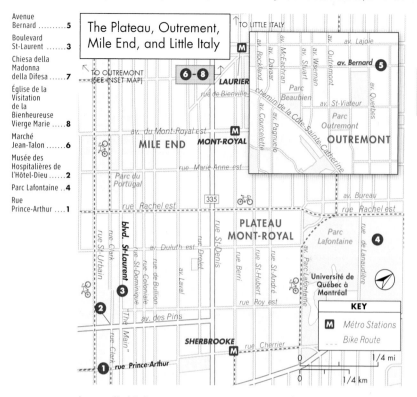

have called it home. Keep your eyes open and you'll see Jewish delis, Hungarian sausage shops, Chinese grocery stores, Portuguese favelas, Italian coffee bars, Greek restaurants, Vietnamese sandwich shops, and Peruvian snack bars. You'll also spot some of the city's trendiest restaurants and nightclubs. The first immigrants to move into the area in the 1880s were Jews escaping pogroms in Eastern Europe. It was they who called the street "the Main," as in Main Street—a nickname that endures to this day. Even Francophone Montrealers sometimes call it "Le Main." ⊠ *The Plateau, Montréal* Ⓜ *St-Laurent, Sherbrooke, or Mont-Royal.*

WORTH NOTING

Musée des Hospitalières de l'Hôtel-Dieu. The nuns of the Religieuses Hospitalières de St-Joseph ran Montréal's Hôpital Hôtel-Dieu for more than 300 years, until the province and the Université de Montréal took it over in the 1970s. The first sisters—girls of good families caught up in the religious fervor of the age—came to New France with Jeanne Mance in the mid-1600s to look after the poor, the sick, and the dying. The order's museum—tucked away in a corner of the hospital the nuns built but no longer run—captures the spirit of that age with a series of meticulously bilingual exhibits. Just reading the excerpts from the letters and diaries of those young women helps you to understand the

ART IN THE MÉTRO

Montréal was ahead of the curve in requiring all construction in the métro system to include an art component, resulting in such dramatic works as Frédéric Back's mural of the history of music in Place des Arts and the swirling stained-glass windows by Marcelle Ferron in Champs-de-Mars. The art nouveau entrance to the Square-Victoria station, a gift from the city of Paris, is the only original piece of Hector Guimard's architectural-design work outside the City of Light.

Operating since 1966, the métro is among the most architecturally distinctive subway systems in the world, with each of its 65 stations individually designed and decorated.

The newer stations along the Blue Line are all worth a visit as well, particularly Outremont, with a glass-block design from 1988. Even Place-d'Armes, one of the least visually remarkable stations in the system, includes a treasure: look for the small exhibit of archaeological artifacts representing each of Montréal's four historical eras (Aboriginal, French, English, and multicultural).

zeal that drove them to abandon the comforts of home for the hardships of the colonies. The museum also traces the history of medicine and nursing in Montréal. ⊠ *201 av. des Pins Ouest, The Plateau, Montréal* ☎ *514/849–2919* ⊕ *www.museedeshospitalieres.qc.ca* ⊠ *C$6* ⊙ *Mid-June–mid-Oct., Tues.–Fri. 10–5, weekends 1–5; mid-Oct.–mid-June, Wed.–Sun. 1–5* Ⓜ *Sherbrooke, then bus 144.*

Parc Lafontaine. You could say that Parc Lafontaine is a microcosm of Montréal: the eastern half is French, with paths, gardens, and lawns laid out in geometric shapes; the western half is English, with meandering paths and irregularly shaped ponds that follow the natural contours of the land. In summer you can take advantage of bowling greens, tennis courts, an open-air theater (Théâtre de Verdure) where there are free events, and two artificial lakes with paddleboats. In winter one lake becomes a large skating rink. The park is named for Sir Louis-Hippolyte Lafontaine (1807–64), a pioneer of responsible government in Canada. His statue graces a plot on the park's southwestern edge. ⊠ *3933 av. Parc Lafontaine, The Plateau, Montréal* ☎ *514/872–9800* ⊕ *www.montreal.com/parks* ⊙ *Daily 9 am–10 pm* Ⓜ *Sherbrooke or Mont-Royal.*

Rue Prince-Arthur. In the 1960s rue Prince-Arthur was the Haight-Ashbury of Montréal, full of shops selling leather vests, tie-dyed T-shirts, recycled clothes, and drug paraphernalia. It still retains a little of that raffish attitude, but it's much tamer and more commercial these days. The blocks between avenue Laval and boulevard St-Laurent are a pedestrian mall, and the hippie shops have metamorphosed into inexpensive Greek, Vietnamese, Italian, Polish, and Chinese restaurants and neighborhood bars. So grab a table, order a coffee or an *apéro*, and watch the passing parade. ⊠ *The Plateau, Montréal* Ⓜ *Sherbrooke.*

OUTREMONT

The gentrification of the Plateau has pushed up rents and driven students, immigrant families, and single young graduates farther north, following the main thoroughfares of boulevard St-Laurent as well as St-Denis. Above the Plateau and next to Parc du Mont-Royal, **Outremont** has long been Montréal's residential Francophone enclave (as opposed to Westmount, always stubbornly English right down to its neo-Gothic churches and lawn-bowling club). It has grand homes, tree-shaded streets, perfectly groomed parks, and two upscale shopping and dining strips along rue Laurier and avenue Bernard. The latter, with wide sidewalks and shady trees, is particularly attractive. The eastern fringes of Outremont are home to Montréal's thriving Hasidic community.

GETTING HERE AND AROUND

By métro, take the Blue Line to Outremont station. You can also get to Outremont from Downtown on Bus 55, which goes along St. Laurent Boulevard, or Bus 80, which goes through Mont-Royal Park along avenue du Parc. Both bus routes can be picked up outside the Place des Arts métro, and you need to get off at rue Laurier and walk west from there. (Outremont begins on the west side of Parc; the east side of Parc is Mile End.)

Alternately, you could stay on Bus 80 for a few more stops until you come to Bernard and then walk west. Both Laurier and Bernard avenues are Outremont's primary hubs for commercial activity. The Outremont métro stop lets you off on avenue Van Horne, another commercial hub but without the fun, interesting boutiques and restaurants of Laurier and Bernard. If you're coming from Downtown and feeling fit you could walk to Outremont in roughly 30–45 minutes, or, for that matter, just hop on a Bixi bicycle, taking the same route as Bus 80 and getting there in half the time.

TOP ATTRACTIONS

Avenue Bernard. If your taste runs to the chic and fashionable, then there is simply no better street for people-watching. Its wide sidewalks and shady trees make it ideal for the kind of outdoor cafés and restaurants that attract the bright and the beautiful. ⊠ *Outremont, Montréal* Ⓜ *Outremont.*

MILE END

In recent years **Mile End** has become one of the hippest neighborhoods in town, and it starts buzzing the moment restaurants open for brunch. Bordering Outremont, this funky area, historically home to Montréal's working-class Jewish community, is now full of inexpensive, often excellent restaurants and little shops selling handicrafts and secondhand clothes. Head east from Parc off streets like Bernard, St. Viateur, and Fairmount. By day it's a great place to take a stroll or sit on a café's *terrasse* (patio) to watch its residents—from artsy bohemians to Hasidic Jews—pass by.

ALL ABOARD THE EXPORAIL!

Exporail. You can rattle around Canada's largest railroad museum in a vintage tram specially built in the 1950s for sightseeing tours in Montréal when the city still had a streetcar system. The museum has more than 120 train cars and locomotives, but if you're a steam buff, you won't want to miss CPR 5935, the largest steam locomotive built in Canada, and CNR 4100, the most powerful in the British Empire when it was built in 1924. To see how the rich and powerful traveled, take a look at Sir William Van Horne's luxurious private car. Of special interest to the kids will be the car that served as a mobile classroom. The museum is south of the city in the town of St-Constant. In the summer, the Agence metropolitain de transport, the commuter rail agency, runs train excursions to the museum from the Gare Lucien-l'Allier next to the Centre Bell. Trains depart at 11 am and return at 4 pm. ⊠ 110 rue St-Pierre, St-Constant ☎ 450/632-2410 ⊕ www.exporail. org ⊒ C$18 ⊘ May 17–June 23, daily 10–5; June 24–Sept. 1, daily 10–6; Sept. 3–Oct. 31, Wed.–Sun. 10–5; Nov.–May 11, weekends 10–5. Outdoor exhibits close an hr earlier.

GETTING HERE AND AROUND
To reach Mile End by public transit, take the métro's Orange Line to Laurier or Bus 55 from Place d'Armes métro station; get off at Fairmount or St. Viateur and walk west from there.

LITTLE ITALY

Farther north is **Little Italy,** which is still home base to Montréal's sizable Italian community of nearly a quarter of a million people, and though families of Italian descent now live all over the greater Montréal area, many come back here every week or so to shop, eat out, or visit family and friends, and the 30-odd blocks bounded by rues Jean-Talon, St-Zotique, Marconi, and Drolet remain its heart and soul. You'll know you've reached Little Italy when the gardens have tomato plants and grapevines, there are sausages and cans of olive oil in store windows, and the heady smell of espresso emanates from cafés.

GETTING HERE AND AROUND
You can take both the Orange and Blue lines to get to Little Italy: get off at Jean-Talon station and walk six short blocks to get to boulevard St-Laurent. Bus 55, which runs north along St-Laurent, will also get you here fairly quickly from Downtown, or you could just take a Bixi bike and get here in roughly 20 minutes. Once here, you can stop for produce and cheese at the Marché Jean-Talon, and you might just see a wedding party outside the Madonna della Difesa church.

TOP ATTRACTIONS
Chiesa della Madonna della Difesa. If you look up at the cupola behind the main altar of Little Italy's most famous church, you'll spot Montréal's most infamous piece of ecclesiastical portraiture. Yes, indeed, that lantern-jaw fellow on horseback who looks so pleased with himself

is Benito Mussolini, the dictator who led Italy into World War II—on the wrong side. The mural, by Guido Nincheri (1885–1973), was completed long before the war and commemorates the signing of the Lateran Pact with Pope Pius XI, one of Il Duce's few lasting achievements. The controversy shouldn't distract you from the beauties of the rest of the richly decorated church. ✉ *6800 av. Henri-Julien, Little Italy, Montréal* ☎ *514/277–6522* ☐ *Free* ⊘ *Daily 10–6* Ⓜ *Beaubien or Jean-Talon.*

Marché Jean-Talon. If you're trying to stick to a diet, stay away: the smells of grilling sausages, roasting chestnuts, and fresh pastries will almost certainly crack your resolve. And if they don't, there are dozens of tiny shops full of Québec cheeses, Lebanese sweets, country pâtés, local wines, and handmade chocolates that will. Less threatening to the waistline are the huge mounds of peas, beans, apples, carrots, pears, garlic, and other produce on sale at the open-air stands. Visit on weekends during the warm summer months, and it will feel as if all of Montréal has come out to shop. ✉ *7070 rue Henri-Julien, Little Italy, Montréal* ☎ *514/277–1588* ⊕ *www.marchespublics-mtl.com* ⊘ *Mon.–Sat 7–6 (to 8 pm Thurs. and Fri.), Sun. 7–5* Ⓜ *Jean-Talon.*

OFF THE BEATEN PATH

Église de la Visitation de la Bienheureuse Vierge Marie. The oldest church on the island, the Church of the Visitation of the Blessed Virgin Mary had its stone walls raised in the 1750s, and the beautifully proportioned Palladian front was added in 1850. Decorating lasted from 1764 until 1837, with stunning results. The altar and the pulpit are as ornate as wedding cakes but still delicate. The church's most notable treasure is a rendering of the Visitation attributed to Pierre Mignard, a painter at the 17th-century court of Louis XIV. Parkland surrounds the church, and the nearby Îles de la Visitation (reachable by footbridge) make for a very good walk. You have to ride the métro to its northern terminus at the Henri-Bourassa station, and then walk for 15–20 minutes through some pretty ordinary neighborhoods to reach this church, but it's worth the trek. ✉ *1847 blvd. Gouin Est, Montréal North, Montréal* ☎ *514/388–4050* ☐ *Free* ⊘ *Fri.–Wed. 8–noon and 1–3; call for tour information (French only)* Ⓜ *Henri-Bourassa.*

PARC DU MONT-ROYAL

Fodor's Choice ★ In geological terms, Mont-Royal is just a bump of basaltlike rock worn down by several ice ages to a mere 760 feet. But in the affections of Montrealers it's a Matterhorn. Without a trace of irony, they call it simply *la Montagne* or "the Mountain," and it's easy to see why it's so well loved.

For Montrealers it's a refuge, a semi-tamed wilderness within the city. It's where you go to get away from it all. And even when you can't get away, you can see the mountain glimmering beyond the skyscrapers and the high-rises—green in summer, gray and white in winter, and gold and crimson in fall.

The nearly 500 acres of forests and meadows were laid out by Frederick Law Olmsted (1822–1903), the man responsible for New York City's Central Park. Olmsted believed that communion with nature could cure body and soul, so much of the park has been left as wild as possible, with narrow paths meandering through tall stands of maples and red oaks. In summer it's full of picnicking families; in winter cross-country skiers and snowshoers take over, while families skate at Lac aux Castors and ride sleds and inner tubes down groomed slopes. If you want to explore with minimum effort, you can hire the services of a horse-drawn carriage (or sleigh in winter).

GETTING HERE AND AROUND

If you're in good shape, you can walk up from Downtown. Climb rue Peel to the entrance to Parc du Mont-Royal and then wheeze your way up the stairway to the top of the mountain. Or you can simply take the métro to the Mont-Royal station and catch Bus 11. If you have a car, there's good parking in Parc du Mont-Royal and at the Oratoire St-Joseph (the latter asks for a contribution of $5 per vehicle Monday to Saturday for anyone not attending a service or coming to pray). Biking up the mountain will test your endurance, but the park has an extensive network of scenic trails.

TIMING

Depending on your interest, you could spend anywhere from a few hours—if you simply just want to see the view—to the entire day here. If you're here for the afternoon, there's a cafeteria in the park for lunch, or you can pick up picnic provisions before you set out.

DID YOU KNOW?

Montréal is a bike lover's city, with miles of paved paths and trails part of the Route Vert, a 5,000-km (3,100-mile) network that covers the province of Québec.

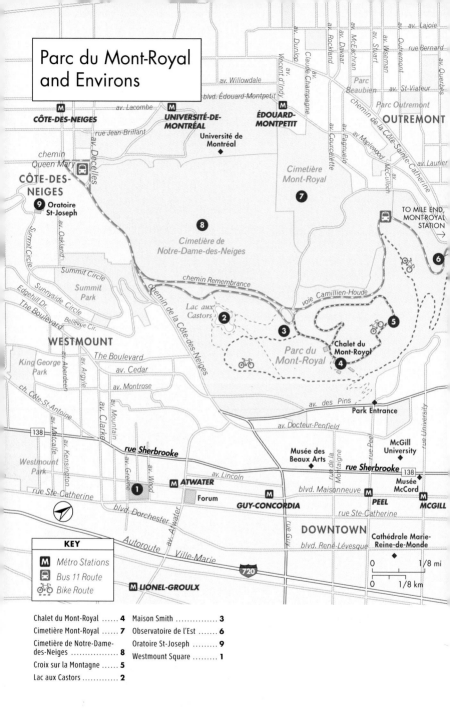

Parc du Mont-Royal and Environs

Chalet du Mont-Royal **4**
Cimetière Mont-Royal **7**
Cimetière de Notre-Dame-des-Neiges **8**
Croix sur la Montagne **5**
Lac aux Castors **2**
Maison Smith **3**
Observatoire de l'Est **6**
Oratoire St-Joseph **9**
Westmount Square **1**

TOP ATTRACTIONS

Chalet du Mont-Royal. No trip to Montréal is complete without a visit to the terrace in front of the Chalet du Mont-Royal. It's not the only place to get an overview of the city, the river, and the countryside beyond, but it's the most spectacular. On clear days you can see not only the downtown skyscrapers, but also Mont-Royal's sister mountains—Monts St-Bruno, St-Hilaire, and St-Grégoire. These isolated peaks, called the Montérégies, or Mountains of the King, rise dramatically from the flat countryside. Be sure to take a look inside the chalet, especially at the murals depicting scenes from Canadian history. ⊠ *Off voie Camillien-Houde, Parc du Mont-Royal, Montréal* ⊕ *www.lemontroyal.qc.ca* ⊠ *Free* ☉ *Daily 9–5* Ⓜ *Mont-Royal, then bus 11 westbound.*

WORTH NOTING

Croix sur la Montagne (*Cross atop Mont-Royal*). Visible from miles away, the 98-foot-high steel cross at the top of Mont-Royal has been a city landmark since it was erected in 1924, largely with money raised through the efforts of 85,000 high-school students. In 1993 the 249 bulbs used to light the cross were replaced with a fiber-optic system. ⊠ *Parc du Mont-Royal, Montréal* ⊕ *www.lemontroyal.qc.ca.*

FAMILY **Lac aux Castors** (*Beaver Lake*). Mont-Royal's single body of water, actually a reclaimed bog, is a great place for kids (and parents) to float model boats in the summertime. In winter, the lake's frozen surface attracts whole families of skaters, and nearby there's a groomed slope where kids of all ages can ride inner tubes. The glass-fronted Beaver Lake Pavilion is a pleasant bistro that serves lunch and dinner. Skate and cross-country-ski rentals are available downstairs. . ⊠ *Off chemin Remembrance, Parc du Mont-Royal, Montréal* ⊕ *www.lemontroyal. qc.ca* Ⓜ *Mont-Royal, then bus 11 westbound.*

Maison Smith. If you need a map of Mont-Royal's extensive hiking trails or want to know about the more than 180 kinds of birds here, the former park keeper's residence is the place to go. It's also a good spot for getting a snack, drink, or souvenir. The pretty little stone house—built in 1858—is the headquarters of Les Amis de la Montagne (The Friends of the Mountain), an organization that offers various guided walks on the mountain and in nearby areas. ⊠ *1260 chemin Remembrance, Parc du Mont-Royal, Montréal* ☏ *514/843–8240* ⊕ *www.lemontroyal.qc.ca* ☉ *Daily 9–6 (hrs may vary slightly by season)* Ⓜ *Mont-Royal, then bus 11 westbound.*

Observatoire de l'Est. If you're just driving across Mont-Royal, be sure to stop for a few moments at its eastern lookout for a view of the Stade Olympique and the east end of the city. Tourists enjoy the location as it's a great photo spot. ⊠ *Voie Camillien-Houde, Parc du Mont-Royal, Montréal* Ⓜ *Mont-Royal.*

CÔTE-DES-NEIGES

Not too many tourists venture north and east of Parc du Mont-Royal but the primarily residential neighborhood of Côte-des-Neiges and the Town of Mount Royal (usually just called TMR) have much to offer.

One of Montréal's most-visited sites—the Oratoire St-Joseph (St. Joseph's Oratory)—sits atop the northern slope of Mont-Royal, dominating the surrounding neighborhood of Côte-des-Neiges. More than 2 million people of all faiths visit the shrine every year. The most devout pilgrims climb the staircase leading to the main door on their knees, pausing on each of its 99 steps to pray.

Even without the Oratoire (as well as the Cimetière de Notre-Dame-des-Neiges, another site worth seeing), Côte-des-Neiges is a district worth visiting. It's also an area where the dominant languages are neither English nor French.

It's largely working-class immigrants who live here—Filipino, Latin American, Southeast Asian, West Indian, Arab, Jewish, Chinese, and most recently people from Eastern Europe and Africa. It's also home to a sizable number of students, many of whom attend the Université de Montréal, as well as other smaller surrounding colleges and universities.

As a result, if you're looking for inexpensive, authentic world cuisine, there's no better place in Montréal to come to than Côte-des-Neiges. It's teeming with ethnic shops and restaurants—Thai, Russian, Korean, Indian, Peruvian, Filipino, and more.

GETTING HERE AND AROUND

Côte-des-Neiges is bordered by avenue Decelles to the north and the Cimetière de Notre-Dame-des-Neiges to the south. It's easy to get here by public transit, either the métro to the Côte-des-Neiges station or the 166 Bus from the Guy-Concordia métro station to chemin Queen-Mary. If you take a car—not a bad idea if you plan to visit the Parc du Mont-Royal as well—it's usually easy to get a parking space at the Oratoire St-Joseph (a contribution of $5 per vehicle is requested Monday to Saturday, except for those attending services or coming to the Oratoire to pray).

WHEN TO GO

Côte-des-Neiges bustles during the day, but is a little quieter at night.

Cimetière
Mont-Royal **3**

Cimetière de
Notre-Dame-
des-Neiges **2**

Oratoire
St-Joseph **1**

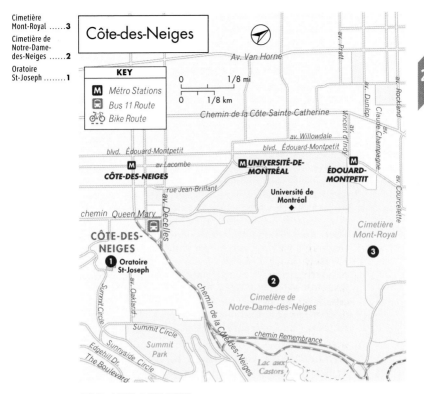

TOP ATTRACTIONS

Fodor'sChoice **Oratoire St-Joseph** (*St. Joseph's Oratory*). Each year some 2 million peo-
★ ple from all over North America and beyond visit St. Joseph's Oratory.
The most devout Catholics climb the 99 steps to its front door on their
knees. It is the world's largest and most popular shrine dedicated to the
earthly father of Jesus (Canada's patron saint), and it's all the work of
a man named Brother André Besette (1845–1937).

By worldly standards Brother André didn't have much going for him,
but he had a deep devotion to St. Joseph and an iron will. In 1870 he
joined the Holy Cross religious order and was assigned to work as a
doorkeeper at the college the order operated just north of Mont-Royal.
In 1904 he began building a chapel on the mountainside across the road
to honor his favorite saint, and the rest is history. Thanks to reports
of miraculous cures attributed to St. Joseph's intercession, donations
started to pour in, and Brother André was able to start work replacing
his modest shrine with something more substantial. The result, which
wasn't completed until after his death, is one of the most triumphal
pieces of church architecture in North America.

The oratory and its gardens dominate Mont-Royal's northwestern
slope. Its copper dome—one of the largest in the world—can be seen
from miles away. The interior of the main church is equally grand,

although it's also quite austere. The best time to visit it is on Sunday for the 11 am solemn mass, when the sanctuary is brightly lit and the sweet voices of Les Petits Chanteurs de Mont-Royal—the city's best boys' choir—fill the nave with music.

The crypt is shabbier than its big brother upstairs but more welcoming. In a long, narrow room behind the crypt, 10,000 votive candles glitter before a dozen carved murals extolling the virtues of St. Joseph; the walls are hung with crutches discarded by those said to have been cured. Just beyond is the simple tomb of Brother André, who was canonized a saint in 2010. His preserved heart is displayed in a glass case in one of several galleries between the crypt and the main church.

High on the mountain, east of the main church, is a garden commemorating the Passion of Christ, with life-size representations of the 14 stations of the cross. On the west side of the church is Brother André's original chapel, with pressed-tin ceilings and plaster saints that is, in many ways, more moving than the church that overshadows it. Note: The oratoire operates a shuttle bus for visitors who aren't up to the steep climb from the main parking lot to the entrance of the crypt church. The main church is several stories above that, but escalators and two elevators ease the ascent. ⊠ *3800 chemin Queen Mary, Côte-des-Neiges, Montréal* 🕾 *514/733–8211, 877/672–8647* ⊕ *www.saint-joseph. org* ⊠ *Free. Parking: $5 per vehicle contribution requested (except for those attending services or coming to pray)* ⊙ *May–Oct., daily 7 am–9 pm; Nov.–Apr., daily 7–5:30* Ⓜ *Côte-des-Neiges.*

WORTH NOTING

Cimetière de Notre-Dame-des-Neiges (*Our Lady of the Snows Cemetery*). At 343 acres, Canada's largest cemetery is not much smaller than the neighboring **Parc du Mont-Royal,** and, as long as you just count the living, it's usually a lot less crowded. You don't have to be morbid to wander the graveyard's 55 km (34 miles) of tree-shaded paths and roadways past the tombs of hundreds of prominent artists, poets, intellectuals, politicians, and clerics. Among them is Calixa Lavallée (1842–91), who wrote "O Canada," the country's national anthem. The cemetery offers some guided tours in summer. Phone ahead for details. ⊠ *4601 chemin de la Côte-des-Neiges, Côte-des-Neiges, Montréal* 🕾 *514/735–1361* ⊕ *www.cimetierenddn.org* ⊙ *Daily 8–5* Ⓜ *Côte-des-Neiges, then bus 165 southbound.*

▌DETOUR   **Duc de Lorraine. A light croissant or rich pastry from the Duc de Lorraine makes for a nice break after visiting the Oratoire St-Joseph. If it's lunchtime, try a meat pie or a quiche, followed by a scoop of homemade ice cream.** ⊠ *5002 Côte-des-Neiges, Côte-des-Neiges, Montréal* 🕾 *514/731–4128* ⊕ *www.ducdelorraine.ca* Ⓜ *Côte-des-Neiges.*

Cimetière Mont-Royal. If you find yourself humming "Getting to Know You" as you explore Mont-Royal Cemetery's 165 acres, blame it on the graveyard's most famous permanent guest, Anna Leonowens (1834–1915). She was the real-life model for the heroine of the Rodgers and Hammerstein musical *The King and I.* The cemetery—established in 1852 by the Anglican, Presbyterian, Unitarian, and Baptist churches—is laid out like a terraced garden, with footpaths that meander between crab-apple trees and past Japanese lilacs. You can also enter the cemetery through a gate on Parc du Mont-Royal, but it's only open 9–4. ✉ *1297 chemin de la Forêt, Côte-des-Neiges, Montréal* ☎ *514/279–7358* 🌐 *www.mountroyalcem.com* ⏲ *May–Aug., weekdays 8–8, weekends 9–8; Sept. and Oct., weekdays 8–6, weekends 9–6; Nov.–Feb., weekdays 8–5, weekends 9–5; Mar. and Apr., weekdays 8–6, weekends 9–6* Ⓜ *Mont-Royale, then bus 11 westbound.*

TOWN OF MOUNT ROYAL (TMR)

The Town of Mount Royal, has long been a primarily English, and for the most part upscale, residential area, filled with classic town houses and many parks. Just north of Outremont and south of Ville St-Laurent, it's a notably pretty area, although not a whole lot goes on here.

GETTING HERE AND AROUND

TMR is a notoriously tricky area to drive to if you don't know Montréal well, and there are no métro stations nearby. The easiest way to get here from Downtown is by taking the commuter train that leaves from Central Station and then getting off at the Mont-Royal stop, at the particularly cute town square. The train ride is notable in itself—it travels directly under "the mountain" (Parc Mont-Royal), through what is the second longest tunnel in the country (about 5 km [3 miles]). It was constructed by the Canadian Northern Railway back in 1910, and was, at that time, considered quite an engineering feat.

HOCHELAGA-MAISONNEUVE

The neighborhood of Hochelaga-Maisonneuve is one of the best spots to go if you're craving green space, plus it has one of Montréal's best markets. In fact, it's worth the trip on the métro's Green Line just to see the four institutions that make up Montréal's Space for Life, an innovative natural science museum complex—the first in the world to link humans with nature. It includes the Jardin Botanique (Botanical Garden); the Insectarium, which houses the world's largest collection of bugs; the Biodôme, a great place to experience different ecosystems under one roof; and the stunning Rio Tinto Alcan Planetarium. Parc Maisonneuve is a lovely green area, and an ideal place for a stroll or a picnic, and don't miss the Stade Olympique (Olympic Stadium), which played host to the 1976 Summer Olympics; the leaning tower that supports the stadium's roof dominates the skyline here and provides a great viewpoint. The rest of the area is largely working-class residential, but there are some good restaurants and little shops along rue Ontario Est.

Until 1918, when it was annexed by Montréal, the east-end district of Maisonneuve was a city unto itself, a booming, prosperous industrial center full of factories making everything from shoes to cheese. The neighborhood was also packed with houses for the almost entirely French-Canadian workforce who kept the whole machine humming.

Maisonneuve was also the site of one of Canada's earliest experiments in urban planning. The Dufresne brothers, a pair of prosperous shoe manufacturers, built a series of grand civic buildings along rue Morgan—many of which still stand—including a theater, public baths, and a bustling market, as well as Parc Maisonneuve. All this was supposed to make working-class life more bearable, but World War I put an end to the brothers' plans and Maisonneuve became part of Montréal, twinned with the east-end district of Hochelaga.

GETTING HERE AND AROUND

It's not necessary to drive to the area, as the Pie-IX and Viau métro stops on the Green Line provide easy access to all the sites, including the Insectarium and the Jardin Botanique. For bikers, it's a straight shot across the path on rue Rachel.

TIMING

If traveling with kids, you'll probably want to dedicate more time to exploring the area to see the sites. One of the city's major markets—Marché Maisonneuve—is on the corner of rue Ontario and avenue Bennett, and is well worth a stop.

TOP ATTRACTIONS

FAMILY **Insectarium.** If you're a little squeamish about beetles and roaches, you might want to give the bug-shape building in the middle of the **Espace pour la Vie Jardin Botanique** (Space for Life Botanical Garden) a pass, but kids especially seem to love it. Considered one of the largest insect museums in North America, with more than 250,000 insects in the collection, the little creatures are either mounted or behind panes of glass thick enough to minimize the shudder factor—a good thing when you're looking at a tree roach the size of a wrestler's thumb. There is, however, a room full of free-flying butterflies, and in February and May the Insectarium releases thousands of butterflies and moths into the Jardin Botanique's main greenhouse. At varying times during the year the Insectarium brings in chefs to prepare such delicacies as deep-fried bumblebees and chocolate-dipped locusts—protein-rich treats that most adults find highly resistible. The Insectarium Metamorphosis project, launched in 2014, will enlarge and renovate the facility and is expected to be completed by 2017. ⊠ *4581 rue Sherbrooke Est, Hochelaga-Maisonneuve, Montréal* ☎ *514/872–1400* ⊕ *www.montrealspaceforlife. ca* ☎ *C$18.75 (includes Jardin Botanique)* ⊙ *Mid-May–Labor Day, daily 9–6; Sept. and Oct., daily 9–9; Nov.–mid-May, Tues.–Sun. 9–5* Ⓜ *Pie-IX or Viau.*

FAMILY

Fodor's Choice

★

Jardin Botanique (*Botanical Garden*). Creating one of the world's great botanical gardens in a city with a winter as harsh as Montréal's was no mean feat, and the result is that no matter how brutal it gets in January there's one corner of the city where it's always summer. With 181 acres of plantings in summer and 10 greenhouses open all year, Space for Life Montréal's Jardin Botanique is the second-largest attraction of its kind in the world (after England's Kew Gardens). It grows more than 26,000 species of plants, and among its 30 thematic gardens are a rose garden, an alpine garden, and—a favorite with the kids—a poisonous-plant garden. You can attend traditional tea ceremonies in the Japanese Garden, which has one of the best bonsai collections in the West, or wander among the native birches and maples of the Jardin des Premières-Nations (First Nations Garden). The Jardin de Chine (Chinese Garden), with its pagoda and waterfall, will transport you back to the Ming Dynasty. A new Glass Pavilion, to be designed along innovative biophilic design principles, is due to open by 2017 and will host horticultural events. ⊠ *4101 rue Sherbrooke Est, Hochelaga-Maisonneuve, Montréal* ☎ *514/872–1400* ⊕ *www.montrealspaceforlife.ca* ☎ *C$18.75 or $16 in winter (includes Insectarium)* ⊙ *May–Aug., daily 9–6; Sept. and Oct., daily 9–9; Nov.–Apr., Tues.–Sun. 9–5* Ⓜ *Pie-IX or Viau.*

Maisonneuve. World War I and the Depression killed early 20th-century plans to turn this industrial center into a model city with broad boulevards, grand public buildings, and fine homes, but just three blocks south of the Olympic site a few fragments of that dream have survived the passage of time. A magnificent beaux arts building, site of the old public market, which has a 20-foot-tall bronze statue of a farm woman, stands at the northern end of tree-lined avenue Morgan. Farmers and butchers have moved into the modern building next door that houses the **Marché Maisonneuve,** which has become one of the city's major markets, along with Marché Jean-Talon and Marché Atwater. The old market is now a community center and the site of summer shows and concerts. Monumental staircases and a heroic rooftop sculpture embellish the public baths across the street. The **Théâtre Denise Pelletier,** at the corner of rues Ste-Catherine Est and Morgan, has a lavish Italianate interior; **Fire Station No. 1,** at 4300 rue Notre-Dame Est, was inspired by Frank Lloyd Wright's Unity Temple in suburban Chicago; and the sumptuously decorated **Église Très-Saint-Nom-de-Jésus** has one of the most powerful organs in North America. The 60-acre **Parc Maisonneuve,** stretching north of the botanical garden, is a lovely place for a stroll. ⊠ *Montréal* Ⓜ *Pie-IX or Viau.*

WORTH NOTING

FAMILY

Biodôme. Not everyone thought it was a great idea to transform an Olympic bicycle-racing stadium into a natural-history exhibit, but the result is one of the city's most popular attractions, part of the Space

DID YOU KNOW?

A crew of more than 100 construction workers came to Montréal for a year to build the Shanghai-style Chinese Garden at the Jardin Botanique, where the Chinese Lantern Festival is held.

Biodôme 4

Château
Dufresne 7

Insectarium 6

Jardin
Botanique 5

Maisonneuve 8

Rio Tinto Alcan
Planetarium 1

Stade
Olympique 2

Tour
Olympique 3

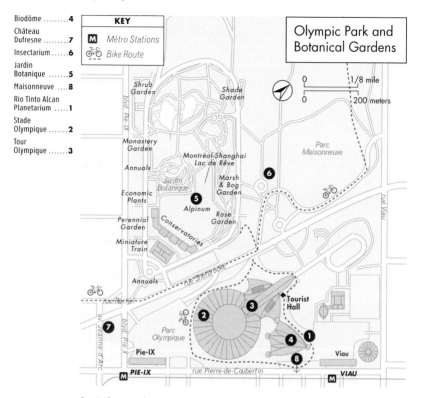

KEY

Ⓜ Métro Stations

🚲 Bike Route

Olympic Park and Botanical Gardens

for Life complex. Four ecosystems—a boreal forest, a tropical forest, a polar landscape, and the St. Lawrence River—are under one climate-controlled dome. You follow pathways through each environment, observing indigenous flora and fauna. New residents of the Biodôme are three Lynx kittens born in captivity in 2013. These little cuties are a hit with kids and adults alike. Between its launch in 2014 and completion in 2017, the Biodôme Renewal project will renovate the exhibits, with a focus on humans' relationship with nature. ■TIP→ Keep in mind that the tropical forest is as hot and humid as the real thing, and the Québec and Arctic exhibits can be frigid. If you want to stay comfortable, dress in layers. ✉ 4777 av. Pierre-de-Coubertin, Hochelaga-Maisonneuve, Montréal ☎ 514/868–3000 ⊕ espacepourlavie.ca ☞ C$18.75 ☼ Late June–early Sept., daily 9–6; early Sept.–early Mar., Tues.–Sun. 9–5, early Mar.–late June, daily 9–5 Ⓜ Viau or Pie-IX.

Château Dufresne. The adjoining homes of a pair of shoe manufacturers, Oscar and Marius Dufresne, provide a glimpse into the lives of Montréal's Francophone bourgeoisie in the early 20th century. The brothers built their beaux-arts palace in 1916 along the lines of the Petit-Trianon in Paris, and lived in it with their families—Oscar in the eastern half and Marius in the western half. Worth searching out are the domestic scenes on the walls of the Petit Salon, where Oscar's wife entertained friends.

Her brother-in-law relaxed with his friends in a smoking room decked out like a Turkish lounge. During the house's incarnation as a boys' school in the 1950s, the Eudist priests who ran it covered the room's frieze of nymphs and satyrs with a modest curtain that their charges lifted at every opportunity. ☒ *2929 rue Jeanne-d'Arc, Hochelaga-Maisonneuve, Montréal* ☎ *514/259–9201* ⊕ *www.chateaudufresne.com* ☒ *C$9* ☼ *Wed.–Sun. 10–5. Tours in English, weekends 2:30* Ⓜ *Viau.*

Rio Tinto Alcan Planetarium. In early 2013, Montréal got a new, ultramodern, C$48 million planetarium, one of only a handful of planetariums worldwide to have two circular theaters—one for astronomy exhibits and the other a high-tech multimedia venue. Part of the Space for Life complex, this state-of-the-art facility promises a futuristic experience unlike any other. The permanent exhibit, EXO: Our Search for Life in the Universe, lets the whole family having fun exploring life on earth and (perhaps) in the universe through interactive and hands-on stations. ☒ *4801 av. Pierre-de-Coubertin, Hochelaga-Maisonneuve, Montréal* ☎ *514/868–3000* ⊕ *espacepourlavie.ca/planetarium* ☒ *C$18.75* ☼ *Late June–early Sept., Sun.–Wed. 9–6, Thurs.–Sat. 9 am–9:30 pm; early Sept.–May, Sun.–Wed. 9–5, Thurs.–Sat. 9–8* Ⓜ *Viau.*

Stade Olympique. Montrealers finished paying for their Olympic stadium (dubbed the "Big O") in the spring of 2006—30 years after the games for which it was built—but they still call it the "Big Owe," and not very affectionately, either. The architecture is dramatic, squatting like a giant flying saucer in the middle of the east end, but it proved to be unworkable and was abandoned by the sports teams it was supposed to house. Now used mostly for trade shows, it offers a tour but there's little to see for the price. But come in summer, on the first Friday of the month, and join the locals who flock to the park outside the stadium to feast from Montréal's food trucks—all of them congregate here for the event. ☒ *4141 av. Pierre-de-Coubertin, Hochelaga-Maisonneuve, Montréal* ☎ *514/252–8687* ⊕ *www.parcolympique.qc.ca* ☒ *Tour C$10* ☼ *Daily 9–6* Ⓜ *Pie-IX or Viau.*

Tour Olympique. The world's tallest tilting structure—take that, Pisa!—is the 890-foot tower that was supposed to hold the Stade Olympique's retractable roof. It looked great on paper, but never worked in practice, and the current roof is a permanent fixture. If you want a great view of the city, however, ride the glass-encased funicular that slides up the outside of the tower to the observatory at the top. On a clear day you can see up to 80 km (50 miles). ☒ *4141 av. Pierre-de-Coubertin, Hochelaga-Maisonneuve, Montréal* ☎ *514/252–4141, 877/997–0919* ⊕ *parcolympique.qc.ca* ☒ *Observation deck C$22.50* ☼ *Mid-June–early Sept., Mon. 1–9, Tues.–Sun. 9–9; Apr.–mid-June and mid-Sept.–Nov., Mon. 1–6, Tues.–Sun. 9–6; Nov.–Mar., Tues.–Sun. 9–5* Ⓜ *Pie-IX or Viau.*

THE ISLANDS

The two islands just east of the city in the St. Lawrence River—Île Ste-Hélène, formed by nature, and Île Notre-Dame, created with the stone rubble excavated from the construction of Montréal's métro—are now used for Montréal's indoor-outdoor playground, Parc Jean-Drapeau.

Expo '67, which the World's Fair staged to celebrate the centennial of the Canadian federation, was brought here by the city's mayor, Jean Drapeau. It was the biggest party in Montréal's history, and it marked a defining moment in its evolution as a modern metropolis.

The spirit of coming here for excitement and thrills lives on. La Ronde, a major amusement park that has the world's highest double wooden roller coaster, is on Île Ste-Hélène. On Île Notre-Dame, there's Casino de Montréal, which includes gaming tables and more than 3,200 slot machines.

For a completely different kind of fun, however, there's much to learn about the Islands' history. At the Stewart Museum at the Old Fort, kids will love watching soldiers in colonial uniforms hold flag-raising ceremonies twice a day, rehearse maneuvers, and even practice drills and fire muskets.

GETTING HERE AND AROUND

Both Île Ste-Hélène and Île Notre-Dame are very accessible. You can drive to them via the Pont de la Concorde or the Pont Jacques-Cartier, take the ferry from the Old Port to Île Ste-Hélène (seasonal), or take the métro from the Berri-UQAM station to Jean-Drapeau.

TIMING

If you're traveling with kids, there's enough here to keep them occupied for a full day, especially in nice weather. Because the Islands are so easy to get to with the ferry, visiting can be tacked on to time spent in Old Montréal.

TOP ATTRACTIONS

FAMILY **Biosphère.** Nothing captures the exuberance of Expo '67 better than the geodesic dome designed by Buckminster Fuller (1895–1983) as the American Pavilion. It's only a skeleton now—the polymer panels that protected the U.S. exhibits from the elements were burned out in a fire long ago—but it's still an eye-catching sight, like something plucked from a science-fiction movie.

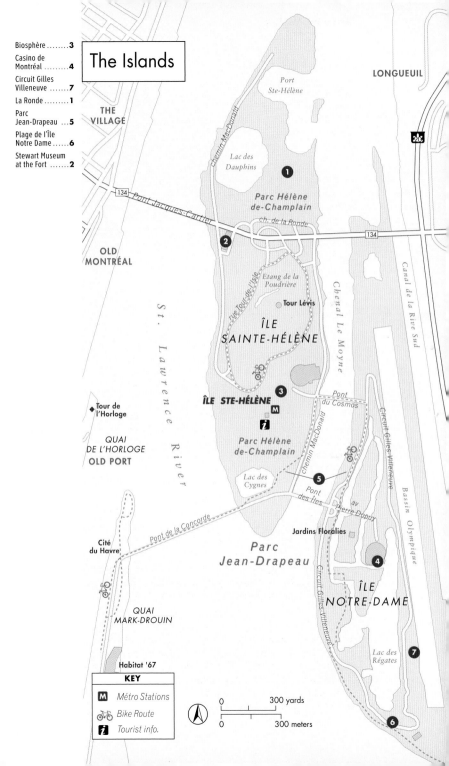

Biosphère **3**

Casino de
Montréal **4**

Circuit Gilles
Villeneuve **7**

La Ronde **1**

Parc
Jean-Drapeau ... **5**

Plage de l'Île
Notre Dame **6**

Stewart Museum
at the Fort **2**

The Islands

LONGUEUIL

THE VILLAGE

Port Ste-Hélène

Lac des Dauphins

Parc Hélène de-Champlain

OLD MONTRÉAL

Pont Jacques-Cartier

ch. de la Ronde

134

chemin MacDonald

Étang de la Poudrière

Tour Lévis

ÎLE SAINTE-HÉLÈNE

Chenal Le Moyne

Canal de la Rive Sud

ÎLE STE-HÉLÈNE

Tour de l'Horloge

QUAI DE L'HORLOGE
OLD PORT

Pont du Cosmos

Parc Hélène de-Champlain

chemin MacDonald

Lac des Cygnes

Pont des Îles

av. Pierre Dupuy

St. Lawrence River

Pont de la Concorde

Cité du Havre

Jardins Floralies

Parc Jean-Drapeau

Circuit Gilles-Villeneuve

Bassin Olympique

ÎLE NOTRE-DAME

QUAI MARK-DROUIN

Lac des Régates

Habitat '67

KEY

M *Métro Stations*

🚲 *Bike Route*

i *Tourist info.*

0 — 300 yards
0 — 300 meters

2

Science of a nonfictional kind, however, is explored in the special environmental center the federal government has built in the middle of the dome. It focuses on the challenges of preserving the Great Lakes and St. Lawrence River system, but it has lively and interactive exhibits on climate change, sustainable energy, and air pollution. Kids and others can use games and interactive displays arranged around a large model of the waterway to explore how shipping, tourism, water supplies, and hydroelectric power are affected.

⚠ **Starting in late 2014 and estimated to last six months, the Biosphère will be closed for major renovations to their exhibit galleries. Call to confirm that it's open before heading out.** ⌧ *Île Ste-Hélène, 160 chemin Tour-de-l'Île, The Islands, Montréal* ☎ *514/283–5000, 855/773–8200* ⊕ *www.biosphere.ec.gc.ca* ⌦ *C$12* ☉ *June–Oct., daily 10–5; Nov.– May, Wed.–Sun. 10–5* Ⓜ *Jean-Drapeau.*

Casino de Montréal. You have to be at least 18 to visit Montréal's government-owned casino, but you don't have to be a gambler. The 24-hour-a-day, fully renovated casino now houses three new bars and four new restaurants, ranging from high-end to deli style. You can even come just to look at the architecture—the main building was the French pavilion at Expo '67. But if you do want to risk the family fortune, there are more than 3,000 slot machines, a keno lounge, a high-stakes gaming area, and 120 tables for playing blackjack, baccarat, roulette, craps, and various types of poker. ⌧ *1 av. du Casino, Île Notre-Dame, The Islands, Montréal* ☎ *514/392–2746, 800/665–2274* ⊕ *www.casino-de-montreal.com* Ⓜ *Jean-Drapeau, then bus 167.*

FAMILY

Fodor'sChoice

★

Parc Jean-Drapeau. Île Ste-Hélène and Île Notre-Dame now constitute a single park named, fittingly enough, for Jean Drapeau (1916–99), the visionary (and spendthrift) mayor who built the métro and brought the city both the 1967 World's Fair and the 1976 Olympics. The park includes La Ronde (a major amusement park), acres of flower gardens, a beach with filtered water, and the Casino de Montréal. There's history, too, at the Old Fort, where soldiers in colonial uniforms display the military methods used in ancient wars. In winter you can skate on the old Olympic rowing basin or slide down iced trails on an inner tube. ⌧ *The Islands, Montréal* ☎ *514/872–6120* ⊕ *www.parcjeandrapeau. com* Ⓜ *Jean-Drapeau.*

Stewart Museum. Housed in the arsenal of Île Ste-Hélène's 1820s Old Fort, the Stewart Museum encompasses two floors full of interesting historical objects. The permanent collection has close to 27 000 artifacts consisting of military objects, images, rare books, maps, pieces of weaponry; all of which documents the history of Montréal, l'Île Ste-Hélène, and the surrounding area, from the early First Nations to today. Open year-round, the Stewart Museum is definitely worth a visit for those interested in the history of New France. ⌧ *20 chemin du Tour-de-l'Île, Île Ste-Hélène, The Islands, Montréal* ☎ *514/861–6701* ⊕ *www.stewart-museum.org* ⌦ *C$10* ☉ *Wed.–Sun. 11–5* Ⓜ *Jean-Drapeau.*

WORTH NOTING

Circuit Gilles Villeneuve. In early June you can join the glitterati of Europe and America in the grandstand to watch million-dollar Formula 1 cars shriek around the 4.3-km (2.7-mile) track—if you're lucky enough and rich enough to get a ticket, that is. This is the kind of crowd that uses Perrier to mop up caviar stains from the refreshment tables. During the off season, the track is accessible to everyone. Locals spend sunny summer weekends cycling, rollerblading, and taking walks around this world famous circuit. ✉ *Île Notre-Dame, Montréal* ☎ *514/350–0000* ⊕ *www.circuitgillesvilleneuve.ca* Ⓜ *Jean-Drapeau.*

FAMILY **La Ronde.** Every year, it seems, this amusement park, at the eastern end of Île Ste-Hélène, adds some new and monstrous way to scare the living daylights (and perhaps your lunch as well) out of you. The most recent addition is DEMON, an extreme ride that will—at high speed (of course)—twist you, twirl you, and turn you upside down, then douse you with water jets. The park also aims to terrify you with such stomach-turning champions as the Endor, the Goliath, the Vampire, Monstre, and Vol Ultime. For the less daring, there are Ferris wheels, boat rides, and kiddie rides. The popular **International Fireworks Competition** is held here on Saturday and Wednesday in late June and July. ✉ *22 chemin Macdonald, Île Ste-Hélène, Montréal* ☎ *514/397–2000, 800/361–4595* ⊕ *www.laronde.com, www.internationaldesfeuxloto-quebec.com* 🎟 *C$58.99, or C$43.99 if purchased online* ⊙ *Late May, weekends 11–8; early June–late June, daily 11–9; late June–late Aug., daily 11–10; Sept., weekends 11–9; Oct., Sat. 11–11, Sun. 11–9. Open later on fireworks nights* Ⓜ *Jean-Drapeau.*

FAMILY **Plage de l'Île Notre-Dame** (*Île Notre-Dame Beach*). The dress code at the neighboring casino might ban camisoles and strapless tops, but here anything seems to go on warm summer days, when the beach is a sea of oiled bodies. You get the distinct impression that swimming is not uppermost on the minds of many of the scantily clad hordes. If you do want to go in, however, the water is filtered and closely monitored for contamination, and there are lifeguards on duty. A shop rents swimming and boating paraphernalia, and there's a restaurant and picnic areas. ✉ *Île Notre-Dame, Montréal* ☎ *514/872–6120* ⊕ *www.parcjeandrapeau.com* 🎟 *C$9* ⊙ *Late June–mid-Aug., daily 10–7; mid-Aug.–Labor Day, Fri.–Sun. noon–7* Ⓜ *Jean-Drapeau.*

NIGHTLIFE

Updated by
Chris Barry

If nightlife in Montréal could be distilled into a cocktail, it would be one part sophisticated New York club scene (with the accompanying pretension), one part Parisian joie-de-vivre (and, again, a dash of snobbery), and one part Barcelonan stamina (which keeps the clubs booming until dawn).

Hot spots are peppered throughout the city. There are compact clusters along rue Crescent, boulevard St-Laurent (known as "The Main"), avenue Mont-Royal, and rue St-Denis. Prominent rue Ste-Catherine plows through town, connecting most of these nighttime niches, and farther east, near Beaudry métro station, it becomes the main drag for the Village, also called Gay Village. For whatever reason, the streets named after saints contain most of the clubs: rue Ste-Catherine, boulevard St-Laurent, rue St-Paul, and rue St-Denis. The Old Port is currently Montréal's hottest neighborhood, with a steady stream of chic venues opening in this cobblestone district.

Montréal's nightlife swings with a robust passion; from the early-evening "5-à-7" after-work cocktail circuit, to the slightly later concerts and supper clubs (restaurant–dance club hybrids where people dance on the tables after eating off them), on into the even later dance club scene; all tastes, cultural backgrounds, and legal ages join the melee. Adult clubs abound in this sexually freewheeling city and are often frequented by mixed groups of people seeking a fun night out on the town. Clubbing is, to say the least, huge in Montréal. Some restaurants are even installing discotheques in their basements.

As for what to wear on a Montréal night out: If you have a daring outfit in your closet that you've hesitated to wear—bring it. Montrealers get absolutely decked to go out on the town to bars and clubs, even if the temperature is below freezing. And remember, most club regulars don't even know where they're going until midnight, so don't go out too early.

PLANNING

EVENTS INFORMATION

Check out Cult MTL (⊕ *www.cultmontreal.com*), which is updated frequently with information on the various goings-on about town. The "Friday Preview" section of the *Gazette* (⊕ *www.montrealgazette.com*), the English-language daily paper, has a thorough list of events at the city's concert halls, clubs, and dance spaces.

The following websites provide comprehensive information about Montréal's nightlife scene: ⊕ *www.tourisme-montreal.org*, ⊕ *www.nightlife. ca*, ⊕ *www.montreal-clubs.com, and* ⊕ *www.bestclubsinmontreal.com*.

HOURS

The bars stop serving around 3 am and shut down shortly thereafter (with the exception of sanctioned "after-hour" haunts), and on the weekends expect them to be packed to the gills until closing. The club scene picks up right after the bars close, and then extends until dawn.

LATE-NIGHT TRANSPORTATION

The best way to get around the city after hours is by taxi. Taxis are generally easy to hail on the street, cost roughly C$10 to C$15 to most nightlife spots, and are available if the white or orange light is on. Another option is to use a car service; before you leave you can get recommendations from your hotel concierge for the closest and most reliable company, which will minimize your wait time. Montréal Dorval Limousine Service (⊕ *www.montreallimo.ca*) is one good option.

The Montréal métro's Green and Orange lines have their last nighttime departures at 12:35 am weekdays, 1 am Saturday, and 12:30 am Sunday; the Yellow Line runs until 1 am weekdays, 1:30 am Saturday, and 1 am Sunday; and the Blue Line takes its last run at 12:15 am daily. For more information, visit ⊕ *www.stm.info*.

TICKETS

For tickets to major pop and rock concerts, you can go to the individual box offices or contact **Admission** (☎ *514/790–1245* ⊕ *www.admission. com*), **Ticketpro** (☎ *514/790–1111 or 866/908–9090* ⊕ *www.ticketpro. ca*), or **Evenko** (☎ *514/790–2525 or 877/668–8269* ⊕ *www.evenko.ca*).

NIGHTLIFE REVIEWS

OLD MONTRÉAL (VIEUX-MONTRÉAL)

Once a tourist trap full of overpriced souvenirs, Old Montréal is now home to a mix of top-notch restaurants and chic lounges. During the summer you can enjoy stunning views of the river from some of the city's best rooftop terraces. Excellent dining can be found along rue St-Paul, while rue McGill is a big part of the 5-à-7 scene.

BARS AND LOUNGES

La Champagnerie. Sharpen your swords! This chic bar for champagne and other sparklers is the perfect place to break open a bottle—literally. The staff like to open the bottles of bubbly with sabers here, a

Montréal
Nightlife

0 ——— 1/2 mile
0 ——— 500 meters

OUTREMONT
Tame thirty-somethings relax over cocktails

MILE END
Hipster spots with decent prices

LE PLATEAU-MONT-ROYAL
Rock & Roll and house dancing clubs abound

LATIN QUARTER
Students plus resto-lounges for young professionals

DOWNTOWN
Densely packed with bars, clubs, and theaters

THE VILLAGE
Gay bars and partying till dawn

OLD PORT
Thriving 5 à 7 scene

CASINO DE MONTRÉAL
Gaming and live musical shows around-the-clock

MONTRÉAL NIGHTLIFE BEST BETS

Best for music: Club Soda	**Best off-the-beaten path:** Le Lab
Best bubbles: La Champagnerie	**Best for a date:** BU
Best water view: Terrasse sur l'Auberge	**Best patio:** Le Sainte-Elisabeth
Best martini: Six Resto Lounge	**Best for expense accounts:** Suite 701
Best comfort food: Baldwin Barmacie	**Best wine bar:** Pullman

3

practice that adds an element of fun to an accessible venue. Finger foods includes oysters, steak (and other kinds of) tartares, and caviar. ✉ *343 rue St-Paul Est, Old Montréal, Montréal* ☎*514/903–9343* ⊕*www. lachampagnerie.ca* ☾ *Closed Mon.* Ⓜ *Champs-de-Mars.*

Modavie Wine Bar. With a Mediterranean menu, an attractive sidewalk terrasse, and a sophisticated interior that places dark wood against stone walls, this jazz bar is pleasing to the eyes *and* ears. Despite being spread out over two floors, the space still feels cozy. Live duos play during the first part of the week, while weekends showcase full bands. There's never a cover charge. ✉ *1 rue St-Paul Ouest, Old Montréal, Montréal* ☎*514/287–9582* ⊕*www.modavie.com* Ⓜ *Champ-de-Mars.*

Philémon Bar. You can grab a glass of one of Philémon's well-priced private import cavas, proseccos, or champagnes to accompany the menu at this sleek bar, which serves more than the usual pub fare (oysters, anyone?). It's packed with locals Thursday through Saturday—in fact, it's become quite the singles hangout. Bouncers keep the ratio of guys to gals at a comfortable level. ✉ *111 rue St-Paul Ouest, Old Montréal, Montréal* ☎*514/289–3777* ⊕*www.philemonbar.com* Ⓜ *Place-d'Armes.*

Suite 701. This bar inside the chic Place-d'Armes Hotel is *the* place for drinks in Old Montréal—try the Moon Light martini, plump with fresh raspberries. You may want to linger over a plate of the crispy gnocchi. Upstairs, a rooftop patio (Terrasse Place d'Armes) overlooks Notre-Dame Cathedral and serves finger food with a whole other selection of cocktails. ✉ *701 côte de la Place-d'Armes, Old Montréal, Montréal* ☎*514/904–1201* ⊕*www.suite701.com* Ⓜ *Place-d'Armes.*

Terrasse sur l'Auberge. For an unbeatable view of the Old Port and numerous Montréal landmarks, head to this unpretentious patio on the roof of the Auberge du Vieux-Port Hotel. Open from the end of May through mid-October (5–11 weekdays, 2–11 on weekends), it's a great place to watch the International Fireworks Festival—if you're early enough to snag a table—and enjoy cocktails and a light tapas menu. The cod croquettes are a must-try, and pair nicely with the clear sangria (made with sparkling wine). ✉ *97 rue de la Commune Est, Old*

When the sun goes down in Montréal, the city's energy gets kicked up a notch, especially in the Old City and the Old Port.

Montréal, Montréal ☎ *514/876–0081* ⊕ *www.terrassesurlauberge.com* Ⓜ *Place-d'Armes or Champs-de-Mars.*

DOWNTOWN

From expensive restaurants to lowly bars, Downtown offers something for every taste and budget. Rue Crescent, with its lively mix of restaurants, pubs, and clubs, is where you'll find most of the action, with neighboring rue Bishop not far behind.

BARS AND LOUNGES

Brutopia. House-brewed concoctions like Raspberry Blond Beer or Scotch Ale attract locals and tourists alike, and lately the kitchen has been serving up delicious tapas-style pub food. In addition to the unique brews, check out the sprawling outdoor seating, the art gallery on the third floor, and nightly live music. A typical crowd at Brutopia is under 30 but older folk shouldn't feel out of place. With live music ranging from traditional Irish folk to the occasional punk or psychedelic '60s garage band, this pub serves as a refreshing alternative to the slightly more upscale, trendy bars and nightclubs that mark the Crescent street strip. ⊠ *1219 rue Crescent, Downtown, Montréal* ☎ *514/393–9277* ⊕ *www.brutopia.net* Ⓜ *Guy-Concordia.*

Fodor'sChoice ★ **Dominion Square Tavern.** Busy nearly every night of the week, this bar with a relaxed 1920s atmosphere is one of the hottest spots downtown for a drink after work, a tasty bite before the hockey game, or an old-fashioned cocktail to unwind and plan the rest of the evening. It opens at 11:30 am weekdays and 4:30 pm weekends. Kitchen closes at midnight daily. ✉ *1243 rue Metcalfe, Downtown, Montréal* ☎ *514/564–5056* ⊕ *www.tavernedominion.com.*

Fodor's Choice ★ **Furco.** Making its name through word of mouth alone, Furco has become one of the trendiest downtown bars, and for good reason. It's all about the industrial-chic interior, the warm amber lighting, and the relaxed, inviting vibe. A nice mix of clientele, great food (the menu changes weekly), and good pours also help make this a popular after-work hangout for locals, and the perfect retreat from the Quartier des Spectacles, a stone's throw away. Furco doesn't take reservations, so go early if you want to nab a seat. ✉ *425 rue Mayor, Downtown, Montréal* ☎ *514/764–3588* ⊕ *www.barfurco.com* Ⓜ *Place des Arts or McGill.*

Le Sainte-Elisabeth. In the Quartier des Spectacles (the local performing-arts district), this European pub is popular in part because of its friendly service and good selection of domestic and imported beers, as well as whiskey and cognac. With one of the city's most beautiful backyard terraces, this is a great place to enjoy the fall colors. ✉ *1412 rue Ste-Elisabeth, Downtown, Montréal* ☎ *514/286–4302* ⊕ *www.ste-elisabeth.com* Ⓜ *Berri.*

Newtown. Once owned by Grand Prix driver Jacques Villenueve (Newtown is his name translated into English), this restaurant and lounge is still trendy with the local folk. The lounge is *the* best spot on Crescent for martinis and people-watching—call to reserve a table on the street. But it's the lesser known rooftop terrasse that really shines on a hot summer day. Club Electric Avenue (⇨ *see below*) is in the basement if you're in the mood for some postdrink dancing. ✉ *1476 rue Crescent, Downtown, Montréal* ☎ *514/284–6555* ⊕ *www.lenewtown. com* Ⓜ *Guy-Concordia.*

Fodor's Choice ★ **Pullman.** At this sophisticated yet relaxed wine bar, let yourself be guided by the expertise of the sommeliers. The tapas-style cuisine is top notch, and the green beans with truffle oil and roasted almonds are great. During cooler months things get going at 4:30 pm, but in summer don't arrive until the sun starts to set. ✉ *3424 av. du Parc, Downtown, Montréal* ☎ *514/288–7779* ⊕ *www.pullman-mtl.com* Ⓜ *Place des Arts.*

Six Resto Lounge. With a prime view of the Quartier des Spectacles, Montréal's performing arts district, this huge terrace overlooking Place des Arts is the perfect place for preshow drinks. In cooler weather you can relax in the purple-and-slate-gray lounge, where the bar takes center stage. Open 5–11 pm. ✉ *Hyatt Regency Hotel, 1255 rue Jeanne-Mance, Downtown, Montréal* ☎ *514/841–2038* ⊕ *www.sixrestolounge.com* Ⓜ *Place des Arts.*

Stogie's Lounge. If the surprisingly trendy interior and views of rue Crescent aren't a big enough draw, then check out the conspicuous glass humidor housing a seemingly infinite supply of imported cigars. Thanks to being grandfathered in, the bar still allows smoking Cubans on-site, despite Québec's tough no-smoking law. ✉ *2015 rue Crescent, Downtown, Montréal* ☎ *514/848–0069* ⊕ *www.stogiescigars.com* Ⓜ *Guy-Concordia or Peel.*

COMEDY CLUBS

The Montréal Just For Laughs comedy festival, which takes place every July, has been the largest such festival in the world since its inception back in 1983.

But Montrealers don't have to wait until summer to get their comedy fix, as there are several Downtown clubs covering all things funny.

Comedy Nest. For decades, this comedy club has been showering Montrealers with humor from some of the biggest names out there: Jim Carrey, Tim Allen, and Russell Peters included. For a mere $5, Open Mic Wednesdays are always good for a laugh and will also secure you one free ticket for the weekend's activities. Get there early to secure a decent spot near the stage (or perhaps away from it) and chow down on some Buffalo Bills chicken wings. ⊠ *Pepsi Forum, 2313 rue Ste-Catherine Ouest, 3rd fl., Downtown, Montréal* ☎ *514/932–6378* ⊕ *www.thecomedynest.com* Ⓜ *Atwater.*

Comedyworks. Popular comedy shows are hosted in a room on the second floor of a local watering hole, the Irish Embassy Pub Grill. The program books both amateur and established comics, both of whom can get fairly risqué on occasion. ⊠ *1238 rue Bishop, 2nd fl., Downtown, Montréal* ☎ *514/398–9661* ⊕ *www.comedyworksmontreal.com* Ⓜ *Guy-Concordia.*

Montréal Improv. The heart of the city's improv comedy scene offers shows in both English and French. Their Friday night Smackdowns, where the audience determines the winner, are definitely good for a laugh and usually sell out quickly. ⊠ *3713 blvd. St-Laurent, Suite 202, Downtown, Montréal* ☎ *514/507–3535* ⊕ *www.montrealimprov.com* Ⓜ *Sherbrooke.*

DANCE CLUBS

Club Electric Avenue. Generation X will get along just fine here, as classics from the '80s and '90s boom out over a devoted, nostalgic crowd. In the basement of the Newtown lounge, these digs have great sound, excellent service, and sexy interior design. It's open Thursday to Saturday from 10 pm. ⊠ *1469 rue Crescent, Downtown, Montréal* ☎ *514/285–8885* ⊕ *www.clubelectricavenue.com* Ⓜ *Guy-Concordia.*

Salsathèque. Though neon lights and disco balls abound, this flashy club is all about the Latin lover—dance lover, that is. Merengue, bachata, and salsa (of course) are the specialties, but themed evenings keep things interesting with r-and-b, reggae, and Top 40 hits. Check the website to learn the week's schedule, and sign up for the guest list while you're about it to avoid a cover. ⊠ *1220 rue Peel, Downtown, Montréal* ☎ *514/875–0016* ⊕ *www.clubsalsatheque.com* ☉ *Closed Mon. and Tues.* Ⓜ *Peel.*

Time Supper Club. Perfect for partying with friends (or making new ones), this institution is known for its bottle service, but don't miss the marvelous martinis. The bartenders mix one of the city's best cosmopolitans. Hot DJs and great acoustics get the party started around 9:30 pm. On Saturday the place plays host to an older crowd. ⊠ *997 rue St-Jacques Ouest, Downtown, Montréal* ☎ *514/392–9292* ⊕ *www.timesupperclub.com* ☉ *Open Thurs.–Sat.* Ⓜ *Bonaventure.*

LIVE MUSIC

Club Soda. The granddaddy of the city's rock clubs has evolved into one of the dominant venues for jazz, reggae, techno, and rhythm and blues. Club Soda is a tall, narrow concert hall with high-tech design and 500 seats—all of them with great sight lines. ✉ *1225 blvd. St-Laurent, Downtown, Montréal* ☎ *514/286–1010* ⊕ *www.clubsoda.ca* Ⓜ *St-Laurent.*

House of Jazz. The food is good but the music is outstanding. For more than 30 years, this institution has been plying the city with the best in jazz, with a little blues and soul thrown in for good measure. A flashy, over-the-top interior that includes mirrored walls adds to the experience. Dress up and be prepared to pay a cover. ✉ *2060 rue Aylmer, Downtown, Montréal* ☎ *514/842–8656* ⊕ *www.houseofjazz.ca* Ⓜ *McGill or Place des Arts.*

McKibbin's Irish Pub. This beautiful old sandstone mansion includes three floors of food, drink, and good Irish *craic* (a Gaelic term that means having fun with amiable companions). This isn't hard to do with more than 20 different stouts, lagers, and ales on tap. There's live entertainment nearly every night of the week, so head to the basement if you're looking for a bit of quiet (or a good chin-wag). The house fries are excellent for noshing, but beware of the Rim Reaper—chicken wings made with the world's hottest pepper. ✉ *1426 rue Bishop, Downtown, Montréal* ☎ *514/288–1580* ⊕ *www.mckibbinsirishpub.com* Ⓜ *Guy-Concordia.*

Fodor's Choice ★ **Upstairs Jazz Bar & Grill.** Five nights a week, the cheerful Joel Giberovitch greets you personally near the entrance to his club, which despite the name is actually downstairs. Giberovitch loves what he does, and the constant stream of local and imported jazz musicians makes this the favored jazz hangout in the city. The eclectic menu makes a nice accompaniment to the live music—try the home-cut fries with smoky mayo. Cover charges start at C$6 and range up to C$45 for name performers during Jazz Fest. The third set is free (usually around 11pm), and other sets are also free if you sit on one of the cozy terrasses. ✉ *1254 rue Mackay, Downtown, Montréal* ☎ *514/931–6808* ⊕ *www.upstairsjazz.com* Ⓜ *Guy-Concordia.*

SUPPER CLUBS

Rosalie. Posh, pricey, and a bit pretentious, this downtown supper club is usually bustling with beautiful people thanks to its central location, large outdoor terrace, and pulsating music. Go late if you're there to party, and early if you're there to drink. If you want to stock up on carbs first, then the pizza, cooked in a wood-fired oven, is worth a visit on its own: it's one of the best in the city. ✉ *1232 rue de la Montagne, Downtown, Montréal* ☎ *514/392–1970* ⊕ *www.rosalierestaurant.com* Ⓜ *Guy-Concordia or Peel.*

THE LATIN QUARTER

Between Downtown and the Gay Village lies the tiny Quartier Latin, known for its theaters, cafés, and student population. (One of the major French universities, UQAM, is located here.) Concentrated on lower rue St-Denis, there are copious bars and a few decent restaurants.

DID YOU KNOW?

Montréal's ever-popular Festival Juste Pour Rire (Just For Laughs Festival) is touted as the world's largest comedy festival.

BARS AND LOUNGES

En Cachette Speakeasy. This Latin Quarter venue brings a touch of sophistication to a neighborhood that's more known for its freewheeling ways. Good music and a relaxed vibe make the strong drinks go down even easier. The snack bar menu features primarily traditional fare like fried calamari, chicken wings, and fish-and-chips. Open Wednesday to Saturday. ⊠ *1765 rue St-Denis, Quartier Latin, Montréal* ☏ *514/419–1986* ⊕ *www.encachette.ca* ☾ *Closed Mon.* Ⓜ *Berri-UQAM.*

THE VILLAGE

Head east along rue Ste-Catherine to enjoy the colorful Gay Village—you'll know you've arrived when you're amid a sea of pretty pink balls and rainbow flags hung in the streets. It's developing a bit of a reputation for fine dining as of late, though it's still mainly known as a place for late-night partying.

GAY AND LESBIAN NIGHTLIFE

Cabaret Mado. Makeup, glitter, and glamorous costumes abound at this nightclub with drag-queen entertainment. Mado herself is a Québec celebrity (so much so that she's immortalized in wax at the Grévin museum inside the Centre Eaton). During the nightly performances, even the clientele may get involved, thanks to karaoke and improv evenings. ⊠ *1115 rue Ste-Catherine Est, The Village, Montréal* ☏ *514/525–7566* ⊕ *www.mado.qc.ca* Ⓜ *Beaudry.*

Fodor's Choice ★ Club Unity. Unity is actually the club's third incarnation on this spot. Small, semiprivate lounges are scattered throughout the two-story complex, and the beautiful rooftop terrace is one of the finest in the Village. Unity is one of the longest running, most popular gay dance clubs in town—although some have been known to complain you'll often find as many straight girls here as you will gay men. Open weekends from 10 pm to 3 am. ⊠ *1171 rue Ste-Catherine Est, The Village, Montréal* ☏ *514/523–2777* ⊕ *www.clubunitymontreal.com* Ⓜ *Beaudry.*

Fodor's Choice ★ Le Drugstore. This mammoth warehouse with six floors of bars, clubs, lounges, and billiards rooms is a mainstay of the city's lesbian scene and a treasure trove of random urban artifacts like vintage subway signs and stoplights. The factory-like complex, part of the former Hotel Bourbon, is popular with gay men, too, with a revolving menu of karaoke, drag shows, and live bands. ⊠ *1366 rue Ste-Catherine Est, The Village, Montréal* ☏ *514/524–1960* ⊕ *www.le-drugstore.com* Ⓜ *Beaudry.*

Sky. This massive complex houses a bar, restaurant, and dance club popular with both gay men and women. The best time to come is during the summer, as the pièce de résistance is the beachlike roof deck with city views and a pool (possibly the hottest destination in the Village). ⊠ *1474 rue Ste-Catherine Est, The Village, Montréal* ☏ *514/529–6969* ⊕ *www.complexesky.com* Ⓜ *Beaudry.*

DID YOU KNOW?

The Montréal International Jazz Festival is in the *Guinness Book of World Records* as "The Largest Jazz Festival in the World."

PLATEAU MONT-ROYAL

The restaurants and bars along St-Denis and Mont-Royal are popular with everyone from rambunctious students to serious food-lovers. Boulevard St-Laurent ("The Main"), especially between rue Sherbrooke and avenue des Pins, is home to the see-and-be-seen crowd, with merrymakers spilling out at all hours of the night.

BARS AND LOUNGES

Fodor'sChoice
★
Big in Japan Bar. Keep your eyes peeled for the red door: there's no sign above this inconspicuous speakeasy. Once you're past the faux suede curtains, the contemporary design and intricate seating plan will win you over—as will the sake and whiskey selection. The miso edamame hummus with fresh vegetables is good, and it pairs nicely with sake (both filtered and unfiltered). Lines form on weekends, but weeknights aren't too bad. ⊠ *4175 blvd. St-Laurent, The Plateau, Montréal* ☎ *438/380–5658* ⊕ *www.biginjapan.ca* Ⓜ *Sherbrooke or St-Laurent.*

Fodor'sChoice
★
Bily Kun. This Czech-themed bar is a favorite hangout of Plateau locals. There's live jazz during the cocktail hour, or you can groove to a DJ later in the evening. Try an absinthe-laced apple cocktail from the extensive alcohol menu as you nibble on a few tapas. Bily Kun soon gets packed, though the high ceilings help alleviate the feeling of claustrophobia. ⊠ *354 av. du Mont-Royal Est, The Plateau, Montréal* ☎ *514/845–5392* ⊕ *www.bilykun.com* Ⓜ *Mont-Royal.*

Fodor'sChoice
★
Le Lab. Fabien Maillard is Montréal's mixologist extraordinaire, and the name of his unpretentious bar is entirely apt. Creating cocktails is his passion and it's shared by the friendly, skilled staff. The potent potions—including a $28 Zombie loaded with liquor—are inspired by everything from old, classic recipes to the fruits of the season. The entire menu changes twice a year, and there are also monthly specials. Call to reserve on weekends; its packed despite being off the beaten track. ⊠ *1351 rue Rachel Est, The Plateau, Montréal* ☎ *514/544–1333* ⊕ *www.lab.mixoart.com* ☉ *Closed Mon.* Ⓜ *Sherbrooke.*

Fodor'sChoice
★
Reservoir. It's all about the beer at this friendly restaurant and bar, and it's all brewed right on the premises. With everything from India pale ales to German-inspired wheat beers, they've got you covered. Packed almost every night of the week, the upstairs patio is the ideal spot for watching locals stroll along the quaint cobblestone avenue. ⊠ *9 av. Duluth Est, The Plateau, Montréal* ☎ *514/849–7779* ⊕ *www. brasseriereservoir.ca* Ⓜ *Sherbrooke.*

DANCE CLUBS

Cactus. Salsa is the favored style of dancing at Cactus, though merengue and samba pop up during the week as well. Thursday through Saturday, the double-decker dance floor of this restaurant, bar, and club is packed with patrons enjoying the rigorously authentic Latin music. You can fuel up on Mexican food at the restaurant downstairs, then dance the calories away. ⊠ *4461 rue St-Denis, The Plateau, Montréal* ☎ *514/849–0349* ⊕ *www.lecactus.ca* Ⓜ *Mont-Royal.*

LIVE MUSIC

Casa del Popolo. One of the city's treasured venues for indie rock, jazz, reggae, blues, folk, and hip-hop, this neighborhood bar is ideal for discovering up-and-coming local acts or forgotten international giants still touring. While you enjoy the music, take a look at the original art and sample some of the tasty vegetarian food. ✉ *4873 blvd. St-Laurent, The Plateau, Montréal* ☎ *514/284–3804* ⊕ *www.casadelpopolo.com* Ⓜ *Mont-Royal.*

Divan Orange. Grab a seat on the "orange sofa" and catch emerging musical talent (both Francophone and Anglophone) at this popular Plateau bar, from Tuesday through Sunday. Credit cards aren't accepted. ✉ *4234 blvd. St-Laurent, The Plateau, Montréal* ☎ *514/840–9090* ⊕ *www.divanorange.org* Ⓜ *Mont-Royal.*

SUPPER CLUBS

Buonanotte. In business on The Main since 1991, this restaurant, lounge, and weekend supper club continues to pull out all the stops. There's top-notch Italian cuisine, a comprehensive wine list, well-known DJs, and even a concierge. Celebrities are known to drop by when in town. ✉ *3518 blvd. St-Laurent, The Plateau, Montréal* ☎ *514/848–0644* ⊕ *www.buonanotte.com* Ⓜ *St-Laurent.*

MILE END

Mile End is becoming more and more well-known for inspired cuisine, affordable lounges, and relaxed bars. And it's slowly becoming a second village to the hipster gay crowd, who tend to forgo the main Village.

BARS AND LOUNGES

Fodor's Choice ★ **Baldwin Barmacie.** Co-owner Alexandre Baldwin named the bar not only after the tiny pharmacy that once occupied this building but also after his grandmother, who worked there—her portrait hangs on the creamy white wall and the downstairs area retains some features from those days. Drinks are served in old-fashioned syrup bottles and milk jugs, and chairs made from scotch barrels add rustic charm. You can sip on a refreshing bourbon punch (there's a great selection of whisky here) as you peruse the menu, which includes some upscale comfort foods—the grilled cheese is delectable. ✉ *115 av. Laurier Ouest, Mile End, Montréal* ☎ *514/276–4282* ⊕ *www.baldwinbarmacie.com* Ⓜ *Laurier.*

Bar Waverly. Named for the street that epitomizes the Mile End, this neighborhood bar has a warm staff, friendly ambience, and a great selection of Scotch. Owners Richard Holder and Olivier Farley have been in the business for years, and it shows. Nightly DJs provide an edgier vibe, while huge floor-to-ceiling windows make it perfect for people-watching. ✉ *5550 blvd. St-Laurent, Mile End, Montréal* ☎ *514/903–1121* ⊕ *www.barwaverly.com* Ⓜ *Laurier.*

La Buvette chez Simone. Arrive early (it opens at 4 pm) at this easygoing wine bar—it's always busy and they don't take reservations. Lots of wines are available by the glass, in 2- and 4-ounce pours, with an emphasis on French varietals. Dress is casual, though the after-work crowd ups the glam factor. Lively but not obnoxious, La Buvette's a great place to catch up with friends. ⊠ *4869 av. du Parc, Mile End, Montréal* ☎ *514/750–6577* ⊕ *www.buvettechezsimone.com* Ⓜ *Laurier or Mont-Royal.*

Fodor'sChoice
★

Royal Phoenix. One of the few gay bars outside of the Village, this hotspot attracts more than its share of hipsters while also being a friendly neighborhood destination. Whether chowing down on the Poutine Royale with pulled pork or dancing to vintage dance music, you'll feel right at home. Try the basil mojito. Closed on Monday. ⊠ *5788 blvd. St-Laurent, Mile End, Montréal* ☎ *514/658–1622* ⊕ *www.royalphoenixbar.com* Ⓜ *Rosemont.*

LIVE MUSIC

Cabaret Playhouse. This former strip club is now a popular music venue with a brand new stage and usually no cover charge, giving Montrealers a chance to discover new bands without breaking the bank. Its "Faggity Ass Fridays" bills itself as a "queer dance party by and for the queer community." ⊠ *5656 av. du Parc, Mile End, Montréal* ☎ *514/276–0594* Ⓜ *Rosemont or Laurier.*

OUTREMONT

While primarily an upscale residential neighborhood, if you take a stroll along avenue Laurier or avenue Bernard you still might find a bit of action if you look hard enough. Technically, the west side of bustling avenue du Parc is in Outremont, although pretty well everyone except the taxman considers it to be Mile End.

BARS AND LOUNGES

BU. Inside Dispensa, a restaurant and food shop on rue Bernard, this wine bar takes over once the daylight hours are gone. The well-priced flights of three wines highlight special imports from different regions on a rotating basis. ⊠ *361 rue Bernard Ouest, Outremont, Montréal* ☎ *514/276–0249, 514/495–8258* ⊕ *www.bu-mtl.com* ☯ *Closed Sun.–Wed.* Ⓜ *Laurier.*

THE ISLANDS

Casino de Montréal, which is on Île Notre-Dame, is several minutes away by car, bicycle, or métro from Downtown. The casino might be the only vestige of nightlife on the islands, but it's worth visiting for the excellent cabaret shows and good selection of bars and restaurants, and, of course, to try your hand at gambling.

CASINOS

Casino de Montréal. Music (including cabaret), food, gambling: there's something for everyone at the Casino de Montréal, which is open around the clock. On Île Notre-Dame, it's easily accessible by car, bicycle, or bus. The casino has more than 3,000 slot machines, a keno lounge, a high-stakes gaming area, and 120 tables for baccarat, craps, blackjack, roulette, and various types of poker, as well as four new restaurants and three new bars. ⊠ *1 av. du Casino, Île Notre-Dame, Montréal* ☎ *514/392–2746, 800/665–2274* ⊕ *www.casinosduquebec.com/montreal* Ⓜ *Jean-Drapeau.*

4

THE PERFORMING ARTS

Updated by
Marcella de
Vincenzo

There's something uniquely Quebecois about the kind of entertainment referred to as a *spectacle*. It's more than just a performance, usually involving some kind of multimedia projection, light show, and, if outdoors, fireworks. It's no wonder, then, that the ultimate spectacle, Cirque du Soleil, was founded in Montréal in the '80s. And it's also hardly surprising that North America's largest French-speaking metropolis should be the continent's capital of French theater.

Montréal is the home of nearly a dozen professional companies and several important theater schools. But there's also a lively English-language theater scene and one of the few remaining Yiddish theaters in North America.

In 2012, the city completed the Quartier des Spectacles, a 70-acre theater district in Downtown with stages for outdoor performances and nearly 80 venues for dance, music, theater, and art.

For a city its size, Montréal offers a remarkable number of opportunities for fans of classical music to get their fill, from operas and symphonies to string quartets.

As for dance, there are several modern dance companies of note, including Montréal Danse, and Québec's premier ballet company, Les Grands Ballets Canadiens.

PLANNING

DRESS CODE
People tend to get somewhat dressed up for the symphony, the opera, and even theater performances in Montréal, perhaps more so than in several large U.S. cities. Men will wear sleek black pants, a button-down, and even a tie. Some women wear dark jeans, but it's not uncommon to see ladies decked out in skirts and dresses with strappy shoes (even in the dead of winter) and carrying clutches.

EVENTS INFORMATION

The bilingual *Nightlife* (⊕ *www. nightlife.ca*) and French-language *Le Voir* (⊕ *www.voir.ca*) list events and reviews, and are free and widely distributed.

Check out the *Gazette*'s "Friday Preview" section (⊕ *www.montreal gazette.com*) for events listings in English.

TICKETS

Tickets for most performances are available at the box offices of the various venues.

La Vitrine Culturelle. Next to the Quartier des Spectacles theater district, la Vitrine Culturelle (literally: Cultural Window) is the perfect place to get information and buy tickets for just about every type of show in town. Great last-minute deals are often available. ✉ *2 rue Ste-Catherine Est, Downtown* ☎ *514/285–4545* ⊕ *www.lavitrine.com* Ⓜ *St-Laurent.*

Ticketmaster. Tickets for theatrical and musical performances, plus a host of other cultural events, can be bought through Ticketmaster. ☎ *514/790–1111, 855/985–5000* ⊕ *www.ticketmaster.ca.*

BEST FREE PERFORMANCES

Several of the outdoor concerts at the **Montréal International Jazz Festival** in July are free, as are summertime performances at the **Théâtre de Verdure** inside Lafontaine Park.

Two of the greatest places to catch free classical music indoors are at **Montréal Christ Church Cathedral**, where organ recitals are given throughout the year, and at the **Basilique Notre-Dame de Montréal**, where there are year-round concerts by chamber and choral groups (regular church entry fee required).

PERFORMING ARTS REVIEWS

CIRCUS

Montréal's reinvention of the ancient art of the circus began in the 1980s, when two street performers, Guy Laliberté and Daniel Gauthier, founded the now world-famous Cirque du Soleil. But it didn't stop there. The city is also home to a huge complex, out beyond Mont-Royal in the St-Michel district, housing Canada's National Circus School, En Piste (Circus Arts National Network), and Cirque du Soleil's head office. The school attracts budding acrobats and clowns from all over the world, as well as several other smaller schools, and puts on several performances throughout the year at the complex's performance venue, TOHU Cité des Arts du Cirque (⊕ *www.tohu.ca*).

FAMILY

Fodor's Choice

★

Cirque du Soleil. This amazing circus is one of Montréal's great success stories. The company—founded in 1984 by a pair of street performers— has completely changed people's idea of what a circus can do. Its shows, now an international phenomenon, use no animals. Instead, colorful acrobatics flirt with the absurd through the use of music, humor, dance, and glorious (and often risqué) costumes.

Cirque du Soleil is Montréal's hometown circus, founded here in 1984. Today there are several troupes across several countries that perform hundreds of shows per year.

The Cirque has companies in Las Vegas and one each in Orlando and Los Angeles—but none in Montréal (though their HQ and a circus school is in the northern part of the city). However, every couple of years one of its international touring companies returns to where it all began, the Old Port, and sets up the familiar blue-and-yellow tent for a summer of sold-out shows. ☎ *514/790–1245, 800/361–4595* ⊕ *www.cirquedusoleil.com.*

Cirque Éloize. This award-winning troupe has been touring the globe since 1993, and with 4,000 performances under its belt, shows no signs of slowing down. Constantly evolving, Cirque Éloize uses artistic mediums like video and music to bring the circus arts to the masses. ☎ *514/596–3838* ⊕ *www.cirque-eloize.com.*

Les 7 doigts de la main. Literally translated as "the seven fingers of the hand," the name is a play on a French expression about working collectively toward a common goal, and these seven fingers—the seven founding partners of the circus—have done just that, building up a world-renowned circus troop over the past decade or so. Combining acrobatics, theater, and dance, they've performed at special events across the globe, including a Royal Variety Performance for Queen Elizabeth II and at the Olympics in Turin and Vancouver. They even made an appearance on *America's Got Talent.* ☎ *514/521–4477* ⊕ *www.7doigts.com.*

CLASSICAL MUSIC

Two symphony orchestras, an opera company of some renown, one of the best chamber orchestras in Canada, and several first-rate choirs make Montréal an ideal destination for music lovers. The music faculties of both McGill University and the Université de Montréal have international reputations, and their campuses' concert halls feature performances by the schools' best talents throughout the academic year. The city's main performance halls are at Place des Arts.

I Musici de Montréal Chamber Orchestra. Arguably the best chamber orchestra in Canada, I Musici, under the direction of Jean-Marie Zeitouni, performs at several places around town. These include the Salle Bourgie at the Musée des Beaux-Arts and the Place des Arts' Nouvelle Salle, but its music is best suited to the wood-paneled **Tudor Hall,** atop the Ogilvy department store. There, about a dozen times a year, you can enjoy a coffee or aperitif while you listen to a late-morning or early-evening concert. ☎ *514/982–6038 tickets* ⊕ *www.imusici.com.*

Opéra de Montréal. This renowned opera company, the largest francophone opera in North America, has a varied schedule of classics, including *Le Nozze di Figaro, Rigoletto,* and *Silent Night.* Seventy-five minutes before each show, the "preOpera" program, done in French with a summary in English, gives attendees a look at the history, music, and artists of the Opéra de Montréal. ⊠ *Place des Arts, 260 blvd. de Maisonneuve, Downtown* ☎ *514/985–2222, 877/385–2222* ⊕ *www. operademontreal.com* Ⓜ *Place des Arts.*

Orchestre Métropolitain du Grand Montréal. The Met may lie in the shadow of the Orchestre Symphonique de Montréal, but its talented conductor and artistic director, Yannick Nézet-Séguin, continues to draw the spotlight. He's in high demand across the world—in addition to his role here, he's the musical director at the Philadelphia Orchestra and the Rotterdam Philharmonic as well as the principal guest conductor of the London Philharmonic Orchestra. His charismatic approach has brought in the crowds since 2000 and produced highly acclaimed performances. Most shows take place at Place des Arts or Maison Symphonique de Montréal. ⊠ *Downtown* ☎ *514/598–0870* ⊕ *www. orchestremetropolitain.com* Ⓜ *Places des Arts.*

Fodor's Choice ★ **Orchestre Symphonique de Montréal.** Under the direction of influential and renowned conductor Kent Nagano, Montréal's beloved OSM plays programs that include masterful renditions of the classics, with contemporary works thrown into the mix. The 2014 season included evenings devoted to Mozart and Schuman, as well as an evening spotlighting the music of Philip Glass, featuring the man himself on piano. The orchestra's home, the Maison symphonique de Montréal is part of the Place des Arts complex (⇨ *see below*) ⊠ *1600 rue St-Urbain, Downtown* ☎ *514/842–9951, 888/842–9931* ⊕ *www.osm.ca* Ⓜ *Place des Arts.*

Place des Arts. Hosting everything from musicals to the symphony to the ballet since 1963, Place des Arts underwent a major facelift and makeover in 2011, to stunning effect. The glass-walled Maison Symphonique concert hall is the permanent home of the Montréal Symphony Orchestra. With state-of-the-art acoustics and only 75 feet between the end of

LATE-NIGHT BITES

Da Emma: Hover over a plate of pasta or roasted lamb at this darkly lit, romantic eatery.

Leméac: One of the best deals in town, their *"fin de soirée"* menu (served from 10 pm to midnight) is C$25, with a choice of 16 starters and 15 mains.

m:brgr: Sometimes nothing but a burger after hours will do, and those at this gourmet Downtown destination hit the spot. The fries are a must.

Rotisserie Panama: For satisfyingly filling and reasonably priced fare, head to this Greek restaurant, which serves some of Montréal's best grilled meat.

Schwartz's Delicatessen: Thanks to this legendary deli's takeout window, you can grab a hot (and huge) smoked-meat sandwich to enjoy back at your hotel room.

⇨ *For full reviews and locations of these restaurants, see Chapter 7, Where to Eat.*

the stage and the last row, it's an intimate place for concerts. The Salle Wilfrid Pelletier performance space is used by three resident companies: the Opéra de Montréal, Les Grands Ballets Canadiens, and the popular Jean Duceppe theater company. The venue's four other performance spaces host dance, theater, and festival events.

The other outdoor stages and other venues that make up the Quartier des Spectacles allow for lots of shows and festivals to be staged in one common area. Even if you don't have tickets to something, you can walk around the Quartier during festival season (pretty much all summer) to take in a variety of shows and concerts for free. ⊠ *175 rue Ste-Catherine Ouest, Downtown* ☎ *514/842–2112, 866/842–2112* ⊕ *www.laplacedesarts.com* Ⓜ *Place des Arts.*

Pollack Concert Hall. McGill University's concert hall showcases the best talents from its formidable music faculty, with concerts by the McGill Symphony, Opera McGill, the McGill Baroque Orchestra, and the Montréal Chamber Orchestra, among others. ⊠ *555 rue Sherbrooke Ouest, Downtown* ☎ *514/398–4547* ⊕ *www.mcgill.ca/music* Ⓜ *McGill.*

Salle Claude-Champagne. This beautiful concert hall hosts more than 150 symphonic and operatic performances every year by the music faculty of the Université de Montréal. The repertoire includes both classic and contemporary works. ⊠ *220 av. Vincent-d'Indy, Outremont* ☎ *514/343–6427* ⊕ *www.musique.umontreal.ca* Ⓜ *Édouard-Monpetit.*

DANCE

Traditional and contemporary dance companies thrive in Montréal, although many take to the road or are on hiatus in summer. Place des Arts, Montréal's main concert hall, is a popular venue for visiting large-scale productions.

Agora de la Danse. More than just a performance space for contemporary dance, this center actively works in the dance community to encourage creativity and experimentation. Hosting acclaimed artists and companies from around the world, the company is also affiliated with the Université du Québec à Montréal dance faculty. ✉ *840 rue Cherrier, Downtown* ☎ *514/525–1500* ⊕ *www.agoradanse.com* Ⓜ *Sherbrooke.*

BJM Danse Montréal. Under Artistic Director Louis Robitaille, BJM Danse Montréal fuses contemporary music and visual arts with extraordinary technique. Performances are held at Place des Arts and Agora de la Danse, and there are free shows at Théâtre de Verdure in Parc Lafontaine during the summer months. ☎ *514/982–6771* ⊕ *www.bjm danse.ca.*

La Fondation de Danse Margie Gillis. Margie Gillis, one of Canada's most exciting and innovative soloists, works with her own company and guest artists to stage performances at Place des Arts, Agora de la Danse, and other area venues. ☎ *514/845–3115* ⊕ *www.margiegillis.org.*

LaLaLa Human Steps. The Casablanca-born choreographer Édouard Lock founded LaLaLa to explore the boundaries of modern dance. The popular troupe has a heavy international schedule, but it also performs at Place des Arts and at Montréal festivals. ☎ *514/277–9090* ⊕ *www. lalalahumansteps.com.*

Fodor's Choice ★ **Les Grands Ballets Canadiens de Montréal.** One of Canada's premier ballet companies, Les Grands have been moving audiences since 1957. Under the artistic direction of Gradimir Pankov, the company has continued to evolve a rich body of both classic and contemporary work. Their annual presentation of *The Nutcracker*, which often sells out, has become a Christmas tradition. Performances take place at the Place des Arts. ☎ *514/842–2112, 866/842–2112 tickets* ⊕ *www.grandsballets.qc.ca.*

Montréal Danse. Lavish sets and dazzlingly sensual choreography have helped make Montréal Danse one of Canada's most popular contemporary repertory companies. They have a busy touring schedule, but also regularly perform at Place des Arts, Agora de la Danse, and the Théâtre de Verdure. ☎ *514/871–4005* ⊕ *www.montrealdanse.com.*

Tangente. For more than 30 years, Tangente has hosted weekly performances of contemporary and experimental dance between September and May—there are currently three venues in the city. They also act as an archive for contemporary dance and experimental performance art, with more than 2,000 files focusing on major international dance schools and festivals, companies and choreographers. Tangente encourages national and international exchanges between dance companies and artists. ☎ *514/525–5584* ⊕ *www.tangente.qc.ca.*

FILM

Although many of the movie theaters that once lined rue Ste-Catherine have closed down in recent years to make way for new, stadium-seating megaplexes like the Cineplex Odeon Forum Cinema, Montrealers remain uniquely privileged in the variety of alternatives that are available.

Ranging from the ultramodern Excentris theater on the Main to the gorgeous art deco confines of the majestic Imperial theater on Bleury Street in Downtown, the city's various venues offer locals the opportunity to

Montréal's world-renowned jazz festival lasts 11 days and features about 500 concerts and shows, more than half of which are free.

enjoy the numerous domestic productions released each year by the province's thriving French-language film industry in addition to the standard Hollywood fare consistently shown at the megaplexes.

Cinéma Banque Scotia. This four-level theater complex is in the center of downtown Montréal. The major attraction is movie-watching in either of the IMAX or the UltraAVX-3D theaters. The food hall offers more than just popcorn—sushi, poutine, and doughnuts are also up for grabs. The lines can be long, so go early or buy tickets online. ✉ *977 rue Ste-Catherine Ouest, Downtown* ☎ *514/842–0549* ⊕ *www. cineplex.com* Ⓜ *Peel.*

Cinéma du Parc. A favorite of Montréal moviegoers for years, this theater focuses on first-run movies from around the world. Retrospectives based on interesting themes and prominent directors are also screened. Located inside La Cité mall, near McGill University, it primarily caters to an Anglophone audience. ✉ *3575 av. du Parc, Downtown* ☎ *514/281–1900* ⊕ *www.cinemaduparc.com* Ⓜ *Place des Arts.*

Cinéma Impérial. Recognized by the Québec government as a historical monument in 2001, this beautiful, old-fashioned movie theater screens independent films, though on a somewhat irregular basis. It plays host to many cultural events, including the Montréal World Film Festival. ✉ *1432 rue Bleury, Downtown* ☎ *514/884–7187* ⊕ *www. cinemaimperial.com* Ⓜ *Place des Arts.*

Cinémathèque Quebecoise. With more than 35,000 films in its collection, and a ticket price of just C$8, Montréal's Museum of the Moving Image is the best place in the city to catch a foreign flick in its original language (with subtitles), in addition to Quebecois and other Canadian productions. The museum also stocks scripts, television shows, and various new media, with a permanent display of old-fashioned cinema equipment. ✉ *335 blvd. de Maisonneuve Est, Latin Quarter* ☎ *514/842–9763* ⊕ *www.cinematheque.qc.ca* Ⓜ *Berri-UQAM.*

Cineplex Odeon Forum Cinemas. With 22 screens showing everything from Hollywood blockbusters to indie flicks, choice is the main draw at this massive theater. That, plus the bowling alley, poolroom, and arcade complex. It used to be the home of Montréal's beloved Canadiens ice hockey team (look for the old seating and hockey memorabilia in the lobby). ✉ *2313 rue Ste-Catherine Ouest, Downtown* ☎ *514/904–1274* ⊕ *www.cinemamontreal.com* Ⓜ *Atwater.*

Excentris. Although two of its three former screening rooms now host live performances by singers, musicians, and dancers, the remaining Cinéma Parallèle is a champion of independant cinema, running avant-garde Canadian and international movies. With lots of candy and organic popcorn on tap, it's a very comfortable place to catch a movie. Excentris plays host to lots of great festivals, including the Festival of New Cinema in October. ✉ *3536 blvd. St-Laurent, The Plateau* ☎ *514/847–2206* ⊕ *www.cinemaexcentris.com* Ⓜ *Sherbrooke or St-Laurent.*

THEATER

There are at least 10 major French-language theater companies in town, some of which have an international reputation. The choices for Anglophones are more limited.

Black Theatre Workshop. The only black English-language company in Québec (and the longest-running in Canada) continues to support and nourish the careers of many prominent artists on the national scene. Expect innovative new productions performed alongside classic plays, such as *A Raisin in the Sun.* Shows take place at the Centaur Theatre and other venues around the city. ✉ *Downtown* ☎ *514/932–1104* ⊕ *www.blacktheatreworkshop.ca.*

Centaur Theatre. Montréal's best-known English-language theater company stages everything from frothy musical revues to serious works, and prominently features works by local playwrights. Its home is in the former stock-exchange building in Old Montréal. ✉ *453 rue St-François-Xavier, Old Montréal* ☎ *514/288–3161, 514/288–1229* ⊕ *www.centaurtheatre.com* Ⓜ *Place-d'Armes.*

Centre Phi. Packed with intimate screening rooms, recording facilities, exhibition spaces, and a performance space, this center promotes artist-driven film, design, and music from locals as well as international artists. Films are in English and French. ✉ *407 rue St-Pierre, Old Montréal* ☎ *514/225–0525, 855/526–8888* ⊕ *www.phi-centre.com* Ⓜ *Place-d'Armes or Square-Victoria.*

Geordie Productions. Promoting itself as a theater for all audiences, this accomplished English company has been delighting kids and adults since 1982. The 2014–15 lineup features productions that include adaptations of *Beneath the Banyon Tree, The Illiad,* and *The Odyssey.*

Most productions are performed at the Centaur Theatre. ✉ *Downtown* ☎ *514/845–9810* ⊕ *www.geordie.ca.*

Mainline Theatre. Operated by the same people who present the Montréal Fringe Festival every summer, the Mainline opened in 2006 to serve the city's burgeoning Anglo theater community and has been going strong ever since. ✉ *3997 blvd. St-Laurent, The Plateau* ☎ *514/849–3378* ⊕ *www.mainlinetheatre.ca* Ⓜ *St-Laurent or Mont-Royal.*

Monument-National. The highly regarded École Nationale de Théâtre du Canada—aka National Theatre School of Canada—supplies world stages with a steady stream of well-trained actors and directors. It works and performs in the historic and glorious old theater that has played host to such luminaries as Edith Piaf and Emma Albani. (Québec's first feminist rallies in the early 1900s also took place here.) Graduating classes perform professional-level plays in both French and English. The theater also plays host to an assortment of touring plays, musicals, and concerts. ✉ *1182 blvd. St-Laurent, Downtown* ☎ *514/871–2224* ⊕ *www.monument-national.qc.ca* Ⓜ *St-Laurent.*

Segal Centre for the Performing Arts. English-language favorites like *Harvey* and *Inherit the Wind* get frequent billing at this Côte-des-Neiges venue, along with locally written works. The center is best-known, however, as the home to the **Dora Wasserman Yiddish Theatre,** which presents such musical works as *The Jazz Singer* and *The Pirates of Penzance* in Yiddish. ✉ *5170 chemin de la Côte-Ste-Catherine, Côte-des-Neiges* ☎ *514/739–2301, 514/739–7944* ⊕ *www.segalcentre.org* Ⓜ *Côte-Ste-Catherine.*

Fodor's Choice **Théâtre du Nouveau Monde.** A season's offerings at this theater might
★ include works by locals Michel Tremblay and Patrice Robitaille as well as works by Shakespeare, Molière, Camus, Ibsen, Chekhov, and Arthur Miller. ✉ *84 rue Ste-Catherine Ouest, Downtown* ☎ *514/866–8668* ⊕ *www.tnm.qc.ca* Ⓜ *St-Laurent.*

Théâtre Ste-Catherine. With around 100 comfortable seats, this independent alternative theater features comedy and improv shows most nights. On Sunday there's a free improv workshop that's open to all, with participants later showing off what they learned as that evening's entertainment. The theater also houses Le Nouveau International, a nonprofit organization run by a thriving community of artists working year-round to produce theater, comedy, improv, films, a bimonthly magazine, and sketch shows. ✉ *264 rue Ste-Catherine Est, Latin Quarter* ☎ *514/284–3939* ⊕ *www.theatresaintecatherine.com.*

Théâtre St-Denis. This is one of several theaters hosting events that are part of the Just For Laughs Festival, and touring Broadway productions, concerts, musicals and dance performances can often be seen here. ✉ *1594 rue St-Denis, Latin Quarter* ☎ *514/849–4211* ⊕ *www. theatrestdenis.com* Ⓜ *Berri-UQAM.*

SHOPPING

Updated by
Vanessa Muri

Montrealers *magasinent* (shop) with a vengeance, whether they're scurrying down busy Ste-Catherine in Downtown checking out department store bargains, or strolling up St-Laurent browsing in boutiques that stock wares from local designers, or buying gourmet food or native crafts at one of the city's markets.

And if you're in the market for a new fur, you've come to the right city. Montréal has a long history of being one of the fur capitals of the world. If you think you might be buying fur, check with your country's customs officials to find out which animals are considered endangered and can't be imported.

The same caveat applies to carvings and other items made of ivory, which can't be imported into the United States or some other countries. And if you do buy Inuit art, make sure to look for the government of Canada's igloo symbol, which attests to the piece's authenticity.

PLANNING

HOURS

Most shops open by 10 am Monday through Saturday and close at 6 pm Monday through Wednesday. Stores stay open until 9 pm on Thursday and Friday, but on Saturday they usually close at 5 pm. On Sunday, most Downtown shops open noon to 5 pm. There are, however, exceptions. Large chain stores in Downtown often stay open weeknights until 9, and boutiques in areas that draw a drinks-and-dinner crowd, such as in the Plateau and in Old Montréal, can stay open even later in summer.

SALES TAX

Visitors must pay 5% in federal tax, called the GST (or TPS in Québec), and an additional 9.975% in Québec tax on most goods and services. Since roughly 2010, a Canadian dollar has been worth more or less the same as the American dollar, meaning that amazing deals can be hard to find. Still, even when the Canuck buck trades at par, there are deals

Montréal Shopping

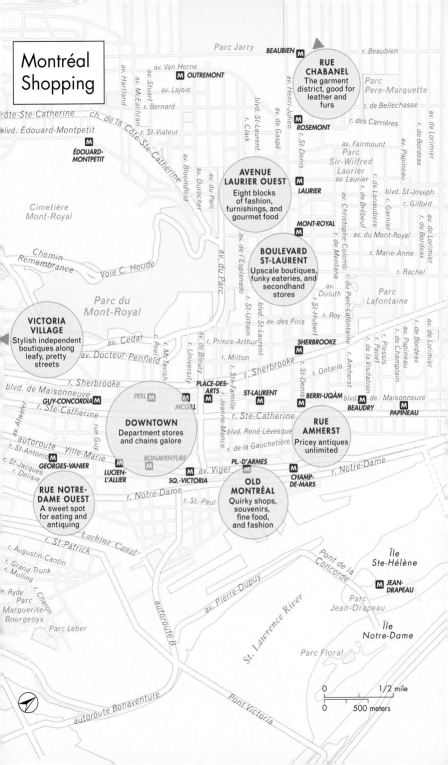

RUE CHABANEL
The garment district, good for leather and furs

AVENUE LAURIER OUEST
Eight blocks of fashion, furnishings, and gourmet food

BOULEVARD ST-LAURENT
Upscale boutiques, funky eateries, and secondhand stores

VICTORIA VILLAGE
Stylish independent boutiques along leafy, pretty streets

DOWNTOWN
Department stores and chains galore

RUE AMHERST
Pricey antiques unlimited

RUE NOTRE-DAME OUEST
A sweet spot for eating and antiquing

OLD MONTRÉAL
Quirky shops, souvenirs, fine food, and fashion

Parc Jarry

BEAUBIEN
OUTREMONT
ROSEMONT
LAURIER
MONT-ROYAL
ÉDOUARD-MONTPETIT
SHERBROOKE
PLACE-DES-ARTS
ST-LAURENT
BERRI-UQÀM
SHERBROOKE
GUY-CONCORDIA
PEEL
MCGILL
BEAUDRY
PAPINEAU
GEORGES-VANIER
BONAVENTURE
LUCIEN-L'ALLIER
SQ.-VICTORIA
PL.-D'ARMES
CHAMP-DE-MARS
JEAN-DRAPEAU

Parc Pere-Marquette
Parc Sir-Wilfrid Laurier
Cimetière Mont-Royal
Parc du Mont-Royal
Parc Lafontaine
Île Ste-Hélène
Parc Jean-Drapeau
Île Notre-Dame
Parc Floral
Parc Marguerite Bourgeoys
Parc Leber

St. Lawrence River
Lachine Canal

Pont de la Concorde
Pont Victoria

autoroute Bonaventure

0 ___ 1/2 mile
0 ___ 500 meters

on certain homegrown items: furs, fast fashion from local chains, and crafty goods that reflect Montréal's funky side.

MONTRÉAL SHOP REVIEWS

OLD MONTRÉAL (VIEUX-MONTRÉAL)

The old part of the city has more than its share of garish souvenir shops, but fashion boutiques and shoe stores with low to moderate prices line rues Notre-Dame and St-Jacques, from rue McGill to Place Jacques-Cartier. With gentrification in the west end of the area, high-end fashion boutiques and spas abound, especially along rue St-Paul Ouest. The area is also rich in art galleries and crafts shops along rue St-Paul and tucked inside the narrow rue des Artistes. Use the Place-d'Armes, Champ-de-Mars, or Square-Victoria métro stations.

ART

DHC/ART. Almost more of a museum than a gallery, this large space showcases great contemporary art. A free iPhone app takes you through the exhibits, and podcasts provide a fascinating look at the artists themselves. ⊠ *451 and 465 rue St-Jean, Old Montréal, Montréal* 🕾 *514/849–3742, 888/934–2278* ⊕ *www.dhc-art.org* ☉ *Closed Mon. and Tues.* Ⓜ *Square-Victoria or Place-d'Armes.*

Galerie Le Chariot. If the friendly and knowledgeable staff doesn't win you over, the vast collection of Inuit and Iroquois art will. With more than 2,000 pieces of sculpture in soapstone and serpentine, authentic drawings, and beautiful jewelry, the hardest part will be choosing what to buy. At least the guaranteed shipping service means you won't have to limit yourself. ⊠ *446 pl. Jacques-Cartier, Old Montréal, Montréal* 🕾 *514/875–6134* Ⓜ *Champ-de-Mars.*

La Guilde Graphique. Get lost for hours inside this stone-and-wood gallery as you scour the vast collection of original prints, engravings, etchings, and oil paintings. ⊠ *9 rue St-Paul Ouest, Old Montréal, Montréal* 🕾 *514/844–3438* ⊕ *www.guildegraphique.com* ☉ *Mon.–Sat. 10–6, Sun. noon–5* Ⓜ *Champ-de-Mars.*

CLOTHING

Boutique Denis Gagnon. This creative designer is much beloved on the Montréal fashion scene—his creations have been exhibited at the Montréal Museum of Fine Arts. In this sleek, subterranean boutique, Gagnon's couture designs stand alongside his ready-to-wear collection. He's also well-known for his shoes. ⊠ *Petit Hotel, 170B rue St-Paul Ouest, Old Montréal, Montréal* 🕾 *514/935–6360* ⊕ *www.denisgagnon. ca* Ⓜ *Place-d'Armes.*

Fodor's Choice   **Espace Pepin.** Talented owner and painter Lysanne Pepin has an eye for
★   design, and as you pass through the gauzy curtains, her boutique-cum-atelier is an intriguing—and beautiful—space to explore. Filled with romantic clothes, funky shoes, and a carefully edited mix of local and international labels, you'll also find eclectic housewares and furniture

Montréal's Best Shopping Streets

Most visitors to Montréal will have Downtown and Old Montréal on the itinerary, but for an authentic experience à la Montréalaise you should also venture into some of the other neighborhoods.

Avenue Laurier Ouest. Shops and boutiques along the eight blocks between boulevard St-Laurent and chemin de la Côte-Ste-Catherine sell medium- to high-end fashions, home furnishings, decorative items, artwork, books, kitchenware, toys and children's items, and gourmet food. There are plenty of restaurants, bars, and cafés in which to rest your feet and check out your purchases. The street is about a 10-minute walk from the Laurier métro station.

Boulevard St-Laurent. Affectionately known as The Main, St-Laurent has restaurants, boutiques, and nightclubs that cater mostly to an upscale clientele. Still, the area has managed to retain its working-class immigrant roots and vitality to some degree: high-fashion shops are interspersed with ethnic-food stores, secondhand clothing and decor boutiques, and hardware stores. Indeed, a trip up this street takes you from Chinatown to Little Italy.

Rue Amherst. Antiques shops began springing up in the Gay Village in the early 1990s, most of them on rue Amherst between rues Ste-Catherine and Ontario. Copious cafés and brunch spots nearby will fuel your quest. The area used to be less expensive than rue Notre-Dame, but it's not always the case these days. Use the Beaudry métro station.

Rue Bernard. Only a few blocks away from the Outremont métro station, this chic villagey street is well worth a detour. The street boasts many sidewalk cafés—called *terrasses* in local parlance—for fine or casual dining, as well as specialty food stores, decor shops, and some of the best ice cream in Montréal at Le Glacier Bilboquet.

Rue Chabanel. The eight-block stretch of Chabanel just west of boulevard St-Laurent is the heart of the city's garment district. The goods seem to get more stylish and more expensive the farther west you go. If you're lucky, you might come across signs for designer sample sales. Many of the city's furriers have also moved into the area. A few places on Chabanel accept credit cards, but bring cash anyway. If you pay in cash, the price will often include the tax. From the Crémazie métro station, take Bus 53 north.

Rue Notre-Dame Ouest. The fashionable place for antiquing is a formerly run-down five-block strip of Notre-Dame between rue Guy and avenue Atwater. Most of the action is at the western end of the strip, as are many of the restaurants and cafés that have sprung up to cater to shoppers. Walk east from Lionel-Groulx métro station.

Victoria Village. The carriage-trade area for wealthy Westmount citizens, who live on the leafy slopes of Mont-Royal, has morphed into a shopping destination for all Montrealers with an eye for style. Independent boutiques offer distinctive home decor, shoes, gifts, stationery, and fashion along rues Victoria and Sherbrooke, with the epicenter between Victoria and Claremont. Cafés and fine specialty food shops also abound. Vendôme is the closest métro station.

5

TOP MONTRÉAL SHOPPING EXPERIENCES

Some of the best deals can be found at **La Maison Simons** department store, where there's something cheap and chic for everyone, from teenyboppers to mesdames and monsieurs on a budget. Along rue Ste-Catherine and in the underground malls, check out trendy Quebecois fashion emporiums, including **Le Château** and **BEDO**. Montréal's luxury lane runs from **Ogilvy** up to **Holt Renfrew** along rue de la Montagne, with designer fashion from **Marie Saint Pierre** and custom pearl jewelry from **Boutique Laura Aline** lining the route.

The path of luxury continues west along rue Sherbrooke, where you'll find the crème de la crème of international fashion and a plethora of art houses, with shops like **Les Créateurs** and **Galerie Walter Klinkhoff.**

Funky fashionistas will want to hit Mile End and the Plateau. In Mile End, hipster territory includes **General 54** and **Unicorn,** with Citizen Vintage for recycled fashions. Moving down Montréal's beloved Main—boulevard St-Laurent—check out vintage, decor, and design shops.

Closer to Downtown, **Boutique 1861** and **M0851** are worth the walk. One-of-a-kind independent shops line avenue Mont-Royal and rue St-Denis.

for home and office. ✉ *350 rue St-Paul Ouest, Old Montréal, Montréal* ☎ *514/844–0114* ⊕ *www.pepinart.com* Ⓜ *Square Victoria.*

Reborn. If you love cutting-edge fashions, don't miss this long, narrow shop. Men and women will love looks by Acne, Jeremy Laing, and Montréal's own superstar, Rad Hourani. Wickedly clever jewelry by Harakiri (also a Montréal designer) ups the avant-garde factor. ✉ *231 rue St-Paul Ouest, Suite 100, Old Montréal, Montréal* ☎ *514/499–8549* ⊕ *www.reborn.ws* Ⓜ *Place-Victoria.*

U&I. Hip men and women flock to this sleek boutique in Old Montréal, which is stocked with avant-garde finds from North America and Europe. Cydwoq, Engineered Garments, and Finsk hang alongside coats from the sleek Montréal label Mackage and pieces from U&I's own label. ✉ *215 St. Paul Ouest, Old Montréal, Montréal* ☎ *514/508–7704* ⊕ *www.boutiqueuandi.com* Ⓜ *Champs de Mars.*

HOUSEWARES

Fodor'sChoice
★
À Table Tout Le Monde. Should you require the most refined disposable plates for a picnic on the mountain (or in your hotel room), you can stop in at this shop and pick up a few Wasara pieces designed in Japan. The sophisticated shop features fine designs from around the world, including Québec's own Jean-Claude Poitras (for organic cotton table runners) and Bousquet (for playful porcelain designs). Of course, it's not all disposable. Quite the contrary. ✉ *361 rue St-Paul Ouest, Old Montréal, Montréal* ☎ *514/750–0311* ⊕ *www.atabletoutlemonde.com* Ⓜ *Place-Victoria.*

MALLS AND SHOPPING CENTERS

Le Scandinave Les Bains Vieux-Montréal. A bastion of urban chic in historic Old Montréal, this spa is especially popular on cold winter days. Inspired by the age-old tradition of public baths, the Scandinave prides itself on offering guests an authentic yet contemporary experience with an accent of privacy and total relaxation. The posh interior of slate, marble, and wood contrasts nicely with the bubbling pool and misty steam rooms. The ultimate meltdown is the zero-stress chamber of absolute quiet and darkness to intensify the peacefulness. All you need to bring along is your bathing suit; the spa provides sandals, bathrobes, and towels. For extra relaxation, sign up for a massage with one of their professional masseuse. ✉ *71 rue de la Commune Ouest, Old Montréal, Montréal* ☎ *514/288–2009* ⊕ *www.scandinave.com* Ⓜ *Place-d'Armes.*

Marché Bonsecours. The silver-domed Marché Bonsecours, the city's main public market in the 1800s, has been restored and renovated with a modern edge. The 15 boutiques inside sell First Nations artwork, Quebecois designer fashions, jewelry, kitchenware, and more. The paintings of Michel Sylvain on display at Art et Antiquités Médius capture eloquent Montréal street scenes. Soak it all up over a cup of coffee from Le Café des Arts or a full-fledged meal from Le Cabaret du Roy. ✉ *350 rue St-Paul Est, Old Montréal, Montréal* ☎ *514/872–7730* ⊕ *www. marchebonsecours.qc.ca* Ⓜ *Champ-de-Mars.*

TOYS

FAMILY **Mortimer Snodgrass.** Kids and adults alike can spend hours in this gadget emporium poring over the original plush toys, temporary tattoos, Fodor'sChoice and funky kitchen gadgets. Don't miss the hilarious card selection ★ tucked underneath the staircase. ✉ *56 rue Notre-Dame Ouest, Old Montréal, Montréal* ☎ *514/499–2851* ⊕ *www.mortimersnodgrass.com* Ⓜ *Place-d'Armes.*

DOWNTOWN

Montréal's largest retail district takes in rues Sherbrooke and Ste-Catherine, boulevard de Maisonneuve, and the side streets between them. Because of the density and variety of the stores, it's the best shopping bet if you're in town overnight or for a weekend. The area bounded by rues Sherbrooke, Ste-Catherine, de la Montagne, and Crescent has antiques and art galleries in addition to designer salons. Fashion boutiques and art and antiques galleries line rue Sherbrooke. Rue Crescent holds a tempting blend of antiques, fashions, and jewelry displayed beneath colorful awnings. Rue de la Montagne is the corridor of chic, between the high-end Holt Renfrew and Ogilvy department stores, with designer boutiques—including top Québec labels—en route. Rue Ste-Catherine is the main shopping thoroughfare, with most of the chain stores and department stores. To get here, take the métro to the Peel, McGill, or Guy-Concordia stations.

ANTIQUES

Antiquités Pour La Table. Armoires and sideboards brimming with fine crystal and china line the walls at this beautiful store, while chandeliers, linens, and other vintage pieces make up the rest of the treasures.

✉ *762 av. Atwater, Downtown, Montréal* ☎ *514/989–8945* ⊕ *www. antiquesforthetable.com* ⊗ *Tues.–Sat. 11–5* Ⓜ *St-Henri.*

Grand Central. "Grand" is the right word to describe this antiques emporium—it's filled to the brim with elegant chandeliers and candelabras, armchairs and secretaries, and other decorative elements from the 18th and 19th centuries. These items would add a touch of refinement to almost any home. ✉ *2448 rue Notre-Dame Ouest, St-Henri, Downtown, Montréal* ☎ *514/935–1467* ⊕ *www.grandcentralinc.ca* ⊗ *Weekdays 9:30–5:30, Sat. 11–5* Ⓜ *Lionel-Groulx.*

Viva Gallery. Unique along the Notre-Dame antiques stretch, this shop sells exquisite Asian furniture—armoires, chests, chairs, and wooden screens with fine carvings—complemented by paintings from Xiaoyang Yu that depict life in Beijing. ✉ *1970 rue Notre-Dame Ouest, Downtown, Montréal* ☎ *514/932–3200* ⊕ *www.vivagalerie.com* ⊗ *Tues., Thurs., and Sat. noon–5* Ⓜ *Lucien-L'Allier.*

ART

Edifice Belgo. Built more than a century ago, Edifice Belgo houses more than two dozen art galleries exhibiting the works of both established and emerging artists. Galerie Roger Bellemare is one of the best galleries for contemporary art, as is Galerie SAS. Galerie Trois Points showcases the work of Montréal and Québec artists. For wearable art, visit designer Véronique Miljkovitch's atelier on the second floor. ✉ *372 rue Ste-Catherine Ouest, Downtown, Montréal* ☎ *514/861–2953* ⊗ *Closed Sun.–Tues.* Ⓜ *Place des Arts.*

Galerie Alan Klinkhoff. The Klinkhoffs know art, and their gallery has been open since 1950. It boasts several floors of Canadian works from both contemporary and historical artists. Hours vary depending on the season. ✉ *1448 rue Sherbrooke Ouest, Downtown, Montréal* ☎ *514/284–9339* ⊕ *www.klinkhoff.com* Ⓜ *Guy.*

BOOKS AND STATIONERY

Essence du Papier. Pretty pens, paper, and journals will call to your inner diarist. The store harkens to a more refined (or at least more analog) time before smartphones and tablets. Imported and handmade stationery, wedding invitations, and birthday cards are among the standouts. Modern desk organizers from Semikolon will tempt you to clean up your home office. ✉ *1 pl. Ville Marie, Downtown, Montréal* ☎ *514/874–9915* ⊕ *www.essencedupapier.com* ⊗ *Mon.–Wed. 8–6, Thurs. and Fri. 8–9, Sat. 9–5* Ⓜ *McGill or Bonaventure.*

Indigo. At this branch of the largest bookstore chain in Canada, a vast selection of classic literature, novels, music, and magazines (in English and French) are sold alongside housewares, fashion accessories, and baby gifts. Famous authors sometimes drop by for book signings, and this convenient location has its own independent café. ✉ *1500 av. McGill College, corner of rue Ste-Catherine, Downtown, Montréal* ☎ *514/281–5549* ⊕ *www.chapters.indigo.ca* Ⓜ *McGill.*

Paragraphe. This shop carries the usual selection of mysteries and thrillers, but also stocks a wide range of Canadian works. It's a favorite with visiting authors, who stop by to read from their latest releases. Sip on a coffee from the adjacent Second Cup coffee shop while you peruse the stacks. ✉ *2220 av. McGill College, Downtown, Montréal* ☎ *514/845–5811* ⊕ *www.paragraphbooks.com* ☉ *Weekdays 8–8, weekends 9–9* Ⓜ *McGill.*

Renaud-Bray. Tucked away in the basement level of the Complexe Desjardins shopping mall, this outlet of the vast French-language book chain is chockablock with French and English books, magazines, and music. ✉ *150 Ste-Catherine Ouest, Downtown, Montréal* ☎ *514/288–4844* ⊕ *www.renaud-bray.com* Ⓜ *Place des Arts.*

Fodor's Choice ★ **The Word.** Deep in the McGill University neighborhood, this small shop is bursting with used books (including first editions) and specializes in philosophy, poetry, and literature. The award-winning Montréal landmark shuns modern technology (including a cash register) in favor of timeless appeal. There's not even a sign, so keep your eyes peeled as you walk along Milton, though the bargain books lining the window are a good clue. ✉ *469 rue Milton, Downtown, Montréal* ☎ *514/845–5640* ⊕ *www.wordbookstore.ca* ☉ *Mon.–Wed. 10–6, Thurs. and Fri. 10–9, Sat. 11–6* Ⓜ *McGill.*

CLOTHING

BEDO. Nailing the trends season after season, BEDO is an affordable way to replenish your wardrobe without breaking the bank. Well regarded by the fashion-obsessed of both sexes, the company collaborated with star designer Denis Gagnon to put out an affordable collection of his avant-garde creations. ✉ *1256 rue Ste-Catherine Ouest, Downtown, Montréal* ☎ *514/866–4962* ⊕ *www.bedo.ca* Ⓜ *Peel.*

Boutique Encore. For years this quaint shop has been supplying Montrealers with lightly used designer goods at surprisingly affordable prices. Expect to find Hermès, Chanel, and Gucci for the ladies, while men can hunt for the likes of Armani and Hugo Boss. ✉ *2145 rue Crescent, Downtown, Montréal* ☎ *514/849–0092* Ⓜ *Peel or Guy-Concordia.*

Buffalo David Bitton. Fans adore the fit of Montrealer David Bitton's jeans, and the reasonable prices don't hurt either. Aside from denim for men and women, there's a full line of trendy clothes and accessories for the gal (and guy) about town. ✉ *1395 rue Ste-Catherine Ouest, Downtown, Montréal* ☎ *514/985–5783* ⊕ *www.buffalojeans.ca* ☉ *Weekdays 10–9, weekends 10–8* Ⓜ *Peel.*

Editorial Boutique. Designer duds happily share space with inexpensive but chic items at this low-key downtown boutique with a devoted cult following. Brands include Citizens of Humanity, Erin Wasson, and Luv U Always, a leggings line from a local design team. ✉ *1455 rue Stanley, Downtown, Montréal* ☎ *514/849–3888* ⊕ *www.editorialboutique.com* Ⓜ *Peel.*

Fodor's Choice ★ **E.R.A. Vintage Wear.** With a reputation as the best vintage shop in the city, this high-end boutique specializes in vintage clothing, shoes, and accessories from the 1920s through the mid-1980s. Each handpicked item is carefully cleaned, repaired, and altered as necessary to give it a more contemporary flavor. High-profile clients like Julianne Moore and Cate Blanchett have been known to drop by. This location is bright, spacious, and loaded with irresistible treasures. ✉ *1001 rue Lenoir,*

Downtown, Montréal ☎ *514/543–8750* ⊕ *www.eravintagewear.tumblr. com* Ⓜ *Place St-Henri.*

Eva B. On the secondhand fashion map for decades, Eva B has all kinds of clothes, shoes, jewelry, and even eyeglasses on offer. Budget at least 30 minutes to scour the labyrinth of racks and the "pool," a large platform in the back where everything is a dollar. Just watch your step; the floor is uneven. Nosh on a samosa or something else from the in-store café if you get hungry in the process. ✉ *2015 blvd. St-Laurent, Downtown, Montréal* ☎ *514/849–8246* ⊕ *www.eva-b.ca* ☯ *Mon.–Sat. 11–9, Sun. noon–8* Ⓜ *St-Laurent.*

Harricana. Yesterday's old fur coats and stoles are transformed into everything from car coats and ski jackets to baby wraps and throw pillows at this designer shop. For summer, vintage scarves become flirty little tops. The recycled furs are sold at dozens of shops, but the best place to see what's available is this combination atelier and boutique. ✉ *3000 rue St-Antoine Ouest, Downtown, Montréal* ☎ *514/287–6517, 877/894–9919* ⊕ *www.harricana.qc.ca* Ⓜ *Lionel-Groulx.*

Harry Rosen. This is Canada's premier high-end menswear destination. Stocked with both casual and formal attire, wallets, watches, and hats, this 22,000-square-foot flagship store caters to the classically tailored male. Brands include 7 For All Mankind, Michael Kors, and Cole Haan. ✉ *Cours Mont-Royal, 1455 rue Peel, Suite 227, Downtown, Montréal* ☎ *514/284–3315* ⊕ *www.harryrosen.com* Ⓜ *Peel.*

Les Créateurs. The long, narrow shop will feel like home to the avant-garde fashionista. For more than 30 years, owner Maria Balla has been offering clothes by the most innovative designers from around the world, including Ann Demeulemeester and Junya Watanabe. ✉ *1444 rue Sherbrooke Ouest, Suite 100, Downtown, Montréal* ☎ *514/284–2102* ⊕ *www.lescreateurs.ca* ☯ *Weekdays 10–6, Sat. 10–5* Ⓜ *Guy-Concordia.*

Fodor's Choice
★ **Marie Saint Pierre.** The leading female designer in Québec (and one who's celebrated throughout Canada), Marie Saint Pierre is known for her signature pleats and ruffles—think sleek and sophisticated rather than frilly. Now she's lending her avant-garde touch to bridal, with a wedding collection that's only available at this flagship boutique. Call ahead, as hours vary. ✉ *2081 rue de la Montagne, Downtown, Montréal* ☎ *514/281–5547* ⊕ *www.mariesaintpierre.com* Ⓜ *Peel or Guy-Concordia.*

Parasuco. Homegrown fashionista Salvatore Parasuco not only opened his first store at age 19, he went on to invent stretch denim. This two-story flagship is bright and spacious, and stocked top to bottom with his signature rocker chic look. Incredibly, designer denim for under $100 can still be bought here. ✉ *1414 rue Crescent, Downtown, Montréal* ☎ *514/284–2288* ⊕ *www.parasuco.com* ☯ *Mon.–Wed. 9:30–6, Thurs. and Fri. 9:30–9, Sat. 9:30–6, Sun. 11–6* Ⓜ *Guy-Concordia or Peel.*

Rudsak. Sleek leather jackets and coats for men and women were the original raison d'être of this cool brand, but chic jumpsuits, classic dresses, and cozy knits highlight how far it has come. The arm candy, including totes, purses, satchels and messenger bags, gets better with age. ⊠ *1400 rue Ste-Catherine Ouest, Downtown, Montréal* ☎ *514/399–9925* ⊕ *www.rudsak.com* Ⓜ *Guy-Concordia.*

Shan. Designed in Montréal and sold around the world, this is couture swimwear at its finest. In a rainbow of colors, these sexy cuts are meant to be displayed—though one of the ethereal cover-ups just might make one reconsider. Men can also shop her collection of swim trunks, briefs, and ready-to-wear. ⊠ *2150 rue Crescent, Downtown, Montréal* ☎ *514/287–7426* ⊕ *www.shan.ca* Ⓜ *Peel or Guy-Concordia.*

Ursula B. Spread out over 5,500 square feet, Ursula B. carries everything from shoes, handbags, and belts to scarves, jewelry, and hats. Find fashion-forward labels like The Row and Mary Katrantzou, sexier designers like Carven and Cushnie et Ochs, and dramatic elegance from Jason Wu. Be sure to head upstairs for the sales section. ⊠ *Les Cours Mont-Royal, 1455 rue Peel, Suite 328, Downtown, Montréal* ☎ *514/282–0294* ⊕ *www.ursulab.com* Ⓜ *Peel.*

CLOTHING: MEN'S ONLY

Fodor'sChoice
★

Henri Henri. The best men's hat store in Canada carries a huge stock of homburgs, fedoras, and derbies, as well as cloth caps and other accessories. Prices range from about C$155 to C$1,000, the top price fetching you a top-of-the-line Panama hat. ⊠ *189 rue Ste-Catherine Est, Downtown, Montréal* ☎ *514/288–0109, 888/388–0109* ⊕ *www. henrihenri.ca* ⊗ *Mon.–Thurs. 10–6, Fri. 10–9, weekends 10–5* Ⓜ *St-Laurent or Berri-UQAM.*

L'Uomo Montréal. You'll come to this store for the selection of European menswear and accessories, but you'll stay for the impeccable service and attention to detail. Expect suits from Kiton and Borrelli, bags from Prada, and ties from Massimo Bizzocchi. It's been called the finest men's store in Canada for a reason. ⊠ *1452 rue Peel, Downtown, Montréal* ☎ *514/844–1008, 877/844–1008* ⊕ *www.luomo-montreal.com* Ⓜ *Peel.*

Tozzi. Known around Montréal as one of the top menswear destinations, Tozzi is a one-stop shop for the dapper gentleman. Suits, polos, jeans, watches, sunglasses, and cologne—this boutique offers just about everything in a minimalist, serene environment. ⊠ *2115 rue Crescent, Downtown, Montréal* ☎ *514/285–4441* ⊕ *www.boutiquetozzi.com* Ⓜ *Guy-Concordia or Peel.*

DEPARTMENT STORES

Fodor'sChoice
★

Holt Renfrew. This upscale department store is Canada's answer to Bergdorf Goodman. Gucci, Chanel, and all the usuals are complemented by up-and-coming designers and Holt's own in-house line. Just try and walk past the wall of handbags on the ground floor without being tempted to buy one or two. Even if your budget doesn't allow for much more than window-shopping, a trip to Café Holt downstairs is a must. Tartines—open-face sandwiches—are made here from bread flown in from Paris's Poilâne bakery and come in several enticing combinations. ⊠ *1300 rue Sherbrooke Ouest, Downtown, Montréal* ☎ *514/842–5111* ⊕ *www.holtrenfrew.com* Ⓜ *Peel or Guy-Concordia.*

La Baie. The Bay is a descendant of the Hudson's Bay Company, the great 17th-century fur-trading company that played a pivotal role in Canada's

5

development. La Baie has been a department store since 1891 and is known for its duffel coats and signature red, green, and white striped blankets. Besides fashions, housewares, and toys, there's also a portrait studio, beauty salon, and spa. ✉ *585 rue Ste-Catherine Ouest, Downtown, Montréal* ☎ *514/281–4422* ⊕ *www.thebay.com* ⊘ *Mon.–Wed. 10–7, Thurs. and Fri. 10–9, Sat. 9–7, Sun. 10–7* Ⓜ *McGill.*

La Maison Simons. Find the *trends du jour* at a great price from the youth-oriented labels on the ground floor of this bustling department store. Upstairs, the fare is more mature, ranging from respectable and affordable twinsets to luxe offerings from the likes of Chloé and Missoni. The store's fashion-forward men's suits and casual wear are also worth checking out. ✉ *977 rue Ste-Catherine Ouest, Downtown, Montréal* ☎ *514/282–1840* ⊕ *www.simons.ca* Ⓜ *Peel.*

Fodor's Choice
★
Ogilvy. Founded in 1865, this department store boasts a vast selection of clothing and accessories for men and women. It hasn't broken with tradition: a kilted piper marches throughout the store at noon daily. The Louis Vuitton boutique is more than 3,000 square feet and has a "bag bar." It's also a good place to rest weary feet. ✉ *1307 rue Ste-Catherine Ouest, Downtown, Montréal* ☎ *514/842–7711, 855/842–7711* ⊕ *www.ogilvycanada.com* Ⓜ *Peel.*

FOOD

Marché Atwater. Heading down Atwater Avenue toward Lachine Canal, you can't miss the art-deco tower of Atwater Market. This is the best spot to pick up local produce, fresh flowers, and gourmet meats and cheeses. Bring a blanket and enjoy a perfect picnic next to the canal. ✉ *138 av. Atwater, Downtown, Montréal* ☎ *514/937–7754* ⊕ *www. marchespublics-mtl.com* ⊘ *Mon.–Wed. 7–6, Thurs. 7–7, Fri. 7–8, weekends 7–5* Ⓜ *Lionel-Groulx.*

JEWELRY

Fodor's Choice
★
Bleu Comme Le Ciel. In France they call costume jewelry *bijoux de fantaisie*, and that's exactly what you'll find here: a fantastic array of colorful crystal baubles. Elegant lines from Ginette NY contrast with the bold bangles of Alexis Bittar. The glass-walled boutique is easy to miss, as it blends into the surrounding building. ✉ *2000 rue Peel, Downtown, Montréal* ☎ *514/847–1128* ⊕ *www.bleucommeleciel.com* Ⓜ *Peel.*

Boutique Laura Aline. Third-generation jewelry designer Aline Papazian and daughter Laura Zakem are intent on changing the perception that pearls are stuffy. Sourcing materials from around the world, they use semiprecious stones, crystals, and diamonds to create unique, contemporary designs. Don't let the buzzer at the door deter you; their jewelry is often quite affordable. ✉ *2017 rue de la Montagne, Downtown, Montréal* ☎ *514/507–6118* ⊕ *www.lauraaline.com* Ⓜ *Peel.*

LINGERIE

La Senza. The two-story flagship of this Québec-based chain is packed with bright, cheerful push-up bras, panties, and negligees. Sleepwear is also available. ✉ *1133 rue Ste-Catherine Ouest, Downtown, Montréal* ☎ *514/281–0101* ⊕ *www.lasenza.com* Ⓜ *Peel.*

MALLS AND SHOPPING CENTERS

Centre Eaton de Montréal. In addition to the 175 stores in downtown's largest mall, there's free Wi-Fi in the spacious lower-level food court. Early 2013 brought the opening of a branch of the Musée Grévin, a wax museum that replicates over a hundred local and international celebrities. ⊠ *705 rue Ste-Catherine Ouest, Downtown, Montréal* ☎ *514/288–3708* ⊕ *www.centreeatondemontreal.com* ⊗ *Weekdays 10–9, Sat. 10–6, Sun. 11–5* Ⓜ *McGill.*

Les Cours Mont-Royal. A variety of chic independent boutiques are mixed in with quality chains like Club Monaco and DKNY in this elegant mall. Drop by Spa Diva or the top-notch salon Pure if you're in need of a beauty break. The elegant atrium sometimes hosts runway shows. ⊠ *1455 rue Peel, Downtown, Montréal* ☎ *514/842–7777* ⊕ *www.lcmr.ca* Ⓜ *Peel.*

Place Ville Marie. Stylish shoppers head to the 80-plus retail outlets in Place Ville Marie, part of the city's vast underground network. Murale is a massive beauty emporium filled with virtually every skin-care product imaginable, including lines for men. ⊠ *Blvd. René-Lévesque and rue University, Downtown, Montréal* ☎ *514/861–9393* ⊕ *www.placevillemarie.com* Ⓜ *McGill or Bonaventure.*

SHOES

Fodor's Choice
★

Browns. This local institution stocks fashionable footwear and accessories for men and women. Besides its own label, Browns carries shoes by Emporio Armani, Michael Kors, Cole Haan, Steve Madden, and Stuart Weitzman. Comfortable couches make shopping a pleasant experience inside this gleaming white-and-silver flagship. ⊠ *1191 rue Ste-Catherine Ouest, Downtown, Montréal* ☎ *514/987–1206* ⊕ *www.brownsshoes.com* ⊗ *Weekdays 10–9, Sat. 10–8, Sun. noon–6* Ⓜ *Peel.*

THE VILLAGE

The Gay Village is known for its excellent furniture stores as much as for its vibrant nightlife. Rue Amherst is nearly overflowing with antiques shops; plenty of unique treasures are just waiting to be discovered, most being midcentury modern. The Beaudry métro station is your best bet.

ANTIQUES

Antiquités Curiosités. A sea of chairs, lamps, and other furnishings awaits you at Antiquités Curiosités, but it's the Victorian-era goodies that are the biggest draw. Retro pieces like rotary phones also tickle the fancy. ⊠ *1769 rue Amherst, The Village, Montréal* ☎ *514/525–8772* Ⓜ *Beaudry.*

Cité Déco. Get your fill of teak armchairs, rococo mirrors, and streamlined furnishings, then put up your feet in one of the many loungers while you ponder your potential purchases. Most of the pieces are from the '30s to the '60s, with some from the '80s thrown in for good measure. ⊠ *1761 rue Amherst, The Village, Montréal* ☎ *514/528–0659* ⊕ *www.citedecomeubles.com* ⊗ *Tues.–Fri. 11–6, Sat. 11–5, Sun. noon–5* Ⓜ *Beaudry.*

THE PLATEAU MONT-ROYAL, MILE END, LITTLE ITALY, AND OUTREMONT

THE PLATEAU

The Plateau has long been recognized as one of North America's hippest neighborhoods, and though trends typically come and go, its cachet endures. Rue St-Denis is home to both independent boutiques and chain stores selling local and international fashion, as well as numerous jewelry stores, all at prices for every budget. Boulevard St-Laurent and avenue Mont-Royal both offer opportunities for vintage shopping, with St-Laurent also known for contemporary furniture and decor stores.

CLOTHING

Aime Com Moi. If the bright fuschia awning doesn't draw you inside, the colorful mannequins will. Promoting young, hip Quebecois designers for more than 15 years, Aime Com Moi caters to trendy women 30 years and up. The shop boasts feminine designs from Annie 50, flirty skirts from Dinh Bá, and colorful recycled creations from Créations Encore. ⊠ *150 av. Mont-Royal Est, The Plateau, Montréal* ☎ *514/982–0088* ⊕ *www.aimecommoi.com* ⊙ *Mon.–Wed. 11–6, Thurs. and Fri. 11–7, Sat. 11–5, Sun. noon–5* Ⓜ *Mont-Royal.*

Fodor'sChoice ★ **Boutique 1861.** This boutique stocks romantic, lacy, and affordable finds from local and international designers, including Arti Gogna and Champagne & Strawberry. With everything white—hardwood floors, couches, and armoires—the boudoir vibe is irresistible. Just look for the pink-and-black cameo signage. The name comes from the smaller branch at 1861 rue Ste-Catherine. ⊠ *3670 blvd. St-Laurent, The Plateau, Montréal* ☎ *514/670–6110* ⊕ *www.1861.ca.*

Boutique Philippe Dubuc. One of the city's favorite menswear designers, Philippe Dubuc's collections are characterized by richly textured fabrics, exquisite tailoring, and lot of black. Head up the wrought-iron steps in search of a fine pair of tapered trousers, one of his signature looks. ⊠ *4451 rue St-Denis, The Plateau, Montréal* ☎ *514/282–1465* ⊕ *www.dubucstyle.com* Ⓜ *Mont-Royal.*

Kanuk. This company's owl trademark has become something of a status symbol among the shivering urban masses. These coats and parkas are built to keep an Arctic explorer warm and dry. Try on coats in a variety of styles and lengths, with optional fur hoodies. Rain gear is also on offer. ⊠ *485 rue Rachel Est, The Plateau, Montréal* ☎ *514/284–4494, 877/284–4494* ⊕ *www.kanuk.com* ⊙ *Late Mar.–early Sept., closed Sun.* Ⓜ *Mont-Royal.*

Fodor'sChoice ★ **M0851.** Sleek, supple leather clothing and bags from the Québec designer Frédéric Mamarbachi have a cult following from Antwerp to Tokyo. The rough-hewn wood floors and concrete walls of this branch give it an industrial-chic vibe. ⊠ *3526 blvd. St-Laurent, The Plateau, Montréal* ☎ *514/849–9759* ⊕ *www.m0851.com* Ⓜ *St-Laurent or Sherbrooke.*

CLOTHING: MEN'S ONLY

Fodor'sChoice ★ **Duo.** This one-stop shop for the style-conscious male might be in an odd location, given that rue Prince Arthur is known for food, not fashion, but that just adds to the cachet. Ultrahip labels like DSquared2 hang

MONTRÉAL'S MARKETS

If food is your first love, head to Montréal's markets, especially in the bountiful days of the autumn harvest.

Marché Jean-Talon in the north end of the city has an Italian flavor; the surrounding streets are home to some of the finest pizza and café lattes anywhere. **Marché Atwater** has a glorious indoor hall, packed with eateries, butchers, bakeries, and fine food emporiums.

The markets are a great place to pick up nonperishables such as jam from Île d'Orléans or cranberries harvested late-September to mid-October; or maple syrup, and butter year-round.

alongside slick suits and limited-edition Nikes. Visiting celebs have been known to pop in from time to time. ⊠ *30 rue Prince-Arthur Ouest, The Plateau, Montréal* ☎ *514/848–0880* ⊕ *www.boutiqueduo.com* Ⓜ *St-Laurent or Sherbrooke*.

FOOD

Fodor'sChoice ★ **La Vieille Europe.** For a taste of the old Main, where generations of immigrants came to shop, look no farther than this deli packed with sausages, cold cuts, cheeses, jams, and atmosphere. Pick up a rich shot of espresso on your way out. ⊠ *3855 blvd. St-Laurent, The Plateau, Montréal* ☎ *514/842–5773* ☉ *Mon.–Wed. 7:30–6, Thurs. and Fri. 7:30 am–9 pm, Sat. 7:30–6, Sun. 9–5* Ⓜ *St-Laurent or Sherbrooke*.

HOUSEWARES

Arthur Quentin. Check out this elegant shop for fine French tableware from Gien and Maintenon. There's also gourmet kitchen gear, as well as designer messenger bags, maps, and pens. ⊠ *3960 rue St-Denis, The Plateau, Montréal* ☎ *514/843–7513* ⊕ *www.arthurquentin.com* Ⓜ *Sherbrooke*.

Zone. This multilevel labyrinth of affordable housewares is especially busy on weekends. It's filled with fine and funky designs for the kitchen, bath, and living room. There is a large location in Westmount as well. ⊠ *4246 rue St-Denis, The Plateau, Montréal* ☎ *514/845–3530* ⊕ *www.zonemaison.com* Ⓜ *Sherbrooke or Mont-Royal*.

LINGERIE

Deuxième Peau. Tucked away in a basement, the tiny "Second Skin" sells a fine assortment of French lingerie. It's hard to miss the curvy mannequins in their ground-floor window, adorned in the likes of Aubade, Chantelle, and Prima Donna. While you're feeling brave and beautiful, kill two birds with one stone and try on a bathing suit. ⊠ *4457 rue St-Denis, The Plateau, Montréal* ☎ *514/842–0811* ⊕ *www.deuxiemepeau.com* Ⓜ *Mont-Royal*.

SHOES

John Fluevog. Unusually curved lines, from the heels of his shoes to the interior design of his funky boutique, have cultivated a devout following for the Canadian shoe designer. Belts and bags are also available, letting you create a quirky yet coordinated outfit. Look to the soles for curious and inspiring messages. ✉ *3857 rue St-Denis, The Plateau, Montréal* ☎ *514/509–1627* ⊕ *www.fluevog.com* Ⓜ *Sherbrooke.*

OUTREMONT

Avenue Laurier in Outremont is a good destination for those in pursuit of a little luxury.

CLOTHING

Billie. One of Montréal's favorite boutiques, Billie has rows of bookcases, drawers, and shelves that give the feeling of raiding your best friend's closet. Look for chic dresses and blouses from Alice + Olivia, cozy sweaters from Repeat Cashmere, and eclectic shoes by Cynthia Vincent. ✉ *1012 av. Laurier Ouest, Outremont, Montréal* ☎ *514/270–5415* ⊕ *www.billieboutique.com* Ⓜ *Laurier.*

Fodor's Choice ★ **Lyla.** Some of the finest lingerie in the city—including brands like Eres and La Perla—is stocked at this lovely little shop. The staff is extremely helpful in finding what fits and flatters. Two other reasons to stop and shop: exquisite fashion from Europe and a great selection of swimsuits and darling cover-ups. ✉ *400 av. Laurier Ouest, Outremont, Montréal* ☎ *514/271–0763* ⊕ *www.lyla.ca* Ⓜ *Laurier.*

Mimi & Coco. You'll want to snap up several of the locally designed T-shirts at Mimi & Coco, perhaps pairing them with luxe knitwear from Italy. Beautiful floor-to-ceiling windows create a bright, inviting interior, even on cloudy days. Come at lunchtime and sample one of the gourmet salads from the in-store counter. ✉ *201 av. Laurier Ouest, Outremont, Montréal* ☎ *514/906–0349* ⊕ *www.mimicoco.com* Ⓜ *Laurier.*

Tilley Endurables. The famous Canadian-designed Tilley hat is sold here—choose from warm- and cold-weather options in a variety of styles. Clever, travel-friendly clothing might also make its way into your suitcase. Think trousers with security pockets for wallets and passports and no-crease fabrics in neutral colors. ✉ *1050 av. Laurier Ouest, Outremont, Montréal* ☎ *514/272–7791* ⊕ *www.tilley.com* Ⓜ *Laurier.*

Fodor's Choice ★ **Très Chic Styling.** Stylish Hervé Léger dresses at two for C$500? Style-savvy co-founders Maryam Rafa and Angelica Koinis believe that women should look good and dress well without having to spend a small fortune. Designer denim and fabulous cocktail dresses for half off (or more) have built their reputation. ✉ *1069 av. Laurier Ouest, Suite 2, Outremont, Montréal* ☎ *514/274–3078* ⊕ *www.tcstyling.com* Ⓜ *Laurier.*

CLOTHING: MEN'S ONLY

Michel Brisson. This is the go-to place for art directors, architects, and other men with an eye for European design from Etro, Jil Sander, or Dries Van Noten. The Laurier store is sleek, with clean lines and lots of gray, while the Old Montréal location injects a bit of warmth with rich wood paneling. ✉ *1074 av. Laurier Ouest, Outremont, Montréal* ☎ *514/270–1012* ⊕ *www.michelbrisson.com* Ⓜ *Laurier.*

FOOD

Yannick Fromagerie. This cheese shop is the go-to destination for the city's top chefs and cheese aficionados. Yannick Achim carries 400 varieties, buying from local dairies and stocking an astonishing international selection. You'll find Pikauba cheese from Québec beside pecorino made with raw sheep's milk and laced with black truffles. Cheese lovers here eagerly trade advice on building the perfect after-dinner cheese plate. ✉ *1218 rue Bernard O., Outremont, Montréal* ☎ *514/279–9376* ⊕ *www.yannickfromagerie.ca* Ⓜ *Outremont.*

MILE END

Just north of the Plateau, the Mile End offers an eclectic mix of artsy boutiques and shops stocked with up-and-coming Montréal designers.

CLOTHING

Bodybag by Jude. When Nicole Kidman wore one of this designer's zip denim dresses, Judith Desjardins's star was set. The designer has a penchant for all things British, so look for cheeky checks and plaids. ✉ *17 rue Bernard Ouest, Mile End, Montréal* ☎ *514/274–5242* ⊕ *www.bodybagbyjude.com* ⊗ *Mon.–Wed. 11–6, Thurs. and Fri. 11–8, Sat. 11–5, Sun. noon–5* Ⓜ *Rosemont.*

Fodor's Choice ★ **Éditions de Robes.** Owner Julie Pesant has stocked her boutique with dresses in a multitude of styles that can easily be dressed up or down with a simple change of accessories. From peplums to lace, satin to jersey, long and short, they're all here. ✉ *178 rue St-Viateur Ouest, Mile End, Montréal* ☎ *514/271–7676* Ⓜ *Laurier.*

General 54. The Mile End neighborhood was made hip by funky shops like this one. The natural-hued clothes—most by local designers—are feminine and elegant, and owner Jennifer Glasgow sells her eponymous clothing line here. The location on The Main is warm and welcoming, with exposed brick and intricately patterned floors. ✉ *5145 blvd. St-Laurent, Mile End, Montréal* ☎ *514/271–2129* ⊕ *www.general54. com* ⊗ *Mon.–Wed. noon–6, Thurs. and Fri. noon–7, weekends noon–6* Ⓜ *Laurier.*

Mousseline. With sizes running from 2 to 22, this place makes finding the perfect fit a snap. Choosing from among the casual wear by designer labels like James Perse, Nobis, and Nolita might be a bit more difficult. Be sure to pick up a comforting sweater from Autumn Cashmere. ✉ *220 av. Laurier Ouest, Mile End, Montréal* ☎ *514/878–0661* ⊕ *www. boutiquemousseline.com* Ⓜ *Laurier.*

Unicorn. Young Québebois designers like Barilà, Valérie Dumaine, and Mélissa Nepton are the stars of this beautiful Mile End boutique, which also stocks unique national and international labels. All the black and white in the window display hints at the minimalist aesthetic within. ✉ *5135 blvd. St-Laurent, Mile End, Montréal* ☎ *514/544–2828* ⊕ *www. boutiqueunicorn.com* ⊗ *Mon.–Wed. 11–6, Thurs. and Fri. 11–8, weekends 11–5* Ⓜ *Laurier.*

Fodor's Choice ★ **Vestibule.** This cheerful boutique is a dream come true for owner Audrey Morissette, who adores all things whimsical and feminine. Uniting her love of fashion and decor, the shop is filled with pretty items ranging from jewelry to clothing to candles, as well as ceramics and other household items. ✉ *5157 blvd. St-Laurent, Mile End, Montréal* ☎ *514/419–3868* ⊕ *www.boutiquevestibule.com* Ⓜ *Laurier.*

LITTLE ITALY

Little Italy is a gourmet shopper's paradise.

FOOD

Fodor's Choice ★ **Marché Jean-Talon.** This is the biggest and liveliest of the city's public markets. On weekends in summer and fall, crowds swarm the half-acre or so of outdoor produce stalls, looking for the fattest tomatoes, sweetest melons, and juiciest strawberries. Its shops also sell sausage, fish, cheese, bread, pastries, and other delicacies. Early in the morning you might rub elbows with the city's top chefs. The market is in the northern end of the city, but is easy to get to by métro. ✉ *7070 av. Henri-Julien, Little Italy, Montréal* ☎ *514/937–7754* ⊕ *www.marchespublics-mtl. com* Ⓜ *Jean-Talon.*

Marché Milano. A huge expansion in 2013 made this popular Italian grocer even more popular, as customers line up for prepared foods at the takeout counter. There's a vast selection of cheeses, oils, vinegars, and baked goods. ■ TIP➔ For some elbow room, go during the week. ✉ *6862 blvd. St-Laurent, Little Italy, Montréal* ☎ *514/273–8558* ⊙ *Mon.–Wed. 8–6, Thurs. and Fri. 8 am–9 pm, weekends 8–5* Ⓜ *Jean-Talon.*

FURS

Labelle Fourrure. This family business has remained a fixture on Montréal's fur map for a century by adapting to the fashions of the day and offering good service and value for your dollar. ✉ *6570 rue St-Hubert, Little Italy, Montréal* ☎ *514/276–3701* ⊕ *www.labellefourrure.com* Ⓜ *Beaubien.*

WESTMOUNT

Stylish locals, quaint architecture, and upscale boutiques make Westmount a chic shopping destination. Rue Sherbrooke Ouest is a pleasant mix of hip shops, florists, and home decor stores. Avenue Victoria is a smaller version of the same, with a few grocery stores and vintage shops thrown in. The closest métro is Vendôme, or you take Bus 24 west from Downtown.

ANTIQUES

Ruth Stalker Antiques. The owner made her reputation finding and salvaging fine pieces of early Canadian pine furniture, but she has also developed a good instinct for such folk art as exquisitely carved hunting decoys, weather vanes, and pottery. Striking leather hatboxes fill the front window. ✉ *4447 rue Ste-Catherine Ouest, Westmount, Montréal* ☎ *514/931–0822* ⊕ *ruthstalkerantiques.com* ⊙ *Tues.–Sat. 11–5* Ⓜ *Atwater.*

ART

Galerie de Bellefeuille. This gallery has a knack for discovering important new talents. It represents many of Canada's top contemporary artists as well as some international ones. Its 5,000 square feet hold a good selection of sculptures, paintings, and limited-edition prints. ✉ *1367 av. Greene, Westmount, Montréal* ☎ *514/933–4406* ⊕ *www.debellefeuille.*

It's well worth the métro ride up to Little Italy's busy Marché Jean-Talon to see French Canadian farmers sell their local produce and prepared food.

com ⊗ Sept.–June, Mon.–Sat. 10–6, Sun. noon–5:30; July and Aug., Mon.–Sat. 10–6 Ⓜ Atwater.

CHILDREN'S CLOTHING

Oink Oink. This pigtail-covered boutique offers three levels of fun for babies, kids, and young adults. Innovative and kooky gifts, books, clothing, and even scooters are available. ⊠ 1343 av. Greene, Westmount, Montréal ☎ 514/939–2634 ⊕ www.oinkoink.ca ⊗ Weekdays 9:30–6, Sat. 9:30–5, Sun. noon–5 Ⓜ Atwater.

CLOTHING

James. The home of hippie-chic in Montréal, this boutique is packed with flowing tunics, embroidered blouses, and white cotton dresses. Add a good mix of designer jeans and funky moccasins by Minnetonka and you'll understand why James is a Victoria Village mainstay. ⊠ 4910 rue Sherbrooke Ouest, Westmount, Montréal ☎ 514/369–0700 ⊕ www. jamesboutique.com ⊗ Mon.–Wed. 10–6, Thurs. and Fri. 10–7, Sat. 10–5:30, Sun. noon–5:30 Ⓜ Vendôme.

JoshuaDAVID. One of Victoria Village's best boutiques may be small, but it's packed with a great selection of contemporary labels, including Diane von Furstenberg, Alexander McQueen, and plenty of Rich & Skinny denim. Rings by Kara Ross add bling to any outfit. ⊠ 4926 rue Sherbrooke Ouest, Westmount, Montréal ☎ 514/788–4436 ⊕ www. joshuadavid.ca ⊗ Weekdays 10–6, Sat. 10–5, Sun. noon–5 Ⓜ Vendôme.

Fodor's Choice **Pretty Ballerinas.** This little boutique showcases beautiful ballerina flats ★ handmade in Spain. Available in a wide variety of colors and styles, you'll find it difficult to limit yourself to just one pair. You'll also find

Barbour handbags—a canvas tote might be the perfect accessory to complement your new flats. ⊠ *392 av. Victoria, Westmount, Montréal* ☎ *514/489–3030* ⊕ *www.prettyballerinas.ca* ⊙ *Weekdays 10–6, Sat. 10–5, Sun. noon–5* Ⓜ *Vendôme.*

Fodor's Choice ★ **TNT.** The 6,000 square feet of women's clothing, shoes, and accessories include an eclectic mix of labels: Stella Forest, Lauren Moshi, and Michael Stars hang near shoes from House of Harlow and Dolce Vita. If your energy flags, a coffee from the Java U inside will help replenish you. ⊠ *4100 rue Ste-Catherine Ouest, Westmount, Montréal* ☎ *514/935–1588* ⊕ *www.tntfashion.ca* ⊙ *Mon.–Wed. 10–6, Thurs. 10–7, Fri. 10–6, Sat. 10–5, Sun. noon–5* Ⓜ *Atwater.*

WANT Apothecary. Under a slick black awning, this boutique keeps its customers coming back with quality goods, doting service, and pleasing surroundings inspired by a 19th-century pharmacy. As well as items from the local leather-goods label WANT, the shop also stocks beauty and skin care products and clothing by Acne, Filippa K, and Nudie Jeans. ⊠ *4960 rue Sherbrooke Ouest, Westmount, Montréal* ☎ *514/484–3555* ⊕ *www.wantapothecary.com* ⊙ *Weekdays 10–6, Sat. 10–5, Sun. noon–5* Ⓜ *Vendôme.*

JEWELRY

Nee Nah. Nina St. Michaels's internationally sourced jewelry collection includes delicate pieces as well bolder items made with beads, stones, metals, and even fabric. ⊠ *361 av. Victoria, Westmount, Montréal* ☎ *514/931–6358* ⊕ *www.neenah.ca* ⊙ *Mon.–Fri. 10–6, Sat. 10–5* Ⓜ *Atwater.*

SHOES

Tony's. Since 1937, Tony's has been one of Westmount's top shoe stores. It might seem small from the outside, but it's filled with fine specimens for men and women—and at good prices, too. ⊠ *1346 av. Greene, Westmount, Montréal* ☎ *514/935–2993, 888/488–6697* ⊕ *www.tonyshoes.com* ⊙ *Weekdays 8–6, Sat. 8–5, Sun. 11–4* Ⓜ *Atwater.*

THE TOWN OF MOUNT ROYAL (TMR)

In the past few years, more and more stores and restaurants have opened on the busy stretch of rue Jean-Talon that forms TMR's southern border.

CLOTHING

Abe & Mary's. On an industrial stretch of Jean-Talon Street, this high-end clothing destination holds racks with Elisabeth and James, Yosi Samra, and vintage couture that could keep you busy for hours, but it's the sample sale section upstairs that makes a visit especially worth the trek. You'll find jewelry, clothing, and shoes at bargain prices. The chic café also beckons. ⊠ *4175 rue Jean-Talon Ouest, Ville Mont-Royal, Montréal* ☎ *514/448–6223* Ⓜ *Namur.*

6

SPORTS AND
THE OUTDOORS

Updated by
Chris Barry

Most Montrealers would probably claim they hate winter, but the city is full of cold-weather sports venues—skating rinks, cross-country ski trails, and toboggan runs—that see plenty of action. During warm-weather months, residents head for the tennis courts, bicycle trails, golf courses, and two lakes for boating and swimming.

You don't have to travel far from Montréal to find good downhill skiing or snowboarding. The many ski centers in the Laurentians and Eastern Townships are within an hour's drive from the city (⇨ *see the Side Trips from Montréal chapter for directions*). As for cross-country, excellent trails can be found right in Parc du Mont-Royal, or on the Islands (Île Sainte-Hélène and Île Notre-Dame).

Despite the bitter winters (or perhaps because of them), Montréal has fallen in love with the bicycle, with enthusiasts cycling year-round. More than 600 km (372 miles) of bike paths crisscross the metropolitan area, and bikes are welcome on the first car of métro trains during off-peak hours.

The city is truly passionate about Canada's national sport, hockey. If you're here during the hockey season, try to catch a Montréal Canadiens game at Centre Bell, or at the very least find yourself a good sports bar.

BIKING

Weather permitting, one of the best ways to discover Montréal is on a bicycle. This is an incredibly bike-friendly metropolis and there are thousands of designated bike paths connecting diverse neighborhoods across the island, running along the river and through parks and forests. If you like to bike but would rather not do it on city streets, ferries at the Old Port can take you to Île Ste-Hélène and the south shore of the St. Lawrence River, where riders can connect to hundreds of miles of trails in the Montérégie region.

SAUTE MOUTON
JET BOATING sur les rapids

Bixi. Available 24 hours a day, seven days per week, April through November, these bikes are a convenient way to explore the city. Public bicycle rental stations are located as far west as Notre-Dame-de-Grace, a western Montréal neighborhood, east to the Olympic Park, and as far south as Parc Jean-Drapeau and even Longueuil (a south shore neighborhood). There's a fee of C$7 for a 24-hour period and C$15 for 72 hours, which include 30 minutes bike rental for each separate trip; extra charges are incurred for longer rides. The transaction is easily done with the swipe of a credit card (a security deposit is also required). Monthly and yearly subscriptions are also available for longer stays. ■TIP→ The bikes are designed for quick (but unlimited) trips, and to minimize extra charges always keep your next Bixi station in mind. ☎514/789–2494, 877/820–2453 ⊕ montreal.bixi.com.

Fodor's Choice ★ **Féria de Vélo de Montréal** (*Montréal Bike Festival*). The biggest bike celebration in North America includes the **Tour la Nuit**, a 22-kilometer (14-mile) ride through the city at night. The week-long festival culminates in as many as 50,000 cyclists taking over the streets for the **Tour de l'Île**, a 50-kilometer (31-mile) ride along a route encircling Montréal. ☎514/521–8356, 800/567–8356 ⊕ www.velo.qc.ca.

Fitz & Follwell Co. This company's bike tour of Montréal highlights is popular, but go deeper and try "Hoods & Hidden Gems" to really learn what makes the city tick. They also offer bike rentals, walking tours, and snow tours in winter. ⊠ 115 av. du Mont-Royal Ouest, The Plateau ☎ 514/840–0739 ⊕ www.fitzandfollwell.ca.

Lachine Canal. The most popular cycling trail on the island begins at the Old Port and winds its way to the shores of Lac St-Louis in Lachine. Pack a picnic lunch; there are plenty of green spaces where you can stop and refuel along the way.

Vélo Montréal. For longer cycling excursions, renting a bike from this company is your best bet. Each rental includes a bicycle helmet, bottle cage, lock, and rear carrier rack. Packages start at C$10 for one hour or C$15 for two hours and go all the way to C$120 for a full week or C$165 for two weeks. They also lease tandem bikes, a fun alternative for couples. ⊠ 3880 rue Rachel Est, Hochelaga-Maisonneuve ☎ 514/259–7272 ⊕ www.velomontreal.com Ⓜ Pie-IX.

BOATING

In Montréal you can climb aboard a boat at a Downtown wharf and be crashing through Class V white water minutes later.

> **TOP FIVE SPORTS EXPERIENCES**
>
> ■ Catch a Montréal Canadiens game.
>
> ■ Bike around the Old Port, then take the ferry across to Parc Jean-Drapeau to finish your ride.
>
> ■ Go white-water rafting on the Lachine Rapids.
>
> ■ Ice-skate for free on Île Ste-Hélène's huge rink.
>
> ■ Hike up to the top of Mont-Royal for a fantastic view of the city.

The Route Verte

Stretches of what's called the most extensive route of biking trails in North America pass right through the very heart of Downtown Montréal.

The Route Verte (Green Route) is a free 5,000-km (3,100-mile) network of paths, shared roadways, and paved shoulders that traverse the province of Québec.

The cycling group Vélo Québec began first talking about the possibility of a province-wide bike network back in the 1980s, but it wasn't until 1995 that the government announced it would fund the C$88.5-million project to be built over the next 12 years.

More than 320 km (200 miles) of the Route Verte cover the streets of the city. It passes through Downtown, stretches up Mont-Royal, hugs the coast near the Lachine Canal, and extends out to Parc Jean-Drapeau, to name just a few of the major areas covered.

For more information, including maps, suggested routes, and other trip-planning tools, check out the website at ⊕ *www.routeverte.com.*

Lachine Rapids Tours. Discover the rapids on a large jet boat—and bring a change of clothes. There are daily departures (every two hours) from May through October, from Clock Tower Pier in the Old Port. The price includes all gear, and the trip lasts an hour. Another option is a 20-minute jaunt around the Islands in a 12-passenger boat that reaches speeds up to 80 kph (50 mph). Boats leave the Old Ports' Jacques Cartier Pier every half hour between 10 am and 6 pm from May to October. Trips are narrated in French and English. ⊠ *47 de la Commune Ouest, Old Montréal* ☎ *514/284–9607* ⊕ *www.jetboatingmontreal.com* 🚢 *Jet boat C$67, Islands trip C$26* Ⓜ *Champ-de-Mars.*

GOLF

Montréal golf enthusiasts have several excellent golf courses available to them, many less than a half-hour drive from Downtown. If you're willing to trek a bit farther (about 45 minutes), you'll find some of the best golfing in the province. For a complete listing of the many golf courses in the area, Tourisme Québec (⊕ *www.bonjourquebec.com*) is the best place to start.

Club de Golf Métropolitain Anjou (*Anjou Metropolitan Golf Club*). One of the longest courses in the province, the Championship course features an undulating landscape with five lakes and some tricky bunkers, all calling for accurate shots. Beginners and improvers can hone their skills on the short Executive course, where more accomplished players will also enjoy a quick round. A clubhouse featuring a steak house and bistro, several banquet halls, a pro shop with an indoor practice range (winter only), and an outdoor driving range all serve to make this a top-notch facility. A dress code is in effect. The club is in Anjou, a 20-minute drive from downtown Montréal. ⊠ *9555 blvd. du Golf* ☎ *514/353–5353* ⊕ *www.golfmetropolitainanjou.com* 🚢 *Championship golf course, C$28–C$44; Executive course, C$15–C$17*

🏌 *Championship golf course: 18 holes, 7005 yards, par 72; Executive course: 11 holes, 2751 yards, par 33.*

The Falcon. Soon after this club opened in 2002, it rapidly became recognized as one of the best courses in Québec. Designed by Graham Cook, it winds through a verdant, well-wooded landscape dotted with water hazards and sand traps, and offers an exciting challenge. Five sets of tees accommodate different skill levels. It's 25 minutes west of downtown in the picturesque and largely Anglophone village of Hudson (which is worth a visit in itself). Recent improvements include a C$2-million clubhouse. Early-bird specials profit those who don't mind a teeing off at 7 am. ✉ *59 rue Cambridge, Hudson* ☎ *450/458–1997* ⊕ *www. falcongolf.ca* 🏷 *Weekdays C$39.58, weekends and holidays C$49.14* 🏌 *18 holes, 7096 yards, par 72.*

Golf Ste-Rose. With lovely views of the Rivière des Mille-Îles, hardwood forests, and myriad ponds, this course may be the most beautiful in Québec. It's a short hop over the bridge to the island of Laval. The course features four sets of tees to accommodate different skill levels. Recently renovated to improve the pace of play, the 18-hole course was designed by John Watson, one of the great names of Canadian golf course architecture. ✉ *1400 blvd. Mattawa, Ste-Rose, Laval* ☎ *450/628–6072, 450/628–3573* ⊕ *www.golfsterose.groupebeaudet. com* 🏷 *C$26–C$48.75* 🏌 *18 holes, 6134 yards, par 70.*

HOCKEY

Ice hockey is nothing short of an institution in Montréal, the city that arguably gave birth to the sport back in the late 19th century. Although variations of the game are said to have been played in other U.S. and Canadian cities as early as 1800, the first organized game of modern hockey was played in Montréal in 1875, and the first official team, the McGill University Hockey Club, was founded in Montréal in 1880. The city's beloved Montréal Canadiens is the oldest club in the National Hockey League and, as Montrealers will be keen to tell you, one of the most successful teams in North American sports history.

McGill University Redmen Hockey. Formed in 1877, this was the first organized hockey club in Canada. It is now one of the top university men's ice hockey programs in Canada, and the Redmen were a Canadian University cup finalist in 2011. Games against cross-town rivals the Concordia Stingers or the UQTR Patriotes are always emotional duels. Home games take place at Percival Molson Stadium. ✉ *475 av. des Pins Ouest, Downtown* ☎ *514/398–7006* ⊕ *www.redmenhockey.com* Ⓜ *McGill.*

Montréal Canadiens. The team meets National Hockey League rivals at the Centre Bell from October through April (and even later if they make the play-offs). The "Habs" (the nickname's taken from Habitants, or early settlers) have won 24 Stanley Cups, although they've been struggling in the standings for several years now and haven't won a cup since the 1992–93 season. Nevertheless, Les Canadiens are a great source of pride to the city's sports fans, and tickets for their local games continue to be a hot commodity. Buy tickets in advance to guarantee a seat.

☒1909 av. des Canadiens-de-Montréal, Downtown ☎877/668–8269, 514/790–2525 ⊕ canadiens.nhl.com Ⓜ Lucien-L'Allier or Peel.

ICE-SKATING

Come the winter months, you don't have to look very far to find an ice-skating rink in Montréal. There are municipally run outdoor—and some indoor—rinks in virtually every corner of the city.

Accès Montréal. For information on the numerous ice-skating rinks (at least 195 outdoor and 21 indoor) in the city, it's best to call or check the city's website. Outdoor rinks are open from December until mid-March, and admission is free. The rinks on Île Ste-Hélène and at the Old-Port are especially large, but there is a C$6 admission charge to skate at the latter. ☎514/872–1111 ⊕ www.ville.montreal.qc.ca.

Atrium le 1000 de la Gauchetière. Inside the tallest building in Montréal, this skating rink lies under a glass atrium, allowing sunlight to shine down on the rink year-round. There is often 2-for-1 admission and specials for tourists on Wednesdays. After working up an appetite, hit any one of the 14 restaurants in the surrounding food court. ☒1000 rue de la Gauchetière, Downtown ☎514/395–0555 ⊕ www.le1000.com ☒C$7.50; skate rental C$7 Ⓜ Bonaventure.

JOGGING

Most city parks have jogging paths, and you can also run the trail along the Lachine Canal.

Parc du Mont-Royal. The gravel Olmsted Road in Parc du Mont-Royal is a superb place for a tranquil jog surrounded by nature. For a panoramic view of downtown, head to the Kondiaronk lookout. ☎514/843–8240 ⊕ www.lemontroyal.qc.ca ☉ Daily 6–midnight Ⓜ Mont-Royal.

RACING

Grand Prix. Every year in early June the Gilles Villeneuve Circuit plays host to this Formula One race, which attracts more than 100,000 fans. Tickets start at C$45.85 for general admission (one day) and C$283.10 for grandstand tickets (three days). Be sure to book your room early for that entire week, as hotels operate at maximum capacity (and maximum cost too). ☒Parc Jean Drapeau, 222 Circuit Gilles Villeneuve, The Islands ☎514/350–0000 ⊕ www.circuitgillesvilleneuve.ca.

SKIING AND SNOWBOARDING

There are pros and cons to skiing in the Eastern Townships and the Laurentians. The slopes in the Townships are generally steeper and slightly more challenging, but it requires more time to get out to them. Also, the Townships' centers tend to be quieter and more family-oriented, so if it's après-ski action you're looking for, you might prefer heading out to a Laurentian hill like Mont St-Sauveur where, for many, partying is as much the experience as is conquering the slopes.

DID YOU KNOW?

Mont-Tremblant is Eastern Canada's largest ski region, with more than 600 acres of skiing and snowboarding terrain.

As for cross-country skiing, you needn't even leave the city to find choice locations to pursue the sport. There's a network of winding trails stretching throughout Parc du Mont-Royal, and the Lachine Canal offers a 12-km (7-mile) stretch of relatively flat terrain, making for both a scenic and relatively simple cross-country excursion.

Tourisme Québec. The "Ski-Québec" brochure available from the tourism office has a wealth of information about skiing in and around the city, and the website has a complete lists of all the hills and trails in the province. ☎ 514/873–2015, 1-877/266–5687 ⊕ www.bonjourquebec.com.

⇨ *For more information on skiing in the Eastern Townships and the Laurentians, see Chapter 9, Side Trips from Montréal.*

CROSS-COUNTRY
Cap-St-Jacques Regional Park. The best cross-country skiing on the island is on the 32 km (20 miles) of trails in the 900-acre Cap-St-Jacques park in the city's west end, about a half-hour drive from downtown. ⊠ 20099 blvd. Gouin Ouest, Pierrefonds ☎ 514/280–6871 ⊕ www.ville.montreal.qc.ca (French only) Ⓜ Henri-Bourassa, then bus 68 west.

Mont-Royal. Within the city itself, "the mountain" (as it's familiarly called) is essentially a toboggan run, but its modest slope makes it ideal for beginners and little ones learning to ski, and a good place to get in a quick cross-country workout. ⊠ Parc du Mont-Royal ☎ 514/843–8240 ⊕ www.lemontroyal.qc.ca.

DOWNHILL
Mont Sutton. A quaint village, a beautiful mountain—lots of glades—and plentiful snow make this the best skiing in the Eastern Townships (and possibly the province). It gets busy, but multiple chairlifts can handle nearly 12,000 people per hour. ⊠ Sutton ☎ 450/538–2545, 866/538–2545 ⊕ www.montsutton.com.

Mont Tremblant. This huge resort is the best in the Laurentians for skiing, though it can be pricey. Sleep, ski, and eat in total comfort—there are plenty of high-end hotels on site, some with luxury spas. The pedestrian village is like something out of Disney, with charming storefronts and colorful rooftops. Four slopes, 95 runs, and 14 lifts await, two hours north of Montréal. ⊠ 1000 Chemin des Voyageurs, Mont-Tremblant ☎ 866/356–2233 ⊕ www.tremblant.ca.

SWIMMING

Most of the city's municipal outdoor pools are open from mid-June through August. Admission is free on weekdays. On weekends and holidays there's a small fee of no more than C$4 at some pools, depending on the borough.

Parc-Plage l'Île Notre-Dame. The west side of Île Notre-Dame is home to the city's man-made beach with probably the cleanest water (tested and monitored) in Montréal, which makes the entrance fee worth it. ⊠ The Islands ☎ 514/872–6120 ⊕ www.parcjeandrapeau.com ⌨ C$9 ☉ Mid-June–mid-Aug., daily 10–7; mid-Aug.–early Sept., daily noon–7 Ⓜ Jean-Drapeau, then bus 167.

WHERE TO EAT

Updated by
Mayssam
Samaha

Montréal has one of Canada's most cosmopolitan restaurant scenes with trendy eateries popping up regularly, their menus heavily influenced by flavors from around the globe and often with an added touch of French flair.

There are top dining destinations to be found all over the city, especially as young chefs move out of Downtown to trendy destinations in Mile End and the Plateau to open new restaurants. Downtown, convenient to many hotels, there are restaurants clustered between rues Guy and Peel and on the side streets that run between boulevard René-Lévesque and rue Sherbrooke. Rue St-Denis and boulevard St-Laurent, between rues Sherbrooke and Jean Talon, have been, and continue to be, convenient areas with the hottest dining strips, with everything from sandwich shops to high-price gourmet shrines. Old Montréal, too, has a collection of well-regarded restaurants, most of them clustered on rue St-Paul, avenue McGill and Place Jacques-Cartier.

You can usually order à la carte, but make sure to look for the table d'hôte, a two- to four-course package deal. It's often more economical, offers interesting specials, and may also take less time to prepare. For a splurge, consider a *menu dégustation*, a five- to seven-course tasting menu. It generally includes soup, salad, fish, sherbet (to cleanse the palate), a meat dish, dessert, and coffee or tea. At the city's finest restaurants, such a meal for two, along with a good bottle of wine, can cost more than C$200 and last four hours.

Menus in many restaurants are bilingual, but some are only in French. If you don't understand what a dish is, don't be shy about asking; a good server will be happy to explain. If you feel brave enough to order in French, remember that in Montréal an *entrée* is an appetizer, and what Americans call an entrée is a *plat principal*, or main dish.

BEST BETS FOR MONTRÉAL DINING

With hundreds of restaurants to choose from, how will you decide where to eat? Here are our favorite restaurants by price, cuisine, and experience. In the first column, Fodor's Choice properties represent the "best of the best" in every price category.

Fodor's Choice ★

BarBounya, $$$$, p. 168

Beautys Luncheonette, $$, p. 162

Blackstrap, $$, p. 176

Bottega Pizzeria, $$, p. 171

Chez l'Épicier, $$$$, p. 147

Joe Beef, $$$$, p. 156

Kazu, $$, p. 156

Kem CoBa, $, p. 169

Labo Culinaire Foodlab, $$, p. 156

La Chronique, $$$$, p. 169

La Croissanterie Figaro, $$, p. 167

Lawrence, $$, p. 170

Le Vin Papillon, $$$, p. 157

Magnan, $$$, p. 158

Olive + Gourmando, $, p. 152

Patisserie Au Kouign Amann, $, p. 164

Patrice Pâtissier, $$, p. 159

Schwartz's Delicatessen, $, p. 166

St-Viateur Bagel & Café, $, p. 166

Su, $$$, p. 176

Toqué!, $$$$, p. 153

Best By Price

$

Café Souvenir, p. 166

De farine et d'eau fraîche, p. 160

Le Gourmet Burger, p. TK

Maison Christian Faure, p. 152

Melina Phyllo Bar, p. 170

Olive + Gourmando, p. 152

Patisserie Rhubarbe, p. 165

Qing Hua Dumplings, p. 159

Schwartz's Delicatessen, p. 166

Sparrow, p. 171

$$

Blackstrap, p. 176

Bottega Pizzeria, p. 171

Dinette Triple Crown, p. 172

Izakaya Iwashi, p. 169

Kazu, p. 156

Labo Culinaire Foodlab, p. 156

La Croissanterie Figaro, p. 167

Lawrence, p. 170

m:brgr, p. 158

Orange Rouge, p. 160

Park, p. 175

Patrice Pâtissier, p. 159

Racines, p. 153

Rotisserie Panama, p. 171

$$$

Bouillon Bilk, p. 154

Chez Victoire, p. 162

Hotel Herman, p. 169

Le Comptoir Charcuteries et Vins, p. 163

Leméac, p. 167

Le Taj, p. 157

L'Express, p. 163

Mezcla, p. 161

Nora Gray, p. 158

Osteria Venti, p. 153

Restaurant Helena, p. 153

Restaurant Le H4C, p. 175

Rumi, p. 165

Van Horne, p. 167

$$$$

Chez l'Épicier, p. 147

Club Chasse et Pêche, p. 147

Garde Manger, p. 151

Joe Beef, p. 156

La Chronique, p. 169

Le Vin Papillon, p. 157

Moishe's, p. 164

Toqué!, p. 153

Best By Cuisine

CAFÉS

Café Olimpico, $, p. 168

Caffé San Simeon, $, p. 172

Maison Christian Faure, $, p. 152

Olive + Gourmando, $, p. 152

Patrice Pâtissier, p. 159

FRENCH

Chez l'Épicier, $$$$, p. 147

La Chronique, $$$$, p. 169

Laloux, $$$, p. 163

Le Mas des Oliviers, $$$, p. 156

L'Express, $$, p. 163

Toqué!, $$$$, p. 153

ITALIAN

Bottega Pizzeria, $$, p. 171

Da Emma, $$$, p. 150

Inferno, $$$, p. 173

Nora Gray, $$$, p. 158

Osteria Venti, $$, p. 153

Ristorante Lucca, $$$, p. 174

POUTINE

La Banquise, $, p. 162

STEAK

Gibbys, $$$$, p. 151

Magnan, $$$, p. 158

Mister Steer, $$, p. 158

Moishe's, $$$$, p. 164

7

EAT LIKE A LOCAL

The combination of multiple cultures and a European flair has resulted in all sorts of dishes and flavors that are unique to Québec. Poutine, *tourtière*, steamies, and smoked meat are all part of the province's charm. Sample what's true to this area and you'll end up learning a lot about La Belle Province and its people.

POUTINE

This classic Quebecois dish is basically a plate of french fries topped with gravy and fresh cheese curds. Although it started out as more of a late-night diner restaurant staple, perfect at the end of a night of drinking, the new trend is for chic restaurants to put all sorts of creative versions on menus.

TOURTIÈRE

Tourtière is a meat pie made with beans and maple syrup. This traditional French Canadian dish doesn't have a specific meat filling but can be made with whatever is available. It is frequently made with pork and/or veal,

but might use wild game, or in coastal regions, it can even be made with fish. It's a filling dish, popular around Christmas and New Year and sugar shack season in spring.

TARTE AU SUCRE (SUGAR PIE)

In English Canada, this sweet dessert is also known as a butter tart. Some describe it as a pecan pie, without the pecans. It's a single crust, with the filling on the bottom, and sometimes there are raisins, too.

SMOKED MEAT

Montréal-style smoked meat is similar to pastrami, but always made with brisket and cured with a blend of spices that generally contains more pepper and less sugar than New York–style pastrami. Served on rye bread, with a smear of mustard, it's a Montréal specialty.

STEAMIES

In Québec, hot dogs are called "steamies"—both the hot dog and the bun are steamed, so the buns are soft and warm. "All-dressed" here means mustard, cabbage (not sauerkraut), onions, and relish—that's all. You can ask for ketchup but you might get a dirty look.

BAGELS

A Montréal bagel is almost a total different bagel species from what you'll find elsewhere. All bagels should be boiled before they're baked but in Montréal, they're boiled in honey water, then cooked in a wood-fired oven, and the result is a sweeter, denser bagel than its New York counterpart.

QUÉBEC CHEESE

There are more than 300 varieties of cheese made in Québec, where permissive raw-milk cheese laws result in delicious and complex varieties from goat, sheep, and cow's milk. Look for Blue Ermite, made by Benedictine monks; it's relatively mild, and said to be a good "introductory" blue cheese.

MAPLE SYRUP

Did you know that Québec produces three quarters of the world's maple

syrup? It's an important part of the Quebecois identity, and in spring, when maple syrup is made, restaurants create entire menus around it. In season, locals will flock to the countryside to have some *tire*—warm maple syrup poured directly on snow (*tire* is French for "taffy").

MEAT AND GAME

The vast forests of Québec are filled with wild game and as a result, carnivores are well fed here with bison, Lac-Brome duck, wild boar, Kamouraska lamb, and elk. Venison and caribou are favorites among chefs. Québec is also home to Canada's biggest foie gras producers, to the delight of many.

ICE WINE

Québec's climate is ideal for making ice wine. The grapes are harvested by hand once the temperature drops to −8°C (17°F), and the frozen grapes are then pressed, resulting in a sweet liquor that pairs wonderfully well with desserts, and some of those Québec-made cheeses.

7

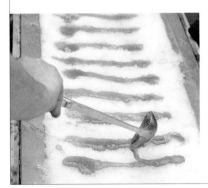

(top left) A Montréal smoked meat sandwich. (top) Montréal bagels. (bottom) Maple syrup being poured on snow to make taffy

MONTRÉAL DINING PLANNER

RESERVATIONS

Reservations are key, especially for weekend dining. Call at least three nights ahead for busy bistros. Because Montrealers eat quite late, it's possible to arrive unannounced before 7 pm and get a table—if you're lucky.

HOURS

Montréal restaurants keep unpredictable schedules. Some are closed Sunday, some are closed Monday, some are open every day. Our reviews note closed days but it can't hurt to call and confirm. Kitchens generally stop taking orders at 10 or 11 pm, but many eateries in the Old Port stay open later in summer, as do hot spots in the Plateau and Mile End. Downtown locations tend to focus on lunch, so they close earlier. Brunch is over by 3 pm.

DINING WITH KIDS

FAMILY   Since smoking was banned in restaurants, it's more common to see kids in bistros, brasseries, and even upscale dining rooms. However, kids under 18 are not allowed in places that have a bar license.

WHAT TO WEAR

Dress up! Women in Montréal take pride in their appearance, which features heels, pretty scarves, dresses, and jewelry. What about men? The standard uniform for hipsters is a fashionable shirt with dark jeans or dress pants. No running shoes, please. Men should also wear a jacket for restaurants in the $$$ range and above.

PRICES

Long live the table d'hôte. This cost-cutting special is a regular feature at many Montréal restaurants. Chefs enjoy changing the three-course special on a daily or weekly basis, so it never gets boring. ■ TIP➔ Upscale restaurants serve elaborate lunch tables d'hôte at cut-rate prices, while some eateries have early-bird or late-night prix-fixe deals. When it comes time to pay, it's not a "given" that you can use your debit card. Many eateries only accept cash or credit.

WHAT IT COSTS IN CANADIAN DOLLARS			
$	**$$**	**$$$**	**$$$$**
Restaurants	under C$12	C$12–C$20	C$21–C$30	over C$30

Restaurant prices are the average cost of a main course at dinner or, if dinner is not served, at lunch.

MONTRÉAL RESTAURANT REVIEWS

Listed alphabetically within neighborhood.

Use the coordinate (✛ B2) at the end of each listing to locate a site on the corresponding map.

OLD MONTRÉAL (VIEUX-MONTRÉAL)

Old Montréal is home to some of the city's hippest and most charming bistros and fine-dining restaurants—all tucked into heritage buildings. Foodies eat wild game and fresh seafood while drinking imported wine. Many of the better restaurants have a reasonable table d'hôte at lunch. It's common to see daily-changing menus written on chalkboards, since market-fresh food is popular.

$$$
FRENCH

✕**Boris Bistro.** Behind a freestanding facade (the remains of a burned-out historic building) is one of the best alfresco dining areas in the city. Like an enchanted forest, the tree-shaded terrace draws crowds to sip strawberry-infused Caipi-Saké or glasses of Kir Royal. The patio tables fill up quickly, but a huge glass wall looking out onto the patio and sidewalk lets diners inside feel like they're outdoors, too. The cheese menu focuses on local offerings and the market-fresh classics, from tartare to duck, fish, and lamb, are extensive. There's even a vegan plate on the menu. Note that children and minors are not allowed to dine in the restaurant, although they're allowed on the terrace if accompanied by an adult. Hours are more limited in the winter months. $ *Average main: C$23* ✉ *465 rue McGill, Old Montréal* ☎ *514/848–9575* ⊕ *www. borisbistro.com* ⊗ *In winter: closed Sun. No dinner Mon. No lunch Sat.* Ⓜ *Square-Victoria* ✛ *D6.*

$$
BRITISH
FAMILY

✕**Brit & Chips.** There's no need to cross the pond because perfectly battered fish and delicious chips can be found right here in Old Montréal. Go with the Brits though and try the malt vinegar on your fries. This long, narrow restaurant hustles during weekday lunch. The cod is a staple but the salmon dipped in Guinness batter is also a menu favorite. For a Canadian touch, try the haddock covered in golden maple syrup batter. End your British experience with the "deep-fried anything" dessert, in which a popular chocolate bar is battered, fried, and served with vanilla ice cream. Brit & Chips now has a second location at 5536A Côte-des-Neiges. $ *Average main: C$12* ✉ *433 rue McGill, Old Montréal* ☎ *514/840–1001* ⊕ *www.britandchips.com* Ⓜ *Square-Victoria* ✛ *D6.*

$$$$
FRENCH
Fodor's Choice
★

✕**Chez l'Épicier.** The menus at this classic French fusion restaurant are printed on brown paper, but the tables have crisp white linens and there's nothing down-market about the seasonal creative dishes: guinea fowl pie, gnudi with house-made ricotta, and the chocolate "club sandwich" dessert with pineapple "fries" that is a crowd favorite and ever-present on the menu. Chef Godbout is a master of his trade and a meal at Chez l'Épicier is a feast for all the senses. If you choose to splurge, which is highly recommended, an C$80, seven-course menu is available. Take a moment to browse through the small section of shelves that showcase some fine terroir ingredients, from top olive oils to tasty spreads. $ *Average main: C$35* ✉ *311 rue St-Paul Est, Old Montréal* ☎ *514/878–2232* ⊕ *www.chezlepicier.com* ⊜ *Reservations essential* Ⓜ *Champs-de-Mars* ✛ *E6.*

$$$$
CANADIAN

✕**Club Chasse et Pêche.** Despite the name—which translates as "Hunting and Fishing Club"—this isn't a hangout for the local gun-and-rod set. On the contrary, it's an ironic reference to the wood-and-leather decor that Chef Claude Pelletier and co-owner Hubert Marsolais inherited

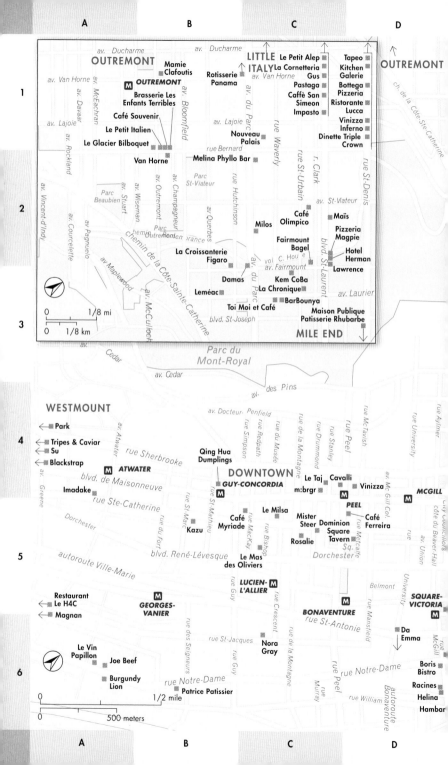

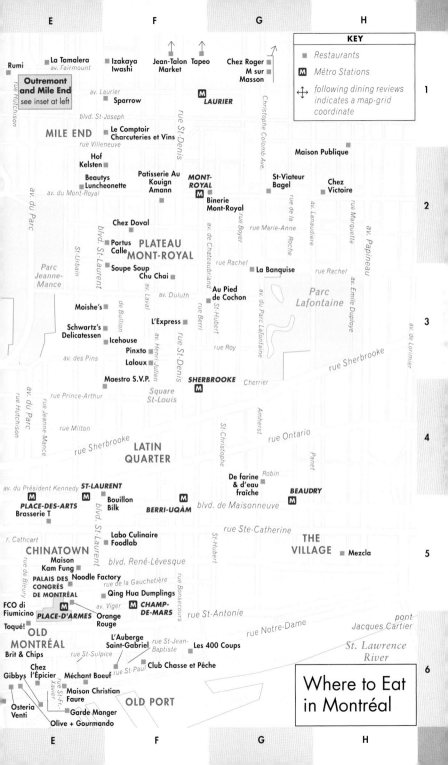

In Old Montréal, there are tons of restaurants with *terrasses* like this one, where you can enjoy the cobblestone streets and stone buildings while eating outside.

from the previous owners. Impeccable service and top-notch ingredients have made this one of the best restaurant in the city. The menu changes often but the dishes are consistently delicious. Don't forget to leave room for dessert, which is prepared by one of the best pastry chefs in town. $ *Average main: C$36* ✉ *423 rue St-Claude, Old Montréal* ☎ *514/861–1112* ⊕ *www.leclubchasseetpeche.com* ⊙ *Closed Sun. and Mon.* Ⓜ *Champ-de-Mars* ✛ *F6.*

$$$
ITALIAN

✕ **Da Emma.** The cellar of what used to be Montréal's first women's prison hardly sounds like the ideal setting for an Italian restaurant, but Grandma Emma's cooking is satisfying enough to drive out any bad vibes from those days. The stone walls and heavy beams make an ideal, catacomblike setting for tasting such Roman specialties as roasted lamb with grilled vegetables, fettuccini with porcini mushrooms, stuffed breast of veal, pasta *al vongole*, and tripe in tomato sauce. Da Emma attracts celebrities like Jake Gyllenhaal, Frida Pinto, and Johnny Depp when they're in town—repeat customers who enjoy the semi-privacy of the covered terrace and private garden. Reservations are recommended. $ *Average main: C$30* ✉ *777 rue de la Commune Ouest, Old Montréal* ☎ *514/392–1568* ⊙ *Closed Sun. No lunch Sat.* Ⓜ *Square-Victoria* ✛ *D6.*

$
ITALIAN
FAMILY

✕ **FCO di Fiumicino.** Pizza *al metro* (by the meter) is a well-known concept in Italy and to many Italians, and FCO di Fiumicino has imported the concept to Montréal. Everything here is made in-house from the pizza dough to the gelato. Try a square of Margherita, with fresh tomatoes and mozzarella, or the Boscaiolo, with its toppings of Italian sausage, mushrooms, and mozzarella. For something a little different, the pizza with pears and Scamorza (a smoked cheese) is delicious. You can enjoy your meal at the long communal table but if the weather's fine, head to the *piazza* across the street to dine alfresco. End your meal with the best gelato in the city; the fresh ricotta and cinnamon flavor is a definitive crowd pleaser. $ *Average main: C$10* ⊠ *451 av. Viger Ouest, Old Montréal* ☏ *514/861–3636* ⊕ *www.thefco.ca* ⊗ *Closed Sat. and Sun.* Ⓜ *Square-Victoria* ✛ *D6.*

$$$$ ✕**Garde Manger.** It's no wonder that chef Chuck Hughes has his own
CANADIAN television show, *Chuck's Day Off,* considering how much charm and skill he possesses, attracting pretty young patrons to his trendy dinner club. And this boy can cook. Popular options include bountiful platters of seafood, rich lobster poutine, and hearty braised short ribs—vegetarians should probably head elsewhere, since fish and meat are featured prominently on the menu. Reservations are essential as the restaurant is small and quite popular. The bar, where flirting is in high gear, is a fun option for dining and hanging out. After 11 pm, the music is cranked up and the party rages until 3 am. Because of their bar permit, children under 18 are not permitted on the premises. $ *Average main: C$35* ⊠ *408 rue St-François-Xavier, Old Montréal* ☏ *514/678–5044* ⊕ *www.crownsalts.com/gardemanger* ⌲ *Reservations essential* ⊗ *Closed Mon. No lunch* Ⓜ *Place-d'Armes* ✛ *E6.*

$$$$ ✕**Gibbys.** Open 365 days per year, Gibbys is one of Montréal's most
STEAKHOUSE famous steak houses and a true culinary landmark. Everything about
FAMILY it is old school, including the 200-year-old historic building with its wooden beams and large fireplaces, white tablecloths, and quality service. Oysters Rockefeller, two-pound lobsters, and some of the best aged steaks in the city are the popular dishes here, not to mention gigantic beef Wellington, creamy clam chowder, and garlicky Caesar salads. The wine list is extensive, as you'd expect, and the cobblestone streets of Old Montréal make for an excellent postprandial stroll. $ *Average main: C$45* ⊠ *298 pl. d'Youville, Old Montréal* ☏ *514/282–1837* ⊕ *www.gibbys.com* ⌲ *Reservations essential* ⊗ *No lunch* Ⓜ *Square-Victoria* ✛ *E6.*

$$$ ✕**Hambar.** As the name suggests, the focus of this restaurant is ham in
CANADIAN all its many incarnations, and Hambar satisfies cravings at all hours. At lunch, if you'd rather grab and go, the back counter prepares sandwiches filled with charcuterie imported from France, Italy, and Spain, along with marinated vegetables made on-site. At dinnertime, you might hobnob with the corporate world dressed to the nines, or sit next to travelers sharing a *salumi* platter in their flip-flops. The menu changes with the seasons, but ham always plays a starring role in both appetizers and mains. The dining room is lovely and airy, with huge windows, and the long communal tables inspire conversation with locals. In summer, you can enjoy a glass of wine from the extensive and well chosen list outside on the terrace. $ *Average main: C$30* ⊠ *Hotel St. Paul, 355 rue McGill, Old Montréal* ☏ *514/879–1234* ⊕ *www.hambar.ca* ⊗ *No lunch weekends* ✛ *E6.*

$$$ ✕**Les 400 Coups.** Located in Old Montréal but away from the main
MODERN tourist areas, this is a low-key destination for an intimate dinner, where
CANADIAN you know the food will be superb and the wine list will have well chosen options. The decor is grandiose and includes a very large mural

taking up one long wall, a vintage tin tile ceiling and the open kitchen located at the back of the dining room. The market fresh menu changes frequently and focuses on local and seasonal products used creatively. Specials like duck magret with buckwheat, carrots, endive, honey, caraway and Nova Scotia trout with yogurt foam, beets, and basil. Lunch is served only on Thursday and Friday. A five-course tasting menu is available at C$75 per person. [$] *Average main: C$30* ✉ *400 Notre-Dame Est, Old Montréal* ☎ *514/985–0400* 🌐 *www.les400coups.ca* ✍ *Reservations essential* 🕒 *Closed Sun. and Mon. No lunch Tues. and Wed.* ✥ *F6.*

$ BAKERY 🍴 **Maison Christian Faure.** Maison Christian Faure has made its elegant home inside a beautifully renovated gray stone, three-story building in Old Montréal. The man himself, pastry chef Chritian Faure, is the recipient of France's highest culinary honor of *Meilleur ouvrier de France* [MOF]. The space has a pastry school on the upper floors while the ground floor is dedicated to take-out or eat-in options. The prominent pastry display holds rows of classics like mille-feuilles (a delicate layered dessert of puff pastry and airy vanilla-scented custard) and seasonal fruit tarts as well as basketfuls of buttery brioches and flaky croissants. The refined French-style *pâtisseries* include a delicious passion and raspberry tart (in season) as well as the best Paris-Brest this side of Paris. Maison Christian Faure also offers a savory and seasonal "chic snacking" menu as well as a great weekend brunch with options like eggs Benedict, French toast, and more. [$] *Average main: C$10* ✉ *355 pl. Royale, Old Montréal* ☎ *514/508–6453* 🌐 *maisonchristianfaure.ca/en* 🕒 *No dinner* ✥ *E6.*

$$$ CANADIAN 🍴 **Méchant Boeuf.** If burgers are your thing, the Hôtel Nelligan's casual dining room is the place for you, with its excellent renditions of comfort food. The mighty Méchant hamburger (an 8-ounce patty with bacon, blue cheese, and caramelized onions) is a winner, but options like the beer-can chicken, crab cakes, hanger steak, and designer poutine are also crowd pleasers. For dessert, two can share the cheesecake. The food may be humble, but the atmosphere is cheeky and chic, with an interior waterfall, brick walls, and an illuminated bar. A DJ spins music Thursday to Sunday, and rock bands perform Tuesday and Wednesday nights. The late-night (after 11 pm) menu offers two courses for C$23. [$] *Average main: C$25* ✉ *Hôtel Nelligan, 124 rue St-Paul Ouest, Old Montréal* ☎ *514/788–4020* 🌐 *www.mechantboeuf.com* 🕒 *No lunch* [M] *Place-d'Armes* ✥ *E6.*

$ CAFÉ FAMILY Fodor's Choice ★ 🍴 **Olive + Gourmando.** Successful yuppies arrive at lunchtime en masse to wait for a table at this bustling bakery and sandwich shop. Owners Dyan Solomon and Éric Girard have a romantic backstory straight out of a movie: they fell in love while working the bread ovens at upscale Toqué! and then branched out on their own. Fittingly, movie stars like Jake Gyllenhaal, Kirsten Dunst, and musician Bono have been spotted here nibbling panini, sour cherry ginger scones, or the chocolate brioche. Fresh crab is flown in for salads, while organic farmers supply heirloom tomatoes. Crowd favorites include Le Cubain panini (pancetta, roasted pork, raw milk Gruyère) and the excellent "Poached egg on your face" breakfast sandwich (spicy poached eggs with herbs and mayonnaise, Comté cheese, speck, and slow-roasted tomatoes). $ *Average main: C$10 ✉ 351 rue St-Paul Ouest, Old Montréal ☎ 514/350–1083 ⊕ www.oliveetgourmando.com ⊙ Closed Sun. and Mon. No dinner* Ⓜ *Square-Victoria ✛ E6.*

$$$

ITALIAN

✕ **Osteria Venti.** Authentic regional Italian cuisine comes to life at this restaurant, housed in a rustic 200-year-old building on a cobblestoned street in historic Old Montréal. You can enjoy delicious dishes from the comfort of your table or take a seat at the bar facing the open kitchen and watch the action. The menu, which features homemade options like ricotta gnocchi, or a juicy porchetta, will not disappoint. All the pastas are homemade and if the spaghetti *al nero di seppia* (spaghetti with squid ink and seafood) is on the menu, you're in luck. Be sure to leave room for dessert; the Venti tiramisu is always an excellent finale. $ *Average main: C$22 ✉ 372 St-Paul Ouest, Old Montréal ☎ 514/284–0445 ⊕ www.osteriaventi.com ᨻ Reservations essential ⊙ Closed Sun. and Mon. No lunch weekends* Ⓜ *Square-Victoria ✛ E6.*

$$$

MODERN
CANADIAN

✕ **Racines.** Racines is located inside an old, long, and narrow diner that's been renovated into a sophisticated and gorgeous new space that is reminiscent of a light box. The tone is set with glazed walls, tan-colored banquettes, vintage chairs, and a lot of warm wood panels. Young chef Simon Mathys hones his craft in the open-air kitchen in the back with an innovative menu of small plates to share, including the agnolotti with rabbit and squash or the scallops with endives and apricots. The raw foie gras with meringue shards is a balanced mélange of sweet and savory, smooth and crunchy. The menu changes often but features mainly local ingredients that are assembled with as little transformation as possible and in surprising combinations. $ *Average main: C$30 ✉ 444 McGill, Old Montréal ☎ 514/544–0444 ⊕ www.racines.ca ᨻ Reservations essential ⊙ Closed Sun. and Mon. No lunch on Sat.* Ⓜ *Square-Victoria ✛ D6.*

$$$$

PORTUGUESE

✕ **Restaurant Helena.** The airy, colorful restaurant is housed inside a welcoming Old Montréal space with alcove windows, brick and stone walls and an intricately decorated ceiling lighting fixture that runs the entire length of the space. The cuisine is traditional Portuguese with plenty of seafood dishes but also a few choices for carnivores. Share a few tapas plates, like the grilled sardines, chouriço sausage or Portuguese style clams before you delve into the main show. The seafood stew with lima beans, squid, shrimps, clams, and mussels, or pork confit with clams are both great choices. Don't forget to leave room for dessert; the *natas*—flaky Portuguese tarts filled with a vanilla-scented luscious custard—are quite delicious. $ *Average main: C$35 ✉ 438 McGill, Old Montréal ☎ 514/878–1555 ⊕ www.restauranthelena.com ᨻ Reservations essential ⊙ Closed Sun. No lunch weekends* Ⓜ *Square-Victoria ✛ D6.*

$$$$

FRENCH

Fodor's Choice

★

✕ **Toqué!.** Toqué is slang for "just a little stubborn," as in star Chef Normand Laprise's insistence on using fresh, local ingredients from the best providers. On the ground floor of a glass tower, this celebrated bastion of fine dining attracts government rainmakers and the expense-account crowd. The menu changes daily, depending on what Laprise and his kitchen crew find at the market, but foie gras, duck, and wild venison are staples. Some clients wouldn't consider ordering anything but the seven-course, C$115 dinner tasting menu. Chitchat at the tables revolves around Laprise's latest award and how lucky everyone is to have gotten a reservation. You can also eat at the somewhat more casual quartz bar, sitting on the comfy bar stools. $ *Average main: C$47* ✉ *900 pl. Jean-Paul-Riopelle, Old Montréal* ☎ *514/499–2084* ⊕ *www.restaurant-toque.com* ⏂ *Reservations essential* ⊘ *Closed Sun. and Mon. and 2 wks at Christmas. No lunch weekends* Ⓜ *Square-Victoria or Place-d'Armes* ✛ *E6.*

DOWNTOWN

From top-quality steak to gourmet burgers, there's lots of meat in Downtown. There's also a nightlife vibe here most evenings. There are rich Indian curries, simple Chinese dumplings, whole-animal cooking, dry-aged beef, designer hamburgers, and updated Italian dishes that stretch the definition. The dress code can be as formal as in Old Montréal or completely toned down and hip—it all depends on where you go.

$$$ ✕ **Bouillon Bilk.** The decor at this restaurant reflects the restaurant's philosophy: a fresh, thoughtful, and simplified (yet not simple) approach to food. The market-based menu changes often and includes dishes that are just as beautiful to look at as they are delicious. House specialties feature local and seasonal products as well as an assortment of Québec cheeses. Try the crab with cucumber, peanuts, pineapple, and mache lettuce or the heartier venison with cauliflower, raisins, chanterelles, and juniper berries. For dessert, try the foie gras with bananas, chocolate, smoked apples and sour cream. The wine selection includes private-import wines. $ *Average main: C$30* ✉ *1595 blvd. St-Laurent, Downtown* ☎ *514/845–1595* ⊕ *www.bouillonbilk.com* ⏂ *Reservations essential* Ⓜ *Saint-Laurent* ✛ *E5.*

MODERN FRENCH

$$ ✕ **Brasserie T.** The team behind Montréal's famous Toqué! restaurant introduced this see-and-be-seen brasserie in the heart of downtown, which is an excellent spot to eat at before or after a show at Place des Arts. A wall of windows keeps things bright and it's an excellent vantage point for looking out over the many festivals that take place in the neighborhood. The seafood platters are popular for sharing but if the salmon tartare (a must-order) is on the menu, you might want to keep that all to yourself. The cured meats are made in-house and are also a favorite for sharing. A terrace is open when the weather's nice. $ *Average main: C$20* ✉ *1425 rue Jeanne-Mance, Downtown* ☎ *514/282–0808* ⊕ *www.brasserie-t.com* ⏂ *Reservations essential* Ⓜ *Place des Arts* ✛ *E5.*

BRASSERIE

$$ ✕ **Burgundy Lion.** This multilevel restaurant filled with young professionals lures patrons with a lively atmosphere and deliciously updated English food. The signature fish-and-chips is deservedly popular, as are other classics like bangers and mash and shepherd's pie. The Burgundy Lion can get boisterous with good cheer in the evening, fueled by the extensive beer list and the more than 200 varieties of whiskey on the menu, and it's a popular spot to watch football (that's soccer to North Americans) and hockey. Classic British breakfasts like

BRITISH
FAMILY

"bubble n' squeak" (cabbage, eggs, onions, and smoked meat) and French toast made with crumpets make for busy weekend mornings. [$] *Average main: C$20* ✉ *2496 rue Notre-Dame Ouest, Downtown* ☎ *514/934–0888* 🌐 *www.burgundylion.com* [M] *Lionel-Groulx* ✥ *A6.*

$$$$ PORTUGUESE 🍴 **Café Ferreira.** Chef Carlos Ferreira and his passionate team put Portuguese food on the Montréal map 18 years ago. A huge mural of antique pottery fragments decorates the pale-yellow walls of this room—an elegant setting for "haute" Portuguese cuisine. Chef Marino Tavares helms the open-concept kitchen, which is renowned for its fish and seafood including the roasted salted cod, seafood bouillabaisse and a whole array of Portuguese-style dishes. You can also make an excellent meal from appetizers like giant shrimp and grilled octopus, or the roasted sardines filets. If you're a wine connoisseur, the impressive list of Portuguese wines is something to behold. **TIP→ If you're dining late at night, the late-night set menu (after 10) for C$23.95 offers great value and has a number of options.** [$] *Average main: C$35* ✉ *1446 rue Peel, Downtown* ☎ *514/848–0988* 🌐 *www.ferreiracafe.com* ✍ *Reservations essential* 🕓 *No lunch weekends. Closed Sun.* [M] *Peel* ✥ *D5.*

$ CAFÉ 🍴 **Café Myriade.** Café Myriade aficionados are willing to wait for a seat at this small café, where the foam on your latte or café au lait is artfully arranged in waves, hearts, or curlicues by award-winning barista Anthony Benda. Benda's delicious coffee is imported from Ethiopia, Guatemala, Brazil, Bolivia, and elsewhere via the famed 49th Parallel Coffee Roasters in Vancouver. Don't drink coffee? Try the molten hot chocolate or the homemade iced tea. Baked goods are sourced from six different local bakeries, all of which are delicious. Myriade now has a second location at 251 St-Viateur West in the hip Mile End neighborhood. [$] *Average main: C$7* ✉ *1432 rue Mackay, Downtown* ☎ *514/939–1717* 🌐 *www.cafemyriade.com* 🕓 *No dinner* [M] *Guy-Concordia* ✥ *C5.*

$$$$ ITALIAN 🍴 **Cavalli.** Pretty young things like to sip cocktails by Cavalli's big front window, which in summer is open to the passing scene on busy rue Peel. The interior—with a black illuminated bar, green and pink velvet chairs, and blond-wood paneling—makes an enticing backdrop. The food is Italian, mostly, with Asian influences. Chef Frank Gioffre marinates Chilean sea bass in miso and serves his mac 'n' cheese with truffles and brioche breadcrumbs. Models order the endive salad, but heartier eaters love the spicy crab cake or the rack of fresh Australian lamb. It's not cheap, but the sceney atmosphere makes this supper club a fun place to hang out. [$] *Average main: C$40* ✉ *2040 rue Peel, Downtown* ☎ *514/843–5100* 🌐 *www.ristorantecavalli.com* 🕓 *No lunch weekends. Closed Sun.* [M] *Peel* ✥ *C4.*

$$ ECLECTIC 🍴 **Dominion Square Tavern.** New owners rescued this bistro a few years ago, throwing out video gambling terminals and big-screen televisions; now, the original floors, lamps, and walls from 1927 set the tone, together with antique chairs and a 40-foot brass bar. Chef Eric Depuis makes everything from scratch, including the ketchup, tonic, and ginger ale. His menu is a bit of everything, ranging from beet salad, corn fritters, and deviled eggs to pulled pork sandwiches and ploughman's fish or meat lunch. End your evening with the sticky toffee pudding with

ice cream, a memorable sweet ending to write home about. Night owls take note: it's open until midnight. Please note that you have to be 18 years old to be admitted in. Reservations are recommended. $ *Average main: C$25* ✉ *1243 rue Metcalfe, Downtown* ☎ *514/564–5056* ⊕ *www.tavernedominion.com* ⊘ *No lunch on weekends* Ⓜ *Peel* ✛ *D5.*

$$$$
FRENCH
Fodor's Choice
★

✕ **Joe Beef.** Dining at Joe Beef is a little like being invited to a dinner party by a couple of friends who just happen to be top-notch chefs. David MacMillan and Frédéric Morin were pioneers in Montréal's modern dining scene until they got tired of living on the edge and opened this gem of a restaurant in the heart of Little Burgundy. Everything written on the chalkboard menu is simple, hearty and just delicious, from the fresh oysters to the organic rib steak and the now famous lobster spaghetti. ■TIP➔ **In summer, the best seat in the house is one of the 25 coveted chairs spread out on the back patio, among the beautiful patches of an organic vegetable garden.** $ *Average main: C$35* ✉ *2491–2501 rue Notre-Dame Ouest, Downtown* ☎ *514/935–6504* ⊕ *www.joebeef.ca* ⌁ *Reservations essential* ⊘ *Closed Sun. and Mon. No lunch* Ⓜ *Lionel-Groulx* ✛ *A6.*

$$
JAPANESE
Fodor's Choice
★

✕ **Kazu.** You could almost walk right by this tiny establishment, but the big giveaway is the line of people waiting to get in. Kazu has created a foodie mania with its fabulous Japanese Izakaya concept. Popular plates include the tuna and salmon rice bowls, or the messy barbecue pork necks—you'll be licking the sauce off your hands, but you won't be sorry. The juicy shrimp burger is an excellent dish to share, and the wonderful ramen topped with barbecue pork, boiled egg, and vegetables a great lunch option. ■TIP➔ **So, how do you beat the line? Arrive at the restaurant 15 minutes before opening time (noon for lunch or 5:30 for dinner) or visit later in the evening, after 8.** $ *Average main: C$15* ✉ *1862 rue St-Catherine Ouest, Downtown* ☎ *514/937–2333* ⊕ *www.kazumontreal.com* ⌁ *Reservations not accepted* ⊟ *No credit cards* ⊘ *Closed Tues. No lunch Sat.* Ⓜ *Guy-Concordia* ✛ *B5.*

$$
INTERNATIONAL
Fodor's Choice
★

✕ **Labo Culinaire Foodlab.** Take cutting-edge experimental art and mix it up with food, and what you get is Labo Culinaire Foodlab. Located on the third floor of Montréal's Society of Arts and Technology [SAT], Foodlab is an ongoing culinary experiment, with rotating themes. One month might be Jerusalem or the South of France, and another month might focus on dishes from Julia Child's cookbook. The decisions are left to Michelle Marek and Seth Gabrielse, the resident chefs and creative masterminds. You can watch them cook in the large open kitchen or, when it's warm, sit outside on one of the most beautiful terraces in town. Foodies come for the consistently excellent and memorable food, and locals love the international feel and regularly head here for drinks after work. Note that children under 18 are only allowed on the outdoor terrace. $ *Average main: C$20* ✉ *Société des Arts Technologiques bldg., 1201 blvd. St-Laurent, Downtown* ☎ *514/844–2033* ⊕ *www.sat.qc.ca/foodlab* ⊘ *No lunch. Closed weekends and Mon.* Ⓜ *St-Laurent* ✛ *F5.*

$$$
BISTRO

✕ **Le Mas des Oliviers.** Search for a textbook definition of "classic French Bistro" and you'll find Le Mas des Oliviers. It's been around since 1966 and the owners pride themselves on the menu items, some of which, like

Joe Beef, known for its excellent organic rib steak and famous lobster spaghetti, is located in Downtown Montréal.

the fish soup, have been on the menu 40-plus years. The dining room looks the part and will transport you to Provence with its white tablecloths, dark wood beams, exposed brick walls, and French art posters on the walls. The staff ups the elegance with vests and ties. Other popular menu staples include lamb shank and veal with mushrooms. Not surprisingly, the kitchen does excellent frogs' legs *à la provençale* and escargots bourguignons. $ *Average main: C$30* ⊠ *1216 rue Bishop, Downtown* ☎ *514/861–6733* ⊕ *www.lemasdesoliviers.ca* ⌂ *Reservations essential* ⊙ *No lunch weekends* Ⓜ *Lucien-L'Allier* ✛ *C5.*

$$
INDIAN
FAMILY

✕ **Le Taj.** The lights are dim and the ambience is warm at Le Taj. This restaurant carries a piece of Montréal's history with its ornate and detailed three-panel mud wall originally made for India's pavilion at Expo '67. The focus here is northern Indian cuisine, which is less spicy and more delicate than that of the south. The Tandoor clay ovens seal in the delicious flavors and keep fish and meat moist. Thalis—full meal platters with a variety of different dishes—are a good way to go if you want to sample different things. Vegetarians are especially happy here, although even meat eaters love the *saag paneer* (Indian white cheese with spinach). The all-you-can-eat lunch buffet is C$16 and the nightly "Indian feast" is C$40. $ *Average main: C$22* ⊠ *2077 rue Stanley, Downtown* ☎ *514/845–9015* ⊕ *www.restaurantletaj.com* ⊙ *No lunch Sat.* Ⓜ *Peel* ✛ *C4.*

$$$$
FRENCH
Fodor's Choice
★

✕ **Le Vin Papillon.** First and foremost a wine bar, this tiny 30-seat spot also dishes out delicious vegetable-centric, market-based cuisine. The cuisine features local and seasonal ingredients, with a special focus on vegetables, and the flavors are simple enough to go well with the stars of the show: the many wines on offer. The homemade bread topped with mushrooms and lobster, the rotisserie whole cauliflower or the Brussels sprouts "a la plancha" are just a few of the dishes that have become crowd favorites. End your meal with an assortment of Québec cheeses. The plates are all meant to be shared while you sip on some of the most unique wines in the city carefully selected from wineries far and close and sometimes only available in very small quantities. **■ TIP→ Reservations are not accepted but to be sure to get a table, get there early, when the restaurant opens at 3 pm.** [$] *Average main: C$40* ✉ *2519 rue Notre-Dame Ouest, Downtown* 🌐 *vinpapillon.com* ✍ *Reservations not accepted* ⏲ *Closed Sun. and Mon. No lunch* ✥ *A6.*

$$$ CANADIAN Fodor's Choice ★ 🍴 **Magnan.** Serving Montrealers since 1932, this tavern is best known for its roast beef. The meat marinates for 20 days and the result is so succulent, it keeps locals raving. This is also a great place to try the traditional French Canadian dish *tourtière*—a meat pie made with pork, veal, and/or beef—which is served with house-made ketchup here. Note that since this is a tavern, no children under 18 are allowed inside, so if you're out with the family, head to the take-out counter and order food to go. Since the restaurant is right on the Lachine Canal (which runs from Old Montréal to Lac St. Louis), it's the perfect spot to sit and enjoy your meal outdoors. [$] *Average main: C$30* ✉ *2602 rue St-Patrick, Downtown* ☎ *514/935–9647* 🌐 *www.maisonmagnan.com* [M] *Charlevoix* ✥ *A6.*

$$ AMERICAN 🍴 **m:brgr.** You can build your own specialty burger here with toppings like apple-wood bacon, grilled pineapple, and even decadent truffle shavings or foie gras. The atmosphere is lively at this trendy "burger bar" that is generally packed with students and families, drawn by the top-notch food and fun atmosphere. Even foodies admit that m:brgr is a cut above, with designer mac 'n' cheese (served with truffle carpaccio, if you want), Angus beef hot dogs, and pulled pork sandwiches. The deep-dish cookies and ice cream is definitely worth sharing for dessert. There are a few tables on the front sidewalk, but the real action is inside. **■ TIP→ A special "fashionably late" menu is available on weekdays from 2 pm to 5 pm and Thursday to Saturday after 10 pm.** [$] *Average main: C$18* ✉ *2025 rue Drummond, Downtown* ☎ *514/906–0408* 🌐 *www.mbrgr.com* ✍ *Reservations essential* [M] *Peel* ✥ *C4.*

$$ AMERICAN FAMILY 🍴 **Mister Steer.** Why mess with a winning formula? The juicy Steer burgers here are old-school 1950s-style fare, and you can order one plain or with cheese and bacon, served slightly *saignant* (rare). Get a side of "Suzie Q" fries for a curly treat. Locals have been eating at this unpretentious spot in the downtown shopping area since 1958; in fact, the decor—orange vinyl booths included—seems to have remained unchanged since then. Mister Steer is especially convenient if you're heading to one of the nearby movie theaters. For a full *Happy Days* effect, order one of their delicious milk shakes to accompany your burger and fries. They're also open for breakfast 7 days a week. [$] *Average main: C$15* ✉ *1198 rue Ste-Catherine Ouest, Downtown* ☎ *514/866–3233* 🌐 *www.mistersteer.com* [M] *Peel* ✥ *C5.*

$$$ ITALIAN 🍴 **Nora Gray.** Nora Gray—a play on one owner's grandmother's name and the chef's family name—specializes in Southern Italian comfort

cuisine. The crowd that fills this casual and lively spot nightly is hip and the simple, modern food and impeccable service keeps them coming back. Start your meal with the fresh homemade ricotta with fennel, celery, and walnuts or the cured tuna with hard-boiled egg and *bottarga* (fermented and dried fish roe). Primis like the spaghetti *alla vongole* (with clams) or the gnocchi with prosciutto and peas are always a great choice, and the sweet-and-sour wild boar with Tuscan cabbage and chickpeas is a generous entrée to have by yourself or share. The classic Old World (mostly Italy and France) wine list is varied and offers several by-the-glass choices. [$] *Average main: C$30* ✉ *1391 rue Saint-Jacques, Downtown* ☎ *514/419–6672* 🌐 *noragray.com* ✍ *Reservations essential* ⏲ *Closed Sun. and Mon. No lunch* [M] *Lucien L'Allier* ✥ *C6.*

$$ MODERN CANADIAN Fodor's Choice ★ 🍴 **Patrice Pâtissier.** Overseen by one of Québec's renowned pastry chefs, Patrice Demers, Patrice Pâtissier is a beautifully designed pastry shop that also doubles as a wine bar with an extensive and well chosen wine list created by Patrice's better half, sommelière Marie-Josée Beaudouin. Pick up a pastry to go at the counter or choose one of the plated desserts to enjoy on-site with or without its wine pairing. Chef Demers' "vert" dessert—a savvy combination of pistachios, green apples, cilantro, olive oil and a white chocolate and yogurt mousse—has become a classic. His *kouign amann*—a French sugar and butter layered dessert from Britanny—is delicious as is the maple *financier*—a nutty-tasting, brown butter cake. There are also several seasonal savory small plates to choose from for a weekday lunch or dinner Thursday to Saturday. The Québec asparagus with squid ink croutons, anchovy mayo, and confit lemons is a classic come springtime, as is the beautiful Nordic shrimp dish with yogurt panna cotta, cucumbers, and sorrel. [$] *Average main: C$20* ✉ *2360 rue Notre-Dame Ouest, Local 104, Downtown* ☎ *514/439–5434* 🌐 *patricepatissier.ca* ⏲ *Closed Mon. No dinner Tues., Wed., and Sun.* [M] *Lionel-Groulx* ✥ *B6.*

7

$ CHINESE FAMILY 🍴 **Qing Hua Dumplings.** Groups of students and other budget-conscious connoisseurs of good food crowd the tables here for soup dumplings just like they make them in northeast China. And the price is right: 15 dumplings for C$9. Demand is high for the lamb-and-coriander dumplings; the boiled shrimp, leek, and egg version; and the fried dumplings with chicken and curry. The coleslaw with carrot and egg is a good starter. Service can be a bit slow, but it's worth the wait. Cash only. [$] *Average main: C$10* ✉ *1019 blvd. St-Laurent, Chinatown* ☎ *438/288–5366* 💳 *No credit cards* [M] *Guy-Concordia* ✥ *B4.*

$$$ ITALIAN 🍴 **Rosalie.** Located inside a historical building in downtown Montréal, the dining room of Rosalie may be trendy, but the menu is classic Italian. With a chef straight from Italy, you know pasta dishes such as Cacio e Pepe (cheese and black pepper) are going to be delicious, though ordering one of the rustic pizzas baked in the wood-burning oven is also a wise choice. Fresh ingredients and perfect tomato sauce make all the difference at this restaurant. The large terrace out front draws crowds for *aperitivo* on late summer afternoons. Thirtysomething professionals pour in after work and often stay for an early supper before heading out on the town. [$] *Average main: C$25* ✉ *1232 rue de la Montagne,*

Downtown ☎ *514/392–1970* ⊕ *www.rosalierestaurant.com* ⊗ *No lunch weekends* Ⓜ *Lucien l'Allier* ✛ *C5.*

CHINATOWN

Montréal's Chinatown may be small but it's packed with big taste, including delicious soup-filled dumplings, delicate and sweet Dragon's Beard candy and a dim sum filled brunch.

$$ ☓ **Maison Kam Fung.** A family-run restaurant for three generations, La
CHINESE Maison Kam Fung is synonymous with dim sum in Montréal. This is
FAMILY the place to come for a noisy dim sum feast where waiters clatter up and down the aisles between tables, pushing a parade of trolleys bearing such treats as firm dumplings stuffed with pork and chicken, and stir-fried squid and shrimp. There are 300 dim sum available, of which 60 are on rotation on any given day. The best way to order is to stop one of the carts as it's going by and point to the dishes you'd like. You can order from a menu, too, but that's not as much fun. In the evening you can order Cantonese and Szechuan dishes until 10 pm. And good news: the Peking duck doesn't require advance notice. Ⓢ *Average main: C$15* ⊠ *1111 rue St-Urbain, Chinatown* ☎ *514/878–2888* ⊕ *www.maisonkamfung.com* Ⓜ *Place-d'Armes* ✛ *E5.*

$$ ☓ **Orange Rouge.** Recently opened in an orange and red building in the
CHINESE heart of Chinatown, Orange Rouge and chef-owner Aaron Langille pay tribute to the neighborhood with the Asian-inspired menu printed on folded paper reminiscent of Chinese restaurant take-out menus. If you are a stickler for authenticity, then Orange Rouge may offend you with its interpretation of certain traditional dishes, but if you are an Asian food aficionado, then it will quickly become a favorite. Chef Langille takes liberties in interpreting Asian dishes and the result is often a combination of familiar flavors with a surprising twist. Order the chrysanthemum salad, an unusual tasting green that is crunchy, slightly herbacious, and bitter. The whole roasted duck is an homage to Chinese-style Peking duck and can be shared by five people. Ⓢ *Average main: C$20* ⊠ *106 De La Gauchetière Ouest, Chinatown* ☎ *514/861– 1116* ⊕ *orangerouge.ca* ⊗ *Closed Sun. and Mon. No lunch Sat.* ✛ *E6.*

THE VILLAGE

A little outside the hustle and bustle of the busy Downtown Montréal core, the Latin Quarter and the Village are quite charming. Primo people-watching can be done at the many cafés in the area. During the summer months (May to September), rue Ste-Catherine in the Village is closed off to cars, which makes it pleasant to explore the shops and restaurants.

$ ☓ **De farine & d'eau fraîche.** This coffee and pastry shop's display is filled
CAFÉ with the cutest cakes and cookies that will charm you into spending a
FAMILY couple of hours here. Owner and pastry chef Marilu Gunji attended pastry school in Japan and worked in some of Montréal and Toronto's best establishments before branching out on her own. De farine & d'eau fraîche serves breakfast, lunch, and brunch in a casual setting

that will make you feel as if you're having high tea in a modern doll house. Try the house specialty: a soft chocolate ball with a crispy exterior filled with rich, vanilla-flavored custard. Note that the decor and tables emblazoned with the café's logo—a heart with "D F + E F" inside—have all been built by the chef's husband, a true testimony to all things sweet. [$] *Average main: C$10* ✉ *1701 rue Amherst, The Village* ☎ *514/522–2777* 🌐 *dfef.ca* 🕓 *No dinner* [M] *Beaudry* ✥ *G4.*

$$$$ LATIN AMERICAN

🍴 **Mezcla.** Mezcla's interpretation of South American cuisine in general, and more particularly Peruvian cuisine, will win any wavering heart the minute the first dish arrives at the table. The simple decor of brick walls and dark wood is offset by the white tablecloth and the dishes' elegant minimalism. Zesty ceviches, beautiful fresh fish *tiraditos* (a Peruvian dish consisting of raw fish or meat slices in a spicy sauce) and savory duck heart *anticuchos* (skewers) rely on local ingredients like Québec duck, venison, lamb, and fish to give them a local twist and a certain *je ne sais quoi.* The restaurant offers several tasting menus: a four-course tasting menu for C$39, a five-course menu for C$49 or a seven-course menu for C$79 that must be ordered by the whole table and are the chef's choice. [$] *Average main: C$35* ✉ *1251 rue de Champlain, The Village* ☎ *514/525–9934* 🌐 *www.restaurantmezcla.com* 🕓 *No lunch weekends. No dinner Mon.* ✥ *H5.*

THE PLATEAU, MILE END, LITTLE ITALY, AND OUTREMONT

7

PLATEAU MONT-ROYAL

Dotted with bistros and cafés, the Plateau has a bohemian edge. Chef-owned eateries favor market cuisine served in a decor of brick walls and hardwood floors. Noisy French-style bistros, like L'Express, are local institutions, as are cafés populated by poets and academics with laptops. There's vegetarian cooking, and Thai, along with sushi and stubborn little bakeries that refuse to mechanize.

$$$ MODERN CANADIAN

🍴 **Au Pied de Cochon.** Not for the timid, the menu at this famous bistro is an ode to nose-to-tail cooking . . . and fat. Martin Picard is one of Québec's most famous chefs and among celebrity chef Anthony Bourdain's favorites. The wild chef doesn't hesitate to serve pigs' feet stuffed with foie gras, pickled tongue, bison tongue, guinea hen liver mousse, a whole pig's head for two, pork hocks braised in maple syrup, or *oreilles-de-crisse* (literally, Christ's ears, or crispy, deep-fried crescents of pork skin) and his now famous duck in a can (a whole duck cooked and served tableside in a sealed can). But it's the foie gras that Picard really loves. He lavishes the stuff on everything, including hamburgers and his own version of poutine. **■ TIP→ Come summer, look for the Au Pied de Cochon food truck on the streets of Montréal from which you can grab one of those famous foie gras poutines or a very decadent APdC donut.** [$] *Average main: C$25* ✉ *536 av. Duluth Est, The Plateau* ☎ *514/281–1114* 🌐 *www.restaurantaupieddecochon.ca* ✍ *Reservations essential* 🕓 *Closed Mon. and Tues. No lunch. No brunch Sat.* [M] *Sherbrooke or Mont-Royal* ✥ *G3.*

$$ ✕**Beautys Luncheonette.** The Schkolnick family have been serving break-
DINER fast and lunch at this Montréal landmark since 1942 and on weekends
FAMILY the line out front can be daunting. The decor hasn't changed much over
Fodor's Choice the years, but you come here for the food. Classic dishes include the
★ Mish Mash omelet, with sliced hot dogs, salami, green peppers, and
fried onions; and the Superbeautys 2 with two eggs, pancakes, bacon
and sausage, home fries, and a toasted bagel. The challah French toast is
also popular, and the Beauty's Special—bagel, lox, and cream cheese—is
a classic. Hyman, the original owner, is now in his 90s but still sits at
the bar to direct patrons to their seats. $ *Average main: C$15* ✉ *93 av.
du Mont-Royal Ouest, The Plateau* ☎ *514/849–8883* ⊕ *www.beautys.
ca* ⬧ *Reservations not accepted* ⊗ *No dinner* M *Mont-Royal* ✛ *E2.*

$ ✕**Binerie Mont-Royal.** That rarest of the city's culinary finds—authentic
CANADIAN Quebecois food—is the specialty at this tiny diner that's been in busi-
ness since 1938. Sit at the long counter and make your way through
a filling breakfast of eggs, ham, toast, and, as the restaurant's name
suggests—beans. These Québec-style signature beans are still made the
old-fashioned way and the owner is more than happy to explain the
steps if you ask. At lunch, there are bowls of stew made with meat-
balls and pigs' feet, *tourtière* (meat pie), and pork and beans. Or opt
for the "Assiette Québécoise" and get a taste of everything. It's cheap
and filling, and the staff is charming, though it could use a slight face-
lift. $ *Average main: C$10* ✉ *367 av. du Mont-Royal Est, The Plateau*
☎ *514/285–9078* ⊕ *www.labineriemontroyal.com* ⊗ *No dinner week-
ends. Closes at 8 pm weekdays* M *Mont-Royal* ✛ *G2.*

$$ ✕**Chez Doval.** This quaint neighborhood restaurant has a bit of a split
PORTUGUESE personality: on the one side, a softly lit dining room for more intimacy
FAMILY and on the other, the more raucous tavern with guitar music, and if
you're lucky, a friendly argument about sports or politics. Food-wise,
it doesn't really matter where you sit: the chicken, sardines, grouper,
and squid—all broiled à-la-Portugaise, on an open charcoal grill behind
the bar—are succulent, simple, and delicious. Good prices attract artists
as well as university kids with visiting parents. $ *Average main: C$15*
✉ *150 rue Marie-Anne Est, The Plateau* ☎ *514/843–3390* ⊕ *www.
chezdoval.com* M *Mont-Royal* ✛ *F2.*

$$$ ✕**Chez Victoire.** The creative menu at this lively neighborhood restau-
MODERN FRENCH rant features French-inspired seasonable and sustainable cuisine. Chez
Victoire is the perfect place to experience the warmth and joie de vivre
of the Plateau-Mont-Royal neighborhood, a beacon of the French cul-
tural diaspora in Montréal. Take a seat at the long bar and order the
house-made charcuterie platter or sit at one of the large booths and
share the classic tomato and mozzarella di buffala salad, the decadent
roasted bone marrow or the famous smoked meat burger. The wine list
focuses on vintages from grapes grown sustainably and organically such
as the Arbois-Pupillin from Pierre Overnoy, a winemaker from the Jura
in France. ■**TIP**➔ **A late-night menu (after 10) is available every night.**
$ *Average main: C$25* ✉ *1453 av. du Mont-Royal Est, The Plateau*
☎ *514/521–6789* ⊕ *chezvictoire.com* M *Mont-Royal* ✛ *H2.*

$ ✕**La Banquise.** Québec is known for poutine—french fries topped with
CANADIAN cheese curds and gravy—and La Banquise has been the place for an
FAMILY authentic poutine experience since 1968. The menu is extensive, with

28 varieties to choose from in either a regular size or, for those who are really hungry, a large size (also great for sharing). If you've never tried poutine before, you might want to go with "La Classique," but there are tempting innovative options, like "La Taquise," with guacamole, sour cream, and tomatoes, and lots of meaty options. La Banquise is open 24 hours, so you can satisfy your poutine craving any time of day or night. La Banquise also serves burgers, sandwiches, salads, and breakfast dishes. $ *Average main: C$9* ✉ *994 rue Rachel Est, The Plateau* ☎ *514/525–2415* ⊕ *www.labanquise.com* Ⓜ *Mont-Royal* ✛ *G3.*

$$$
FRENCH

✕ **Laloux.** Serious foodies keep Laloux on their must-eat list, and it's not hard to see why: the prices are good and the food is refined in an elegant decor reminiscent of a high-end French restaurant. The cuisine is fresh and based on very local ingredients like immature juniper berries, sea buckthorn, and local honeycomb. The restaurant takes pride in its exemplary environmental approach like an Ocean Wise certification, a composting program, and organic or sustainably-produced ingredients. The seasonal menu changes often but the duck magret or seared scallops are always a good bet. For a more casual atmosphere, head over to Bar Laloux next door for a great three-choice, C$20 table d'hôte in a mid-century Scandinavian decor. $ *Average main: C$25* ✉ *250 av. des Pins Est, The Plateau* ☎ *514/287–9127* ⊕ *www.laloux.com* ⌚ *Reservations essential* ⊙ *No lunch weekends* Ⓜ *Sherbrooke* ✛ *F3.*

$$$
MODERN
CANADIAN

✕ **Le Comptoir Charcuteries et Vins.** The team at this casual spot know their stuff, and they proudly display their knowledge on the plate. The house-made charcuterie uses whole hogs in a nose-to-tail philosophy and has a loyal local following. The privately-imported, natural wine choices are made specifically to pair well with the menu offerings. The dining room is modern and paired down, with blond-wood counters, exposed brick, and chalkboard menus, which change nightly. The best seat in the house is the bar counter from which you can observe the action in the tiny open kitchen. The charcuteries platters are perfect as appetizers, to share or as a main meal if you order the larger size. Sunday brunch at Le Comptoir is a coveted affair so reservations are highly recommended. $ *Average main: C$30* ✉ *4807 blvd. St-Laurent, Mile End* ☎ *514/844–8467* ⊕ *www.comptoircharcuteriesetvins.ca* ⌚ *Reservations essential* ⊙ *No brunch Sat. No lunch Mon. or weekends* Ⓜ *Laurier* ✛ *F1.*

$$$
FRENCH
FAMILY

✕ **L'Express.** L'Express is the closest thing Montréal (and maybe even Canada) has to a Parisian bistro. Service is fast and efficient—most of the waiters have been here for 20 or 30 years—prices are reasonable, and the food is good, even if the tiny tables barely have room to accommodate the crowds. The city's celebrity chefs congregate here for dinner after hours and breakfast before hours, which speaks volumes about the quality and authenticity. The steak tartare with french fries, salmon with sorrel, and calves' liver with tarragon are marvelous. Don't expect the menu to change—diners would have a conniption. Jars of gherkins, fresh baguettes, and aged cheeses make the pleasure last longer, as do the reasonably priced bottles of imported French wine. Kids are warmly welcome. $ *Average main: C$22* ✉ *3927 rue St-Denis, The Plateau* ☎ *514/845–5333* ⊕ *www.restaurantexpress.ca* ⌚ *Reservations essential* Ⓜ *Sherbrooke* ✛ *F3.*

$$$ SEAFOOD 🍴 **Maestro S.V.P.** The oysters here are imported from all over the world, so you can compare the subtle differences between, say, a delicate little bivalve from Kumamoto, Japan, and a big meaty Kawakawa from New Zealand. A free lesson in shucking techniques comes with the order. Famous guests, from Leonard Cohen and William Hurt to Laura Linney and Bo Derek, have signed their oyster shells which are displayed in frames. If oysters aren't your thing, don't despair: you can also order grilled salmon, king crab, calamari, or *moules et frites* (mussels and french fries). Tuesday through Thursday, the menu features smaller, tapas-style portions perfect for sharing. [$] *Average main: C$30* ✉ *3615 blvd. St-Laurent, The Plateau* ☎ *514/842–6447* 🌐 *www.maestrosvp.com* ✍ *Reservations essential* ⏲ *No lunch* [M] *Sherbrooke* ✥ *F4.*

$$ CANADIAN 🍴 **Maison Publique.** Local celebrity chef Derek Dammann teamed up with the famed British chef Jamie Oliver to open this pub-style restaurant. The interior is dark and cozy, and a long counter takes up one side of the space—it's fun to sit here because you get a prime view of the tattooed chefs in action. The menu is posted on the wall and changes frequently based on what's in season. Foie gras toast with gherkins or baked oysters covered in cheese and marmite are both excellent dishes, as is Welsh rarebit: a slice of brioche covered with a sauce made from porter beer, béchamel, and melted cheese. The breakfast quiche, available at brunch on the weekends, is fabulous, as is the roasted bone marrow served with the "brunch for 2." [$] *Average main: C$20* ✉ *4720 rue Marquette, Mont-Royal* ☎ *514/507–0555* 🌐 *www.maisonpublique.com* ⏲ *Closed Mon. and Tues. No lunch* [M] *Laurier* ✥ *D3.*

$$$$ STEAKHOUSE 🍴 **Moishe's.** Elegant and old-school, Moishe's is one of Montréal's premier steak houses. Since 1938, the Lighter family has been hands-on when it comes to selecting and aging their own steaks. The specialty is grilled meat, accompanied by Moishe's famous buttery Monte Carlo potato—the inside of a potato is scooped out, mixed with milk, butter, cream, and chives and then put back into the skin. Fresh oysters are a great way to start, and the traditional Caesar salad is good accompaniment to the main event. Lamb chops and various fresh fish preparations are available, but make no mistake, this is a steak house. The C$25 "Three Hours to Midnight" special (after 9 pm) Thursday through Saturday is a great deal. [$] *Average main: C$35* ✉ *3961 blvd. St-Laurent, The Plateau* ☎ *514/845–3509* 🌐 *www.moishes.ca* ✍ *Reservations essential* [M] *St-Laurent* ✥ *F3.*

$ BAKERY Fodor's Choice ★ 🍴 **Patisserie Au Kouign Amann.** This small bakery makes some of the best croissants in Montréal, and the aroma of freshly baked pastries and quiches is transporting. The eponymous Kouign Amann is a delicious, multilayered butter and sugar cake but it's the croissants that will make your visit to Montréal memorable. Owner Nicholas comes from Brittany and is passionate about his pastries. He might even suggest the proper way to eat a croissant if he sees you doing it the "wrong" way—according to him, it tastes best if you break it in half and bite through the many layers, although some schools of thought would have you bite off an end and proceed from there. Whatever you do, don't let him see you unpeel a croissant. There are only two tables here so take your order to go and sit across the street on the steps of the church.

The patisserie is open from 7 am every morning. Ⓢ *Average main: C$10* ✉ *322 av. du Mont Royal Est, The Plateau* ☎ *514/845–8813* ▭ *No credit cards* ☉ *No dinner* Ⓜ *Mont-Royal* ⊹ *F2.*

$ ✕ **Patisserie Rhubarbe.** This little bakery is a Montréal treasure and locals
CAFÉ   come from around the city to pick up fantastic desserts made by chef
FAMILY   and owner Stephanie Labelle. The lemon tarts are gorgeous to look at, of course, taste terrific. Another favorite is the absolutely delicious Paris-Brest, which is filled with seasonal and airy flavors. Desserts here are a bit smaller in size than other bakeries but the intense flavors are worth every bite. Weekend brunch means simple and easy menu items in a calm and warm ambience. The exquisite brioche French toast with apples and caramel is always a great choice, and the scrambled eggs with truffle oil is a winner. Rhubarbe also serves afternoon tea every Friday from 2 to 5. Ⓢ *Average main: C$10* ✉ *5091 rue de Lanaudière, Mont-Royal* ☎ *514/903–3395* ⊕ *www.patisserierhubarbe. com* ⌕ *Reservations not accepted* ☉ *Closed Mon. and Tues. No dinner* Ⓜ *Laurier* ⊹ *D3.*

$$$ ✕ **Pintxo.** You don't dine at Pintxo—you graze. And what a lovely pas-
SPANISH   ture it is, too, with bare brick walls, white tablecloths, and a welcoming wine display near the door. Pintxos (pronounced "pinchos") are the Basque version of tapas of about two bites each, best enjoyed with a good beer or a glass of Spanish wine. There are about 15 pinxtos on the menu every night, ranging from tiny stacks of grilled vegetables to more substantial dishes such as smoked duck tartare, foie gras, chorizo, octopus, and the crowd-pleasing strawberry gazpacho. Traditionally, pintxos are not shared and it takes about six of them to make a meal. If creating your dinner one bite at a time doesn't appeal, there are larger dishes on the menu, too, such as black cod and beef cheeks braised in wine. Ⓢ *Average main: C$28* ✉ *256 rue Roy Est, The Plateau* ☎ *514/844–0222* ⊕ *www.pintxo.ca* ⌕ *Reservations essential* ☉ *No lunch Sat.–Tues.* Ⓜ *Sherbrooke* ⊹ *F3.*

$$$$ ✕ **Portus Calle.** A sunny decor greets you at this fabulous Portuguese
PORTUGUESE   restaurant run by celebrated chef Helena Loureiro. The many *petiscos* (tapas) such as *caldo verde* soup (traditional potatoes and chorizo soup), *chouriço* (pork) sausage, or a grilled seafood platter for two encourage sharing and tasting. The house specializes in fish and seafood, which are served tapas-style or as main meals. It's hard to go wrong at this Portuguese spot when the ingredients are top quality: fresh fish arrives daily and vegetables are local and market-fresh. If you're an aficionado, the selection of more than 7,000 well-chosen Portuguese wines and ports is impressive. Ⓢ *Average main: C$38* ✉ *4281 blvd. St-Laurent, The Plateau* ☎ *514/849–2070* ⊕ *www.portuscalle.ca* ⌕ *Reservations essential* ☉ *No lunch weekends. Closed Sun.* Ⓜ *Mont-Royal* ⊹ *F2.*

$$$ ✕ **Rumi.** With a menu inspired by the ancient spice route, Rumi attracts
MIDDLE EASTERN   a mix of chatty travelers, students, and foodies who appreciate eclectic
FAMILY   food. Start with Persian black tea, then order small dishes of *hodja* (puréed eggplant) and *wali* (feta with basil), which are eaten with Uzbecki-style naan bread or pita baked in the traditional Indian tandoor oven. The dahl soup is popular, as is the Layla salad (cucumbers, tomatoes, and basil, in a pomegranate vinaigrette) and the sweet and

savory Tabriz dish—roasted Cornish hen stuffed with prunes, apricots, cranberries, and orange. In summer, the outdoor terrace is great for people-watching. Rumi also serves weekend brunch. [$] *Average main: C$25* ✉ *5198 rue Hutchison, Outremont* ☎ *514/490–1999* 🌐 *www.restaurantrumi.com* 🕓 *No lunch Mon.* [M] *Outremont or Parc* ✥ *E1.*

$ CANADIAN FAMILY Fodor's Choice ★

🍴 **Schwartz's Delicatessen.** Schwartz's has no frills and could use a decor update, but that's all really beside the point because eating here is all about the thick sandwiches. The cooks do such a good job of curing, smoking, and slicing beef brisket that even when it's 20 below zero, locals don't mind lining up to get a seat at the city's most famous deli. Fodorites agree, it's worth the wait for the smoked meat sandwich on rye, with fries. Both Angelina Jolie and Halle Berry couldn't resist the medium-fat sandwich. Try to avoid lunch and dinner hours, as the wait is long. If you're in a rush, use the take-out counter next door. [$] *Average main: C$10* ✉ *3895 blvd. St-Laurent, The Plateau* ☎ *514/842–4813* 🌐 *www.schwartzsdeli.com* ✍ *Reservations not accepted* 💳 *No credit cards* [M] *Sherbrooke* ✥ *F3.*

$ CAFÉ Fodor's Choice ★

🍴 **St-Viateur Bagel & Café.** Even expatriate New Yorkers have been known to prefer Montréal's light, crispy, and slightly sweet bagel to its heavier Manhattan cousin. (The secret? The dough is boiled in honey-sweetened water before baking in a wood-burning oven.) With coffee and smoked salmon, these bagels make a great breakfast, or a snack at any time of the day. The wood-fired brick ovens at the original location—at 263 rue St-Viateur Ouest, in Mile End—have been operating since 1957. Keep in mind that although that location is open 24/7, it just serves bagels to go; there are no tables for dining in. [$] *Average main: C$6* ✉ *1127 av. Mont-Royal Est, The Plateau* ☎ *514/528–6361* 🌐 *www.stviateurbagel.com* 💳 *No credit cards* [M] *Laurier* ✥ *G2.*

OUTREMONT

Outremont caters to affluent French-speaking professionals with restaurants that look as good as the food being served. There are plenty of charming outdoor terraces in the warm months.

$$$ CANADIAN

🍴 **Brasserie Les Enfants Terribles.** With its cavernous corner spot on Outremont's trendy avenue Bernard, sophisticated yet playful decor, and artfully prepared comfort food, Les Enfants Terribles is always a good bet for quality food and excellent people-watching. The menu at this brasserie-with-a-twist is a mix of high-class cuisine and comfort food favorites: shepherd's pie; fish-and-chips; braised shortribs; mushroom risotto; and mac 'n' cheese. On weekends when the weather's nice, Montrealers flock to the large outdoor terrace to enjoy the breakfast menu available until 3 pm. The kitchen stays open to serve after-theater customers on show nights at nearby Théâtre Outremont. The photos on the menu and clear thumbprints engraved on the glasses are from Brûlé's very own *enfants terribles.* [$] *Average main: C$25* ✉ *1257 av. Bernard Ouest, Outremont* ☎ *514/759–9918* 🌐 *www.lesenfantsterriblesbrasserie.ca* 🕓 *No breakfast weekdays* [M] *Outremont* ✥ *B1.*

$$ BISTRO

🍴 **Café Souvenir.** From media moguls to Olympic medalists, a wide range of clientele can be found here, nibbling crepes with Chantilly cream or sipping double espressos. Breakfast and brunch are served daily and the weekend edition is the signature meal at this Parisian-style eatery, where omelets and *croque matins* (an egg and cheese croissant sandwich) come with generous mounds of fresh fruit. Diners exchange sections of the *New York Times* and check their iPhones, happy to chat at the breakfast bar or at the bistro tables. On sunny and warm Montréal days, try to get a table outside on the small terrace. For a casual evening meal, regulars rave about the hamburgers, the quesadillas, and the Caesar salad with chicken. $ *Average main: C$15* ✉ *1261 rue Bernard Ouest, Outremont* ☎ *514/948–5259* 🌐 *www.cafesouvenir.com* [M] *Outremont or Parc* ✣ *B1.*

$$ BISTRO FAMILY Fodor's Choice ★ 🍴 **La Croissanterie Figaro.** The self-proclaimed "un coin perdu de Paris" (a lost corner of Paris) is famous for its wraparound patio, Parisian vibe, and 100-year-old corner building. It's hard to know which architectural detail to admire first—the art deco chandelier, the art nouveau bar imported from Argentina, the "gilded" tables, the copper vats, the stained glass, or the woodwork. It's fun to watch for local television stars while you nibble a homemade croissant and nurse a large bowl of café au lait. Although this is a full bistro serving three meals every day of the week, it shines brightest in the morning, when you can order the Special Bonjour croissant with ham and cheese, or other hearty sandwiches. Evenings feature unique daily cocktails. Early birds and night owls are equally served since La Croissanterie opens at 7 am and closes at 1 am every day of the week. $ *Average main: C$15* ✉ *5200 rue Hutchison, Outremont* ☎ *514/278–6567* 🌐 *www.lacroissanteriefigaro.com* [M] *Outremont* ✣ *B3.*

$$$ BISTRO FAMILY 🍴 **Leméac.** On a popular street corner, this French bistro creates good karma by heating its outdoor terrace for eight months of the year. The other winning move is the late-night special: between 10 pm and midnight, the table d'hôte menu (an appetizer and a main) is just C$27. Regulars gravitate toward classic dishes such as the calf liver, salmon or beef tartare, grilled Cornish hen, and hanger steak—all served with aplomb on white linen tablecloths. It's no secret that the fries at Leméac are world-class, as is the weekend brunch. Leave room for dessert: The Pain Perdu, a thick slice of brioche with caramel and maple, is a specialty. $ *Average main: C$30* ✉ *1045 rue Laurier Ouest, Outremont* ☎ *514/270–0999* 🌐 *www.restaurantlemeac.com* [M] *Outremont* ✣ *B3.*

$$$ ITALIAN 🍴 **Le Petit Italien.** Two key factors conspire to make this a great Montréal dining spot: a fabulous terrace for warm summer evenings, and savory Italian comfort food at reasonable prices. One wall of this modern bistro is lined with glass mason jars containing the house tomato sauce, reminding diners that everything served at Le Petit Italien is prepared from scratch. One bite of the linguine *buongustaio* pasta dish, with guanciale, chicken, grapes, basil, and a white wine sauce, and you're a believer. $ *Average main: C$25* ✉ *1265 rue Bernard Ouest, Outremont* ☎ *514/278–0888* 🌐 *www.lepetititalien.com* 🕒 *No lunch weekends* [M] *Parc or Outremont* ✣ *B1.*

$$$ MODERN CANADIAN 🍴 **Van Horne.** The tiny 28-seat restaurant is decorated in neutral tones yet stuns with its choice of imposing and unique art pieces like a collection of colorful Roy Lichtenstein plates or a massive door panel of the Iranian pavilion from Expo 67. The menu is concise with only four

appetizers, four main meals, and two dessert choices, but everything on it is quite refined. A five-course tasting menu is available for $59. Since seating is limited at this small restaurant, reservations are highly recommended. Ⓢ *Average main: C$30* ✉ *1268 av. Van Horne, Outremont* ☎ *514/508–0828* ⊕ *www.vanhornerestaurant.com* ⏤ *Reservations essential* ⊗ *Closed Sun. and Mon.* Ⓜ *Outremont* ✛ *B2.*

MILE END

Rue Bernard and rue Laurier tend to cater to successful young couples and are popular with the brunch crowd. Hipster chefs and restaurant owners have been opening up more and more new places to dine along the aforementioned streets as well as rue St-Viateur and avenue Fairmount.

$$$$
MEDITERRANEAN
Fodor's Choice
★

✕ **BarBounya.** The menu at BarBounya features Mediterranean cuisine with a focus on *meze*, small dishes served hot or cold and meant to be ordered in large quantities for sharing. The atmosphere is casual at this restaurant where the seating is communal and the service friendly yet flawless. The local lamb tartare spiced with cumin has become a classic, as has the Imam bayildi, a braised eggplant topped with a mélange of onions, tomatoes and ricotta. BarBounya also serves a Mediterranean-inspired lunch on Thursdays and Fridays and a delicious brunch on weekends. Don't miss out on the homemade *kaymak* (fresh milk curd) topped with honey and served as part of the lavish brunch spread. In the summer, the sunny terrace is a great spot for people-watching. Ⓢ *Average main: C$35* ✉ *234, av. Laurier W, Mile End* ☎ *514/439–8858* ⊕ *www.barbounya.com* ⏤ *Reservations essential* ⊗ *Closed Mon. No dinner Sun. No lunch Tues. and Wed.* ✛ *C3.*

$
CAFÉ
FAMILY

✕ **Café Olimpico.** Open every day from 7 am to midnight, Café Olimpico is a popular spot for great Italian coffee and a Montréal landmark. Families, hipsters, and business people head here in the morning before work or school, and the place really gets jammed on weekend mornings, though it's large enough to accommodate a crowd. The line at the bar to order your drink may be long but the baristas know their craft and the clink of spoons in saucers and the grinding of the espresso machine is welcoming background music for anyone who takes coffee seriously. This is a great place to get a real feel for Montréal. Ⓢ *Average main: C$3* ✉ *124 rue St-Viateur Ouest, Mile End* ⊕ *www.cafeolimpico.com* ⊟ *No credit cards* ✛ *C2.*

$$$
MIDDLE EASTERN

✕ **Damas.** If you've never had Syrian food, which is difficult to find in North America, you're in for a treat. The ambience is colorful and cozy, and dishes like *fatta* (yogurt, tahini, pita, pistachios, pine nuts, and herbs) along with a variety of meats or vegetables are delicious and have earned Damas rave reviews from Montrealers. Appetizers like the hummus with lamb and the *kibbeh nayeh* (raw minced beef mixed with bulgur) are perfect for sharing, then you might want to split a grilled meat or fish dish for two. Add a glass of Arak—a traditional, anise-flavored drink—or wine from their list of Mediterranean imports to bring it all together. Ⓢ *Average main: C$25* ✉ *5210 av. du Parc, Mile End* ☎ *514/439–5435* ⊕ *www.restaurant-damas.com* ⏤ *Reservations essential* ⊗ *No lunch* ✛ *C2.*

$$$ CANADIAN

🍴 **Hotel Herman.** Hipster chefs with a French Canadian focus on terroir make creativity the key word at the trendy Hotel Herman (which is not in a hotel, in case you were wondering). The menu is small and seasonal, with cheese varieties that focus on local artisans and fresh oysters that arrive daily. The marinated trout with smoked crème fraîche, trout eggs, and pumpernickel croutons is so popular it's become a permanent fixture on the menu. A must is the bread and butter, both made daily in-house. For dessert, the chocolate terrine for two is sublime: it's often topped with unusual seasonal ingredients like Jerusalem artichokes and bacon caramel. The list of organic, natural, and biodiverse wines is affordable and changes often. Reservations are recommended. [$] *Average main: C$30* ✉ *5171 blvd. St-Laurent, Mile End* ☎ *514/278–7000* 🌐 *www.hotelherman.com* ✍ *Reservations essential* 🕒 *Closed Tues. No lunch* ✥ *C2.*

$$ JAPANESE

🍴 **Izakaya Iwashi.** This Japanese-style pub serves little plates to share and delicious bowls of ramen. Iwashi (which translates as sardine in Japanese) started as a pop-up café but was so popular that it quickly launched as a permanent restaurant. Dishes such as seared mackerel and friend chicken have become some of the city's best izakaya (or pub) food. There are daily specials and house sake-based cocktails, like the sakerinha with sake, cucumber syrup, and lime juice. Note that Iwashi only operates as an izakaya after 6 pm; before then, the space is used as Café Sardine and serves excellent coffee and donuts. [$] *Average main: C$20* ✉ *9 av. Fairmount Est, Mile End* ☎ *514/802–8899* 🌐 *cafesardine.com* 🕒 *Closed Sun. and Mon.* ✥ *F1.*

$ CAFÉ FAMILY Fodor's Choice ★

🍴 **Kem CoBa.** There is one word that describes this ice-cream shop: delicious. Vincent and Ngoc, the owners and chefs, as well as husband and wife, opened this colorful spot to showcase their ice-cream creativity. The flavors change frequently based on what the chefs find at the market, but the lightly salted butter ice cream is a staple, and locals love it. If you think it sounds a little strange, partner it up with the apple sorbet and you'll have yourself an apple pie on a cone. Or give the soft serve a taste; tart raspberry swirled with creamy vanilla is bliss inducing, so is the almond milk and sour cherry. There aren't any preservatives or artificial flavorings here, just all-round natural goodness. [$] *Average main: C$5* ✉ *60 av. Fairmount Ouest, Mile End* ☎ *514/419–1699* 🌐 *www.kemcoba.com* 🕒 *Closed Oct.–Apr.* [M] *Laurier* ✥ *C3.*

$$$$ MODERN CANADIAN Fodor's Choice ★

🍴 **La Chronique.** It's an elegant place with white walls and high ceilings flooded with light but people don't come here for the ambience; they come for the excellent food. Without fuss or fanfare, La Chronique has steadily been one of the best French restaurants in town since it opened in 1995. The cuisine seamlessly blends lightened French fare with seasonal and local ingredients. If you are a foie gras fan, the seared foie gras served with seasonal fruit is easily the best in town. **■ TIP→ This is an excellent place to splurge on the prix-fixe tasting menu—five courses are C$85 at dinner, or try the more affordable three-course prix-fixe lunch menu for C$31.** [$] *Average main: C$42* ✉ *104 rue Laurier Ouest, Mile End* ☎ *514/271–3095* 🌐 *www.lachronique.qc.ca* ✍ *Reservations essential* 🕒 *Closed Mon. No lunch weekends* [M] *Laurier* ✥ *C3.*

$$ ✗ **Lawrence.** There are lines outside this hip-and-trendy establishment
CANADIAN   before the restaurant opens for weekend brunch. The chef's British
Fodor's Choice   background means that the homemade scones and clotted cream here
★   are to die for and must be ordered as a prebrunch snack. Other brunch
options include scrambled eggs with crème fraîche and smoked trout
and deviled kidneys on toast or pig's trotters for the more adventur-
ous eaters. The dinner menu changes regularly. If the pork chop with
seasonal sides or the braised lamb with aioli are available for dinner,
you're in luck. The Lawrence team just opened up Boucherie Law-
rence, a butcher shop a couple of doors up on St-Laurent with meat
sourced from small, local producers. The sandwiches are made on
homemade bread and filled with the house meats and sausages. $ *Av-
erage main: C$20* ✉ *5201 blvd. St-Laurent, Mile End* ☎ *514/503–
1070* ⊕ *www.lawrencerestaurant.com* ☽ *Closed Mon. No dinner Sun.*
Ⓜ *Laurier* ✛ *C3.*

$ ✗ **Melina Phyllo Bar.** It may be in the heart of Mile End, but this "phyllo
GREEK   bar" looks like it was transported directly from Athens, with food arriv-
FAMILY   ing on checkered cobalt-blue wax paper. It's all about take-out here,
though warm temperatures allow for two tables out front. The delicious
spanakopita, with a perfect crunchy exterior, makes an excellent lunch
on the go. The menu is brief, but every item is well made, including
the Melina sandwich, with its spicy feta spread, kalamata hummus,
cucumbers, tomatoes, and *graviera* (Swiss-like cheese). Another must-
try, the *bougatsa*, is a warm custard-filled phyllo pastry with cinnamon.
$ *Average main: C$10* ✉ *5573 av. du Parc, Mile End* ☎ *514/270–1675*
Ⓜ *Parc* ✛ *C2.*

$$$$ ✗ **Milos.** Don't let the nets and floats hanging from the ceiling fool you:
GREEK   Milos is no simple taverna (a fact reflected in the prices, which some
argue are exorbitant). The main dish is usually the catch of the day
grilled over charcoal and seasoned with parsley, capers, and lemon juice,
but appetizers like grilled vegetables or shrimp, or the sliced zucchini
and eggplant with lightly fried saganaki cheese and tzaziki, are a good
way to start. Fish are priced by the pound and often displayed, along
with the vegetables, in the restaurant's colorful, open-market interior.
There are meaty options, too. ■TIP➡ If you're on a budget, consider
the affordable fixed-price three-course late-night menu available from
Thursday to Saturday between 10 and midnight for C$25.13; or the
three-course fixed-price lunch menu for C$25.14. $ *Average main:
C$40* ✉ *5357 av. du Parc, Mile End* ☎ *514/272–3522* ⊕ *www.milos.
ca* ⌥ *Reservations essential* ☽ *No lunch weekends* Ⓜ *Parc* ✛ *C2.*

$$ ✗ **Nouveau Palais.** Hipsters head to Nouveau Palais for the '70s diner
AMERICAN   decor (wood paneling and vinyl seats) and the simple, delicious, and
FAMILY   classic dishes. The Palace Hamburger is gaining a reputation among
Montrealers as one of the best the city has to offer, and the sweet-potato
pie also has fans. Another reason hipsters love it here: in addition to
weekend brunch (the fried chicken and waffles are strongly recommended), and daily lunch and dinner, Nouveau Palais stays open until 3
am. Winneburger, the Nouveau Palais food truck offers a more diminu-
tive yet just as delicious version of the famous burger, and makes the
rounds around Mile End, so keep your eyes peeled. $ *Average main:*

C$15 ✉ *281 rue Bernard Ouest, Mile End* ☎ *514/273–1180* ⊕ *www. nouveaupalais.com* ⊙ *Closed Mon. No dinner Sun.* Ⓜ *Rosemont or Beaubien* ⊹ *C1.*

$$ ✕ **Pizzeria Magpie.** Although a few inspired appetizers are available, it's
PIZZA really all about the pizza and oysters at this unpretentious, casual spot.
FAMILY Tucked away on a small side street in Mile End, this classic pizzeria with white-washed walls and pressed tin ceiling turns out some of the best wood-burning oven pizza the city has to offer. Favorites include the Magpie Margherita with *bocconcini* (small mozzarella cheese balls), fresh basil, and San Marzano tomatoes, and the three-cheese meatball pizza. Start with fresh oysters; they have a fantastic selection at affordable prices. The simple homemade desserts are a sure hit as well. Ⓢ *Average main: C$15* ✉ *16 rue Maguire, Mile End* ☎ *514/507–2900* ⊕ *www.pizzeriamagpie.com* ⊙ *Closed Mon. No lunch Tues. or weekends* Ⓜ *Laurier* ⊹ *C2.*

$$ ✕ **Rotisserie Panama.** Some of the best grilled meat in Montréal is what
GREEK attracts big, noisy crowds to Rotisserie Panama. The dining room is
FAMILY simple, with beige walls and blue checkered tablecloths, but the roasted chicken and crispy lamb chops are excellent, as is the grilled red snapper and sea bass. Sides of *horta*—boiled bitter greens with lemon—and roasted Greek-style potatoes make any meal complete. Extended families come on the weekend for the roasted baby lamb, which is truly delicious. A meal at Panama wouldn't be complete without a heaping plate of *loukoumades*, Greek-style balls of fried dough smothered in honey. Best of all, the prices are extremely reasonable. Ⓢ *Average main: C$16* ✉ *789 rue Jean-Talon Ouest, Mile End* ☎ *514/276–5223* ⊕ *www. rotisseriepanama.com* Ⓜ *Parc* ⊹ *B1.*

$$ ✕ **Sparrow.** The aviary decor motifs are welcoming at this lunch and
MODERN breakfast spot, where you can get a traditional English breakfast. Noon
AMERICAN favorites include the designer grilled-cheese sandwich, the burger with hand-cut fries, and the delicious seasonal specials. Coffee aficionados appreciate that Sparrow gets its beans from Café Myriade downtown. Sparrow uses local and sustainable products, the meat is certified organic, hormone and antibiotic-free, and ground in house for the famous Sparrow burgers. Look for seasonal menus, like the delicious sugar shack brunch menu in April. ■TIP➔ **Every Friday to Sunday, 11 am to 7 pm, head upstairs to Sparrow's sister, Cardinal Tea Room for scrumptious tea sandwiches and cakes served on lovely vintage plates.** Ⓢ *Average main: C$13* ✉ *5322 blvd. St-Laurent, Mile End* ☎ *514/507– 1642* ▭ *No credit cards* ⊙ *Closed Sun. for dinner* ⊹ *F1.*

LITTLE ITALY

Little Italy offers a nostalgic look back at what La Bella Italia used to be 30 years ago, as old men congregate in front of their favorite café and chat about politics and last night's soccer game. Restaurants turn out traditional pizza and pasta dishes while younger chefs are making their mark by putting a modern spin on familiar dishes.

$$ ✕ **Bottega Pizzeria.** Nobody questions the authenticity of the Neapoli-
PIZZA tan style pizza here, seeing as there's a 3,500-kilogram wood-burning
Fodor's Choice pizza oven made from Vesuvian rock in the kitchen. It cooks pizza in
★ 90 seconds flat, at 500 degrees Celsius (932 °F). There are just a few

pizza options but all are fabulous and made with fresh tomatoes, vegetables, and top quality salumi. Another reason to go to Bottega is the array of tapas-style appetizers, called *sfizi*—meatballs, eggplant, grilled peppers, and *arancini* (stuffed fried rice balls). The kitchen is open until midnight, so the city's top chefs often come by for their dinner after work. The gelato is also excellent, and you can also get it to go, with a cookie. $ *Average main: C$20* ⊠ *65 rue St-Zotique Est, Little Italy* ☎ *514/277–8104* ⊕ *www.bottega.ca* ⌂ *Reservations essential* ⊘ *Closed Mon. No lunch* Ⓜ *Beaubien* ✛ *D1.*

$ × **Caffè San Simeon.** In the heart of Little Italy, Caffè San Simeon really
CAFÉ   feels like a trip to *la dolce vita*. This spot is filled with regulars chatting away in Italian, and has quickly become one of the city's best places to get an espresso, latte, cappuccino, or the signature smooth Malibu—a lukewarm drink shorter than a cappuccino but longer than a macchiato and made by combining a short shot of espresso with frothed milk. Visit a few times and you won't even have to order, the experienced baristas will prepare your drink when they see you walk in. It's open from 6 am to midnight (or later) every day of the week. There are a few pastries available if you are peckish but the main reason to seek out this Little Italy *caffè* is their excellent brew. $ *Average main: C$5* ⊠ *39 rue Dante, Little Italy* ☎ *514/272–7386* ⊕ *www.caffesansimeon.com* ▭ *No credit cards* Ⓜ *Jean-Talon* ✛ *C1.*

$$$ × **Chez Roger.** A French bistro with a modern feel, this is a great place
BISTRO   to get a fabulous dinner in Montréal. The côte de bœuf dish for two with mashed potatoes and seasonal vegetables is popular, as is the fish-and-chips. For a little theater flair with your meal, the beef and salmon tartares are prepared tableside. Should you arrive a little earlier than your reservation time, head next door to Bar Roger while you wait: on warm summer evenings you can sip your drink outside while perched on a stool just in front of the restaurant. $ *Average main: C$25* ⊠ *2316 rue Beaubien Est, Rosemont* ☎ *514/593–4200* ⊕ *www.barroger.com* ⊘ *No lunch* Ⓜ *D'Iberville* ✛ *G1.*

$$ × **Dinette Triple Crown.** Chef and Kentucky native Colin Perry has brought
SOUTHERN   Southern cuisine to Montréal and it's a hit. He and his girlfriend and co-
FAMILY   owner, Nicole Turcotte, a native Montrealer, have built a huge following with their tiny restaurant (a counter with eight stools). Fried chicken with fluffy mashed potatoes and gravy, braised greens, hush puppies, and biscuits, along with pulled pork sandwiches and brisket, will have you speaking with a southern drawl in no time. There are also daily specials and desserts. If the weather's nice, tell the hipsters behind the counter that you'd like to have your meal in Little Italy Park across the street and they'll provide the picnic basket, cutlery, dishes, and a table-cloth—just don't forget to return the basket. $ *Average main: C$15* ⊠ *6704 rue Clarke, Little Italy* ☎ *514/272–2617* ⌂ *Reservations not accepted* ⊘ *Closed Wed.* Ⓜ *Jean-Talon or Beaubien* ✛ *D1.*

$$$ × **Gus.** Eclectic may be the best way to describe the food at Gus, as the
ECLECTIC   dishes combine a French bistro feel with a little bit of the American South. The seasonings are down to a science here, and the proof is in the homemade ketchups, hot sauces, and salsas that are generously

offered at each table. As with many restaurants, the menu changes with the seasons, the products, and the chef's inspiration but the Caesar salad made *à-la-minute* is a popular constant. The meat and seafood are carefully sourced so any of the nightly available options are always a great choice. Reservations are recommended at this popular, small neighborhood steak house. [$] *Average main: C$27* ✉ *38 rue Beaubien Est, Little Italy* ☎ *514/722–2175* 🌐 *www.restaurantgus.com* 🕘 *Closed Sun. No lunch Mon.–Wed.* [M] *Beaubien* ✥ *C1.*

$$$ ITALIAN 🍴 **Inferno.** Dark wood on the walls, tables, and floors fill the dining room of this Little Italy eatery. At the corner of rue Dante and rue St-Dominique, many say the food at this trendy neighborhood restaurant is paradise found, a play on Dante Aligheri's 14th-century epic poem "The Divine Comedy." The house-made pastas change frequently, depending on what's available at the Jean-Talon market up the street. Meat options such as the grilled pork chop with honey and truffle sauce, and the fresh fish dishes showcase the creativity of the chefs, though the restaurant is particularly known for its tripe preparations, demonstrating Inferno's ability to maintain Italian traditions while adding a modern edge. [$] *Average main: C$25* ✉ *6850 rue St-Dominique, Little Italy* ☎ *514/274–0666* 🌐 *www.restaurantinferno.com* ✍ *Reservations essential* 🕘 *Closed Sun. and Mon.* [M] *Jean-Talon* ✥ *D1.*

$$$ BISTRO 🍴 **Kitchen Galerie.** With its small ingredient-based menu, this homey bistro is an example of excellence through simplicity. The chefs do everything—the shopping, the chopping, the cooking, the greeting, and the serving, and the focus is on meats, fish, and vegetarian dishes all inspired by what local farmers bring to the adjacent Jean-Talon market that morning. The open kitchen turns out classic French bistro market cuisine, including rib-eye steak for two and their now famous *pot de foie gras,* a foie gras mousse placed in a Mason jar and steam cooked inside a dishwasher for perfect consistency, then served with a muscat gelée. The long 20-foot banquet table is a fun place to sit—the communal seating encourages diners to talk to their neighbors—though there are smaller tables as well. [$] *Average main: C$30* ✉ *60 rue Jean-Talon Est, Little Italy* ☎ *514/315–8994* 🌐 *www.kitchengalerie.com* ✍ *Reservations essential* 🕘 *No lunch. Closed Sun. and Mon.* [M] *Jean-Talon* ✥ *D1.*

$ CAFÉ FAMILY 🍴 **La Cornetteria.** This lovely little bakery that feels like it's been transported from Italy specializes in the Italian version of the croissant: the *cornetto.* Owner Alex Fica makes the pastries fresh every day and offers them plain or filled with Nutella, ricotta cream, or almond paste. They're the perfect accompaniment to a great Cornetteria cappuccino. If you're in town in March, ask about *zeppole*—deep-fried donuts filled with ricotta—which are made once a year all around Italy and by Italian Montrealers in celebration of St. Joseph. The cannoli, filled with a light and sweet ricotta cream, are also delicious but for those who prefer savory bites, try the delicious speck and *stracchino* (a mild, fresh Italian cheese) sandwich on homemade foccacia bread. The bakery closes at 6 pm. [$] *Average main: C$4* ✉ *6528 blvd. St-Laurent, Little Italy* ☎ *514/277–8030* 🌐 *www.lacornetteria.com* 💳 *No credit cards* 🕘 *No dinner* [M] *Beaubien* ✥ *C1.*

7

$$ MIDDLE EASTERN FAMILY

🍴 **Le Petit Alep.** This casual Middle Eastern spot is comfortable and homey but still has style, with music, ivy, exposed-stone walls and a lovely *terrasse* come summer. The menu is perfect for grazing and excellent sharing options include the *mouhamara* (pomegranate and walnuts spread), *sabanegh* (spinach and onions pies), *fattouche* (a salad with pita chips and mint), and *yalandji* (vine leaves stuffed with rice, chickpeas, walnuts, and tomatoes). There are Armenian dishes, too, like the salad with cumin and *flefle* (hot peppers). Delicious kebabs dominate the main courses, with the moderately spiced *Terbialy* a popular favorite. Daily specials are available every day. [$] *Average main: C$15* ✉ *191 rue Jean-Talon Est, Little Italy* ☎ *514/270–6396* 🌐 *www.petitalep.com* 🕒 *Closed Sun. and Mon.* [M] *Jean-Talon or de Castelnau* ✥ *C1.*

$$$ CANADIAN FAMILY

🍴 **Pastaga.** Critically acclaimed chef, owner, and TV personality Martin Juneau and his partner are creative and grounded when it comes to the menu at their restaurant Pastaga. Juneau's signature dish of crispy pork belly marinated in brown sugar (or maple when in season) won him the best chef in Canada award at the Gold Medal Plates in 2011 and is a mainstay on the seasonal menu. Another must is the excellent chopped liver "à la juive" (Jewish style), with soft and creamy chopped liver, hard-boiled egg, crunchy bagel chips, and tart-marinated onions. The all-natural wine list will have you discover some unusual bottles. The restaurant is popular so reservations are strongly suggested. If you want to watch the chefs at work, ask for a seat at the bar—though if you really want to be at the center of the action, reserve the chef's table inside the large kitchen. [$] *Average main: C$30* ✉ *6389 blvd. St-Laurent, Little Italy* ☎ *438/381–6389* 🌐 *www.pastaga.ca* 🕒 *No lunch Mon.–Thurs.* [M] *Beaubien* ✥ *C1.*

$$$ ITALIAN

🍴 **Ristorante Lucca.** Small and cozy, Ristorante Lucca is one of the go-to places in Little Italy for the definitive Italian dining experience. And it never disappoints: the food is always top-notch with great market ingredients purchased at Marché Jean-Talon up the street and solid traditional dishes. Some of the most popular choices are the veal chops served with spinach and polenta, and the seafood linguini. The decor is simple: wooden table are clustered around deep terra-cotta-colored walls. It's perfect for a romantic meal but make reservations as it does get busy. [$] *Average main: C$30* ✉ *12 rue Dante, Little Italy* ☎ *514/278–6502* 🌐 *www.restaurantlucca.ca* ✍ *Reservations essential* 🕒 *Closed Sun. No lunch Sat.* [M] *Jean-Talon* ✥ *D1.*

$$$ SPANISH

🍴 **Tapeo.** Bringing tapas uptown, this Spanish-inspired eatery is a chic yet casual place to drink imported wines and share a few small plates. The Tapeo version of the classic *patatas bravas* (fried potato cubes) served with a spicy tomato sauce and aioli is always a good choice, as are the roasted vine tomatoes and the grilled chorizo. For an unforgettable meal, book the chef's table in the open kitchen, where you can watch the action and get special attention; there's seating for 18 people. For dessert, order the house *churros,* the Spanish equivalent of donuts, dusted with sugar and served with a side of warm chocolate sauce for dipping; a true classic! [$] *Average main: C$30* ✉ *511 rue Villeray, Little Italy* ☎ *514/495–1999* 🌐 *www.restotapeo.com* ✍ *Reservations essential* 🕒 *Closed Mon.* [M] *Jarry or Jean-Talon* ✥ *D1.*

$$ ITALIAN FAMILY 🍴 **Vinizza.** The name, a portmanteau of *vino* (wine) and pizza, is an immediate cue to what the focus is at Vinizza. And you can't go wrong with their pizza, cooked to perfection in a wood-burning oven, or fresh pasta made on-site. The ingredients are superb and fresh, purchased from Marché Jean-Talon right outside the door. We recommend starting with fried calamari, then sharing the divine linguini with seafood and a "ca'pummarola 'ncopp" pizza—with tomato, basil, and fresh mozzarella. An additional incentive to dine here is that for every main dish sold, a donation is made to l'Accueil Bonneau to help feed Montréal's homeless. There's another location of Vinizza downtown at 2044 rue Metcalfe. [$] *Average main: C$20* ✉ *150 rue Jean-Talon Est, Little Italy* ☎ *514/904–2250* 🌐 *www.vinizza.com* ✍ *Reservations essential* 🕒 *No lunch weekends* [M] *Jean-Talon* ✥ *D4.*

WESTMOUNT

This area is predominantly Anglophone. You'll see polished moms in Prada sunglasses pushing strollers, as well as dressed-down locals walking their dogs along rue Sherbrooke and avenue Greene. There aren't a lot of restaurants here, but you may need some sustenance after hitting the area's hip and trendy boutiques.

$$$ JAPANESE FUSION 🍴 **Park.** Sustainable, organic, and fresh every day is the philosophy chef Antonio Park prides himself on when it comes to sushi. The menu is eclectic, with excellent sushi, sashimi, noodles, and Japanese dishes mixed with a variety of influences from the chef's multiple backgrounds—Korean, Argentinian, and Canadian. You can leave the inspiration to the chef and opt for a *omakase* menu (chef's choice)—the lunch version is C$50; dinner starts at C$65. Bibimbap, a Korean dish of multigrain rice, poached egg, vegetables, and tofu, is an excellent choice. Brunch standouts include a homemade kimchi BLT on focaccia bread. [$] *Average main: C$20* ✉ *378 av. Victoria, Westmount* ☎ *514/750–7534* 🌐 *www.parkresto.com* ✍ *Reservations essential* 🕒 *Closed Sun.* ✥ *A4.*

$$ MODERN CANADIAN 🍴 **Restaurant le H4C.** Le H4C's market cuisine is first and foremost product-driven and inspired by local and seasonal ingredients like snow crab, Québec halibut, asparagus or fiddleheads. It's housed inside a beautiful old bank building topped by a clock tower in the heart of Saint-Henri. The old bank vault is still used as a walk-in cellar while the rest of the room has been revamped into a great dining room with stone walls, warm wood panels and tables, and elegant black leather chairs. Northern winters can be harsh in terms of product availabilities yet the chef manages to created refined and inspired plates such as the ricotta *gnuddi* (a ricotta-based gnocchi or dumpling) with mushrooms or the pear, black olive, orange and fennel dessert that have been dubbed real "chefs d'œuvres" by local food lovers and fans. The brunch menu is just as creative and includes house-made beignets, jams and spreads, a foie gras parfait, and a riff on the classic pancakes with theirs being made with apples, a homemade yogurt, and maple syrup. Reservations are recommended. [$] *Average main: C$28* ✉ *538 Place Saint-Henri* ☎ *514/316–7234* 🌐 *www.leh4c.com* 🕒 *Closed Sun. and Mon. No brunch Sat. No lunch* [M] *Place St-Henri* ✥ *A5.*

VERDUN

Low rent and proximity to Downtown make Verdun attractive to small chef-owned restaurants. Choices run the gamut from fast food to high-end restaurants, with interesting ethnic eats as well.

$$
SOUTHERN
Fodor's Choice
★

✕ **Blackstrap.** Southern barbecue is the name of the game at this popular, self-serve spot owned and operated by a champion pit master honing his skill behind the smoker and Missouri-imported barbecue pits. Pork, brisket, chicken and ribs all get a secret-rub treatment and are then cooked slowly for up to 16 hours. Try the excellent braised greens or the top-notch "burnt ends" poutine topped with charred, fatty, and smoky bits of brisket. Blackstrap uses meat sourced from local Québec farms and the restaurant's bread is made by a local artisanal bakery. $ *Average main: C$15* ✉ *4436 rue Wellington, Verdun* ☎ *514/507–6772* ⊕ *www.blackstrapbbq.ca* ⌂ *Reservations not accepted* Ⓜ *De l'Église* ✛ *A4.*

$$$
TURKISH
Fodor's Choice
★

✕ **Su.** The vibrant blue and white decor of this airy restaurant will make you feel like you've been transported to the Mediterranean, and owner Fisun Ercan is recognized as one of the most authentic Turkish chefs in Montréal. Everything served here is fresh and made in-house. Start off by ordering a selection of *mezzes* (appetizers) to share, like the *zeytinyagli enginar* (artichoke bottoms topped with carrots, fava beans and dill) or the *sudjuk* (homemade lamb sausages), then move on to hearty mains. The house *manti*, which is basically homemade ravioli stuffed with meat and served with a yogurt sauce, is delicious, and the baklava is as authentic as it comes on this side of Turkey. ■ TIP➜ **There are a lot of options available for vegetarians.** $ *Average main: C$28* ✉ *5145 rue Wellington, Verdun* ☎ *514/362–1818* ⊕ *www.restaurantsu. com* ⊗ *Closed Mon. and Sun. No lunch Tues.–Fri.* Ⓜ *De l'Eglise, bus 61 west* ✛ *A4.*

ROSEMONT

The neighborhood of Rosemont is just east of the Plateau.

$$$
BISTRO

✕ **M sur Masson.** The menu at M sur Masson is filled with dishes that are satisfyingly traditional but with enough creative twists to keep food lovers interested. The French onion soup is one of the best around, making use of a deep-flavored Swiss Gruyère des Grottes, and if veal liver is your thing, this is the place to order it. The old cheddar poutine is the house specialty and makes a definitely satisfying lunch. The dining room, lined with wooden benches and globe-shaped light fixtures, is appropriately bistro-esque. If you're coming for Sunday brunch, be sure to reserve a table. $ *Average main: C$25* ✉ *2876 rue Masson, Rosemont* ☎ *514/678–2999* ⊕ *www.msurmasson.com* ⌂ *Reservations essential* ⊗ *No lunch weekends. No brunch Sat.* ✛ *G1.*

WHERE TO STAY

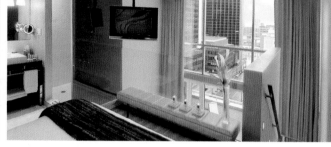

Updated by
Joanne Latimer

Montréal is a city of neighborhoods with distinct personalities, which creates a broad spectrum of options when it comes to deciding on a place to stay. The Downtown core has many of the big chain hotels you'd find in any city, while Old Montréal, the Plateau, and other surrounding areas have unique *auberges* (inns) and boutique hotels.

Most of the major hotels in Downtown—the ones with big meeting rooms, swimming pools, and several bars and restaurants—are ideal for those who want all the facilities along with easy access to the department stores and malls on rue Ste-Catherine, the museums of the Golden Square Mile, and nightlife on rues Crescent and de la Montagne. If you want something a little more historic, consider renting a room in one of the dozen or so boutique hotels that occupy the centuries-old buildings lining the cobbled streets of Old Montréal. Most of them offer all the conveniences along with the added charm of stone walls, casement windows, and period-style furnishings.

If your plans include shopping expeditions to avenue Mont-Royal and rue Laurier with maybe a few late nights at the jazz bars and dance clubs of Boulevard St. Laurent and rue St-Denis, then the place to bed down is in one of Plateau Mont-Royal's small but comfortable hotels. Room rates in the area tend to be quite reasonable, but be careful: The hotels right in the middle of the action—on rue St-Denis for example—can be noisy, especially if you get a room fronting the street.

PLANNING

RESERVATIONS

Montréal is always hosting a festival or an international convention, so the hotels are consistently booked. This takes tourists by surprise. Many of the quaint auberges have a small number of rooms, so they fill up fast. It's necessary to book months ahead for the Grand Prix, the Jazz Festival, the World Film Festival, and all holiday weekends.

	NEIGHBORHOOD VIBE	PROS	CONS
Old Montréal	Horse-drawn carriages, boutique hotels, designer clothes, and historic architecture; very touristy, although it quiets down at night.	Quaint; easy access to bike paths; nice to walk along the waterfront; several hip restaurants are at the Old Port.	Can be desolate in the late evening outside hotel lobbies; parking is scarce; depending on the exact location, métro and bus access can be limited.
Downtown	Montréal's center for hustle and bustle, centering on always-crowded rue Ste-Catherine and boulevard René Lévesque.	Extremely convenient; big-name hotel chains; central location; garage parking; perfect for families as well as business travelers.	Traffic congestion can be unpleasant; not as many dining options as other neighborhoods, and what is there tends to be at either extreme—fast food or very pricey (and not always worth it).
The Latin Quarter	Hopping with university kids and moviegoers, this area boasts a crazy mix of cafés, handmade chocolate shops, and folks carrying library books.	Quick stroll to main festival artery; easy métro access; right between the Plateau and Downtown; local characters abound.	Uneven gentrification means dodgy pockets; litter; bad roads.
The Plateau and Environs	Scattered auberges and B&Bs host the artsy crowd and academics, with streets filled with local boutiques and hip restaurants; perfect for strolling.	Stumbling distance to the best bistros and pubs; unique shopping that focuses on local designers and craftspeople.	Limited métro and taxi access; limited hotel selections; can be noisy at night; panhandlers galore.
Mont-Royal and Environs	There are only a few hotels in this quiet section of the city, located in the shadow of the immense Parc du Mont-Royal.	Unhurried pace; lots of green space; lower rates.	Limited métro access; few dining options.

■TIP→ From mid-November to early April rates often drop, and throughout the year many hotels have two-night, three-day, double-occupancy packages at substantial discounts.

FACILITIES

When pricing accommodations, ask what's included. You can assume that all rooms have private baths, phones, and TVs unless otherwise noted. If no meals are included in the room rate, "No meals" is stated toward the end of the review. Breakfast is noted when it's included in the rate.

Most hotels are wired, with a business center in the lobby. Smaller auberges may not have televisions and air-conditioning, but often have Wi-Fi.

Bathtubs, plush bathrobes, and fluffy white duvets are popular here for winter comfort. Bigger hotels have day spas and health clubs, as well as some of the city's finest restaurants.

WITH KIDS

Most of the chain hotels—Hilton, for example—have great pools. Avoid smaller auberges, however, because noise travels and the charming ambience doesn't go far with children. Hotels in the Old Port are popular with families because they're near the Centre des Sciences de Montréal and the Lachine Canal bike path.

Given that they are in a major city, the hotel rooms here are generous. Budget rooms and auberges are the exception, with rooms measuring less than 300 square feet. Otherwise, expect standard sizes of about 400–700 square feet.

PARKING

Parking is a sore point in Old Montréal. Your car will feel like a tank on the narrow streets, and you can expect to pay heftily for valet service in this part of town. Elsewhere, there's often parking available under the large-scale hotels. This is a blessing in winter, when you don't want to shovel snow and de-ice your car. If possible, avoid taking your car.

PRICES

Aside from during the Grand Prix, the World Film Festival, and the Jazz Festival, it's possible to get a decent hotel room in high season for C\$200 to C\$300. Take advantage of web-only deals and ask about promotions.

WHAT IT COSTS IN CANADIAN DOLLARS			
\$	**\$\$**	**\$\$\$**	**\$\$\$\$**
Hotels	under C\$160	C\$160–C\$200	C\$201–C\$250	over C\$250

Hotel prices are the lowest cost of a standard double room in high season.

MONTRÉAL HOTEL REVIEWS

Reviews are listed alphabetically within neighborhoods.

Hotel reviews have been shortened. For full information, visit Fodors. com.

Use the coordinate (✢ B2) at the end of each listing to locate a site on the corresponding map.

OLD MONTRÉAL (VIEUX-MONTRÉAL)

Let's start with the name. Nobody says "Old Town." That's an American phrase. You may call it Old Montréal, but street signs say "Vieux-Montréal," in French. Either way, it's full of charm—from narrow, cobblestone streets to horse-drawn carriages. You can find boutique hotels, auberges, and cozy bed-and-breakfasts nestled inside heritage buildings. Most properties have exposed beams, stone walls, wooden floors, and thick, casement windows. History buffs find this area pleasing, as do people who want to wander around boutiques and art galleries. But remember, this is no place for stilettos. Bring your walking shoes

BEST BETS FOR MONTRÉAL LODGING

Fodor's offers a selective listing of quality lodging experiences in every price range, from the city's best budget beds to its most sophisticated luxury hotels. Here, we've compiled our top recommendations by price and experience. The very best properties—in other words, those that provide a particularly remarkable experience in their price range—are designated in the listings with the Fodor's Choice logo.

Fodor's Choice ★

ALT Montréal Griffin-town, $, p. 184
Auberge du Vieux-Port, $$$, p. 184
Épik Montreal, $$, p. 184
Hotel 10, $$$, p. 191
Hôtel Gault, $$$, p. 184
Hôtel Le St-James, $$$$, p. 185
Hôtel Nelligan, $$$, p. 185
Le Petit Hôtel, $$$, p. 185
Le Place d'Armes Hôtel & Suites, $$$, p. 185
Loews Hôtel Vogue, $$$, p. 190
Ritz-Carlton Montréal, $$$$, p. 190
Sofitel Montréal, $$, p. 190
W Montréal, $$$$, p. 186

Best by Price

$

ALT Montréal Griffin-town, p. 184

Hôtel Terrasse Royale, p. 192

$$

Delta Montréal, p. 188
Épik Montreal, p. 184
Hilton Montréal Bonaventure, p. 188
Hôtel Chez Swann, p. 188
Hôtel St. Paul, p. 185
Sofitel Montréal, p. 190

$$$

Auberge du Vieux-Port, p. 184
Hotel 10, p. 191
Hôtel Gault, p. 184
Hôtel Nelligan, p. 185
Le Petit Hôtel, p. 185
Le Place d'Armes Hôtel & Suites, p. 185
Loews Hôtel Vogue, p. 190

$$$$

Hôtel Le St-James, p. 185
Le Saint-Sulpice, p. 186
Ritz-Carlton Montréal, p. 190
W Montréal, p. 186

Best by Experience

BEST CELEBRITY RETREAT

Le Saint-Sulpice, $$$$, p. 186
Loews Hôtel Vogue, $$$, p. 190
Ritz-Carlton Montréal, $$$$, p. 190
Sofitel Montréal, $$, p. 190

BEST HOTEL BAR

Hôtel Nelligan, $$$, p. 185
InterContinental Montréal, $$, p. 185
Le Place d'Armes Hôtel & Suites, $$$, p. 185
Ritz-Carlton Montréal, $$$$, p. 190

BEST FOR ROMANCE

Auberge du Vieux-Port, $$$, p. 184
Épik Montreal, $$, p. 184
Hôtel Nelligan, $$$, p. 185

Le Petit Hôtel, $$$, p. 185

BEST BOUTIQUE HOTELS

Hôtel Le St-James, $$$$, p. 185
LHOTEL, $$, p. 186

BEST HIPSTER HOTELS

ALT Montréal Griffin-town, $, p. 184
Hotel 10, $$$, p. 191
Hôtel Chez Swann, $$, p. 188
Hôtel St. Paul, $$, p. 185
W Montréal, $$$$, p. 186

BEST INTERIOR DESIGN

Hôtel Chez Swann, $$, p. 188
Hôtel Gault, $$$, p. 184
W Montréal, $$$$, p. 186

BEST POOLS

Delta Montréal, $$, p. 188
Hilton Montréal Bonaventure, $$, p. 188

BEST NEW HOTELS

ALT Montréal Griffin-town, $, p. 184
Hotel 10, $$$, p. 191
Hôtel Chez Swann, $$, p. 188
Le Petit Hôtel, $$$, p. 185
Le St-Martin Hôtel Particulier, $$$$, p. 190

8

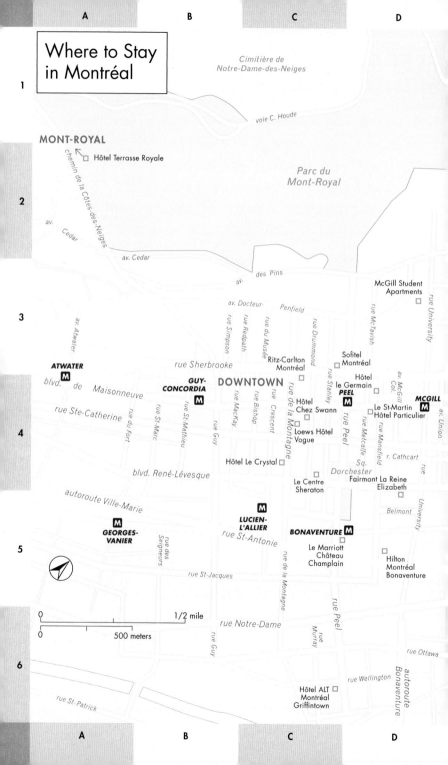

Where to Stay in Montréal

Cimitière de Notre-Dame-des-Neiges

voie C. Houde

MONT-ROYAL

Hôtel Terrasse Royale

chemin de la Côtes-des-Neiges

Parc du Mont-Royal

av. Cedar

av. Cedar

des Pins

av. Docteur-Penfield

McGill Student Apartments

rue McTavish

av. McGill Col.

rue University

av. Atwater

rue Simpson

rue Redpath

rue du Musée

rue Drummond

Sofitel Montréal

Hôtel le Germain

ATWATER
Ⓜ

rue Sherbrooke

Ritz-Carlton Montréal

rue Stanley

PEEL
Ⓜ

Le St-Martin Hôtel Particulier

MCGILL
Ⓜ

av. Union

blvd. de Maisonneuve

GUY-CONCORDIA
Ⓜ

DOWNTOWN

rue Metcalfe

rue Mansfield

rue Ste-Catherine

rue St-Marc

rue St-Mathieu

rue MacKay

rue Bishop

rue Crescent

rue de la Montagne

rue Peel

Hôtel Chez Swann

Loews Hôtel Vogue

r. Cathcart

rue Guy

Hôtel Le Crystal

blvd. René-Lévesque

Sq. Dorchester

Fairmont La Reine Elizabeth

rue University

autoroute Ville-Marie

GEORGES-VANIER
Ⓜ

rue des Seigneurs

LUCIEN-L'ALLIER
Ⓜ

rue St-Antonie

Le Centre Sheraton

Belmont

BONAVENTURE
Ⓜ

Le Marriott Château Champlain

Hilton Montréal Bonaventure

rue St-Jacques

rue de la Montagne

0   1/2 mile
0   500 meters

rue Notre-Dame

rue Guy

rue Murray

rue Peel

rue Ottawa

Hôtel ALT Montréal Griffintown

rue Wellington

autoroute Bonaventure

rue St-Patrick

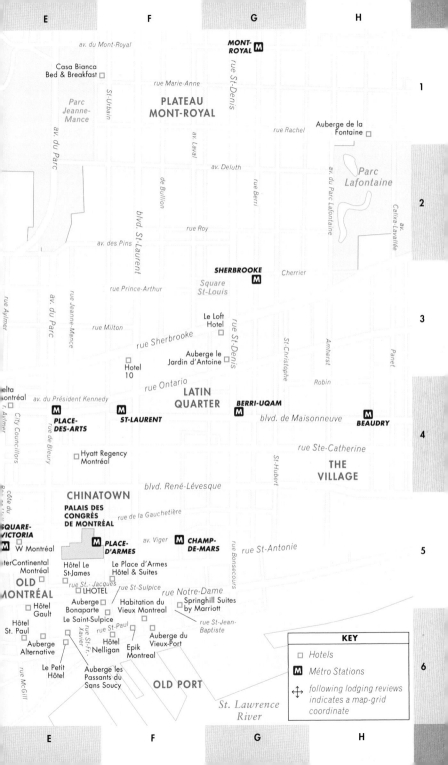

and expect to stumble upon film crews and the occasional Hollywood actor taking a smoke break. I'm talking to you, Brad Pitt.

$ HOTEL Fodor's Choice ★ **ALT Montreal Griffintown.** Savvy young hipsters and budget-conscious artsies flock to ALT in Griffintown (and its sister in Brossard) because of the exceptional style and comfort provided for the miraculous (set) rate of $149 a night. **Pros:** razzle-dazzle lobby design; Starbucks in lobby; underground parking; family-owned feel in a modern context. **Cons:** no valet; no king-size beds or tubs; guests are "forced" to experience Montréal's array of restaurants. [$] *Rooms from: C$149* ✉ *120 rue Peel, Old Montréal* ☎ *514/375–0220* 🌐 *althotels.ca* 🛏 *154 rooms* 🍴 *No meals* ✥ *C6.*

$$ B&B/INN **Auberge Bonaparte.** Stately and distinguished, Bonaporte feels like a private library tucked inside a 19th-century building, with a romantic inn upstairs; keep heading upward and you'll find the newly expanded rooftop terrace, with great views. **Pros:** luxury car service to airport for $50; free access to two local gyms; dazzling solarium; perfect for theater lovers—the Centaur Theatre is next door. **Cons:** downstairs restaurant can be a bit noisy on weekends; not suitable for rambunctious kids. [$] *Rooms from: C$195* ✉ *447 rue St-François-Xavier, Old Montréal* ☎ *514/844–1448* 🌐 *www.bonaparte.ca* 🛏 *30 rooms, 1 suite* 🍴 *Breakfast* [M] *Place-d'Armes* ✥ *F5.*

$$$ B&B/INN Fodor's Choice ★ **Auberge du Vieux-Port.** With stone and brick walls, casement windows, wood floors, and exposed beams, this elegant auberge is a magnet for romantics who appreciate the view of the river and a welcoming staff. **Pros:** warm staff; expansive rooftop deck with retractable cover; multijet showers. **Cons:** occasional bouts of noise in street-facing rooms; smallest rooms can feel claustrophobic. [$] *Rooms from: C$229* ✉ *97 rue de la Commune Est, Old Montréal* ☎ *514/876–0081, 888/660–7678* 🌐 *www.aubergeduvieuxport.com* 🛏 *45 rooms* 🍴 *Breakfast* [M] *Place-d'Armes or Champ-de-Mars* ✥ *F6.*

$$ B&B/INN Fodor's Choice ★ **Épik Montreal.** With its rustic stone walls and exposed beams, this inn was the first of its kind in the Old Port when it opened as the Auberge les Passants du Sans Soucy back in 1989, and the new owners are honoring its tradition of calm excellence. **Pros:** exquisitely personal service; guests can use refrigerator downstairs; restaurant in lobby serves three meals a day. **Cons:** rooms need to be booked far in advance; not suitable for lively kids; only select rooms have tubs. [$] *Rooms from: C$160* ✉ *171 rue St-Paul Ouest, Old Montréal* ☎ *514/842–2634* 🌐 *www.epikmontreal.com* 🛏 *9 rooms, 1 suite* 🍴 *Breakfast* [M] *Square-Victoria or Place-d'Armes* ✥ *F6.*

$$$ HOTEL Fodor's Choice ★ **Hôtel Gault.** A heritage boutique hotel with serious design chops, the Gault attracts movie stars and style mavens, none of whom would ever guess it was a cotton factory in the 1800s. **Pros:** Fodorites love the intimate vibe; iPads to borrow at front desk; 24/7 room service; DVDs to rent. **Cons:** a bit hard to find; $35 valet; no pool. [$] *Rooms from: C$249* ✉ *449 rue Ste-Hélène, Old Montréal* ☎ *514/904–1616, 866/904–1616* 🌐 *www.hotelgault.com* 🛏 *30 suites* 🍴 *No meals* [M] *Square-Victoria* ✥ *E5.*

$$$$ HOTEL FAMILY Fodor's Choice ★ 🏨 **Hôtel Le St-James.** Rock royalty frequents this lavishly furnished luxury hotel, which has also pampered European nobility, the business elite, and Hollywood moguls who appreciate the splendor. **Pros:** civility reigns; lush experience and stately lobby; kids get milk and cookies at check-in. **Cons:** rue St-Jacques is very quiet after 6 pm; dog rate starts at $40 per day. [$] *Rooms from: C$400* ✉ *355 rue St-Jacques, Old Montréal* ☎ *514/841–3111, 866/841–3111* 🌐 *www.hotellestjames.com* 🛏 *23 rooms, 38 suites, 1 apartment* 🍴 *No meals* [M] *Square-Victoria* ✥ *E5.*

$$$ HOTEL Fodor's Choice ★ 🏨 **Hôtel Nelligan.** There's a cultivated air of refinement echoing through this ultraromantic hotel, a landmark on rue St-Paul named after Québec's most passionate poet, Émile Nelligan. **Pros:** cozy rooms; great views from the rooftop terrace and restaurant; lively bar right on rue St-Paul; huge bath tubs. **Cons:** weekend wedding traffic; valet parking is $28 plus tax. [$] *Rooms from: C$239* ✉ *106 rue St-Paul Ouest, Old Montréal* ☎ *514/788–2040, 877/788–2040* 🌐 *www.hotelnelligan.com* 🛏 *44 rooms, 59 suites, 2 penthouses* 🍴 *No meals* [M] *Place-d'Armes* ✥ *F6.*

$$ HOTEL 🏨 **Hôtel St. Paul.** Forget fussy oil paintings or rococo furniture—behind its 19th-century facade the St. Paul keeps the focus on modern silk, stone, and raw-metal accents, much admired by its fashionable guests, who rave about the serenity and panoramic Old Port views. **Pros:** free Wi-Fi everywhere; lobby fireplace; great location. **Cons:** under-lit hallways and elevators can be spooky; fur throws and off-white sofas in lobby need refreshing. [$] *Rooms from: C$195* ✉ *355 rue McGill, Old Montréal* ☎ *514/380–2222, 866/380–2202* 🌐 *www.hotelstpaul.com* 🛏 *96 rooms, 24 suites* 🍴 *No meals* [M] *Square-Victoria* ✥ *E6.*

$$ HOTEL 🏨 **InterContinental Montréal.** On the edge of Old Montréal, this award-winning luxury hotel is part of the Montréal World Trade Center, drawing international business travelers and design-savvy tourists. **Pros:** iPod alarm clocks; easy underground access to shopping and nightlife; new Java U café in lobby. **Cons:** business-oriented (convention center is across the street); a bit posh for families with youngsters. [$] *Rooms from: C$179* ✉ *360 rue St-Antoine Ouest, Old Montréal* ☎ *514/987–9900, 800/361–3600* 🌐 *www.montreal.intercontinental.com* 🛏 *334 rooms, 23 suites* 🍴 *No meals* [M] *Square-Victoria or Place-d'Armes* ✥ *E5.*

$$$ HOTEL FAMILY Fodor's Choice ★ 🏨 **Le Petit Hôtel.** Couples seeking a hideaway can find it at this quiet boutique hotel that marries modern design with old stone walls and exposed beams. **Pros:** fun design; two free bicycles available; chic lobby café expanded next door; cribs, playpens, and babysitters available. **Cons:** smallish bathrooms have no tubs; the $28 fee for valet parking is steep, but it's the going rate. [$] *Rooms from: C$229* ✉ *168 rue St-Paul Ouest, Old Montréal* ☎ *514/940–0360, 877/530–0360* 🌐 *www.petithotelmontreal.com* 🛏 *28 rooms* 🍴 *Breakfast* [M] *Square-Victoria* ✥ *E6.*

$$$ HOTEL FAMILY Fodor's Choice ★ 🏨 **Le Place d'Armes Hôtel & Suites.** Three splendidly ornate Victorian commercial buildings were merged to create Old Montréal's largest boutique hotel, pleasing jetsetters and business execs alike with rooms that combine old-fashioned grandeur with sleek modern furnishings. **Pros:** best spa in town; new Japanese tavern serves *hamachi bibimbap* (marinated

yellowtail). **Cons:** late sleepers may be disturbed by the noontime Angelus bells at the basilica; steep approach from métro is slippery in winter; no pool. [$] *Rooms from: C$239* ✉ *55 rue St-Jacques, Old Montréal* ☎ *514/842–1887, 888/450–1887* 🌐 *www.hotelplacedarmes.com* 🛏 *80 rooms, 53 suites* 🍴 *No meals* [M] *Place-d'Armes* ✣ *F5.*

$$$$ HOTEL 🏨 **Le Saint-Sulpice.** Celebrities emerging from limousines outside, the Basilique Notre-Dame-de-Montréal next door, and a chic lobby lounge opening onto a courtyard garden that's one of the rare green spots in Old Montréal's stony landscape—these all add to the appeal of this winning hotel. **Pros:** in-room massage service; excellent celebrity-spotting; easy access to the Basilique Notre-Dame de Montréal. **Cons:** church bells on Sunday morning may disturb late sleepers; too fancy for kids to run around. [$] *Rooms from: C$269* ✉ *414 rue St-Sulpice, Old Montréal* ☎ *514/288–1000, 877/785–7423* 🌐 *www.lesaintsulpice.com* 🛏 *108 suites* 🍴 *Multiple meal plans* [M] *Place-d'Armes* ✣ *F6.*

$$ HOTEL 🏨 **LHOTEL.** Fashion mogul George Marciano, the man behind Guess? jeans, bought this opulent hotel in the financial district to double as a personal art gallery and opulent guest house for his well-heeled friends (note the Ferraris parked outside). **Pros:** pop art galore; big high-ceiling rooms; lively bar in lobby with new boutique; buffet continental breakfast served in a deco setting. **Cons:** pop art lurking inside a Grande Dame exterior isn't for everyone; street parking is scarce; rue St-Jacques is deadly dull after 6 pm. [$] *Rooms from: C$185* ✉ *262 rue St-Jacques Ouest, Old Montréal* ☎ *514/985–0019, 877/553–0019* 🌐 *www.lhotelmontreal.com* 🛏 *41 rooms, 14 suites* 🍴 *Breakfast* [M] *Square-Victoria* ✣ *E5.*

$$$ HOTEL FAMILY 🏨 **Springhill Suites by Marriott.** Handy and quiet, with large rooms and underground parking—all rarities in Old Montréal—this fairly basic all-suites hotel attracts families, government employees, and business travelers who want standardized service in an old world location. **Pros:** free, bountiful breakfast with healthy options; saltwater pool; Häagen-Dazs, Lean Cuisines, and gluten-free items for sale in the lobby. **Cons:** not much style for the money; difficult access on a narrow street; poor views. [$] *Rooms from: C$225* ✉ *445 rue St-Jean-Baptiste, Old Montréal* ☎ *514/875–4333, 888/287–9400* 🌐 *www.springhillsuites.com* 🛏 *124 suites* 🍴 *Breakfast* [M] *Champ-de-Mars* ✣ *F5.*

$$$$ HOTEL Fodor's Choice ★ 🏨 **W Montréal.** The luxurious W chain's first Canadian hotel arrived in 2004, inside the old Bank of Canada building, but you'd never suspect it was a decade old after being greeted by the cubic water fountain and glowing red walls of the lobby. **Pros:** guests feel like rock stars; good people-watching; sexy bathrooms; fastest room service in town; pet program. **Cons:** $15 per night fee for in-room WiFi (it's free in the lobby); lobby noisy at night; showers afford no privacy. [$] *Rooms from: C$299* ✉ *901 Square Victoria, Old Montréal* ☎ *514/395–3100* 🌐 *www.whotels.com/montreal* 🛏 *152 rooms, 28 suites* 🍴 *No meals* [M] *Square-Victoria* ✣ *E5.*

CLOSE UP

Lodging Alternatives

There are many reasons for travelers to consider apartment rentals or other lodging alternatives, but we tend to recommend hotel suites instead. Why? Unfortunately, apartment rental scams in Montréal are prevalent—especially when booked online. In some published reports, potential guests have arrived to find that the apartment they rented doesn't exist, or that they're paying for an illegal sublet. (Note: Never wire money to an individual's account.)

There are, however, reputable providers of short- and long-term rentals; our favorites are below. Most will fill advanced grocery orders, for a service fee.

LOFT AND APARTMENT RENTALS
Fully furnished lofts—some with closed bedrooms—and apartments are available through these esteemed companies:

Habitation du Vieux Montréal. Habitation du Vieux Montréal rents out five apartments in one building in the Old Port on St. Laurent Boulevard at the corner of St. Paul. Completely independent, each unit is fully equipped—from kitchen to bathroom to bedding. Guests appreciate the welcome basket of teas and coffees, plus the new flat-screens. Expect street noise at night in the summer. Prices range from $130 to $275 a night. ☎ 514/892–1238 ⊕ www. habitationvieuxmontreal.ca ⊹ F6.

Lofts du Vieux-Port. This agency has 24 apartment-style lofts scattered throughout the Old Port. The lofts are chic and sexy, with a mix of antiques and modern design, attracting film people, sports stars, and others who like the room-service option and

laundry service. No elevators, but valets carry your luggage. Short- and long-term rentals. ☎ 514/876–0081 ⊕ www.loftsduvieuxport.com.

STUDENT HOUSING
McGill Student Apartments. From mid-May to mid-August, backpackers and families stay in these apartments in a former hotel that's off of the McGill campus. Smug budget travelers congratulate themselves for finding this gem. Use of the school's swimming pool, and gym facilities costs a little bit extra. The university cafeteria is open during the week, serving breakfast and lunch. Rates start at $99 for a private room with a double bed. Rates reach $149 for a suite. ☎ 514/398–5200 ⊕ www.mcgill. ca/students/housing/summer.

B&BS
Some B&Bs are off the grid. They prefer to remain private and hush-hush. To find them, simply walk the streets of the Village, specifically rues St-Andre, St-Christophe, and St-Timothée, below rue Sherbrooke. Or, ask any of the friendly locals, who'll be more than glad to point you in the direction of their friend's B&B. ⇨ *For more information on B&Bs, see Travel Smart Montréal and Québec City.*

—Joanne Latimer

8

DOWNTOWN

The hub for countless festivals, Downtown is a convenient place to unpack your bags. This is where you'll find the major chain hotels, with underground parking, pools, and all the amenities that families enjoy. A few new boutique hotels have appeared in recent years, providing more options for couples without kids. From Downtown, it's just a short trip—via bike path, métro or taxi—to the city's other neighborhoods of interest, so this is a good central point from which to see the city.

$$ HOTEL FAMILY **Delta Montréal.** Government employees and jazz festival performers cycle through the Delta regularly, ignoring the airport-like lobby to revel in rooms that overlook the mountain or downtown. **Pros:** gym has a play area for kids; excellent soundproofing; kids have their own check-in procedure. **Cons:** a lobby makeover's overdue; no safes in room; Restaurant Aroma is OK but no place for a date. [$] *Rooms from: C$199 ✉ 475 av. du Président-Kennedy, Downtown ☎ 514/286–1986, 877/286–1986 🌐 www.deltamontreal.com 🛏 447 rooms, 9 suites 🍴 No meals [M] McGill or Place des Arts ✣ E4.*

$$$ HOTEL **Fairmont Le Reine Elizabeth.** Built to impress international guests during Expo 67, this was also the iconic setting for John and Yoko's second "bed-in for peace" of 1969, but it's hardly stuck in the past, and will certainly please eco-conscious guests. **Pros:** chic gym open 24 hours; easy access to trains and métro; electric car docking station. **Cons:** $16 per day for Wi-Fi except for President's Club members (it's free to join); lobby is drab and as busy as a train station; conventioneers abound. [$] *Rooms from: C$239 ✉ 900 blvd. René-Lévesque Ouest, Downtown ☎ 514/861–3511, 800/441–1414 🌐 www.fairmont.com 🛏 937 rooms, 100 suites 🍴 No meals [M] Bonaventure ✣ D5.*

$$ HOTEL FAMILY **Hilton Montréal Bonaventure.** Two and a half acres of rooftop gardens and an open-air swimming pool set the Hilton apart from the usual corporate hotels and make it a great place to take the family, and the location atop the Place Bonaventure exhibition center couldn't be more convenient. **Pros:** almost every room has a view of the rooftop garden; easy access to the métro and the Underground City; year-round pool heated by the kitchen's steam; in-room spa services; free Wi-Fi. **Cons:** lots of business traffic; ground-floor entrance—with elevator ride to reception—isn't so welcoming. [$] *Rooms from: C$189 ✉ 900 rue de la Gauchetière, Downtown ☎ 514/878–2332, 800/267–2575 🌐 www.hilton.com 🛏 395 rooms, 15 suites 🍴 Multiple meal plans [M] Bonaventure ✣ D5.*

$$ HOTEL **Hôtel Chez Swann.** Young culture vultures are tripping over themselves to get a room at this boutique hotel—the name's a reference to Proust—to bask in its dramatic and quirky interior design. **Pros:** hip design; in-room spa treatments; downtown location; spin room; free phone calls within North America. **Cons:** no bath tubs; no pets; not suitable for kids. [$] *Rooms from: C$170 ✉ 1444 rue Drummond, Downtown ☎ 514/842–7070 🌐 www.hotelchezswann.com 🛏 7 rooms, 16 suites 🍴 Breakfast [M] Peel ✣ C4.*

$$$ HOTEL **Hôtel Le Crystal.** It's no wonder A-list performers stay here, considering Le Crystal's dramatic style and luxury suites, which pamper travelers with spa-style bathrooms and separate soaking tubs. **Pros:** best city

view from the treadmills; near Centre Bell and best shopping streets; saltwater pool; outdoor year-round whirlpool hot tub. **Cons:** not suitable for kids; rather formal; right on the sidewalk of a busy intersection. $ *Rooms from: C$229* ⊠ *1100 de la Montagne, Downtown* ☎ *514/861–5550* ⊕ *www.hotellecrystal.com* ⇨ *131 suites* ⫶◎⫶ *No meals* Ⓜ *Lucien-L'Aller* ✛ *C4.*

$$$
HOTEL

⫶⫱⫶ **Hôtel le Germain.** The lobby in this sleek boutique hotel is peppered with models, record producers, and all varieties of international hipsters, who delight in stylish room details like bedding designed by Québec fashion icon Marie Saint Pierre. **Pros:** free Wi-Fi; top chef Daniel Vézina heads the restaurant; deluxe continental breakfast included; quiet location in the heart of downtown; connectivity panels project your laptop onto a 42-inch screen. **Cons:** on a charmless urban street; parking is scarce, and the valet is $25; the lobby is starting to bore regulars. $ *Rooms from: C$239* ⊠ *2050 rue Mansfield, Downtown* ☎ *514/849–2050, 877/333–2050* ⊕ *www.hotelgermain.com* ⇨ *99 rooms, 2 suites* ⫶◎⫶ *Multiple meal plans* Ⓜ *Peel or McGill* ✛ *D4.*

$$
HOTEL

⫶⫱⫶ **Hyatt Regency Montréal.** The Hyatt is *the* place to stay for the Just For Laughs Festival and the International Jazz Festival in July—it overlooks the Place des Arts plaza where most of the festivals' free events are staged—and is in a good location the rest of the year, too. **Pros:** great location for concert lovers; easy access to the Underground City; indoor pool and lounge; dinner served until 11:30 pm. **Cons:** strange approach to lobby via elevator; $9.95–$12.95 per day for in-room Wi-Fi; no lunch served; networking and careerism rules the bar and reception areas, so this might not be the best hotel to get away from it all. $ *Rooms from: C$169* ⊠ *1255 rue Jeanne-Mance, Downtown* ☎ *514/982–1234, 800/361–8234* ⊕ *www.montreal.hyatt.com/property* ⇨ *605 rooms, 11 suites* ⫶◎⫶ *No meals* Ⓜ *Place des Arts or Place-d'Armes* ✛ *E4.*

$
HOTEL
FAMILY

⫶⫱⫶ **Le Centre Sheraton.** At this magnet for conventioneers, hockey fans, and businesspeople, the lobby bar draws boisterous guests for drinks and networking, and the morning crowd shares newspapers at the in-house Starbucks café. **Pros:** "Sheraton Link" digital hub in lobby; huge gym with new terrace and views; meal deals and restaurant distractions for kids; close to the Centre Bell for hockey and concerts. **Cons:** lobby marred by convention signs; no in-hotel access to the métro; executive club lounge on the 37th floor costs $50 more. $ *Rooms from: C$159* ⊠ *1201 blvd. René-Lévesque Ouest, Downtown* ☎ *514/878–2000, 800/325–3535* ⊕ *www.sheraton.com/lecentre* ⇨ *785 rooms, 40 suites* ⫶◎⫶ *No meals* Ⓜ *Bonaventure or Peel* ✛ *C4.*

$$$
HOTEL

⫶⫱⫶ **Le Marriott Château Champlain.** An icon from the 1967 Olympics, this 36-floor skyscraper overlooking Place du Canada attracts business guests and families alike with its electronic gadgetry, indoor links to the métro and Underground City, and great views. **Pros:** expansive views; park-side location; top three floors have private lounges. **Cons:** a favorite for parties, proms, and receptions; off-putting reception desk. $ *Rooms from: C$249* ⊠ *1050 rue de la Gauchetière Ouest, Downtown* ☎ *514/878–9000, 800/200–5909* ⊕ *www.marriott.com* ⇨ *578 rooms, 33 suites* ⫶◎⫶ *No meals* Ⓜ *Bonaventure* ✛ *C5.*

8

$$ HOTEL FAMILY

Le St-Martin Hôtel Particulier. Sober and chic, this tasteful hotel is in a great location for shopping and restaurants, and the year-round heated pool makes it good for families. **Pros:** windows have excellent soundproofing; kids under 12 stay for free; soaker tubs and TV in bathrooms; very good restaurant. **Cons:** reception is just steps from the sidewalk and gets crowded at checkout; no spa; small outdoor pool often in shade. [$] *Rooms from: C$199* ✉ *980 blvd. de Maisonneuve Ouest, Downtown* ☎ *514/843–3000, 877/843–3003* 🌐 *www.lestmartinmontreal.com* 🛏 *71 rooms, 42 suites* 🍴 *Multiple meal plans* [M] *Peel* ✣ *D4.*

$$$ HOTEL FAMILY Fodor's Choice ★

Loews Hôtel Vogue. Serious shoppers like the location (a five-minute walk from Holt Renfrew, Ogilvy, and other high-end boutiques) and the luxury of this downtown boutique hotel, a celebrity haunt that in 2014 spent C$10 million making the facade, lobby, and guest rooms super sexy. **Pros:** laptop-friendly tub chairs in the lobby; huge bathrooms with flat-screen TVs and phones; toys available for kids, and under 12s eat free in high season. **Cons:** higher speed Wi-Fi is $14.95; valet parking costs $35. [$] *Rooms from: C$249* ✉ *1425 rue de la Montagne, Downtown* ☎ *514/285–5555, 800/465–6654* 🌐 *www.loewshotels.com* 🛏 *126 rooms, 16 suites* 🍴 *No meals* [M] *Peel* ✣ *C4.*

$$$$ HOTEL Fodor's Choice ★

Ritz-Carlton Montréal. Montréal's grandest hotel, in the Golden Square Mile, was extensively renovated in 2012, but preserved important elements—the Palm Court (now housing a Dom Perignon bar), the Oval Room, the garden—alongside additions like a Daniel Boulud restaurant and an infinity pool. **Pros:** revived style, but still plenty of history; state-of-the-art bathrooms; high-end shopping and galleries within a five-minute walk; infinity pool with patio. **Cons:** poor métro access; Sherbrooke Street can be barren on weeknights. [$] *Rooms from: C$425* ✉ *1228 rue Sherbrooke Ouest, Downtown* ☎ *514/842–4212, 800/363–0366* 🌐 *www.ritzmontreal.com* 🛏 *98 rooms, 31 suites* 🍴 *No meals* [M] *Peel or Guy-Concordia* ✣ *C4.*

$$ HOTEL Fodor's Choice ★

Sofitel Montréal. At the foot of Mont Royal, in the heart of downtown, this exquisite 17-story hotel uses its understated elegance, top-notch details, and convenient location to attract a well-heeled international crowd that includes Hollywood A-listers and diplomats. **Pros:** renovated state-of-the-art gym; copious breakfast and brunch options. **Cons:** no pool; scarce street parking; valet parking costs an impressive $35 plus tax; obstructed views in the east-facing rooms. [$] *Rooms from: C$199* ✉ *1155 rue Sherbrooke Ouest, Downtown* ☎ *514/285–9000* 🌐 *www.sofitel.com* 🛏 *241 rooms, 17 suites* 🍴 *No meals* [M] *Peel* ✣ *C3.*

THE LATIN QUARTER

Bustling with moviegoers and university kids rushing to cafés and libraries, the Quartier Latin is alive with expectation. No, it isn't as pristine as the Old Port, since gentrification has been slow and uneven, but it's full of local flavor—artisanal chocolate shops, gastropubs, and hippie shops. The panhandlers are funny, not dangerous, and beg in two languages.

$ B&B/INN 🏨 **Auberge le Jardin d'Antoine.** Traditionally styled furniture and hardwood floors give this small hotel plenty of shabby-chic charm, but its best selling point is its location right on rue St-Denis, among the Latin Quarter's trendy restaurants, movie theaters, and poutine joints. **Pros:** lively neighborhood; some rooms have been upgraded; secure luggage room for late departures; good coffee machines in rooms. **Cons:** a quarter of the rooms are unrenovated and outdated; the lively location means it can be noisy. [$] *Rooms from: C$105* ✉ *2024 rue St-Denis, Latin Quarter* ☎ *514/843–4506, 800/361–4506* 🌐 *www.aubergelejardindantoine.com* 🛏 *25 rooms* 🍴 *Breakfast* [M] *Berri-UQAM* ⊕ *G3.*

$$$ HOTEL Fodor's Choice ★ 🏨 **Hotel 10.** After a major renovation of its rooms, the former Hotel Opus has been reclaiming its place in a center of cool, right across the street from such hot spots as Globe and Buonanotte. **Pros:** Avis Budget car rental counter; classic art deco building; 24-hour gym. **Cons:** drivers must choose between iffy street parking or $28 valet; weekend party atmosphere can be alienating for some; not skewed to appeal to kids. [$] *Rooms from: C$229* ✉ *10 rue Sherbrooke Ouest, Latin Quarter* ☎ *514/843–6000, 866/744–6346* 🌐 *www.hotel10montreal.com* 🛏 *122 rooms, 14 suites* 🍴 *No meals* [M] *St-Laurent* ⊕ *F3.*

$$$ HOTEL 🏨 **Le Loft Hotel.** Inside an art deco landmark, this chic hotel has loft-like rooms with high ceilings and lots of space, as well as sleek Ikea kitchens, funky art, and wide views of the cityscape. **Pros:** 10-foot ceilings; great for entertaining; superior soundproofing. **Cons:** street parking is scarce; a bit hard to find. [$] *Rooms from: C$229* ✉ *334 Terrasse St-Denis, Latin Quarter* ☎ *888/414–5638* 🌐 *www.lofthotel.ca* 🛏 *29 rooms* 🍴 *Breakfast* [M] *Berri-UQAM* ⊕ *G3.*

8

THE PLATEAU MONT-ROYAL

Full of artists and academics, the Plateau is a bustling neighborhood with a high density of bistros, brewpubs, martini bars, cupcake emporiums, designer boutiques, and parks. This is no place for quiet contemplation. In the summer, join the crowds at outdoor markets and street fairs. There aren't many places to stay, but they include some lovely auberges and B&Bs.

$ B&B/INN FAMILY 🏨 **Auberge de la Fontaine.** A winner of the city's Prix Ulysse for the best three-star hotel, this turn-of-the-20th-century residence overlooks Parc Lafontaine and one of the city's major bicycle trails. **Pros:** joggers paradise; park-side location on a bicycle trail; near restaurants; kids under 12 stay for free. **Cons:** outdated lobby is a little sad; some rooms are unrenovated and quite small; parking can be difficult. [$] *Rooms from: C$159* ✉ *1301 rue Rachel Est, The Plateau* ☎ *514/597–0166, 800/597–0597* 🌐 *www.aubergedelafontaine.com* 🛏 *18 rooms, 3 suites* 🍴 *Breakfast* [M] *Mont-Royal* ⊕ *H1.*

$$ B&B/INN 🏨 **Casa Bianca Bed & Breakfast.** Popular with love-struck couples with friends on The Plateau, this renovated mansion is an ode to French Renaissance Revival architecture and promotes an organic vegetarian ethic. **Pros:** free Wi-Fi; yoga classes; private terrace with flowers; facing Mont-Royal and public tennis courts (fee). **Cons:** only five rooms, so book early; creaky hardwood floors; no soundproofing in bedrooms;

some might miss bacon at breakfast. [$] *Rooms from: C$179* ✉ *4351 av. de l'Esplanade, The Plateau* ☎ *514/312–3837, 866/775–4431* 🌐 *www.casabianca.ca* 🛏 *3 rooms, 2 suites* 🍴 *Breakfast* [M] *Mont-Royal* ✥ *F1.*

CÔTES-DES-NEIGES

With its street-side fruit markets, bookstores, and multicultural vibe, Côtes-des-Neiges has much to offer the more relaxed tourist who isn't looking for a hipster hot spot. The mom-and-pop restaurants serve a United Nations of food choices, too, alongside a thriving Irish pub (McCarold's) and the ubiquitous Starbucks outlets.

$ HOTEL 🏨 **Hôtel Terrasse Royale.** Near the Oratoire St-Joseph, this serviceable hotel in a busy neighborhood attracts tourists and families who enjoy ethnic markets and restaurants where you can dine cheaply and well. **Pros:** practical kitchens; breakfast downstairs is only $3.85; multilingual neighborhood; easy access to métro. **Cons:** noisy; glum exterior; lobby needs a renovation. [$] *Rooms from: C$119* ✉ *5225 chemin de la Côte-des-Neiges, Côte-des-Neiges* ☎ *514/739–6391, 800/567–0804* 🌐 *www.terrasse-royale.com* 🛏 *56 rooms* 🍴 *No meals* [M] *Côte-des-Neiges* ✥ *A2.*

SIDE TRIPS FROM MONTRÉAL

WELCOME TO SIDE TRIPS FROM MONTRÉAL

TOP REASONS TO GO

★ **Ski at Mont-Tremblant:** Heading 150 km (90 miles) north of Montréal takes you to some of the best skiing east of the Rockies, as well as fine hotels and restaurants, a lively ski village, and great golf courses.

★ **Take a driving tour of Eastern Township wineries:** The vineyards here resemble those in the Niagara Region and Okanagan Valley.

★ **Visit Abbaye St-Benoit-du-Lac:** The Benedictine monks built this splendid church—with its fairy-tale castle bell tower—on the shores of Lake Memphrémagog.

★ **Spend a night among wolves in Parc Omega:** Go with an experienced guide to explore the lives of these great predators in their natural habitat—the magnificent Outaouais region.

★ **Go leaf peeping . . . anywhere:** From mid-September through mid-October the entire Laurentians, Eastern Townships, and Outaouais are ablaze with spectacular fall foliage.

1 The Laurentians. With its ski hills and lakes, this is sheer paradise for those looking for a quick break from the hustle and bustle of urban life. Quaint villages, many steeped in colorful history, line the delightful countryside—all hardly a stone's throw away from the center of Montréal.

2 The Outaouais. The ruggedly beautiful Outaouais is an excellent place to go camping and spot wildlife—and that's especially true of Gatineau and Parc Omega.

GETTING ORIENTED

The Laurentians resort area begins 60 km (37 miles) north of Montréal. The Eastern Townships start approximately 80 km (50 miles) east of the city in a southern corner of the province. The Outaouais lies about 110 km (68 miles) to the west, bordering Ontario. All three are an easy drive from Montréal.

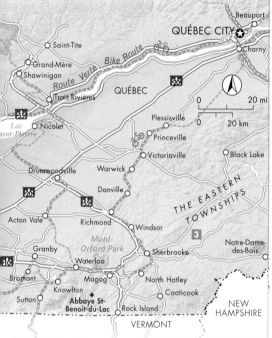

3 The Eastern Townships. A favorite ski and sun destination for those looking to get away from it all, this is also an increasingly popular culinary tourism destination for its artisan food producers and wineries. Settled by British Loyalists fleeing the American Revolution, the region's redbrick villages, charming bed-and-breakfasts, and excellent regional dining are a blend of New England and Nouvelle France.

9

Updated by
Marcella De
Vincenzo

In the minds of many who live here, one of Montréal's greatest attributes is its proximity to the sheer physical beauty of the surrounding countryside. From downtown Montréal you can head in pretty well any direction and within an hour or so, you'll be, if not in the wilderness, then at least in the thick of cottage country. The three most popular side-trip destinations from Montréal are the Laurentians, the Eastern Townships, and the Outaouais—each possessing its own distinct characteristics and flavor.

Most people traveling to this region do so by car, making it easy to spend as much or as little time in any given area as desired. However, Québec has created the Route Verte (Green Route), a 5,000-km (3,100-mile) network of bike trails in the southern part of the province. Many of the trails are currently open for access.

RESTAURANTS

Although you're not likely to find much in the way of quality ethnic dishes, the major towns in the region serve a variety of cuisines at a range of prices, with French and regional specialties dominating the higher end of the price scale. The Eastern Townships are particularly strong on regional cuisine using local artisanal ingredients.

HOTELS

Accommodations here range from resort hotels to cozy *auberges* (inns). Hotels and inns often require a minimum two-night stay on weekends in high season, so ask in advance. Many inns—especially in high season—include two meals, usually breakfast and dinner, in the cost of a night's stay.

Hotel reviews have been shortened. For full information, visit Fodors. com.

WHAT IT COSTS IN CANADIAN DOLLARS			
	$	$$	$$$	$$$$
Restaurants	under C$12	C$12–C$20	C$21–C$30	over C$30
Hotels	under C$160	C$160–C$200	C$201–C$250	over C$250

Restaurant prices are the average cost of a main course at dinner or, if dinner is not served, at lunch. Hotel prices are the lowest cost of a standard double room in high season.

THE LAURENTIANS

The Laurentians (les Laurentides) range is a delightful year-round destination for getting outdoors, whether it's for golf and white-water rafting in the summer or skiing and dog sledding in the winter. Along with its stunning natural beauty, it's also known for its authentic Québec food—all of this to be found less than an hour's drive from downtown Montréal, traffic allowing.

The main tourist region, which actually encompasses only a small part of the Laurentian mountain range, is divided into two major regions: the Lower Laurentians (les Basses Laurentides) and the Upper Laurentians (les Hautes Laurentides). But don't be fooled by the designations; they don't signify great driving distances. The rocky hills here are relatively low, but many are eminently skiable, with a few peaks above 2,500 feet. Mont-Tremblant, at 3,150 feet, is the region's highest.

The P'tit Train du Nord—the former railroad line that's now a 200-km (124-mile) "linear park" used by cyclists, hikers, skiers, and snowmobilers—made it possible to transport settlers and cargo easily to the Upper Laurentians. It also opened up the area to skiing by the early 1900s. Before long, trainloads of skiers replaced settlers and cargo as the railroad's major trade. At first a winter weekend getaway for Montrealers who stayed at boardinghouses and fledgling resorts, the Upper Laurentians soon began attracting international visitors.

Ski lodges and private family cottages for wealthy city dwellers were accessible only by train until the 1930s, when Route 117 was built. Today there's an uneasy peace between the longtime cottagers, who want to restrict development, and resort entrepreneurs, who want to expand. At the moment, commercial interests seem to be prevailing. A number of large hotels have added indoor pools and spa facilities, and efficient highways have brought the country even closer to the city—45 minutes to St-Sauveur, 1½–2 hours to Mont-Tremblant.

The resort area begins at St-Sauveur-des-Monts (Exit 60 on Autoroute 15) and extends north to Mont-Tremblant. Beyond, the region turns into a wilderness of lakes and forests best visited with an outfitter. Fishing guides are concentrated around Parc du Mont-Tremblant. To the first-time visitor, the hilly areas around St-Sauveur, Ste-Adèle, Morin Heights, Val-Morin, and Val-David up to Ste-Agathe-des-Monts form a pleasant hodgepodge of villages, hotels, and inns that seem to blend one into another. Tourisme Laurentides in Mirabel provides information and offers a daily lodging-booking service. Its main information center is at the Porte du Nord complex at Exit 51 on Autoroute 15.

PLANNING

WHEN TO GO

The Laurentians are a big skiing destination in winter, but the other seasons all have their own charms: you can drive up from Montréal to enjoy the fall foliage; to hike, bike, play golf, camp, or fish; or to engage in spring skiing—and still get back to the city before dark. The only slow periods are early November (aka "mud season"), when there isn't much to do, and June, when the area has plenty to offer but is plagued by black flies. Control programs have improved the situation somewhat.

GETTING HERE AND AROUND

Autoroute 15 is the fastest and most direct route from Montréal to the most in-demand spots in the Laurentians. This limited access highway peters out at Ste-Agathe and morphs into Autoroute 117, which runs all the way to Rouyn-Noranda. Exit numbers on Autoroute 15 reflect the distance from Montréal. Autoroute 15 starts at the New York–Québec border where it connects to Interstate 87, so it's also the most direct route for most visitors from the United States. The highway crosses into Montréal on the Champlain Bridge and follows the Décarie and Metropolitan expressways across the island. Visitors arriving from Boston and points east on Interstate 91 can follow Autoroute 55 from the border north to Autoroute 10 (the Autoroute des Cantons de l'Est) and then drive west until it merges with Autoroute 15 at the Champlain Bridge.

VISITOR INFORMATION

Contact **Tourisme Laurentides (Porte du Nord)** ✉ *1000 Hwy. 15 N, St-Jérôme, Québec* ☎ *450/224–7007 from Montréal area, 800/561–6673 from rest of North America.*

OKA

40 km (25 miles) west of Montréal.

If you like apples and delicious cheese, Oka is sure to be a highlight of your trip. It was once the home of Cistercian monks, but the urban sprawl has driven them from their abbey, on the shores of Lac des Deux-Montagnes, to seek solace farther north in St-Jean-de-Matha in the Lanaudière region, but the cheese they made famous is still produced by a private firm here and is available in local shops. The rolling hills around the little town of Oka are where you'll find many of the apple orchards. If you love cider, follow the *Route des Vergers*, stopping at various properties along this "Orchard Route" to sample the local wares. There's also a winery on the route: La Roche des Brises, whose whites and reds include the port-like *L'été Indien* (Indian Summer).

GETTING HERE AND AROUND

To get from Montréal to Oka, take Autoroute 15 North to Autoroute 640 West.

Parc National du
Mont-Tremblant

The Laurentians
and the Outaouais

EXPLORING

La Roches des Brises. You can tour the vineyard (reservations are required), taste the award winning wines for C$7, and dine in the adjacent four-star restaurant serving the best in regional cuisine. Across the road overlooking some of the grapevines is an appealing five-room bed-and-breakfast with a spa. It's worth the trip, even if it's only to take in the splendor of the exceptionally lovely grounds. ⊠ *2007 rue Principale, St-Joseph-du-Lac* ☎ *450/472–2722, 450/472–3477* ⊕ *www. rochedesbrises.com* ◷ *Mid-Feb.–Dec.*

Parc d'Oka (*Oka National Park*). Beautifully surrounded by low hills, this park has a lake fringed by a sandy beach and plenty of opportunities for outdoor sports, including hiking and biking trails, kayaking, canoeing, fishing, and, in winter, snowshoeing and cross-country skiing. Locals also consider it to be one of the top camping destinations. Administered by the province along environmentally conscious lines—they implemented the Ecological Integrity Monitoring Program (EIMO) in 2004—it has nearly 900 campsites, and you can rent bicycles, cross-country skis, snowshoes, canoes, and kayaks from the office. Note that the strip at the far eastern end of the beach is "clothing optional," or, in effect, "clothing nonexistent." ⊠ *2020 chemin*

Oka ☏ *450/479–8365, 800/665–6527 activities* ⊕ *www.sepaq.com* 🖃 *C$7.50* ⊘ *Daily 8–sunset.*

Hudson. A quick detour on the ferry (C$10 one-way; ⊕ *traverseoka. qc.ca*) across Lac des Deux-Montagnes brings you to this small town with old houses now used for art galleries, boutiques, and Christmas shops. In winter there's an "ice bridge": basically a plowed path across a well-frozen lake. Taking a walk across the bridge is a singular experience. If you happen to visit on a Saturday from May to October, make a stop at the popular Finnegan's Market (⊕ *www.finnegansmarket.com*). Open from 9 to 4, the flea market sells antiques, jewelry, crafts, and preserves, among other goods. ⊠ *Hudson.*

ST-SAUVEUR-DES-MONTS

85 km (53 miles) north of Oka, 63 km (39 miles) north of Montréal.

Just a 45-minute drive from Montréal (or 90 minutes when the traffic's heavy, as it frequently is), St-Sauveur is probably the busiest little town in Québec, especially on weekends. Its rue Principale bristles with bars and restaurants that serve everything from lamb brochettes and spicy Thai stir-fries to steaks and burgers. On summer weekends, the street is so jammed with cars and the sidewalks so packed with visitors that it's sometimes called Crescent Street North after the action-filled street in Montréal. Despite the glitz and the sea of condos that surround it, however, the town has managed to retain a bit of rural charm in its fine old church and veranda-fronted clapboard homes.

St-Sauveur in winter is no less busy. The "mountains" surrounding the town hardly qualify as Alpine—none has a vertical drop of more than 700 feet—but they're close to Montréal, well serviced by lifts, and lit at night, so the winter sports scene here is very lively. Whether you ski or not, the après-ski scene in St-Sauveur is worth sampling.

GETTING HERE AND AROUND
Take Highway 15 north from Montréal and get off at Exit 60. The best way to explore the main street is to find a parking lot and walk around. Driving through town is difficult in winter, impossible in summer.

VISITOR INFORMATION
Contact Tourist Welcome Bureau of Pays-d'en-Haut ⊠ *605 chemin des Frênes, Piedmont* ☏ *800/898–2127, 450/227–3417* ⊕ *www.lespaysdenhaut.com.*

EXPLORING

FAMILY **Mont-St-Sauveur Water Park.** Slides, a giant wave pool, a wading pool, and snack bars will all keep the kids occupied here. The river rafting attracts an older, braver crowd; the nine-minute ride follows the natural contours of steep hills. On the tandem slides, plumes of water flow through figure-eight tubes and makes for a great time. But if you'd rather stay dry, take an adventure through the trees on their zip line or enjoy a fast ride with the Viking Alpine Coaster. ⊠ *350 rue St-Denis* ☏ *450/227–4671* ⊕ *www.mssi.ca* 🖃 *C$35.66* ⊘ *Early June–early Sept., daily 10–5 (to 7 mid-June–late Aug.).*

Musée du ski des Laurentides. The Laurentians are one of the oldest ski regions in North America, and ski buffs will enjoy this little museum tracing the long history of this area with great photos, artifacts, and some interesting models of early ski lifts. It also houses the Temple de la Renomée du ski (the Ski Hall of Fame). ⊠ *30 rue Filion* ☎ *450/227–2564* ⊕ *www.museeduskideslaurentides.com* ⊐ *Free* ⊙ *Wed.–Sun. 11–6.*

WHERE TO EAT AND STAY

$$$
FRENCH
✕ **Le Carré Des Saveurs.** Whether you need to refuel after a shopping trip along St-Sauveur's quaint and charming main street or just want to enjoy some authentic French cuisine, this is a good place to do either. The menu features other European dishes as well, such as gazpacho and lobster-filled ravioli, and to sweetly round off the meal, you could do no better than choose the dark chocolate fondant cake, made with 75% cocoa from Tanzania—absolutely to die for. ⓢ *Average main: C$25* ⊠ *206 rue Principale, St-Sauveur* ☎ *450/744–1766* ⊕ *carre-dessaveurs. com* ⌓ *Reservations essential* ⊙ *Closed Mon.*

$$
B&B/INN
⌂ **Relais St-Denis.** Once a wartime refuge for well-heeled English children and their governesses, this lovely inn and spa now offers everyone a refuge from everyday stress, with a fireplace and a whirlpool bath in every room and a year-round outdoor heated pool and steam room. **Pros:** variety of spa services and in-room massage packages; kitchenette in all rooms and suites; walking distance to restaurants, outlet shopping, and activities. **Cons:** not much for kids to do. ⓢ *Rooms from: C$139* ⊠ *61 rue St-Denis* ☎ *450/227–4766, 888/997–4766* ⊕ *www. relaisstdenis.com* ⌔ *18 rooms, 24 suites* ⍨ *No meals.*

SHOPPING
SHOPPING CENTERS

Fodor'sChoice
★
Factoreries St-Sauveur. If you feel like shopping and can't resist a bargain, this could be your dream destination. With 35 stores, including Jones New York, Guess, Parasuco, and Rockport selling designer clothing at reduced prices, there's really no reason not to go. ⊠ *100 rue Guindon* ☎ *450/240–0880, 800/363–0332* ⊕ *www.tangeroutlet. com/saintsauveur.*

Rue Principale. Small fashion boutiques, restaurant terraces and cute gift shops adorned with bright awnings and flowers, line this popular shopping street.

SPORTS AND THE OUTDOORS
SKIING

Mont St-Sauveur International (MSSI). The hills surrounding St-Sauveur might be relatively low, but this vibrant ski resort is long-established and perennially popular for good reason. It has an extensive skiable area, good snowmaking and lift capacity, and many trails that are lit at night, making it possible for energetic Montrealers to drive up after work for a couple hours of skiing. Most of the village's ski operations belong to MSSI, which also owns hills in other nearby towns, but Mont-St-Sauveur is the largest, with a 700-foot vertical drop and 142 acres of skiable terrain. Seventeen of its 38 trails are for beginners and intermediates, 16 are for experts, and 5 are rated extreme. Mont-Avila has

One of the most popular times to visit the region is in fall, when the mountains are splashed with a spectrum of warm yellows, oranges, and reds.

13 trails (2 beginner, 3 intermediate, 5 difficult, 3 extremely difficult), a snow park, a fun tubing park, and the Viking, a toboggan-style ride in a cart that twists and turns on a track through the forest. ✉ *350 av. St-Denis, St-Sauveur* ☎ *450/227–4671, 514/871–0101* ⊕ *www.mssi.ca.*

Station de Ski Mont-Habitant. More than 55 years in operation, Mont-Habitant is one of the last of the independent ski operations in St-Sauveur. This mountain has always been a favorite with families and with beginner and intermediate skiers since the vertical drop is just 600 feet and the 10 trails are relatively gentle. Mont-Habitant also has St-Sauveur's only beach, which makes it very popular in the summer. ✉ *12 chemin des Skieurs* ☎ *450/227–2637, 866/887–2637* ⊕ *www. monthabitant.com* ☉ *Weekdays 9–5, weekends 8:30–5.*

MORIN HEIGHTS

10 km (6 miles) west of St-Sauveur-des-Monts, 73 km (45 miles) northwest of Montréal.

If Saint-Sauveur is too busy and overdeveloped for your liking, Morin Heights is a great alternative, with plenty of restaurants, bookstores, boutiques, and craft shops to explore free from the crowds. The town's British architecture and population reflect its settlers' heritage; most residents here speak English.

In summer, windsurfing, swimming, and canoeing on the area's two lakes—Claude and Lafontaine—are popular. In fall and winter, come for the foliage and the alpine and Nordic skiing.

GETTING HERE AND AROUND

From Montréal to Morin Heights, take Autoroute 15 North, then take Exit 60.

WHERE TO EAT AND STAY

$$$$
FRENCH
Fodor'sChoice
★

⤬ **Auberge Restaurant Clos Joli.** If you're looking for superior French cuisine and are prepared to pay top dollar for it, this family-owned and operated establishment fits the bill. The award-winning chef, gets creative with seasonal and local ingredients in her five-course table d'hôte dinner menu. Any dish with game such as lamb, rabbit, or salmon, will be memorable, and anything featuring venison will be legendary. If you rent a room for the night, breakfast will be included the next morning. $ *Average main: C$45* ✉ *19 chemin Clos Joli* ☎ *450/226–5401, 866/511–9999* ⊕ *www.aubergeclosjoli.net* ⟐ *Reservations essential* ⊘ *No lunch.*

$$$
B&B/INN

⛳ **Refuge Morin Heights.** In a beautiful wooded area near a small, pristine lake, this charming auberge is one of the best-equipped spa destinations in the Laurentians, and its outdoor terrace is one of the most pleasant places to relax in the entire region. **Pros:** some rooms have beautiful views of the Rivière du Nord; spectacular spa; whirlpool baths and fireplaces in some units. **Cons:** isolated from village; close to highway. $ *Rooms from: C$235* ✉ *500 Rte. 364* ☎ *866/996–1796, 450/226–1796* ⊕ *www.spalerefuge.com* ⟐ *27 rooms* ⦿*Breakfast.*

SHOPPING

SPAS

Amerispa Spa Nordique. Only 45 minutes outside of Montréal, this is a great place to escape and unwind. Hidden in a Laurentian forest of maples, firs, and birches is a beautifully rustic pavilion housing a spa with hot tubs and cold pools, eucalyptus-scented steam baths, and thermal and Nordic waterfalls. The Elixir Ice Cider Massage and companion body wrap gets good reviews. ✉ *160 Watchorn St.* ☎ *450/226–7722, 866/263–7477* ⊕ *www.amerispa.ca* ⊘ *Daily 10–9.*

STE-ADÈLE

12 km (7 miles) north of Morin Heights, 85 km (53 miles) north of Montréal.

This town has a lot to offer, with attractions and activities to please families, outdoors enthusiasts, and visitors who want to experience something of the local culture. With a permanent population of more than 10,000, it's the largest community in the lower part of the Laurentians, and has good boutiques, restaurants, summer theater (performed in French), and art galleries. Active types can find horseback riding, golf, and lengthy bike trails in summer and skiing in winter.

GETTING HERE AND AROUND

From Montréal to Ste-Adèle, take Autoroute 15 North and then take Exit 67.

VISITOR INFORMATION

Contact Tourist Welcome Bureau of Pays-d'en-Haut ✉ *1490 rue St-Joseph (Exit 67 off Hwy. 15 N)* ☎ *450/229–3729* ⊕ *www.lespaysdenhaut.com.*

EXPLORING

FAMILY   **Au Pays des Merveilles.** Fairy-tale characters such as Snow White, Little Red Riding Hood, and Alice in Wonderland wander the grounds, playing games with children. Small fry may also enjoy the petting zoo, amusement rides, wading pool, and puppet show. A ride called Le Petit Train des Merveilles (the Little Train of Wonders) is a nod to the historic train that launched the tourism industry in the Laurentians. There are 45 activities, enough to occupy those ages two to eight for about half a day. Check the website for discount coupons. The theme park is completely accessible to strollers and wheelchairs. ✉ *3795 rue de la Savane* ☎ *450/229–3141* ⊕ *www.paysmerveilles.com* 💲 *C$17.35* ☉ *Mid-June–late Aug., daily 10–6.*

WHERE TO EAT AND STAY

$$$$ ✕ **La Clef des Champs.** French-influenced cuisine is served at this roman-
FRENCH FUSION   tic restaurant tucked amid trees, with a main focus on fresh fish and seafood. The prix-fixe menu (the only option) includes dishes such as poached lobster, shrimp provençales and grilled organic salmon. The dessert selection is small but enticing, with palate-cleansers like sorbet and fresh fruits alongside richer treats like crème brûlée and profiteroles with Grand Marnier. 💲 *Average main: C$40* ✉ *875 chemin Pierre-Péladeau* ☎ *450/229–2857* ⊕ *www.restaurantlaclefdeschamps.com* 🍴 *Reservations essential* ☉ *Closed Mon. during low season. No lunch.*

$ 🛏 **Le Chantecler.** A favorite with Montrealers, and a good choice for
HOTEL   active types wanting to expend some energy, this rustic place in the Laurentians, near the lovely Lac Ste-Adèle, offers a good range of year-round activities. **Pros:** friendly, helpful staff; lakeside rooms. **Cons:** fills up early due to its outstanding reputation. 💲 *Rooms from: C$109* ✉ *1474 chemin Chantecler* ☎ *450/229–3555, 888/916–1616* ⊕ *www.lechantecler.com* 🛏 *150 rooms, 29 suites* 🍽 *Multiple meal plans.*

SPORTS AND THE OUTDOORS

GOLF

Club de Golf Chantecler. Every hole here will provide breathtaking panoramic views of the surrounding Laurentian scenery. Opened in 1950, his semiprivate club offers a mountainside course with long and narrow fairways and three sets of tees for different skill levels. Just one hour from Montréal, it's easy and convenient for a day trip. ✉ *2520 chemin du Club* ☎ *450/476–1339, 450/229–3742* ⊕ *www.groupebeaudet.com* 💲 *C$31.60–C$40.38* ⛳ *18 holes, 5885 yards, par 72.*

SKIING

Ski Mont-Gabriel. Part of the Mont St-Sauveur International (MSSI) chain of ski resorts, Mont Gabriel has five lifts, 18 superb downhill trails, which are primarily for intermediate and advanced skiers, and a vertical drop of 656 feet. It's about 19 km (12 miles) northeast of Ste-Adèle. ✉ *1501 chemin du Mont-Gabriel* ☎ *450/227–1100, 514/871–0101* ⊕ *www.skimontgabriel.com.*

VAL-DAVID

33 km (20 miles) west of Ste-Adèle, 82 km (51 miles) north of Montréal.

Val-David is a major destination for mountain climbers, hikers, and campers. It's also a place that many Québec artists and artisans call home, a fact suggested by the several galleries and marvelous art shops in town.

GETTING HERE AND AROUND

The village is just a couple of kilometers east of Exit N6 on Autoroute 15, making it easy to get to by car, but it's also accessible by bicycle: Le P'tit Train du Nord cycling trail runs right through town.

VISITOR INFORMATION

Contact **Tourist Bureau of Val-David** ✉ *2579 rue de l'Église* ☎ *888/322-7030, 819/324-5678* 🌐 *www.valdavid.com.*

EXPLORING

FAMILY **Village du Père Noël** (*Santa Claus Village*). Santa is not just for Christmas here. In his summer residence kids can sit on his knee and speak to him in French or English, then have fun in the grounds, which contain bumper boats, a petting zoo with goats, sheep, horses, and colorful birds; games; and a large outdoor pool in the summer. There is a snack bar, but visitors are encouraged to bring their own food (there are numerous picnic tables). During the cold winter months, the park transforms into a winter wonderland with skating rinks and tubing fun for the kids. ✉ *987 rue Morin* ☎ *819/322-2146, 800/287-6635* 🌐 *www.noel.qc.ca* 🎟 *C$20* 🕒 *Early June–late Aug., daily 10–6; check website for winter schedule.*

WHERE TO EAT

$$ CANADIAN FAMILY Fodor's Choice ★ 🍴 **Au Petit Poucet.** For a true Quebecois treat, stop by this rustic cabin for breakfast or lunch. It's a big draw with tourists as well as locals. Meat pies, maple-smoked ham, egg dishes, homemade chutneys, and the restaurant's famous country bread (also homemade) are all on the menu. A gift shop at the front sells many of its products—and you *will* want to take some home. [$] *Average main: C$20* ✉ *1030 rte. 117* ☎ *819/322-2246, 888/334-2246* 🌐 *www.aupetitpoucet.com* 🕒 *No dinner.*

SHOPPING

CERAMICS

1001 Pots. One of the most interesting events in Val David is this ceramic exhibition, held from July through mid-August. On view is the Japanese-style pottery of 1001 Pots' founder, Kinya Ishikawa—as well as pieces by up to 100 other ceramists. Ishikawa's studio also displays work by his wife, Marie-Andrée Benoît, who makes fish-shaped bowls with a texture derived from pressing canvas on the clay. There are workshops for adults and children throughout the exhibition and there is always at least one artisan on site. While you're there, take the time to enjoy tea in one of the three beautiful gardens and learn the art of the Japanese tea ceremony. ✉ *2435 rue de l'Église* ☎ *819/322-6868* 🌐 *www.1001pots.com* 🎟 *C$2 for exhibition* 🕒 *July–mid-Aug., daily 10–6; call for hrs rest of yr.*

9

HOUSEHOLD

Atelier Bernard Chaudron, Inc. If you're looking for an interesting conversation piece to bring back home with you, check out master craftsman Bernard Chaudron's hand-forged, lead-free pewter household objects that include oil lamps, hammered-silver beer mugs, pitchers, candleholders, and animal-themed knife rests. ✉ *2449 chemin de l'Île* ☎ *819/322–3944, 888/322–3944* 🌐 *www.chaudron.ca* 🕒 *Daily 10–4.*

SPORTS AND THE OUTDOORS

SKIING

Centre de Ski Vallée-Bleue. Family-run and family-focused, this ski hill suits everyone, from beginners to advanced level skiers and snowboarders, with 19 trails, three lifts, and a verticle drop of 365 feet. ✉ *1418 chemin Vallée-Bleue* ☎ *866/322–3427* 🌐 *www.vallee-bleue.com.*

STE-AGATHE-DES-MONTS

5 km (3 miles) north of Val-David, 96 km (60 miles) northwest of Montréal.

The wide, sandy beaches of Lac des Sables are the most surprising feature of Ste-Agathe-des-Monts, a tourist town best known for its ski hills. Water activities include canoeing, kayaking, swimming, and fishing. Ste-Agathe is also a stopover point on the Linear Park, the bike trail between St-Jérôme and Mont-Laurier.

GETTING HERE AND AROUND

From Montréal to Ste-Agathe-des-Monts, take Autoroute 15 North. Take Exit 89 to reach QC–329 South, and then take QC–117.

VISITOR INFORMATION

Contact Tourist Bureau of Ste-Agathe-des-Monts ✉ *24 rue St-Paul* ☎ *819/326–3731, 888/326–0457* 🌐 *www.sainte-agathe.org.*

WHERE TO STAY

$ HOTEL 🏨 **Auberge Watel.** If you're looking for a room with a double-size Jacuzzi, a fireplace, and a balcony with a superb view of Lac des Sables, try this distinguished, white-painted hotel, which is also convenient for the boutiques and cultural activities in Ste-Agathe. **Pros:** adjacent to three beaches; indoor and outdoor pools; year-round outdoor spas. **Cons:** not all rooms have a Jacuzzi, fireplace, and lake view. [$] *Rooms from: C$120* ✉ *250 rue St-Venant* ☎ *819/326–7016, 800/363–6478* 🌐 *www.hotelspawatel.com* 🛏 *31 rooms* 🍴 *Some meals.*

SPORTS AND THE OUTDOORS

BOAT TOURS

***Alouette V* and *VI*.** These sightseeing boats offer guided 50-minute tours of Lac des Sables. They run at least seven times a day from mid-June to mid-August and five times a day from mid-August to mid-October. The first boat leaves the dock at 11:30 am. ✉ *Municipal Dock, rue Principale* ☎ *819/326–3656, 866/326–3656* 🌐 *www.croisierealouette.com* 🎟 *C$17.*

MONT-TREMBLANT

25 km (16 miles) north of Ste-Agathe-des-Monts, 100 km (62 miles) north of Montréal.

At more than 3,000 feet, Mont-Tremblant is one of the highest peaks in the Laurentians and a major draw for skiers. The resort area at the foot of the mountain (called simply Tremblant) is spread around 14-km (9-mile) -long Lac Tremblant and is consistently—and justifiably—ranked among the top ski resorts in eastern North America.

The hub of the resort is a pedestrians-only village that gives an architectural nod to the style of New France, with dormer windows and colorful steep roofs on buildings that house pubs, restaurants, boutiques, sports shops, a movie theater, self-catering condominiums, and hotels. A historical town this is not: built for the resort, it may strike you as a bit of Disney in the mountains.

GETTING HERE AND AROUND

The easiest way to get here is by car. Drive north on Autoroute 15 until it ends just beyond Ste-Agathe-des-Monts and then continue on Route 117 (a four-lane highway) for another 30 km (18 miles) to the Mont-Tremblant exit (Exit 119). The resort's parking lots are vast, but they fill up quickly. A shuttle bus links them to the main resort and ski area. Mont-Tremblant has two tourist offices, one in the village and one in the downtown area.

VISITOR INFORMATION

Contact Tourisme Mont-Tremblant ✉ *5080 Montée Ryan* ☎ *877/425–2434, 819/425–2434* ⊕ *www.tourismemonttremblant.com* ✉ *48 chemin de Brebeuf, Exit 117, Rte. 117* ☎ *877/425–2434, 819/425–3300.*

EXPLORING

FAMILY **Parc National du Mont-Tremblant.** This vast wildlife sanctuary has more
Fodor'sChoice than 400 lakes and rivers and is home to nearly 200 species of birds and
★ animals, so is great for wildlife watching. Cross-country skiers, snowshoers, and snowmobilers enjoy the park's trails in winter and camping, fishing, canoeing, and hiking are the popular summer activities. The park was once the home of the Algonquins, who called this area Manitonga Soutana, meaning "mountain of the spirits." ☎ *800/665–6527* ⊕ *www.sepaq.com* ✉ *C$7.50.*

La Diable Visitors' Centre. The park entrance closest to Mont-Tremblant is at the La Diable Visitors' Centre, just beyond the village of Lac-Supérieur and about a half-hour drive from the resort. ✉ *3824 chemin du Lac Supérieur, Lac Supériéur* ☎ *819/688–2281 visitor center, 800/665–6527 Sépaq (government national park agency)* ⊕ *www. sepaq.com/pq/mot.*

WHERE TO EAT

$$$ ✕ **Auberge du Coq de Montagne.** Five minutes from the ski slopes and
ITALIAN right on Lac Moore, this restaurant, which opens onto a terrace during the summer months, has garnered much praise for its Italian dishes. These include tried-and-true favorites such as veal marsala and veal *fiorentina* (cooked with spinach and cheese). Hosts Nino and Kay are reputed to be some of the friendliest folks you'll ever meet. $ *Average*

main: C$25 ✉ *2151 chemin du Village* ☎ *819/425–3380* ✍ *Reservations essential* ⏲ *No lunch.*

$$ CANADIAN FAMILY 🍴 **Creperie Catherine.** This is a great place to refuel in the Mont-Tremblant area if you want to take a break from the hustle and bustle of the Village. Ten minutes by car, this restaurant was recently part of the popular Food Network TV show *You Gotta Eat Here*, and rightly so, as they offer some of the best and most creative crepe dishes. Breakfast is available all day, so you can enjoy the Catherine's Special (eggs, ham, and cheese) any time, or sample the escargot crepe with their signature béchamel sauce. To satisfy that sweet tooth, their take on the banana split makes it simple and delicious. [$] *Average main: C$15* ✉ *977 rue Labelle* ☎ *819/681–4888* 🌐 *www.creperiecatherine.ca.*

$$$$ FRENCH 🍴 **Restaurant Le Cheval de Jade.** "The Jade Horse" is quite haute—an elegant dining room with lace curtains, white linens, and ivory china—and the food is the real thing. Local ingredients and organic produce are used to create classic French fare such as grilled beef filet mignon, bouillabaisse, and tiger prawns flambéed with rum. The Discovery menu (C$82) has included seared duck, foie gras, and smoked salmon; the Gastronomic menu (C$97) might feature snow crab and Matane shrimp cake or perhaps Québec veal sweetbreads, along with cheeses, and deer filet. [$] *Average main: C$40* ✉ *688 rue de St-Jovite* ☎ *819/425–5233* 🌐 *www.chevaldejade.com* ✍ *Reservations essential* ⏲ *Closed Sun. and Mon. No lunch.*

WHERE TO STAY

$$$ HOTEL FAMILY Fodor's Choice ★ 🏨 **Fairmont Tremblant.** The classy centerpiece of the Tremblant resort area takes its cues from the grand 19th-century railroad "castle hotels" scattered throughout Canada. **Pros:** poolside barbecue during the summer; dogs (under 50 lbs.) allowed; easy access to ski hills and the village. **Cons:** it's in the fairly busy village rather than more scenic grounds; valet parking $21 plus tax, and public parking (fees may apply) a 10-minute walk away. [$] *Rooms from: C$229* ✉ *3045 chemin de la Chapelle* ☎ *819/681–7000, 800/257–7544* 🌐 *www.fairmont.com/tremblant* 🛏 *252 rooms, 62 suites* 🍽 *Breakfast.*

$$ HOTEL 🏨 **Hôtel du Lac.** Just down the lakeside road from the ski station at Mont-Tremblant, this is a rustic but comfortable European-owned hotel with excellent facilities and magnificent views of Mont-Tremblant. **Pros:** excellent service; complimentary shuttle to the ski hills; beautiful, tranquil grounds with on-site activities and private beach; three restaurants. **Cons:** not within walking distance of town. [$] *Rooms from: C$179* ✉ *121 rue Cuttle* ☎ *819/425–2731, 800/567–8341* 🌐 *www.clubtremblant.com* 🛏 *122 suites* 🍽 *Some meals.*

$$ HOTEL FAMILY 🏨 **Le Grand Lodge.** At this Scandinavian-style log-cabin hotel, on 13½ acres on the shore of Lac Ouimet, you'll find great year-round amenities and activities for families and sports lovers and a resorty feel that survives its busy conference trade schedule. **Pros:** friendly staff; good food; peaceful environment; ice rink and ice path in winter; very family-friendly; private beach on the lake. **Cons:** no facilities for people with disabilities. [$] *Rooms from: C$179* ✉ *2396 rue Labelle* ☎ *819/425–2734, 800/567–6763* 🌐 *www.legrandlodge.com* 🛏 *11 rooms, 101 suites* 🍽 *Breakfast.*

SPORTS AND THE OUTDOORS
GOLF
Mont-Tremblant. The same company that operates the ski resort also runs two of the most challenging and popular championship golf courses in Québec. **Le Géant** (the Giant) was designed by Thomas McBroom to take full advantage of the fantastic scenery. **Le Diable** (the Devil), with long narrow fairways and strategically placed red sand bunkers, was designed by Michael Hurdzan and Dana Fry. Also at Le Diable, you can find the reputable Tremblant Golf Academy. ☎ 866/356–2233 ⊕ *www.tremblant.ca* 🖾 *Le Diable, C$119 weekdays, C$129 weekends; Le Géant, C$109 weekdays, C$119 weekends* 🏌 *Le Diable, 18 holes, 7056 yards, par 71; Le Géant, 18 holes, 6836 yards, par 72.*

SKIING
Mont-Tremblant. With a 2,116-foot vertical drop, 654 acres of skiable terrain, 95 trails, 18 acres of ramps and jumps for snowboarders, and enough state-of-the-art snowmaking equipment to blanket a small city, Mont-Tremblant is truly one of the great ski resorts of North America, arguably the best east of the Rockies. Its 14 lifts—including two heated gondolas and five high-speed, four-passenger chairlifts—can handle 27,230 skiers an hour. It has some of the toughest expert runs on the continent, but it also has long, gentle runs like the 6-km (3.7-mile) Nansen and dozens of exciting trails for intermediate skiers. Its altitude and location, as well as all that snowmaking equipment, gives it some of eastern Canada's most reliable ski conditions, especially now that winters are getting warmer. All this doesn't come cheap, mind you. A day lift ticket costs about C$79, but for serious skiers there is no better mountain in Québec. ⊠ *1000 chemin des Voyageurs* ☎ *866/356–2233, 819/681–3000* ⊕ *www.tremblant.ca.*

NIGHTLIFE AND PERFORMING ARTS
Festi Jazz. Tons of fun and completely free, the very popular five-day jazz festival in early August draws in at least 15,000 tourists and locals to Mont-Tremblant. The concerts take place under the stars on two outdoor stages and in at least 10 restaurants, bars, and hotels in the Village or Saint Jovite (downtown area). ☎ *514/994–0543* ⊕ *www.jazzmttremblant.com.*

Festival International du Blues de Tremblant (*Tremblant International Blues Festival*). People don't just flock to Mont-Tremblant for outdoor fun. This place is becoming a music lovers' paradise, especially for 10 days in July when the Blues Festival takes place with more than 130 shows. Artists such as Otis Taylor, JJ Grey & Mofro, and Thornetta Davis entertain fans on outdoor stages and in intimate clubs right in the Village. ☎ *819/681–3000* ⊕ *www.tremblantblues.com.*

THE OUTAOUAIS
First settled in the mid-19th century and long known for its logging, the Outaouais (pronounced: ewt–away) region is now a nature lover's paradise as well, with 20,000 lakes, countless rivers, 400 km (249 miles) of hiking trails, and 2,730 km (1,696 miles) of snowmobile trails.

DID YOU KNOW?

Mont-Tremblant's alpine pedestrian village has a wide variety of shops and restaurants housed in buildings with classic and colorful Quebecois mansard roofs.

RENTING A SKI CHALET IN MONT-TREMBLANT

If you think you'd like to spend more than a few days in the Laurentians you might want to consider renting a chalet from a private owner. There are generally plenty to choose from, and not only is a private rental often less expensive than staying at a hotel, it's a lot homier as well, especially if you are traveling with children. And even with the many restaurants in Mont-Tremblant, every once in a while it's nice to buy groceries and come home to cook your own dinner.

Options range from cozy little cottages for four to multibedroom properties where you could have a real house party with family and friends. If you fill a place to capacity the cost can be very competitive,

particularly if you don't mind being outside the main hub of the resort or out of the peak season. Some places offer weekend rates as well as renting by the week. Very good sources for chalet rentals in this part of the province are the websites ⊕ www.chalets-mont-tremblant. com and ⊕ www.chaletsauquebec. com, and the Montréal pages for ⊕ craigslist.com and ⊕ kijiji.ca are full of posts advertising private chalet rentals in the Laurentians. If you'd prefer to go through a third party, most area real estate agents broker short and long-term cottage and chalet rentals as well. Try Remax Laurentides at 286 Principal in St-Sauveur (☎ 450/227–8411) for starters.

To fully experience the majesty of the Outaouais wilderness you could spend close to a week here, but simply driving to any of the region's major provincial parks is a good one-day journey. Montebello, a little country village on the banks of the Ottawa River, is only an hour-and-a-half drive from Montréal, and is where you'll find Le Château Montebello, the largest log structure ever built. From there you can find excursions to take you to the surrounding countryside or if you'd prefer, you can simply take in nearby Omega Park, a safari adventure where you'll bear witness to many of the region's creatures interacting within their natural environment. It encompasses an enormous body of land located in the southwest corner of the province.

PLANNING

WHEN TO GO
The Outaouais is beautiful at any time of year, but unless you're looking to spend several days there it's best to go in summer and stay in the lower region, around Montebello. Making your way up to the provincial parks in the north is a lengthy journey at best, but in winter, potentially hazardous road conditions could well add several more hours to your trip.

GETTING HERE AND AROUND
To get to the Outaouais take Autoroute 15 North roughly 40 km (25 miles) until you get to Autoroute 50 West heading toward Lachute. Drive another 70 km (43 miles) past Lachute and you'll soon be in Montebello. Continue on another 15 km (9 miles) to reach Gatineau.

VISITOR INFORMATION

Contact **Tourisme Outaouais** ✉ *103 rue Laurier, Gatineau* ☎ *819/778–2222, 800/265–7822* ⊕ *www.tourismeoutaouais.com.*

MONTEBELLO

130 km (80 miles) west of Montréal.

Located on the banks of the Ottawa River, this little village is best known for the Fairmont Le Château Montebello, a spectacular hotel touted as the largest log cabin in the world. Given the town's relative proximity to Ottawa, the nation's capital, more than a few world leaders and dignitaries have visited Montebello for one of the many international summits hosted by the Château since it was built in 1930. The Outaouais in general is well-known for the rugged beauty of its wilderness, and even in this more populated southern section of the region there's still excellent fishing, hunting, canoeing, hiking, and wildlife-spotting, with a series of hiking paths starting right beside the Château Montebello. Even if an expedition into the bush isn't quite your thing, you can still get up close to the local wildlife in a more controlled environment at Parc Omega, home to a wide variety of indigenous species and domestic animals.

GETTING HERE AND AROUND

From Montréal, take Autoroute 50 West for 130 km (80 miles); it's about a 90-minute trip.

VISITOR INFORMATION

Contact **Montebello Tourist Information Office** ✉ *Gare de Montebello, 502-A rue Notre-Dame* ☎ *819/423–5602, 800/265–7822* ⊕ *www.tourismeoutaouais. com.*

EXPLORING

FAMILY **Parc Omega.** In the 1,800 acres of hills, valleys, rivers, and streams that make up the park, visitors drive along designated trails to view wild animals roaming free in their beautiful natural environment. These include bear, Alpine ibexes, buffalo, wolves, elk, and more. There are also walking trails among non-aggressive species like white-tailed deer, with golf-cart rental available in summer to save the leg-work. Also in summer, you can visit farm animals in the restored 19th-century Léopold's Farm and see a birds of prey show. ✉ *399 Rte. 323 N* ☎ *819/423–5487* ⊕ *www.parc-omega.com* 💰 *C$23–C$26, depending on season* ☉ *Late June–early Sept., daily 9–7; mid-May–late June and early Sept.–mid-Oct., daily 10–6; mid-Oct.–mid-May, daily 10–5. Last admission 4 year-round.*

WHERE TO EAT AND STAY

$ ✕ **La Belle Bédaine Casse-Croûte.** If you're looking for elegant dining keep
CANADIAN on going, but if you're after a bit of local color, a cold beer, a good burger, a steamie (hot dog), or maybe a sample of Québec's famed poutine, then La Belle Bédaine (which translates as "the happy belly") is just the place. Its good and basic menu comes with a terrace overlooking the river. $ *Average main: C$7* ✉ *664 rue Notre-Dame* ☎ *819/423–5053* ▭ *No credit cards.*

9

$$ ✕ **Le Napoleon.** In what is basically a one-street town, this restaurant's
ITALIAN reputation for serving outstanding food at affordable prices stands out,
and the knowledgeable, personable waitstaff does, too. Though the
cuisine is primarily Italian, some Mediterranean, French, and Quebe-
cois influences are also in evidence, backed up by a fairly extensive
and reasonably priced wine list. In the warmer seasons you can eat out
on the covered terrace, while the fireplace inside makes those colder,
harsher evenings downright cozy. Lunch is only available in the sum-
mer. $ *Average main: C$19* ⊠ *489 rue Notre-Dame* ☎ *819/423–5555*
⊕ *www.le-napoleon.com* ⊗ *No lunch, except in summer (dates vary).*

$$$$ ⛱ **Fairmont Le Château Montebello.** On a bank of the Ottawa River, with
HOTEL its own marina, this grand log-built hotel provides extreme luxury, local
FAMILY flavor, great views, and heaps of activities—no wonder it's an annual
Fodor'sChoice family destination for many well-heeled Canadians. **Pros:** great place
★ to bring children; indoor tennis; magnificent fireplace in lobby; state-
of-the-art conference facility. **Cons:** small bathrooms; 75-minute drive
from Montréal; no nearby restaurants of note; pricey, and a C$17 per
room per night resort fee is added to your bill at checkout. $ *Rooms
from: C$279* ⊠ *392 rue Notre-Dame* ☎ *819/423–6341* ⊕ *www.
fairmont.com/montebello* ⊃ *211 rooms* ❖ *Multiple meal plans.*

$ ⛱ **Hotel Domaine Monté-Bello.** Comfortable and budget-friendly, this hotel
HOTEL may be considerably less grand than the nearby Château Montebello,
but it's quaint and most rooms have lovely views of the Ottawa River.
Pros: standard of hospitality is first-rate; close to Parc Omega. **Cons:**
guests in lower-priced rooms have to share a bathroom. $ *Rooms from:
C$89* ⊠ *696 rue Notre-Dame* ☎ *819/423–5096, 877/420–5096* ⊕ *www.
domainemontebello.com* ⊃ *5 rooms, 6 suites, 1 log cabin* ❖ *No meals.*

GATINEAU

205 km (127 miles) west of Montréal.

This town on the northern edge of the Ottawa River is best known for
the nearby Gatineau Park and the many outdoor activities that can be
done here. For more history, visit the Canadian Museum of History,
which emphasizes the changes the country has undergone, from the
prehistoric past to the present day. From Gatineau, it's a short walk
over the Alexandra Bridge to visit Ottawa, the nation's capital. The
view from either side of the river is stunning.

GETTING HERE AND AROUND
From Montréal, take Autoroute 50 west for 205 km (127 miles); it's
about a two-hour trip.

VISITOR INFORMATION
Contact Gatineau Tourist Information Office ⊠ *103 rue Laurier* ☎ *819/778–
2222, 800/265–7822* ⊕ *www.tourismeoutaouais.com.*

EXPLORING
FAMILY **Canadian Museum of History.** Formerly known as the Canadian Museum
of Civilization, this superb institution officially changed its name in
2013 when it received C$25 million in funding from the Canadian gov-
ernment in order to renovate and expand. More than 50,000 square feet

of the existing museum will be renovated, and a new Canada History Hall will be added, showcasing people and events that have shaped Canada over the years. Some areas will remain open throughout the work, but it's scheduled to fully reopen on July 1, 2017, for the 150th anniversary of Canada's Confederation. Areas that will remain open include the most popular exhibit, the National Aboriginal Collection, which has some 2,000 objects on display. Also staying open are the Children's Museum, Grand Hall, and IMAX Theatre, but call before you go to check on any temporary closures. ✉ *100 rue Laurier* ☎ *819/776–7000, 800/555–5621* 🌐 *www.historymuseum.ca* 🎟 *C$13* 🕒 *June–Sept., daily 9:30–6 (to 8 Thurs.); Oct.–May, daily 9:30–5 (to 8 Thurs.).*

FAMILY **Gatineau Park.** This massive park—nearly 364 square km (140 square miles)—brings nature lovers from all over throughout the year. You can hike up King Mountain on a challenging trail that takes you 300 meters (980 feet) above the Ottawa Valley, explore Lusk Cave, go camping, view the Luskville Falls, or swim at one of the six beaches here (there are also 50 lakes). In winter the cross-country skiing trails cover approximately 200 km (125 miles) of the park. From June to mid-October, you can use the park's south entrance on Taché Boulevard; stop at the reception center for visitor information. ☎ *819/827–2020* 🌐 *www.canadascapital.gc.ca/places-to-visit/gatineau-park.*

WHERE TO EAT AND STAY

$$ CANADIAN 🍴 **Edgar.** Wonderful homemade pastries that include lemon-curd doughnuts and pear-and-almond tarts have brought renown to this little place (only 11 seats), but there's more to it than that. Breakfast and lunch are always busy, and weekend brunch, served until 2 pm, brings a line out the door, but take-out meals are available, too, and can be ordered in advance. Favorite dishes include poached eggs with duck confit, and potatoes in brown butter. Note that Edgar may close for a week or more in summer. [$] *Average main: C$20* ✉ *60 rue Bégin* 🌐 *www.chezedgar.ca* 🕒 *No dinner. Closed Mon.*

$$$$ HOTEL 🏨 **Moulin Wakefield Mill Hotel and Spa.** Part heritage mill with original features, part modern environmentally-friendly building, this waterside hotel and spa on the edge of Gatineau Park has lots of character, wonderful views of the MacLaren Falls, and plenty of pampering on offer. **Pros:** walking distance to Gatineau Park; great views; pets allowed. **Cons:** hotel caters mostly to adults; expensive. [$] *Rooms from: C$299* ✉ *60 chemin Mill* ☎ *888/567–1838, 819/459–1838* 🌐 *www.wakefieldmill.com* 🛏 *42 rooms* 🍽 *Breakfast.*

THE EASTERN TOWNSHIPS

The Eastern Townships (also known as les Cantons de l'Est, and formerly as l'Estrie) refers to the southeast corner of the province of Québec, which borders Vermont, New Hampshire, and Maine, and is known for its mountains, spas, charming small towns, lush forests, and many vineyards. In winter, the Townships are the place to be for serious ski and snowboard enthusiasts, boasting many of the province's highest peaks and most challenging trails. In summer, boating, swimming, sailing, golfing, in-line skating, hiking, and bicycling take over. And every

9

fall the inns are booked solid with visitors eager to take in the brilliant foliage. Fall is also a good time to visit the wineries (although most are open all year). Because of its mild microclimate, the Townships area has become one of the more prominent wine regions in Canada, with a dozen of Québec's 33 commercial wineries.

There remains a sizable, albeit dwindling, English population here, mostly the descendants of Empire Loyalists who fled first the Revolutionary War and later the newly created United States of America. The Loyalists were followed, around 1820, by the first wave of Irish immigrants. Some 20 years later the potato famine sent more Irish pioneers to the Townships. The area became more Francophone after 1850, as French Canadians moved in to work on the railroad and in the lumber industry, but the region still looks more like New England than New France, with redbrick villages, tidy Protestant churches, and white clapboard farmhouses with big verandas. During the late 19th century, English families from Montréal and Americans from the border states began summering at cottages along the lakes.

PLANNING

WHEN TO GO
The Eastern Townships are best in fall, when the foliage is at its peak; the region borders Vermont and has the same dramatic colors. It's possible to visit wineries at this time, but you should call ahead, since harvest is a busy time.

GETTING HERE AND AROUND
For the Eastern Townships, take Autoroute 10 Est (the Autoroute des Cantons de l'Est) from Montréal, or U.S. 91 from New England, which becomes Autoroute 55 as it crosses the border into the Eastern Townships.

VISITOR INFORMATION
Contact **Tourisme Cantons-de-l'Est** ⊠ *20 rue Don-Bosco Sud, Sherbrooke* ☎ *800/355–5755* ⊕ *www.easterntownships.org.*

BROMONT

78 km (48 miles) east of Montréal.

The boating, camping, golf, horseback riding, swimming, tennis, biking, canoeing, fishing, hiking, cross-country and downhill skiing, and snowshoeing available here make this a place for all seasons. Bromont has the only night skiing in the Eastern Townships—and there's even a slope-side disco, Le Bromontais. The town also has more than 100 km (62 miles) of maintained trails for mountain bikers.

GETTING HERE AND AROUND
Bromont is about one hour from Montréal on Autoroute 10. Get off at Exit 78.

VISITOR INFORMATION
Contact **Bromont Tourism Office** ⊠ *15 blvd. de Bromont* ☎ *877/276–6668, 450/534–2006* ⊕ *www.tourismebromont.com.*

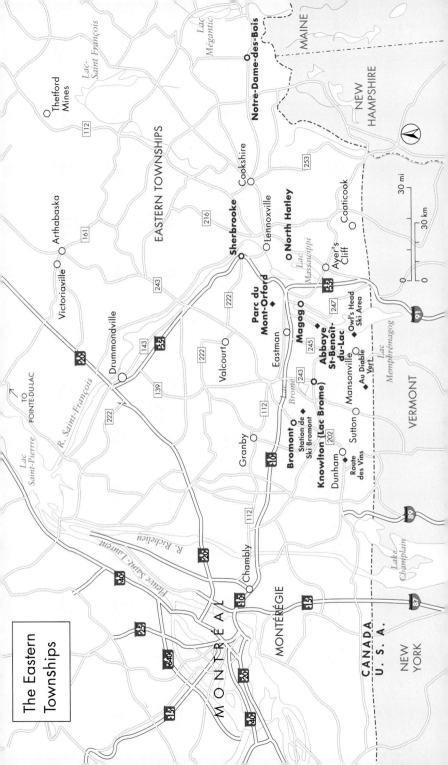

The Eastern Townships

EXPLORING

Route des Vins (*Wine Route*). Make sure you bring along a designated driver for this Wine Route, which includes 21 wineries. Map out your chosen stops then travel from one to the next to learn about their history, local products and, best of all, sample the wine. Most wineries have an area outdoors where you to enjoy a picnic. Call for hours as they can change from one season to the next. ☎ *888/811–4928* 🌐 *www.laroutedesvins.ca.*

Vignoble Domaine Côtes d'Ardoise. This winery, opened in 1980, was one of the first to set up shop in the area, and is considered to be the oldest vineyard still in operation in Québec. On nearly 30 acres of land, 50,000 vines go to produce some award winning reds, whites, rosés, and ice wines. Visit for a tasting and enjoy a picnic on the grounds. From July through October, a sculpture garden showcases the works of more than 80 artists, primarily from the area. ✉ *879 rue Bruce (Rte. 202), Dunham* ☎ *450/295–2020* 🌐 *www.cotesdardoise.com* 🕒 *Mid-June–Oct., weekdays 10–5, weekends 10–6; Nov.–mid-June, Wed.–Sun. 10–5.*

Vignoble Les Trois Clochers. This lovely winery is another great stop along the wine route. It produces a dry, fruity white from Seyval grapes as well as several other white, red, and ice wines and a nonalcoholic juice. In addition to the tastings, you can take a tour of the grounds (reservations required), stroll along the trails, and stop for a picnic before you move on to the next stop. ✉ *341 chemin Bruce (Rte. 202), Dunham* ☎ *450/295–2034* 🌐 *www.3clochers.com* 🕒 *Late June–Oct., Mon and Tues. noon–6, Wed.–Sun. 10–6; Nov.–mid-June, Wed.–Sun. 10–5.*

Vignoble de l'Orpailleur. Established in 1982, this vineyard produces 11 wines, including an ice wine that won two gold medals at the 2014 Finger Lakes International competition. Tours are given three times a day during the summer and you can stop by the museum, where you'll learn about the hisory and production of wine, from the cultivation of the vines to the bottling process. The patio restaurant is a nice place to take a break. ✉ *1086 rue Bruce (Rte. 202), Dunham* ☎ *450/295–2763* 🌐 *www.orpailleur.ca* 🕒 *May–Oct., daily 9–5; Nov.–Apr., daily 10–4:30.*

WHERE TO STAY

$ HOTEL 🏨 **Auberge Château Bromont.** Among the rolling hills of the Townships and with great views of the local countryside from every room, this modern hotel is part of the Domaine Château-Bromont complex, and well priced, considering all the amenities available. **Pros:** outstanding views from each room; friendly staff; close to ski hill and golf course. **Cons:** lack of an elevator makes it difficult for guests on the upper floors, especially those with ski equipment. [$] *Rooms from: C$150* ✉ *95 rue de Montmorency* ☎ *888/276–6668* 🌐 *www.chateaubromont.com* 🛏 *40 rooms* 🍴 *Breakfast.*

$ HOTEL 🏨 **Hôtel Château Bromont.** Massages, algae wraps, and aromatherapy are just a few of the services at this European-style resort, which also includes a large, Turkish-style *hammam* (steam room) and the Château Bromont Golf Course. **Pros:** outdoor hot tubs; friendly staff. **Cons:** some rooms are small, so check what you're getting when you book;

windows facing the interior do not open and those rooms can feel claustrophobic. $ *Rooms from: C$160* ⊠ *90 rue Stanstead* ☎ *450/534– 3433, 888/276–6668* ⊕ *www.chateaubromont.com* ⇆ *156 rooms, 8 suites* ☉ *Multiple meal plans.*

SHOPPING

MARKETS

Fodor'sChoice **Bromont Five-Star Flea Market.** The gigantic sign on Autoroute 10 is hard
★ to miss. More than 1,000 vendors at this indoor flea market sell T-shirts, household gadgets, and much more, on weekends (9–5) from April to the end of October. Shoppers come from as far away as Vermont. ⊠ *16 rue Lafontaine* ☎ *888/689–1255.*

SPAS

Fodor'sChoice **Balnea Réserve Thermale.** Tucked in a forest and overlooking a lake,
★ this strikingly contemporary spa takes advantage of its location with airbeds that float among lily pads, and tiers of sundecks with gorgeous views. In addition to steam rooms, saunas, and baths, Balnea also has 30 body treatments: you can bliss out with the Abenaki Native ritual, a chocolate massage, or yoga. Full and half-day spa packages are available. In summer, great meals are available: over a 10-week period, ten top Montréal chefs spend a week each in the kitchen and create their own menu. ⊠ *319 chemin Lac Gale* ☎ *866/734–2110* ⊕ *www.balnea. ca* ☉ *Mon.–Wed. 11–9, Thurs.–Sun. 10–10.*

SPORTS AND THE OUTDOORS

GOLF

Royal Bromont. Designed by Graham Cooke, one of the most reputable golf course architects, the Royal Bromont was built in 1992 and is located in the center of Bromont. All 18 holes provide wonderful views of the surrounding mountains and, from novice to expert, this golf course is considered to be one of the top places to play. In 1994 the Royal Bromont hosted the Canadian PGA Championships. ⊠ *400 chemin Compton* ☎ *450/534–4653, 888/281–0017* ⊕ *www.royalbromont. com* ⛳ *C$27–C$72* ⛳ *18 holes, 7036 yards, par 72.*

SKIING

FAMILY **Station de Ski Bromont.** Not many metropolises in eastern North America can boast a 1,300-foot ski mountain within an hour's drive of downtown. That height and proximity has made Bromont very popular with Montréal day-trippers and weekenders. But Bromont's 156 trails (102 of them lighted at night) and nine lifts can handle the crowds quite comfortably. Like many other ski hills, Bromont operates as a year-round resort. In summer and early fall, you can take a mountain bike to the summit aboard a chairlift and test your nerves on one of 19 downhill trails, two of which are labeled "easy"—the rest are "hard" to "extreme." Part of the ski hill is converted into the **Bromont Aquatic Park** in summer, with a 24,000-square-foot wave pool and 25 rides and slides. ⊠ *150 rue Champlain* ☎ *450/534–2200, 866/276–6668* ⊕ *www. skibromont.com* ⛳ *Skiing C$40–C$55 per day; Aquatic Park C$34.79; mountain biking $40 per day, chairlift $22 per ascent* ☉ *Late May–mid-Oct, open from 10 am; closing times vary (Aquatic Park: mid-June–late Aug. only). Call for winter sports details.*

9

VENUE

Parc Équestre Olympique Bromont. If you love horses and competitions, the Bromont Equestrian Center is the place to visit. Once an Olympic site, it hosts show jumping, dressage, and pony club events, and, in July, the annual International Bromont Equestrian competition. By 2016 the new International Center for Training and Competition will be completed, including an indoor arena with seating for 2,000 spectators that will allow for year-round events. ⊠ *450 chemin de la Gaspe* ☎ *450/534–0787, 450/534–3255* ⊕ *www.internationalbromont.org.*

KNOWLTON (LAC BROME)

49 km (29 miles) northeast of Bromont, 101 km (63 miles) southeast of Montréal.

Knowlton is the quintessential Eastern Townships resort town, with Loyalist-era buildings, old inns, great antiques shops, and enticing pastry shops. It's managed to retain its particular identity, with a main street full of stores selling antiques, art, clothes, and gifts. Interesting little restaurants have taken residence in renovated clapboard houses painted every color of the rainbow. A frequent feature on most menus here is Brome Lake duck, served in many different ways. These internationally renowned birds are raised at a farm on the shores of Brome Lake just a few miles outside town. The main regional tourist office is in Foster, one of the other old villages that constitute Lac Brome, but walking maps of Knowlton are available from many local businesses.

GETTING HERE AND AROUND

To get from Montréal to Knowlton, take Autoroute 10 Est, head toward Autoroute 15 Sud, and take Exit 90 for QC–243.

VISITOR INFORMATION

Contact Lac Brome Tourism Office ⊠ *696 rue Lakeside, Lac Brome* ☎ *450/243–6111* ⊕ *www.cclacbrome.com.*

EXPLORING

Musée Historique du Comté de Brome. Here's a wonderful opportunity to learn about the Loyalists who settled the area after fleeing the American Revolution. Several buildings, including the former County Courthouse dating back to 1859, the old fire hall (fire station), and a former school, house an eclectic collection that include 19th-century farm tools, Native Canadian arrowheads, and a military collection that includes uniforms and a World War 1 Fokker aircraft. The museum also maintains the Tibbits Hill Pioneer School, a stone schoolhouse built in 1834 to serve rural families—kids can find out what education was like in the mid-19th century. ⊠ *130 rue Lakeside* ☎ *450/243–6782* ⊕ *www.bromemuseum. com* ⊡ *C$5* ⊙ *Mid-May–mid-Oct., Mon.–Sat. 10–4:30, Sun. 11–4:30; Tibbits Hill School and the Old Court House: Sun. 1–4.*

WHERE TO STAY

$

B&B/INN

Fodor's Choice

★

Auberge Knowlton. A local landmark since 1849, when it was a stagecoach stop, this lovely old inn is a special-occasion venue for locals and a delightful option for visitors who relish period style and good regional cuisine. **Pros:** within walking distance of Knowlton's main

DID YOU KNOW?

Mont-Tremblant's 2,116-foot vertical drop and 94 trails make this Laurentian peak one of the top ski destinations in Canada.

attractions; dog-friendly; storage, repair kits for bicycles; fine restaurant. **Cons:** on the main road through town, so not the most scenic location; no elevator. [$] *Rooms from: C$125* ✉ *286 chemin Knowlton, Lac Brome* ☎ *450/242–6886* 🌐 *www.aubergeknowlton.ca* 🛏 *12 rooms* 🍴 *No meals.*

NIGHTLIFE AND PERFORMING ARTS

Fodor's Choice ★ **Théâtre Lac Brome.** This local theater company stages plays, musicals, and productions of classic Broadway and West End hits from mid-June to Labour Day. It hosts professional and amateur English-language productions, but has also dabbled in bilingual productions as well as contemporary works by Canadian playwrights. The 175-seat, air-conditioned theater is behind the Knowlton Pub. ✉ *9 Mount Echo Rd.* ☎ *450/242–2270, 450/242–1395* 🌐 *www.theatrelacbrome.ca.*

SHOPPING

ANTIQUES

Camlen. Cameron and Helen Brown (get it? Cam + len) import gorgeous antiques from China and Eastern Europe and also create reproductions using old wood. Their passion for, and dedication to the art of furniture making is reflected in the high standard of workmanship. ✉ *110 Lakeside Rd.* ☎ *450/243–5785* 🌐 *www.camlenfurniture.com* 🕒 *Daily 10–5:30.*

CLOTHING

Rococo. Owners Carla Hadlock and Anita Laurent—the latter a former model—know fashion and style, and have many contacts in the business, so their collection of clothing and accessories includes many items obtained straight from manufacturers. You'll love the prices, too, which are a fraction of what you'd pay in a large retail store. ✉ *293 Knowlton Rd.* ☎ *450/243–6948* 🕒 *Daily 10–5:30.*

ABBAYE ST-BENOÎT-DU-LAC

132 km (82 miles) southeast of Montréal.

At this impressive abbey, a bell juts above the trees like a fairy-tale castle. Combine its calm and peaceful surroundings with the chance to pick up some of the products sold here, including sparkling apple wine and some of the best cheese in Québec, and you have an expedition that makes for a very memorable experience.

GETTING HERE AND AROUND

To get to the abbey from Magog, take Route 112 and follow the signs for the side road (Rural Route 2, or rue des Pères) to the abbey.

EXPLORING

Fodor's Choice ★ **Abbaye St-Benoît-du-Lac.** Built by the Benedictines in 1912 on a wooded peninsula on Lac Memphrémagog, the abbey is home to upwards of 50 monks. They sell apples and sparkling apple wine from their orchards, as well as cheeses: Ermite (which means "hermit"), St-Benoît, and ricotta. Gregorian prayers are sung daily, and some masses are open to the public; call for the schedule. Dress modestly if you plan to attend vespers or other rituals, and avoid shorts. If you wish to experience a few days of retreat, there are guesthouses for both men and women. Reserve well in advance (a contribution of C$60 per night, which includes meals, is suggested). ⊠ *1 rue Main, St-Benoît-du-Lac* ☎ *819/843–4080, 819/843–2861 store* ⊕ *www.st-benoit-du-lac.com* ⊗ *June–mid-Oct., Mon.–Sat. 9–10:45, 11:45–6, Sun. 12:15–6; mid-Oct.–May, Mon.–Sat. 9–10:45, 11:45–5.*

PARC DU MONT-ORFORD

19 km (12 miles) north of Abbaye St-Benoît-du-Lac, 115 km (72 miles) east of Montréal.

In addition to a multitude of year-round outdoor activities, such as hiking, camping, fishing, and snowmobiling, the provincial park here also serves as a nature reserve.

The annual music performances that make up the Festival Orford always draw crowds to the foot of Mont-Orford.

GETTING HERE AND AROUND

From Montréal, go east on Highway 10 (Autoroute des Cantons de l'Est), take Exit 115 onto QC–112 and go north onto QC–141 (chemin du Mont-Orford). Coming from the east, leave Highway 10 at Exit 118 and go north on QC–141.

EXPLORING

Festival Orford. Every summer, from the end of June to mid-August, a celebration of music and art brings classical music, jazz, and chamber orchestra concerts to Parc du Mont-Orford. It's organized by the Orford Arts Centre, which has been teaching students the art of classical music and performance since 1951. ⊠ *3165 chemin du Parc* ☎ *819/843–3981, 800/567–6155 in Canada* ⊕ *www.arts-orford.org.*

FAMILY **Parc du Mont-Orford.** The amount of activities seem almost endless at this 58-square-km (22-square-mile) park. Summertime sees hikers, campers, beach lovers, and canoers enjoying the grounds and in winter, show-shoers and cross-country skiers take over. White-tailed deer and blue herons share the park with tourists. The scenery in the fall is spectacular, with vibrant orange, yellow, and red hues spreading across the landscape. ⊠ *3321 chemin du Parc, Canton d'Orford* ☎ *819/843–9855, 800/665–6527* ⊕ *www.sepaq.com/pq/mor/.*

WHERE TO STAY

$$ **Estrimont Suites & Spa.** With a Nordic waterfall, Scandinavian baths,
HOTEL and relaxation yurt, plus nearby golf courses, riding stables, and ski hills, this attractive complex fits the bill for an active or relaxing break. **Pros:** very reasonably priced spa packages; excellent place for conferences or business retreats; two outdoor hot tubs in scenic surroundings. **Cons:** only one suite is wheelchair accessible. $ *Rooms from: C$170* ⊠ *44 av. de l'Auberge (Rte. 141 Nord)* ☎ *800/567–7320, 819/843–1616* ⊕ *www.estrimont.ca* ⌇ *95 suites* ❄ *Breakfast.*

9

MAGOG

11 km (6 miles) south of Parc du Mont-Orford, 118 km (74 miles) east of Montréal.

This bustling town is at the northern tip of Lac Memphrémagog, a large body of water that reaches into northern Vermont. Its sandy beaches are a draw, and it's also a good place for boating, bird-watching, sailboarding, horseback riding, dog sledding, in-line skating, golfing, bass fishing, and snowmobiling. You might even see Memphré, the lake's sea dragon, on one of the many lake cruises—there have been more than 100 sightings since 1816.

In recent years this formerly depressed textile town has enjoyed something of an economic and cultural rebirth, partially due to the substantial number of artists who have chosen to relocate to this welcoming, and relatively inexpensive, region of the province. The streets downtown are lined with century-old houses that have been converted into boutiques, stores, and eateries.

GETTING HERE AND AROUND

From Montréal to Magog, take Autoroute 10 Est, keep left toward Autoroute 15 Sud, and then take Exit 118 for QC–141.

VISITOR INFORMATION

Contact **Memphrémagog Tourism Office** ✉ *55 rue Cabana* ☎ *819/843–2744, 800/267–2744* 🌐 *www.tourisme-memphremagog.com.*

EXPLORING

Le Cep d'Argent. The wines from this vineyard have won many awards, including four at a recent Finger Lakes International Wine Competition. The whites are very good, and the dessert wine—similar to a port and flavored with a little maple syrup—goes well with the local cheese. You can take a guided tour of the vineyard and winery, with tasting of six different wines for C$19—or C$29 for the VIP visit. In the new Interpretation Center you can learn about the traditional ways of making champagne. ✉ *1257 chemin de la Rivière* ☎ *819/864–4441, 877/864–4441* 🌐 *www.cepdargent.com* 🕒 *Daily 10–5.*

WHERE TO STAY

$$ B&B/INN 🏨 **Auberge l'Étoile Sur-le-Lac.** The rooms at this popular inn on Magog's waterfront are modern and have appealing furnishings, including some with fireplaces, but, best of all, the majority have water views. **Pros:** right on Lac Memphrémagog; various packages available; direct access to the popular cycling Route Verte; Magog attractions all within comfortable walking distance. **Cons:** not recommended for guests who are looking for isolated, peaceful surroundings. [$] *Rooms from: C$175* ✉ *1200 rue Principale Ouest* ☎ *819/843–6521, 800/567–2727* 🌐 *www.etoile-sur-le-lac.com* 🛏 *51 rooms, 1 suite, 8 condos* 🍴 *Some meals.*

$$ HOTEL 🏨 **Spa Eastman.** The oldest spa in Québec, once a simple health center, has evolved into a bucolic haven for anyone seeking rest and therapeutic treatments, including lifestyle and weight-management counseling. **Pros:** dinner included in room rate; a totally relaxing and peaceful respite; hair spa; wheelchair-accessible rooms. **Cons:** no phone or TV might prove too isolating for some. [$] *Rooms from: C$175* ✉ *895*

chemin des Diligences, Eastman ☎ *450/297–3009, 800/665–5272* ⊕ *www.spa-eastman.com* ⇆ *45 rooms* �◎ *Some meals.*

NIGHTLIFE AND PERFORMING ARTS

Auberge Orford. Come by boat and you can moor right alongside this patio bar that overlooks the Magog River. Sometimes there's live entertainment, but when musicians aren't around, the flocks of ducks lining up alongside the café to beg crumbs from patrons' plates is an entertaining sight in itself. ⊠ *20 rue Merry Sud* ☎ *819/843–9361.*

Café St-Michel. In a century-old building, this chic pub, outfitted in shades of charcoal and ebony, serves Tex-Mex food, pasta, and local beers. Its patio bar, at Magog's main intersection, may not be not peaceful, but it's a great spot to watch the world go by. *Chansonniers* (singers) belt out popular hits for a full house on Friday and Saturday evenings starting at 6 pm. ⊠ *503 rue Principale Ouest* ☎ *819/868–1062* ⊕ *www. cafestmichel.com.*

Le Vieux Clocher de Magog. Originally built in 1881 as a Methodist church, and converted into a theatre by local impresario Bernard Caza 100 years later, this theater headlines well known comedians and singers such as Claude Dubois and Gilles Vigneault. Most performances are in French. ⊠ *64 rue Merry Nord* ☎ *819/847–0470* ⊕ *www.vieux clocher.com.*

Microbrasserie La Memphré. Named after the monster said to lurk in Lake Memphrémagog, La Memphré dates back to the 1800s, when it belonged to Magog's first mayor. Now a microbrewery, it serves Swiss-cheese fondue, sausages with sauerkraut, and panini—all good accompaniments for a cold one. Hope for a train to go by when you're in the restaurant, if you hear the horns, a pitcher of house beer is only $10! ⊠ *12 rue Merry Sud* ☎ *819/843–3405* ⊕ *www.lamic.ca.*

SPORTS AND THE OUTDOORS

GOLF

Golf Owl's Head. This course, close to the Vermont border, has some spectacular views. Laid out with undulating fairways, bent-grass greens, and 64 sand bunkers, the course, designed by Graham Cooke, is surrounded by mountain scenery. The clubhouse, a stunning timber-and-fieldstone structure with five fireplaces and 45-foot-high ceilings, is a popular watering hole. ⊠ *40 chemin du Mont-Owl's Head, Mansonville* ☎ *450/292–3666, 800/363–3342* ⊕ *www.owlshead.com* ⊑ *C$50 weekdays, C$60 weekends* ♟ *18 holes, 6701 yards, par 72.*

Manoir des Sables golf course. Between Mount Orford and Lake Memphremagog, this resort course comes with some of the best scenery in the Eastern Townships and has been voted a favorite course in Québec. The best views are from the second, third, and fourth holes. Several water hazards are dotted around the course, with streams cutting across more than half the fairways and ponds calling for accurate shots onto some greens. ⊠ *90 av. des Jardins, Magog-Orford* ☎ *819/847–4299, 800/567–3514* ⊕ *www.hotelsvillegia.com* ⊑ *$32.70–$36.50* ♟ *18 holes, 6352 yards, par 71.*

Mont-Orford Golf Club. This venerable course in the heart of the national park winds through forested land, with the peak of Mont-Orford visible from many of its greens. There are some tricky holes—look out for the pond to the right of the fairway and an uphill putt on the 5th, the two streams cutting across the 8th, and the sharp dog-leg on the 13th. All in all, it's a satisfying challenge and an exceptionally scenic course to play. ✉ *3074 chemin du Parc* ☎ *819/843–5688, 866/673–6731* 🌐 *www.mt-orford.com* 🎟 *$34 weekdays, $39 weekends* ⛳ *18 holes, 6095 yards, par 72.*

SKIING

Owl's Head Ski Area. On the Knowlton Landing side of Lake Memphrémagog, Owl's Head is great for skiers seeking sparser crowds—and the views from its peak are truly exceptional. It has eight lifts, a 1,772-foot vertical drop, and 50 trails, including a 4-km (2½-mile) intermediate run, the longest such run in the Eastern Townships. It's also one of the least expensive hills in the Townships. ✉ *40 chemin du Mont-Owl's Head* ☎ *450/292–3342, 800/363–3342* 🌐 *www.owlshead.com.*

NORTH HATLEY

10 km (6 miles) east of Magog, 133 km (83 miles) east of Montréal.

North Hatley, the small resort town on the tip of Lac Massawippi, has a theater as well as some excellent inns and restaurants. Set among hills and farms, it was discovered by rich vacationers in the early 1900s, and has been drawing visitors ever since. It was particularly popular with magnates from the American South who were looking for a cool summer refuge that wasn't controlled by the Yankees. The result is that some of the village's most majestic buildings are more reminiscent of Georgia than Vermont.

GETTING HERE AND AROUND

From Montréal to North Hatley, take Autoroute 10 Est to Autoroute 15 Sud, and then take Exit 121 to get on to Autoroute 55 Sud. Take Exit 29 for QC–108.

WHERE TO EAT AND STAY

$$ AMERICAN 🍴 **Pilsen Pub.** Massawippi pale and brown ales and a vast selection of microbrews and imports are all on tap here. Good pub food—pasta, homemade soups, burgers, and the like—is served both in the upstairs dining room and in the tavern. There are three terraces at this waterfront restaurant, so you'll be sure to enjoy the fantastic view of the Massawippi River. It's a popular place and can get busy at lunch, so try to get there by noon. [$] *Average main: C$20* ✉ *55 rue Principale* ☎ *819/842–2971* 🌐 *www.pilsen.ca* 🕒 *Everyday 11:30 am–3 am.*

$$ HOTEL 🏨 **Manoir Hovey.** Overlooking Lac Massawippi, with a private beach, this elegant retreat feels rather like a private estate, with many activities, such as tennis, boating, and bicycling, included in the room rate. **Pros:** lakeside setting; secluded; historic buildings; wheelchair accessible. **Cons:** main restaurant overpriced; grounds often taken over by weddings on weekends; 10% tax added to Saturday night room rate. [$] *Rooms from: C$190* ✉ *575 chemin Hovey* ☎ *819/842–2421,*

800/661–2421 ⊕ www.manoirhovey.com ⇆ 37 rooms, 6 suites, 1 cottage ⎹⃝⎸ *Some meals.*

NIGHTLIFE AND PERFORMING ARTS

Fodor's Choice
★
Piggery. Enriching the Townships' cultural landscape since 1965, this theater, in a former pig barn in the mountains, is known for showcasing English-language plays, with a focus on Canadian playwrights. Concerts, magic shows, and comedy acts also feature in a season that runs mid-May through October. ⊠ *215 chemin Simard* ☎ *819/842–2431* ⊕ *www.piggery.com.*

SHERBROOKE

21 km (12 miles) northeast of North Hatley, 130 km (81 miles) east of Montréal.

Sherbrooke bills itself as the *Reine des Cantons de l'Est* (Queen of the Eastern Townships), and with a population of more than 150,000, it's far and away the region's largest and most important city. The Loyalists who founded the city in the 1790s and who named it for Sir John Coape Sherbrooke, one of Canada's pre-Confederation governors-general, used the power of the Rivière St-François to build a strong industrial base. Though the city's economic importance has waned, it still has significant manufacturing and textile plants, and Wellington street, in the downtown area, is experiencing a significant face-lift, with trendy restaurants, bars, and clubs now occupying once vacant lots.

A highlight of the town is the many beautifully painted murals on the sides of downtown buildings, and you can follow a self-guiding 6-km (3¾-mile) tour of them, starting from the tourist office on rue King.

GETTING HERE AND AROUND

Sherbrooke is easy to get to by car via Autoroute 10. From the United States, it's an easy stop on the way to Montréal if you cross the border via Interstate 91 and take Autoroute 55. There are also frequent bus connections between Montréal and Sherbrooke. The city is large and quite hilly, so getting around on foot can be difficult. However, there's a well-developed bus system.

VISITOR INFORMATION

Contact Sherbrooke Tourism Office ⊠ *785 rue King Ouest* ☎ *819/821–1919, 800/561–8331* ⊕ *www.tourismesherbrooke.com.*

EXPLORING

FAMILY **Musée de la Nature et des Sciences.** Fun and educational for the whole family, this natural history museum utilizes imaginative multisensory displays with state-of-the-art light and sound effects—the buzzing of mosquitoes may be *too* lifelike—and hands-on displays to enhance the experience. Long-running temporary exhibits include Terra Mutantes, a geological experience portraying the birth of the Appalachian Mountains, and AlterAnima, exploring animal life in a mythical forest. Both will be available until May or June 2020. ⊠ *225 rue Frontenac* ☎ *819/564–3200, 877/434–3200* ⊕ *www.naturesciences.qc.ca*

🏛 *C$13.50* 🕑 *Mid-June–mid-Sept., daily 10–5; mid-Sept.–mid-June, Wed.–Sun. 10–5.*

Musée des Beaux-Arts de Sherbrooke. This fine-arts museum has a permanent exhibit on the history of art in the region from 1800 to the present. More than 10 exhibits per year are staged in its three galleries, with an emphasis on artists from the Eastern Townships. ✉ *241 rue Dufferin* ☎ *819/821–2115* ⊕ *www.mbas.qc.ca* 🏛 *C$10* 🕑 *Mid-June–early Sept., daily 10–5; mid-Sept.–early June, Tues.–Sun. noon–5.*

WHERE TO EAT

$$$ ✕ **Auguste.** Québec celebrity chef Danny St-Pierre placed the town of
MODERN Sherbrooke firmly on the foodie map when he opened this restaurant in
CANADIAN 2008, and it continues to impress. Local ingredients take pride of place
FAMILY on the menu, in dishes such as the starter of trout tartar with chips, and main courses like veal liver plate or pork shoulder with apricots, carrots, and fava beans. An absolute must is the *pouding chômeur* (poor man's pudding), a classic French Canadian dessert in which maple syrup or caramel is poured over cake and served warm. The short—but guaranteed to please—children's menu is free Sunday to Wednesday from 5 to 7 pm. 💲 *Average main: C$30* ✉ *82 rue Wellington N* ☎ *819/565–9559* ⊕ *www.auguste-restaurant.com* 🕑 *No brunch weekdays.*

NIGHTLIFE AND PERFORMING ARTS

Centennial Theatre. On the campus of Bishops University, this 600-seat theater presents a roster of jazz, classical, and rock concerts, as well as opera, dance, mime, and children's theater. ✉ *2600 rue College* ☎ *819/822–9692* ⊕ *www.centennialtheatre.ca.*

SHOPPING

CRAFTS

Boutique des Métiers d'Art. Stop in this charming little shop filled with crafts made by artists from the Eastern Townships. Jewelry, kitchenware, and clothing are just a few of the items you'll want to take home. ✉ *121 rue Frontenac* ☎ *819/823–0221* ⊕ *www.metiersdartestrie.com* 🕑 *Wed.–Sun. 11–5.*

NOTRE-DAME-DES-BOIS

72 km (43 miles) east of Sherbrooke, 204 km (127 miles) east of Montréal.

Notre-Dame-des-Bois is a sleepy little one-street village just north of the Maine border. It sits in the shadow of one of the region's tallest and steepest mountains—Mont-Mégantic, which soars 576 meters (1,890 feet) above the surrounding plain, with a height of 3,601 feet above sea level. In 2007, the Mont-Mégantic Observatory area was declared the first International Dark-Sky Reserve, in recognition of the lack of light pollution that provides some of the clearest night skies in Québec, a quality that attracts stargazers, both professional and amateur.

GETTING HERE AND AROUND

Count on a three-hour journey from Montréal, some of it over paved but bumpy secondary roads. To get here, follow Autoroute 10 east past Sherbrooke to its end near Ascot Corner, then follow Route 112 to East

Angus, then Route 253 to Cookshire, and finally Route 212 through L'Avenir to Notre-Dame-des-Bois. If you want to make the journey comfortably, plan to stay overnight somewhere rather just coming for the day.

EXPLORING

Astrolab du Mont-Mégantic (*Mont-Mégantic's Observatory*). Both amateur stargazers and serious astronomers head to his observatory, located in a beautifully wild and mountainous area that in 2007 became the first ever International Dark-Sky Reserve. The observatory is at the summit of the Townships' second-highest mountain (3,601 feet above sea level and 1,890 feet above the surrounding landscape), whose northern face records annual snowfalls rivaling any in North America. A joint venture of the University of Montréal and Laval University, the observatory has a powerful telescope, the largest on the East Coast. In the Astrolab at the welcome center at the mountain's base, you can view an exhibition and a multimedia show to learn about the night sky. ✉ *Parc Mégantic, 189 Rte. du Parc* ☎ *819/888–2941* 🌐 *www.astrolab-parc-national-mont-megantic.org* 🎟 *Observatory: C$17.20 daytime, C$19.50 at night; Astrolab: C$17.20 daytime, C$19.50 at night; additional C$7.50 to enter Parc Mégantic* ✍ *Reservations essential* 🕒 *Mid-May–mid-June, weekends noon–5, astronomy evenings Sat. 8 pm; mid-June–late Aug., daily noon–4:30, astronomy evening daily 8 pm; Sept.–mid-Oct., weekends noon–4:30, astronomy evening Sat 7:30 pm.*

Parc du Mont-Mégantic. If you're short on time or don't feel like a hike you can take a shuttle bus to the top of Mont-Mégantic for spectacular views of Québec, Maine, New Hampshire, and on really clear days, Vermont. But if you want the full experience, walk up. The park has 50 km (31 miles) of hiking trails that are also open in winter to snowshoers and cross-country skiers. For a real adventure, you can stay overnight in one of the park's rustic shelters. ✉ *189 rte. du Parc* ☎ *819/888–2941, 800/665–6527* 🌐 *www.sepaq.com* 🎟 *C$7.50.*

WHERE TO STAY

$ B&B/INN Fodor's Choice ★ 🏨 **Aux Berges de l'Aurore.** From its lofty perch, this delightful century-old inn has spectacular views day and night—it's within the International Dark Sky Reserve—and is less than a minute's drive from Mont Mégantic National Park and the Astrolab. **Pros:** stunning scenery; close to area activities; delicious breakfasts; hiking trails on the property. **Cons:** compulsory C$2 gratuity at breakfast; minimum two-night stay holiday weekends and some other times. [$] *Rooms from: C$120* ✉ *139 rte. du Parc* ☎ *819/888–2715* 🌐 *www.auberge-aurore.qc.ca* 🛏 *3 rooms, 2 suites* 🍴 *Multiple meal plans.*

QUÉBEC CITY

WELCOME TO QUÉBEC CITY

TOP REASONS TO GO

★ **See the Château Frontenac:** Even if you're not staying at Québec City's most famous landmark, make sure to pop into one of the world's legendary hotels.

★ **Dine at world-class restaurants:** High-end bistros; hip, hole-in-the-wall cafés; and amazing breweries: Québec City has it all.

★ **Explore La Citadelle:** Québec City's highest perch is the largest fortified base in North America, and site of the daily Changing of the Guard in summer.

★ **Play on the Plains of Abraham:** With cross-country skiing and sledding in winter and picnicking, concerts, and in-line skating in summer, this huge park is a popular place for outdoor fun.

★ **Experience Carnaval de Québec:** Dance at the Ice Palace, catch the night parade, or sluice down a snow slide. For three weekends in January and February, the city hosts one of the biggest winter festivals in the world.

1 Upper Town. Crowning Cap Diamant and partially surrounded by the Fortifications, a 5-km-long (3-mile-long) wall, Upper Town hosts the city's main attractions, including the majestic Château Frontenac and La Citadelle, a star-shaped fortress. The sweeping views of the St. Lawrence River, the Laurentian Mountains to the north, and the Appalachians to the south are all enchanting.

2 Lower Town. A maze of cobblestone streets with tucked-away cafés, artisan shops, and crêperies characterizes Lower Town, but there's also modern flair thrown in, as converted warehouses have become chic hotels, hip boutiques, and art galleries.

3 Outside the Old City. There's an entire city to explore beyond the Old City that many visitors never see. Rue St-Jean, avenue Cartier, the Grande-Allée, and the St-Roch district all have restaurants, shops, and nightlife well worth checking out.

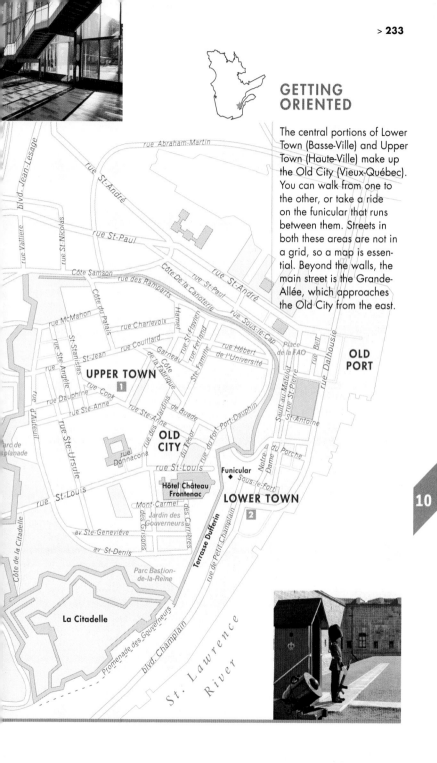

GETTING ORIENTED

The central portions of Lower Town (Basse-Ville) and Upper Town (Haute-Ville) make up the Old City (Vieux-Québec). You can walk from one to the other, or take a ride on the funicular that runs between them. Streets in both these areas are not in a grid, so a map is essential. Beyond the walls, the main street is the Grande-Allée, which approaches the Old City from the east.

A WALK THROUGH QUÉBEC CITY'S HISTORY

Exploring Québec City's history can be an all-consuming pastime, and a rewarding one. The walk outlined here takes you through much of it, but feel free to pursue the Old City's inviting little detours.

Outside the Old City

The best place to begin a journey through the history of New France is at the end. Start your tour at the **Wolfe Monument,** on the far west side of the **Plains of Abraham.** It was here in 1759 that British General James Wolfe extinguished France's dreams of a North American empire and set off the English-French divergence that has both enriched and plagued Canada's history.

The Plains of Abraham was where the famous battle took place. Today it's a pleasant and expansive city park with trees, lawns, and meandering paths with sweeping views of the St. Lawrence River.

Make your way over to the Fortifications and the Old City via the northern side of the Plains of Abraham, along the **Grande Allée** and then to the residential neighborhood of **Montcalm,** home to gorgeous 19th-century neo-Gothic and Queen Anne–style mansions and **Hôtel du Parlement.**

The Fortifications

The end of the Grand Allée is Porte St-Louis. Turn right down the Côte de la Citadelle, which leads to **La Citadelle.** Something of a microcosm of Canada's cultural tensions, the fortress is home to the Royal 22e Régiment. Don't miss the daily changing of the guard ceremony.

Upper Town

Beyond **Porte St-Louis,** you could imagine yourself in 17th- and 18th-century France. Steep-roofed houses with small windows crowd a tangle of narrow, curving streets

and the rattle of horse-drawn carriages on ancient cobblestones adds to the illusion.

The **Maison Jacquet** on rue St-Louis looks exactly as it did when it was built in 1677 and the **Maison Kent** was once the home of Queen Victoria's father, the Duke of Kent. **Le Couvent des Ursulines** at 12 rue Donnacona is now a museum featuring an exhibit of magnificent lace embroidery created by Ursuline nuns in the 19th and early 20th century.

Québec City's most famous building, the **Fairmont Le Château Frontenac,** is at the beginning of **Terrasse Dufferin,** which is worth a stroll up and down for sweeping views of the St. Lawrence River before you get on the funicular to reach Lower Town.

Lower Town

Once at the base of this cable-connected elevator, you end up in the 17th-century **Maison Louis-Jolliet,** built before he paddled off to explore the Mississippi River. From here, it's a short walk to **Place Royale,** a square graced by a statue of the Sun King Louis XIV, and considered to be the birthplace of New France. The last jaunt is along **rue du Petit-Champlain,** the oldest street in the city, lined with cafés.

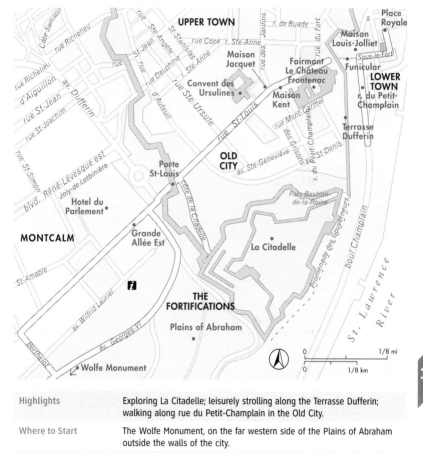

Highlights	Exploring La Citadelle; leisurely strolling along the Terrasse Dufferin; walking along rue du Petit-Champlain in the Old City.
Where to Start	The Wolfe Monument, on the far western side of the Plains of Abraham outside the walls of the city.
Length	About 3 km (2 miles).
Where to End	On rue du Petit-Champlain, in the Lower Town section of the Old City.
Best Time to Go	If you want to avoid crowds in summer, go on a weekday morning.
Worst Time to Go	A cold winter day.
Editor's Choice	Strolling along the tree-lined streets off Grande Allée in Montcalm; riding the funicular from Upper Town to Lower Town; standing in historic Place Royale.

Updated by
Rémy Charest

Québec City's alluring setting atop Cape Diamond (Cap Diamant) evokes a past of high adventure, military history, and exploration. This French-speaking capital city is the only walled city north of Mexico. Visitors come for the delicious and inventive cuisine, the remarkable historical continuity, and to share in the seasonal exuberance of the largest Francophone population outside France.

The historic heart of this community is the Old City (Vieux-Québec), comprising the part of Upper Town (Haute-Ville) surrounded by walls and Lower Town (Basse-Ville), which spreads out at the base of the hill from Place Royale. Many sets of staircases and the popular funicular link the top of the hill with the bottom. Cobblestone streets, horse-drawn carriages, and elaborate cathedrals here are charming in all seasons. The Old City earned recognition as an official UNESCO World Heritage site in 1985, thanks largely to city planners who managed to update and preserve the 400-year-old buildings and attractions without destroying what made them worth preserving. The most familiar icon of the city, Fairmont Château Frontenac, is set on the highest point in Upper Town, where it holds court over the entire city.

Sitting proudly above the confluence of the St. Lawrence and St. Charles rivers, the city's famous military fortification, La Citadelle, built in the early 19th century, remains the largest of its kind in North America. In summer, visitors should try to catch the Changing of the Guard, held every morning at 10 am; you can get much closer to the guards here than at Buckingham Palace in London.

Enchanting as it is, the Old City is just a small part of the true Québec City experience. Think outside the walls and explore St-Roch, a downtown hot spot, which has artsy galleries, foodie haunts and a bustling square. Cruise the Grande-Allée and avenue Cartier to find a livelier part of town dotted with nightclubs and fun eateries. Or while away the hours in St-Jean-Baptiste, a neighborhood with trendy shops and hipster hangouts.

QUÉBEC CITY PLANNER

WHEN TO GO

Winter is formidable, but the city stays alive—especially during the popular Winter Carnival. Spring is short and sweet with the *cabanes à sucre* bringing fresh maple goodies. In summer, the city's terraces and courtyards open and everyone comes out to enjoy the sunshine. In late September and early October, the region's foliage blazes with color.

GETTING HERE AND AROUND

The Funiculaire du Vieux-Québec, a small elevator up the side of the steep embankment, travels between Upper and Lower towns. Another option, and a good workout, is to take one of the sets of stairs that start in Upper Town and end at the Quartier du Petit Champlain in Lower Town. Renting a car isn't recommended unless you're taking day trips outside the city.

AIR TRAVEL

If you're flying in, Jean-Lesage International Airport is about 19 km (12 miles) northwest of downtown. Driving into town, take Route 540 (Autoroute Duplessis) to Route 175 (boulevard Laurier). The ride takes about 30 minutes. Taxis are available immediately outside the airport exit near the baggage-claim area. A ride into the city costs about C$34.

BUS TRAVEL

The electric Écolobus, which shuttles around Vieux-Québec, costs C$2 and runs every 10 minutes in both directions.

CAR TRAVEL

Montréal and Québec City are linked by Autoroute 20 on the south shore of the St. Lawrence River and by Autoroute 40 on the north shore. On both highways, the ride between the two cities is about 240 km (150 miles) and takes about three hours. U.S. I–87 in New York, U.S. I–89 in Vermont, and U.S. I–91 in New Hampshire connect with Autoroute 20, as does Highway 401 from Toronto. Driving northeast out of Montréal on Autoroute 20, follow signs for Pont Pierre-Laporte (Pierre Laporte Bridge) as you approach Québec City. After you've crossed the bridge, turn right onto boulevard Laurier (Route 175), which becomes the Grande-Allée.

10

TRAIN TRAVEL

VIA Rail, Canada's passenger rail service, has service between Montréal and Québec City. The trip takes less than three hours. One-way tickets cost C$89, but early reservation rates can be as low as C$29. A taxi from the train station to the Fairmont Le Château Frontenac is about C$7.

VISITOR INFORMATION

Québec City Tourist Information ⊠ *12, rue Sainte-Anne, Upper Town, Québec City* ☎ *418/641–6290, 877/783–1608* ⊕ *www.quebecregion.com.*

UPPER TOWN

No other place in Canada has so much history squeezed into such a small spot. Upper Town was a barren, windswept cape when Samuel de Champlain decided to build a fort here nearly 400 years ago. Now it's a major tourist destination surrounded by cannon-studded stone ramparts.

Home to many of the city's most famous sites, Upper Town's Old City offers a dramatic view of the St. Lawrence River and the countryside, especially from a ride on the funicular (C$2), or while walking along the Terrasse Dufferin, in front of the Château Frontenac. Historic buildings that house bars, cafés, and shops, along with hotels and bed-and-breakfasts, line the neighborhood's winding streets. A 5-km-long (3-mile-long) wall neatly splices off this section of the city with entrances on rues St-Jean and St-Louis, Vieux-Québec's two main thoroughfares. The wall itself is a national historic monument. It began as a series of earthworks and wooden palisades built by French military engineers to protect the Upper Town from an inland attack following the siege of the city by Admiral Phipps in 1690. Over the next century, the French expended much time, energy, and money to strengthen the city's fortifications. After the fall of New France, the British were equally concerned about strengthening the city's defenses and built an earth-and-wood citadel atop Cap Diamant. Slowly, the British replaced the wooden palisades that surrounded the city with the massive cut-stone wall that has become the city's trademark attraction. The crowning touch to the fortifications came after the War of 1812, with the construction of the cut-stone, star-shaped citadel, perched high on Cap Diamant.

Like La Citadelle, most of the many elegant homes that line the narrow streets in Upper Town are made of granite cut from nearby quarries in the 1800s. The stone walls, copper roofs, and heavy wooden doors on the government buildings and high-steepled churches in the area also reflect the Upper Town's place as the political, educational, and religious nerve center of both the province and the country during much of the past four centuries.

GETTING HERE AND AROUND
Many people begin their tours in Upper Town, taking in the Château Frontenac, which is probably Québec City's top site, as well as the spectacular views. The Fortifications border this section of the city. Walk

Québec City's Terrasse Dufferin offers unobstructed views of the St. Lawrence River, with the peaks of the Laurentians and the Appalachians visible in the distance.

along rue d'Auteuil, between rues St-Louis and St-Jean to get a good sense of where the wall divides the Old City.

If coming from Lower Town, take the funicular. Otherwise, consider braving one of the many staircases that connect the top of the hill to the bottom and bypass the line, which gets long in the summer. Shops and restaurants provide the opportunity for a quick rest along the way.

TIMING

Plan to spend a whole day visiting the many sights and shops clustered around the Château Frontenac. Rue St-Jean offers plenty of lunch options. Or do as the locals do: grab a sandwich and head to a bench in one of the area's lovely parks.

Mark out at least a half-day for walking the walls of La Citadelle—set out early in the morning to catch the Changing of the Guard at 10 am in summer. Afterward, picnic on the Plains, or try one of the many terraces on the Grande Allée and avenue Cartier.

TOP ATTRACTIONS

Basilique Cathédrale Notre-Dame de Québec (*Our Lady of Québec Basilica Cathedral*). François de Laval, the first bishop of New France, once ruled a diocese that stretched all the way to the Gulf of Mexico. Laval's original cathedral burned down and has been rebuilt several times, but the current basilica still has a chancel lamp that was a gift from Louis XIV, the Sun King.

The church's ornate interior includes a canopy dais over the Episcopal throne, a ceiling of painted clouds decorated with gold leaf, and richly colored stained-glass windows. The large crypt was Québec City's first

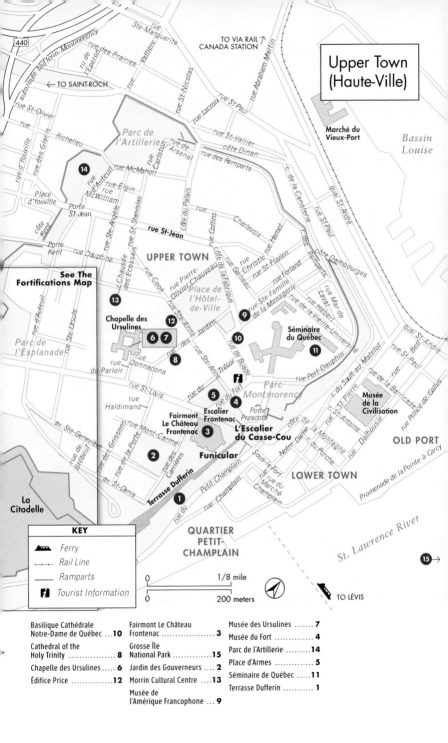

Upper Town (Haute-Ville)

440

← TO SAINT-ROCH

TO VIA RAIL
CANADA STATION ↑

rue Ste-Marguerite

rue Vallière

autoroute Dufferin-Montmorency

rue de l'Eperon

rue des Prairies

rue St-Olivier

rue St-Nicolas

rue Lacroix

rue St-Paul

rue Abraham-Martin

Marché du
Vieux-Port

Bassin
Louise

rue St-Vallier

côte Dinan

rue des Remparts

Parc de
l'Artillerie

rue de
Carleton Arsenal

rue McMahon

rue d'Auteuil

rue Elgin

rue McWilliam

14

Place
d'Youville

Porte
St-Jean

côte Kent

Porte
Kent

rue Dauphine

rue St-Jean

rue Ste-Angèle

rue St-Stanislas

rue des Écossais

La Chaussée

rue Cook

rue du Palais

rue Collins

Charlevoix

rue Christie

rue St-Flavien

rue Garneau

rue Ste-Famille

rue Ferland

rue Hamel

rue Hébert

rue de la Vieille-Université

côte Dambourges

côte de la Canoterie

quai St-André

quai St-Paul

rue Mar de

rue Laval

rue de la Barricade

rue St-Paul

quai St-André

rue Prince-of-Galles

UPPER TOWN

See The
Fortifications Map

13

rue d'Auteuil

rue Ste-Ursule

Parc de
l'Esplanade

Chapelle des
Ursulines

12

6 **7**

8

rue Donnacona

rue
du Parloir

rue St-Louis

rue
Haldimand

av. Ste-Geneviève

rue de Brébeuf

rue des Grisons

rue de la Porte

rue Mont-Carmel

côte de la Fabrique

Place de
l'Hôtel-
de-Ville

rue Pierre-
Olivier-Chauveau

rue des Jardins

rue Ste-Anne

9

rue Ste-Famille
de la Ménagerie

10

rue de Buade

Séminaire
du Québec

11

rue Port-Dauphin

rue du Fort

rue du Trésor

Parc
Montmorency

r. du Sault au Matelot

rue St-Pierre

rue de la Barricade

Musée
de la
Civilisation

OLD PORT

5

4

Porte
Prescott

Fairmont
Le Château
Frontenac

3

Escalier
Frontenac

L'Escalier
du Casse-Cou

côte de la Montagne

Notre-Dame

rue St-Antoine

r. St-Pierre

rue Dalhousie

2

rue Carrières

Funicular

Porte
St-Louis

av. St-Denis

Petit-Champlain

rue du
Marché
Champlain

Sous-le-Fort

rue du Porche

LOWER TOWN

La
Citadelle

Terrasse Dufferin

1

rue du

rue Petit-Champlain

Promenade de la Pointe-à-Carcy

St. Lawrence River

**QUARTIER
PETIT-
CHAMPLAIN**

KEY

- 🚢 Ferry
- ⊢⊣ Rail Line
- —— Ramparts
- 🛈 Tourist Information

0 _____ 1/8 mile
0 _____ 200 meters

TO LÉVIS

15 →

Basilique Cathédrale
Notre-Dame de Québec ...**10**

Cathedral of the
Holy Trinity **8**

Chapelle des Ursulines **6**

Édifice Price **12**

Fairmont Le Château
Frontenac **3**

Grosse Île
National Park **15**

Jardin des Gouverneurs **2**

Morrin Cultural Centre **13**

Musée de
l'Amérique Francophone ... **9**

Musée des Ursulines **7**

Musée du Fort **4**

Parc de l'Artillerie **14**

Place d'Armes **5**

Séminaire de Québec **11**

Terrasse Dufferin **1**

cemetery; more than 900 bodies are interred here, including 20 bishops and four governors of New France. Samuel de Champlain may be buried near the basilica: archaeologists have been searching for his tomb since 1950. There are information panels that allow you to read about the history of this church. If you prefer, guided tours of the cathedral and crypt (by appointment only) are also available. The Centre d'animation François-de-Laval uses videos and pictures to illustrate the life of Québec's first bishop and founder of Canada's Catholic Church. A "holy door" was added to the church in 2014, as a special form of pilgrimage. ⊠ *16 rue de Buade, Upper Town* ☎ *418/692–2533 church* ⊕ *notredamedequebec.org* ⌨ *Basilica free, guided tour C$3* ☉ *Oct.– May, daily 7:30–4; June–Sept. 7:30–8:30; guided tours May–Oct., upon reservation Nov.–Apr.*

Chapelle des Ursulines (*Ursuline Chapel*). Founded in 1639, the Couvent des Ursalines itself is the oldest institution of learning for women in North America. Its chapel is where French general Louis-Joseph Montcalm was buried after he died in the 1759 battle that decided the fate of New France. The chapel houses the finest examples of woodcarving anywhere in Québec, gilded by the nuns themselves. In 2001, Montcalm's remains were transferred to rest with those of his soldiers at the Hôpital Général de Québec's cemetery, at 260 boulevard Langelier. The exterior of the Ursuline Chapel was rebuilt in 1902, but the interior contains the original chapel, which took sculptor Pierre-Noël Levasseur from 1726 to 1736 to complete. Girls still study academics with the Ursulines, who are also famous for their handmade lace. ⊠ *2 rue du Parloir, Upper Town* ☎ *418/694–0694* ⌨ *Free* ☉ *Chapel May–Oct., Tues.–Sat. 10–11:30 and 1:30–4:30, Sun. 1:30–4:30.*

Fodor's Choice ★ **Fairmont Le Château Frontenac.** The most photographed landmark in Québec City, this imposing turreted castle with a copper roof owes its name to the Comte de Frontenac, governor of the French colony between 1672 and 1698. Samuel de Champlain was responsible for Château St-Louis, the first structure to appear on the site of the Frontenac; it was built between 1620 and 1624 as a residence for colonial governors. In 1784 Château Haldimand was constructed here, but it was demolished in 1892. The original portions of the hotel opened the following year, one in a series of château-style hotels built at the time across Canada to attract wealthy railroad travelers. It was remarkably luxurious for the time: guest rooms contained fireplaces, bathrooms, and marble fixtures, and a special commissioner purchased antiques for the establishment. The hotel was designed by New York architect Bruce Price, who also worked on Québec City's train station, Gare du Palais. The addition of a 20-story central tower in 1924 completed the hotel. Since then the Château, as it's simply called by locals, has accumulated a star-studded guest roster, including Queen Elizabeth II, Princess Grace of Monaco, Alfred Hitchcock, and Ronald Reagan, as well as Franklin Roosevelt and Winston Churchill, who met here in 1943 and 1944 for two wartime conferences. ⊠ *1 rue des Carrières, Upper Town* ☎ *418/692–3861* ⊕ *www.fairmont.com/frontenac.*

Fortifications of Québec National Historic Site. In the early 19th century this was just a clear space surrounded by a picket fence and poplar trees.

THE HISTORY OF QUÉBEC CITY

Québec City was founded by French explorer Samuel de Champlain in 1608, and is the oldest municipality in the province. In the 17th century the first French explorers, fur trappers, and missionaries arrived to establish a colony.

French explorer Jacques Cartier arrived in 1535, but it was Champlain who founded "New France" some 70 years later, and built a fort on the banks of the St. Lawrence (called Place Royale today).

The British were persistent in their efforts to dislodge the French from North America, but the colonists of New France built forts and other military structures, such as a wooden palisade (defensive fence) that reinforced their position on top of the cliff. It was Britain's naval supremacy that ultimately led to New France's demise. After capturing all French forts east of Québec, General James Wolfe led his army to Québec City in the summer of 1759.

After a months-long siege, thousands of British soldiers scaled the heights along a narrow cow path on a moonless night. Surprised to see British soldiers massed on a farmer's field so near the city, French general Louis-Joseph Montcalm rushed out to meet them in what became known as the Battle of the Plains of Abraham. The French were routed in the 20-minute skirmish, which claimed the lives of both Wolfe and Montcalm. The battle symbolically marks the death of New France and the birth of British Canada.

British rule was a boon for Québec City. Thanks to more robust trade and large capital investments, the fishing, fur-trading, shipbuilding, and timber industries expanded rapidly. As the city developed and diversified, the quality of people's lives also greatly improved.

Wary of new invasions from its former American colonies, the British also expanded the city's fortifications. They replaced the wooden palisades with a massive stone wall and built a star-shaped fortress. Both structures still stand.

The constitution of 1791 established Québec City as the capital of Lower Canada, a position it held until 1840, when the Act of Union united Upper and Lower Canada and made Montréal the capital. When Canada was created in 1867 by the Act of Confederation, which united four colonial provinces (Québec, Ontario, New Brunswick, and Nova Scotia), Québec City was named the province's capital city, a role it continues to play. In Québec, however, the city is known officially as *la capitale nationale*, a reflection of the nationalist sentiments that have marked Québec society and politics since the 1960s.

The French began building ramparts along the city's cliffs as early as 1690 to protect themselves from British invaders. However, the colonists had trouble convincing the French government to take the threat of invasion seriously, and when the British invaded in 1759 the walls were still incomplete. The British, despite attacks by the Americans during the American Revolution and the War of 1812, took a century to finish them—and they never saw armed conflict. From June to early October, the park is the starting point for walking the city's 5 km (3

Kids will love watching the Royal 22nd Regiment's Changing of the Guard every summer day at 10 am, from June 24 until the first Monday in September.

miles) of walls. There are two guided tours (adults C$9.80); one starts at the interpretation center and the other begins at Terrasse Dufferin.

Fodor's Choice
★
Jardin des Gouverneurs (*Governors' Park*). In this small park just south of the Château Frontenac stands the **Wolfe-Montcalm Monument,** a 50-foot-tall obelisk that is unique because it pays tribute to both a winning (English) and a losing (French) general. The monument recalls the 1759 battle on the Plains of Abraham, which essentially ended French rule here. British general James Wolfe lived only long enough to hear of his victory; French general Louis-Joseph Montcalm died shortly after Wolfe, with the knowledge that the city was lost. On the south side of the park is **avenue Ste-Geneviève,** lined with well-preserved Victorian houses dating from 1850 to 1900. Many have been converted to inns, B&Bs, and hotels. ⊠ *Upper Town.*

Fodor's Choice
★
La Citadelle. Built at the city's highest point, on Cap Diamant, the Citadelle is the largest fortified base in North America still occupied by troops. The 25-building fortress was intended to protect the port, prevent the enemy from taking up a position on the Plains of Abraham, and provide a refuge in case of an attack. Having inherited incomplete fortifications, the British completed the Citadelle as protection against French and, eventually, American attacks. However, by the time it was finished in 1832, the attacks against Québec City had ended.

Since 1920 the Citadelle has served as a base for Canada's most storied French-speaking military formation, the Royal 22e Régiment (Royal 22nd Regiment), known across Canada as the Van Doos, from the French "vingt-deux" (twenty-two). Firearms, uniforms, and decorations from as far back as the 17th century are displayed in the **Musée Royal**

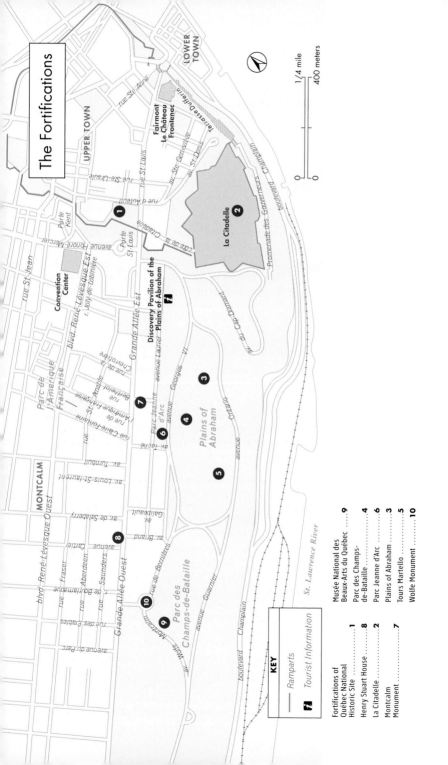

The Fortifications

UPPER TOWN

LOWER TOWN

Fairmont
Le Château
Frontenac

Convention
Center

La Citadelle ②

Discovery Pavilion of the
Plains of Abraham

Plains of Abraham

Parc de
l'Amérique
Française

MONTCALM

Parc des
Champs-de-Bataille

St. Laurence River

Porte Kent
Porte St-Louis
Porte Honoré-Mercier

rue Ste-Anne
rue St-Louis
rue Ste-Ursule
av. Ste-Geneviève
av. St-Denis
Terrasse Dufferin
rue d'Auteuil
Côte de la Citadelle
avenue Honoré-Mercier
rue St-Jean
blvd. René-Lévesque Est
Grande Allée Est
r. Joly de Lotbinière
rue de la Chevrotière
rue Berthelot
rue de l'Amérique Française
rue Ste-Amélie
av. Cartier
rue Claire-Fontaine
rue de la
av. Turnbull
av. Louis-St-Laurent
av. de Salaberry
avenue Cartier
av. Aberdeen
blvd. René-Lévesque Ouest
rue Fraser
rue Saunders
rue de Bernières
rue de Boursmaque
rue des Érables
avenue du Parc
Grande Allée Ouest
rue Montcalm
rue Wolfe
avenue Garnier
boulevard Champlain
Promenade des Gouverneurs
boulevard Champlain
avenue Laurier
avenue George VI
avenue Ontario
avenue Taché
avenue Garnier
av. Briand
av. Galipeault
av. du Cap-Diamant

1 ❶
2 ❷
3 ❸
4 ❹
5 ❺
6 ❻
7 ❼
8 ❽
9 ❾
10 ❿

1/4 mile
0
0   400 meters

KEY

——— Ramparts

🛈 Tourist Information

Fortifications of
Québec National
Historic Site **1**

Henry Stuart House **8**

La Citadelle **2**

Montcalm
Monument **7**

Musée National des
Beaux-Arts du Québec **9**

Parc des Champs-
de-Bataille **4**

Parc Jeanne d'Arc **6**

Plains of Abraham **3**

Tours Martello **5**

Wolfe Monument **10**

22e Régiment (Royal 22nd Regiment Museum) in the former powder magazine, built in 1750. If weather permits, you can watch the changing of the guard, a ceremony in which troops parade before the Citadelle in red coats and black fur hats, and a band plays. The regiment's mascot, a well-behaved goat, also watches the activity. The queen's representative in Canada, the governor-general, has a residence in the Citadelle, and it's open for tours in summer. Québec City's oldest military building, the Cape Diamond Redoubt, was constructed in 1693 under the supervision of the engineer Josué Boisberthelot de Beaucours and is now included in the guided tours. A guide must accompany visitors to the Citadelle, as it is a military base. ⊠ *Côte de la Citadelle, Upper Town* ☎ *418/694–2815* ⊕ *www.lacitadelle.qc.ca* ⛉ *C$10* ⊙ *May–Oct., daily 9–6; Nov.–Mar., daily 10–5, bilingual tour daily, group reservations available daily. Changing of the Guard June 24–1st Mon. in Sept., daily at 10 am; Beating of the Retreat June 24–1st Mon. in Sept., Sat. at 7 pm.*

Montcalm Monument. France and Canada jointly erected this monument honoring Louis-Joseph Montcalm, the French general who gained his fame by winning four major battles in North America. His most famous battle, however, was the one he lost, when the British conquered Québec City on September 13, 1759. Montcalm was in the north, at Beauport, when he learned that the British attack was imminent. He quickly assembled his troops to meet the enemy and was wounded in battle in the leg and stomach. Montcalm was carried into the walled city, where he died the next morning. The monument depicts the standing figure of Montcalm, with an angel over his shoulder. ⊠ *Cours du Général-De Montcalm, Upper Town.*

Musée des Ursulines. The former residence of Madame de la Peltrie, the laywoman who helped found the convent, is now a museum providing an informative perspective on the Ursuline nuns. It includes an exhibition on the nuns' work in education during the 19th and 20th centuries. The Ursulines are famous for their lace, and it took a nun nine years of training to attain the level of a professional lace embroiderer. The museum contains magnificent examples of their ornate work, such as altar frontals with gold and silver threads intertwined with semiprecious jewels. ⊠ *12 rue Donnacona, Upper Town* ☎ *418/694–0694* ⊕ *www.museedesursulines.com* ⛉ *C$8* ⊙ *May–Sept., Tues.–Sat. 10–5; Oct.–Apr., Tues.–Sun. 1–5.*

10

Musée National des Beaux-Arts du Québec (*National Museum of Fine Arts of Québec*). This neoclassical beaux arts structure showcases more than 22,000 traditional and contemporary pieces of Québec art. The original building houses 5,635 objects, including works by Jean-Paul Riopelle (1923–2002), Jean-Paul Lemieux (1904–90), Alfred Pellan (1906–1988) and Horatio Walker (1858–1938) that are particularly notable, as well as legions of other artifacts. The museum's dignified building in Parc des Champs-de-Bataille was designed by Wilfrid Lacroix and erected in 1933 to commemorate the 300th anniversary of the founding of Québec. Incorporated within is part of an abandoned prison dating from 1867. A hallway of cells, with the iron bars and courtyard, has been preserved as part of a permanent exhibition on the prison's history. A new, modern wing is set to open in the fall of 2015. ⊠ *Parc* *des Champs-de-Bataille, Upper Town* ☎ *418/643–2150* ⊕ *www.mnba. qc.ca* ✉ *C$18* ⊙ *Sept.–May, Tues. and Thurs.–Sun. 10–5, Wed. 10–9; June–Aug., Thurs.–Tues. 10–6, Wed. 10–9.*

Parc de l'Artillerie (*Artillery Park*). Nineteenth-century British officers knew how to party in style, if the ornate china and regimental silver glittering in the beautifully restored officers' mess in this national historic site are anything to go by. They and their families didn't live too badly, either, as you'll see if you visit the gardens and rooms of the restored **Officers' Quarters,** all decorated in the style of the 1830s.

In July and August you can sample a taste (literally) of life in the lower ranks by trying a piece of chewy "soldier's bread" baked in an outdoor oven, share in a tea ceremony, or watch a costumed actor in a French uniform of the 18th century demonstrate shooting with a flintlock musket. Artillery Park's four buildings all have long histories. The Officers' Quarters, for example, were built in 1817, and are housed in the Dauphin Redoubt, which, as the name suggests, were virtually impenetrable to enemy attacks. The British took it over in 1759, and from 1785 until 1871 it served as the mess for the officers of the Royal Artillery Regiment. The old iron foundry houses a magnificent scale model of Québec City built in 1808, allowing visitors to get a sense of the city as it looked then, as well as its geography, and history. ✉ *2 rue d'Auteuil, Upper Town* ☎ *888/773–8888, 418/648–7016* ⊕ *www.pc.gc. ca/fra/lhn-nhs/qc/fortifications/index.aspx* ✉ *C$3.90, $9.80 for guided tour* ⊙ *Apr.–mid-May, by reservations only; mid-May–mid-June, daily 10–5; mid-June–Labor Day, daily 10–6; day after Labor Day–early Oct., daily 10–5.*

Parc des Champs-de-Bataille (*Battlefields Park*). These 250 acres of gently rolling slopes have unparalleled views of the St. Lawrence River. Within the park and west of the Citadelle are the Plains of Abraham. The park hosts the popular Summer Festival and Winter Carnival and many other shows and activities throughout the year. ✉ *835 av. Laurier, Upper Town* ⊕ *www.ccbn-nbc.gc.ca/en.*

Fodor's Choice
★
Parc Jeanne d'Arc. An equestrian statue of Joan of Arc is the focus of this park, which is bright with colorful flowers in summer. A symbol of military courage and of France itself, the statue stands in tribute to the heroes of 1759 near the place where New France was lost to the British. The park also commemorates the Canadian national anthem, "O Canada"; it was played here for the first time on June 24, 1880. ✉ *avs. Laurier and Taché, Upper Town.*

QUICK
BITES
Chez Ashton. As far as fast food goes, nothing is more Quebecois than poutine, that rough-and-ready dish made of fries, cheese curds, and gravy. In Québec City, the favorite spot for poutine is Chez Ashton, a regional chain founded in 1969 that's been making hurried lunchers and late-night snackers happy ever since. Also well worth trying here is a hot-dog du lac, a "steamie" (steamed hot dog) with mayo, cabbage, and a few fries on top. ✉ *54 Côte du Palais, Upper Town* ☎ *418/692–3055* ⊕ *www.chezashton.ca.*

L'Inox. Beer has been brewed in Québec since the early 1600s, and L'Inox carries on the tradition with a combination brewpub and museum. A large, sunny terrace is open in summer. L'Inox serves many of its own beers, as well as other beverages, alcoholic and not. Tours of the brewery are available for groups of eight or more. ✉ *655 Grande Allée Est, Upper Town* ☎ *418/692–2877* ⊕ *www.inox.qc.ca.*

Place d'Armes. For centuries, this wide square was used for parades and military events, although today, it's mostly strollers and buskers and visitors enjoying restaurant terraces. On its West side stands the majestic **Ancien Palais de Justice** (Old Courthouse), a Renaissance-style building from 1887. The plaza is on land that was occupied by a church and convent of the Récollet missionaries (Franciscan monks), who in 1615 were the first order of priests to arrive in New France. The Gothic-style **fountain** at the center of Place d'Armes pays tribute to their arrival. ✉ *Rues St-Louis and du Fort, Upper Town.*

FAMILY

Fodor's Choice

★

Plains of Abraham. This park, named after Abraham Martin, who used the plains as a pasture for his cows, is the site of the famous 1759 battle that decided New France's fate. People cross-country ski here in winter and in-line skate in summer. At the **Discovery Pavilion of the Plains of Abraham,** check out the multimedia display, "Odyssey: A Journey Through History on the Plains of Abraham," which depicts 400 years of Canada's history. ✉ *Discovery Pavilion of the Plains of Abraham, 835 av. Wilfrid-Laurier, Level 0 (next to Drill Hall), Upper Town* ☎ *418/649–6157 for Discovery Pavilion and bus-tour information* ⊕ *www.ccbn-nbc.gc.ca* ✉ *Discovery Pavilion C$14 for 1-day pass (summer only), bus tour and Odyssey exhibition included* ☉ *Discovery Pavilion July–Labor Day, daily 8:30–5:30; day after Labor Day–June, weekdays 9:30–5, Sat. 9–5, Sun. 10–5.*

Terrasse Dufferin. This wide boardwalk with an intricate wrought-iron guardrail has a panoramic view of the St. Lawrence River, the town of Lévis on the opposite shore, Île d'Orléans, the Laurentian Mountains to the north, and the edge of the Appalachians to the south. It was named for Lord Dufferin, governor of Canada between 1872 and 1878, who had this walkway constructed in 1878. Château St-Louis, whose remains can be seen under the walkway, was home to the governors from 1626 to 1834, when it was destroyed by fire. (⇨ *See St-Louis Forts and Châteaux National Historic Site below.*) There are 90-minute tours of the fortifications that leave from here. The **Promenade des Gouverneurs** begins at the boardwalk's western end; the path skirts the cliff and leads up to Québec's highest point, Cap Diamant, and also to the Citadelle. ✉ *Upper Town.*

10

St-Louis Forts and Châteaux National Historic Site. Venture under the Terrasse Dufferin to see archaeological treasures from the official residence and power base of the French and British governors. Two-year excavations, completed in 2007, unearthed objects from the first château, built under the direction of Governor Montmagny, to the time the Château St-Louis burned in 1834. Wine bottles, kitchenware—even remains of walls and doorframes—give clues to the luxurious life of the governors, who were among the most powerful men in the nation. Don't miss the guided tours and activities, such as chocolate tasting from a centuries-old recipe (details available at the kiosk on the Terrasse Dufferin). History buffs might consider attending one of the in-depth archaeology conferences held here. ⊠ *Terrasse Dufferin, Upper Town* ☏ *418/648–7016* ⊕ *www.pc.gc.ca* ⊠ *C$3.90* ☉ *Late May–mid-Oct., daily 10–6.*

Wolfe Monument. This tall monument marks the place where the British general James Wolfe died in 1759. Wolfe landed his troops about 3 km (2 miles) from the city's walls; 4,500 English soldiers scaled the cliff and began fighting on the Plains of Abraham. Wolfe was mortally wounded in battle and was carried behind the lines to this spot. ⊠ *Rue de Bernières and av. Wolfe-Montcalm, Upper Town.*

WORTH NOTING

Cathedral of the Holy Trinity. The first Anglican cathedral outside the British Isles was erected in the heart of Québec City's Upper Town between 1800 and 1804. Its simple, dignified facade is reminiscent of London's St. Martin-in-the-Fields, and the pediment, archway, and Ionic pilasters introduced Palladian architecture to Canada. The land on which the cathedral was built was originally given to the Récollets (Franciscan monks from France) in 1681 by the king of France for a church and monastery. When Québec came under British rule, the Récollets made the church available to the Anglicans for services. Later, King George III ordered construction of the present cathedral, with an area set aside for members of the royal family. A portion of the north balcony is still reserved for the use of the reigning sovereign or his or her representative. The church houses precious objects donated by George III, and numerous plaques honor distinguished members of the local English community. The cathedral's impressive rear organ has 3,058 pipes. Even more impressive is the smaller English Chamber Organ, built in 1790, which was donated to the cathedral for the Bicentenial Celebrations in 2004. ⊠ *31 rue des Jardins, Upper Town* ☏ *418/692–2193* ⊕ *www. cathedral.ca* ⊠ *Free* ☉ *June 24–Labor Day, Mon.–Thurs. 9–5, Fri. and Sat. 9–8, Sun. noon–5; morning services year-round in English weekdays at 8:30 am, Sun. at 11 am, in French Sun. at 9:30 am.*

Édifice Price. Styled after the Empire State Building, the 17-story, art deco structure was the city's first skyscraper. Today it is an official residence of the premier of Québec—he uses the top two floors. Built in 1929, it served as headquarters of the Price Brothers Company, a lumber firm founded by Sir William Price. ⊠ *65 rue Ste-Anne, Upper Town.*

Grosse Île National Park. For thousands of immigrants from Europe in the 1800s, the first glimpse of North America was the hastily erected quarantine station at Grosse Île—Canada's equivalent of Ellis Island. During the time Grosse Île operated (1832–1937), 4.3 million immigrants passed through the port of Québec. For far too many passengers on disease-racked ships, particularly the Irish fleeing the potato famine, Grosse Île became a final resting place. Several buildings have been restored to tell the story of the tragic period of Irish immigration. It's necessary to take a boat tour or ferry to visit the park (some day-long

cruises depart from Québec City), and you should reserve in advance. ☎ *418/234–8841 Parks Canada, 888/773–8888* ⊕ *www.grosseile.ca* ✉ *C$49.50, including boat tour or ferry* ⊙ *May 3–Oct. 12, daily 9–6.*

Croisières Lachance. Croisières Lachance runs a ferry that departs from Berthier-sur-Mer to Grosse Île for C$49.50, which includes admission to the island. From Québec City, head south on the Pont Pierre-Laporte (Pierre Laporte Bridge) and follow Autoroute 20 east for about an hour to Berthier-sur-Mer. Follow the signs to the marina. ☎ *888/476–7734* ⊕ *www.croisiereslachance.ca.*

Croisières Le Coudrier. Croisières Le Coudrier has tours that depart from Québec City's Old Port, Lévis, Île d'Orléans, and Ste-Anne-de-Beaupré for Grosse Île. Tours cost C$73.50, which includes admission to the island. ☎ *888/600–5554* ⊕ *www.croisierescoudrier.qc.ca.*

Henry Stuart House. If you want to get a firsthand look at how the well-to-do English residents of Québec City lived in a bygone era, this is the place. Built in 1849 by the wife of wealthy businessman William Henry, the Regency-style cottage was bought in 1918 by the sisters Adèle and Mary Stuart. Active in such philanthropic organizations as the Red Cross and the Historical and Literary Society, the sisters were pillars of Québec City's English-speaking community. They also maintained an English-style garden behind the house. Soon after Adèle's death in 1987 at the age of 98, the home was classified a historic site for its immaculate physical condition and the museum-like quality of its furnishings, almost all of them Victorian. Guided tours of the house and garden start on the hour and include a cup of tea and piece of lemon cake. ✉ *82 Grande Allée Ouest, Upper Town* ☎ *418/647–4347* ⊕ *www.maisonhenrystuart.qc.ca* ✉ *C$8* ⊙ *Mid-June–Labor Day, Tues.–Sun. 11–4; day after Labor Day–early June, available for groups of 6 or more with reservations.*

Morrin Cultural Centre. This stately gray-stone building has served many purposes, from imprisoning and executing criminals to storing the national archives. Built between 1808 and 1813, it was the first modern prison in Canada. Two blocks of half a dozen cells remain intact and are open to visitors. The scaffold used to hang criminals is long gone.

When the jail closed in 1868, the building was converted into Morrin College, one of the city's first private schools, and the **Literary and Historical Society of Québec** moved in. Founded in 1824, this forerunner of Canada's National Archives operates an active lending library and has a superb collection that includes some of the first books printed in North America. The college is no longer in operation, but historical and cultural talks are held in English, and tours of the building are available. Don't miss the Victorian-era library and College Hall. ✉ *44 rue Chaussée des Ecossais, Upper Town* ☎ *418/694–9147* ⊕ *www.morrin.org* ✉ *Library free; guided tours C$8* ⊙ *Library: Sun., Wed., Fri. noon–4, Tues., Thurs. noon–8, Sat. 10–4. Guided tours in English late May–early Sept., Mon.–Sat. 11 and 3, Sun. 1:30. Tours for groups by arrangement.*

Musée de l'Amérique Francophone. A former student residence of the Séminaire de Québec houses this museum that focuses on the history of the

QUÉBEC CITY'S BEST WALKING TOURS

Tours Voir Québec. This company offers English- and French-language (and Spanish from June through September) walking tours of the Old City, starting at C$22.95. They also have a murder mystery tour based on Louise Penny novels, as well as a popular food tour with tastings at various establishments for C$37.95. ⊠ *12 rue St-Anne, Upper Town* ☎ *418/694–2001, 866/694–2001* ⊕ *www.toursvoirquebec.com.*

Ghost Tours of Québec. Costumed actors lead ghoulish 90-minute evening tours of Québec City murders, executions, and ghost sightings. The tours (C$20) are available in English or French, from May through October. After the walk, you can buy a copy of *Ghost Stories of Québec*, which has stories not told on the tours. ⊠ *34 blvd. Champlain, Lower Town* ☎ *418/692–9770* ⊕ *www.ghosttoursofquebec.com.*

La Compagnie des Six-Associés. This company gives several historical theme-driven walking tours year-round for groups, and in the summer for individuals, starting at C$17. A tour-ending drink is included with some of the tours. Moving well beyond standard fare, the themes cover topics such as "Doctors, Healers, and Gravediggers," "Crime and Punishment," and "Lust and Drunkenness." ⊠ *820 blvd. Charest Est, Upper Town* ☎ *418/692–3033* ⊕ *www.sixassocies.com.*

French in North America. Among other things, you can view about 20 of the museum's 400 landscape and still-life paintings, some from as early as the 15th century, along with French colonial money and scientific instruments drawn from collections created by the priests for the education of their students, starting in 1806. The attached former chapel is used for exhibits, conferences, and cultural activities. There's a great exhibition called "On the Road," about the Francophones' journey across North America. ⊠ *2 côte de la Fabrique, Upper Town* ☎ *418/692–2843* ⊕ *www.mcq.org* C$8 ☉ *June 24–early Sept., daily 9:30–5; early Sept.–June 23, Tues.–Sun. 10–5.*

Musée du Fort. A 30-minute sound-and-light show reenacts the area's important battles, including the Battle of the Plains of Abraham and the 1775 attack by American generals Arnold and Montgomery. The museum's permanent expositions feature a history on soldiers' weaponry, uniforms, and military insignia; a glossary of lesser-known New France facts; and a diorama on the background of the show and building. A 400-square-foot replica of the city—complete with ships, cannons, and soldiers lined up for battle is the highlight of museum and helps guests visualize the area's strategic importance. ⊠ *10 rue Ste-Anne, Upper Town* ☎ *418/692–2175* ⊕ *www.museedufort.com* C$8 ☉ *Feb., Mar., and Nov., Thurs.–Sun. 11–4; Apr.–Oct., daily 10–5; Dec. 26–Jan. 2, daily 11–4; closed Nov. 28–Dec. 25 and Jan. 4–27.*

Séminaire de Québec. Behind iron gates, next to the Notre-Dame-de-Québec cathedral, lies a tranquil courtyard surrounded by austere stone buildings with rising steeples; these structures have housed classrooms and student residences since 1663. François de Montmorency Laval, the first bishop of New France, founded Québec Seminary to train priests in the new colony. In 1852 the seminary gave birth to Université Laval, the first Francophone university in North America. In the 1950s the university moved to a larger campus in suburban Ste-Foy.

Today priests still live on the premises, and Laval's architecture school occupies part of the building. The on-site **Musée de l'Amérique franco-phone** gives tours of the seminary grounds and the interior in summer. Tours start from the museum, at 2 côte de la Fabrique. The small Second Empire–style **Chapelle Extérieure,** at the west entrance of the semi-nary, was built in 1888 after fire destroyed the 1750 original. Joseph-Ferdinand Peachy designed the chapel; its interior is patterned after that of the Église de la Trinité in Paris. ⊠ *1 côte de la Fabrique, Upper Town* ☎ *418/692–2843, 866/710–8031* 🖄 *C$7; free Tues., Nov.–Mar.* ⊙ *Tours late June–Labor Day, daily 9:30–5; Sept.–late June, daily 10–5.*

Tours Martello (*Martello Towers*). Of the 16 Martello towers in Canada, four were built in Québec City because the British government feared an invasion after the American Revolution. In summer, visitors can tour Martello Tower No. 1, and watch a presentation on the history of the four structures. A haunted maze is held for youngsters on Halloween at Martello Tower No. 2, at avenues Taché and Laurier, and a mystery dinner show is available by reservation. Martello Tower No. 3, which guarded the westward entry to the city, was demolished in 1904. Martello Tower No. 4, on rue Lavigueur overlooking the St. Charles River, isn't open to the public. ⊠ *Battlefields Park, Upper Town* ☎ *418/648–4071 for information on towers* ⊕ *www.ccbn-nbc.gc.ca* 🖄 *C$14 for day pass to tower, Discovery Pavilion on Plains of Abraham, and a bus tour of park* ⊙ *Daily 10–5.*

LOWER TOWN

Seeing all the bustle and upscale commerce here, it's hard to imagine that 40 years ago, this area was run-down and looking for a new lease on life. Today, after exploring Place Royale and its cobblestone streets, you can walk along the edge of the St. Lawrence River and watch the sailboats and ships go by, shop at the market, or kick back on a *terrasse* (patio) with a local craft beer. Rue Petit-Champlain also has charming places to stop and listen to street musicians, and the scene near the Old Port starts buzzing as soon as the sun goes down.

If there's a cradle of French civilization in North America, you're standing in it when you visit Lower Town. In 1608 Champlain chose this narrow, U-shaped spit of land sandwiched between the frigid waters of the St. Lawrence River and the craggy heights of Cap Diamant as the site for his settlement. Champlain later abandoned the fortified *abitation* (residence) at the foot of Cap Diamant and relocated to the more easily defendable Upper Town.

However, the area continued to flourish as a bustling port and trading center for French merchants, fur traders, and *coureurs des bois* (woodsmen), and France's Native American allies. It was also the base from which dozens of military campaigns and fact-finding missions were launched into the heart of the continent. A bust of France's Sun King, Louis XIV, was erected in the main square, Place du Marché, which was renamed Place Royale in 1686. Destroyed by British cannons that were set up on the opposite shore during the siege of 1759, the port and buildings were rebuilt by the British, and the area quickly regained its role as Canada's leading commercial and business center.

Lower Town went into an economic tailspin in the late 1800s, becoming a slum whose narrow streets were lined with pawnshops, rough-and-tumble taverns, and smoky brothels that catered to sailors and lumberjacks. This lasted until the 1960s, when it received a multimillion-dollar face-lift that remade it into a sanitized version of its 1700s self. Today, once-dilapidated houses and warehouses contain busy boutique hotels, stylish boutiques, chic art galleries, and popular restaurants and bars. Bounded by the Dufferin-Montmorency Highway to the west, the St. Charles River to the north, the St. Lawrence River to the east, and Petit Champlain shopping area to the south, the Lower Town is also home to approximately 850 people.

10

GETTING HERE AND AROUND

Because Lower Town is the oldest part of the city, many prefer to see it first to get a sense of how the city developed chronologically. If coming from Upper Town, head down L'Escalier Casse-Cou, a stairway steep enough to earn that name, which means "Breakneck Stairs." Have your camera or phone ready, as the top of the staircase is where to snap that quintessential Petit-Champlain photo.

TIMING

You'll need one full day to see the area surrounding two of the city's most famous squares, Place Royale and Place de Paris. Pause for lunch before touring the Musée de la Civilisation and the antiques district.

TOP ATTRACTIONS

Église Notre-Dame-des-Victoires (*Our Lady of Victory Church*). The fortress shape of the altar is no accident; this small but beautiful stone church is linked to a bellicose past. Grateful French colonists named it in honor of the Virgin Mary, whom they credited with helping French forces defeat two British invasions: one in 1690 by Admiral William Phipps and the other by Sir Hovendon Walker in 1711. The church itself was built in 1688, making it the city's oldest—it has been restored twice since then. Several interesting paintings decorate the walls, and a model of *Le Brezé*, the boat that transported French soldiers to New France in 1664, hangs from the ceiling. The side chapel is dedicated to Ste. Geneviève, the patron saint of Paris. ✉ *32 rue Sous-le-Fort, Lower Town* ☎ *418/692–1650* ⊕ *www.notredamedequebec.org* ✉ *Free, C$2 for guided tours* ☉ *Early May–late Oct., daily 9–5; late Oct.–early May, daily 10–4; closed to visitors during Mass (Sun. at 10:30 and noon), marriages, and funerals.*

L'Escalier Casse-Cou. The steepness of the city's first iron stairway, an ambitious 1893 design by city architect and engineer Charles Baillairgé, is ample evidence of how it got its name: Breakneck Steps. The 59 steps were built on the site of the original 17th-century stairway that linked the Upper Town and Lower Town. There are shops and restaurants at various levels. ✉ *Lower Town.*

Maison Chevalier. This old stone house (which is actually three houses brought together) was built in 1752 for the shipowner Jean-Baptiste Chevalier. Its classic French style is one rich aspect of the urban architecture of New France. The double-thick walls, high chimneys, vaulted cellars, original wood beams, and stone fireplaces are noteworthy. An exhibition displays typical interior design from the 18th and 19th centuries, featuring artifacts from the Museum of Civilization vaults. ✉ *50 rue du Marché-Champlain, Lower Town* ☎ *418/646–3167* ✉ *C$5.50* ☉ *June 24–early Sept. and Dec. 26–Jan. 3, daily 9:30–5; early Sept.–mid-Oct., Tues.–Sun. 10–5; mid-Oct.–Dec. 23 and Jan. 3–May 6, weekends 10–5.*

Maison Louis-Jolliet. Louis Jolliet, the first European to see the Mississippi River, and his fellow explorers used this 1683 house as a base for westward journeys. Today it's the lower station of the funicular. A monument commemorating Louis Jolliet's 1672 trip to the Mississippi stands in the park next to the house. The house is at the foot of the Escalier

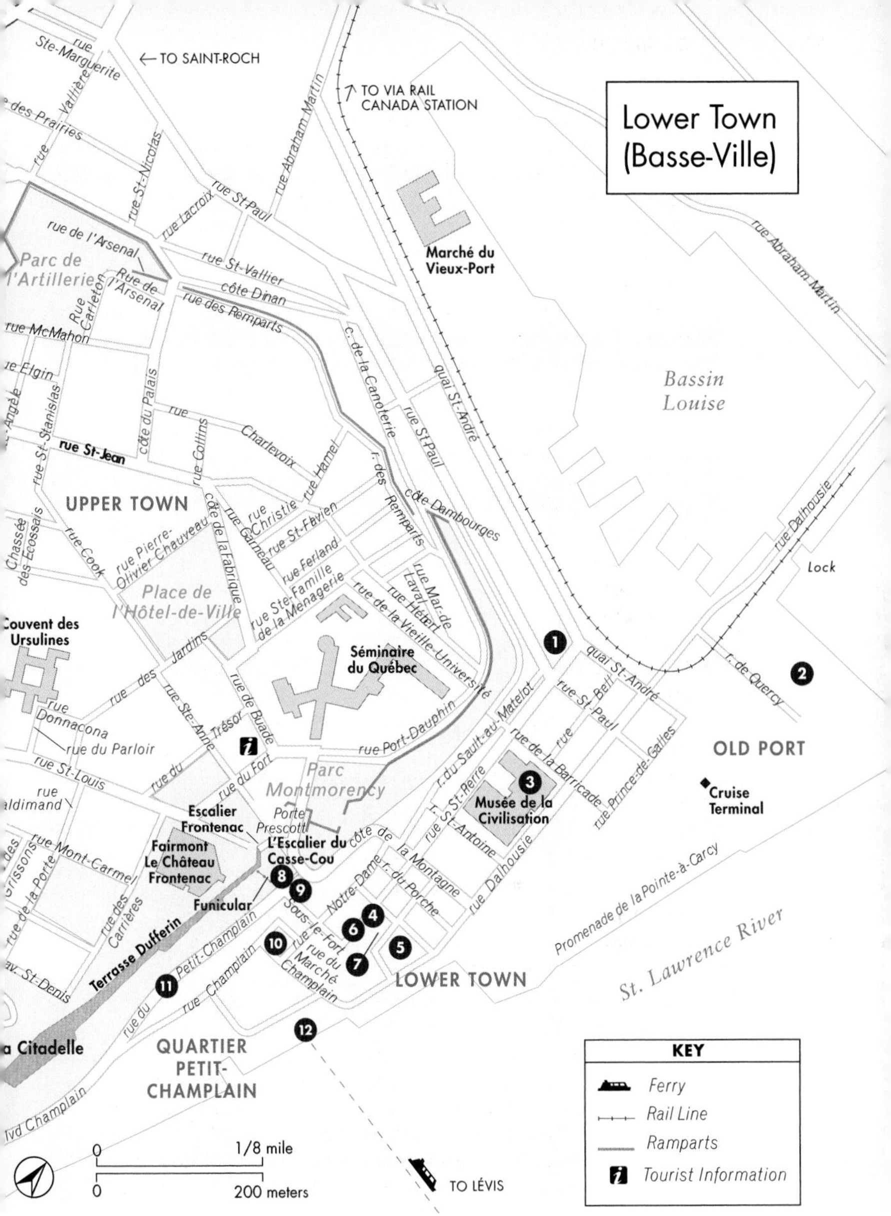
Lower Town (Basse-Ville)
TO SAINT-ROCH
TO VIA RAIL CANADA STATION
Marché du Vieux-Port
Bassin Louise
rue Ste-Marguerite
rue Vallière
rue des Prairies
rue St-Nicolas
rue Abraham-Martin
rue Lacroix
rue St-Paul
rue de l'Arsenal
Parc de l'Artillerie
Rue de l'Arsenal
rue St-Vallier
côte Dinan
rue des Remparts
Rue Carleton
rue McMahon
rue Elgin
rue St-Stanislas
côte du Palais
rue Charlevoix
rue Collins
rue St-Jean
c. de la Canoterie
quai St-André
rue St-Paul
r. des Remparts
côte Dambourges
rue Hamel
rue Christie
rue St-Flavien
rue Ferland
UPPER TOWN
Chaussée des Écossais
rue Cook
rue Pierre-Olivier-Chauveau
rue Garneau
côte de la Fabrique
rue Ste-Famille
rue Mar-de-Laval
rue Hébert
rue de la Vieille-Université
Place de l'Hôtel-de-Ville
rue de la Ménagerie
Couvent des Ursulines
Séminaire du Québec
rue des Jardins
rue Donnacona
rue du Parloir
rue Ste-Anne
rue de Buade
rue du Trésor
rue Port-Dauphin
rue du Sault-au-Matelot
rue St-Paul
rue Bell
quai St-André
rue de la Barricade
rue Dalhousie
Lock
r. de Quercy
OLD PORT
rue St-Louis
rue Haldimand
rue du Fort
Parc Montmorency
Escalier Frontenac
Porte Prescott
Musée de la Civilisation
rue Prince-de-Galles
Cruise Terminal
rue des Grisons
rue Mont-Carmel
Fairmont Le Château Frontenac
L'Escalier du Casse-Cou
côte de la Montagne
r. St-Pierre
r. St-Antoine
rue Dalhousie
rue de la Porte
rue des Carrières
Funicular
Sous-le-Fort
Notre-Dame
r. du Porche
Promenade de la Pointe-à-Carcy
Terrasse Dufferin
rue du Petit-Champlain
rue du Marché Champlain
St. Lawrence River
av. St-Denis
rue Champlain
LOWER TOWN
La Citadelle
QUARTIER PETIT-CHAMPLAIN
blvd Champlain
0 1/8 mile
0 200 meters
TO LÉVIS
KEY
Ferry
Rail Line
Ramparts
Tourist Information

Antiques district **1**
Boutique des Métiers d'Art du Québec **7**
Église Notre-Dame-des-Victoires **6**
L'Escalier Casse-Cou **9**
Maison Chevalier **10**
Maison Louis-Jolliet **8**
Musée de la Civilisation **3**
Old Port **2**
Place de Paris **5**
Place Royale **4**
Québec-Lévis Ferry **12**
Rue du Petit-Champlain ...**11**

One of Lower Town's top sights is the Place Royale, also one of the oldest public squares in the country.

Casse-Cou (Breakneck Staircase). ✉ *16 rue du Petit-Champlain, Lower Town* ⊕ *www.funiculaire-quebec.com.*

FAMILY

Fodor's Choice

★

Musée de la Civilisation (*Museum of Civilization*). Wedged between narrow streets at the foot of the cliff, this spacious museum with a striking limestone-and-glass facade was designed by architect Moshe Safdie to blend into the landscape. Its campanile (bell tower) echoes the shape of the city's church steeples. Two excellent permanent exhibits at the museum examine Québec's history. "People of Québec, Now and Then" engagingly synthesizes 400 years of social and political history—including the role of the Catholic church and the rise of the Québec nationalist movement—with artifacts, time lines, original films and interviews, and news clips. It's a great introduction to the issues that face the province today. The "Nous, les Premières Nations" (We, the First Nations) exhibit looks at the 11 aboriginal nations that inhabit Québec. Several of the shows, with their imaginative use of artwork, video screens, computers, and sound, appeal to both adults and children. ✉ *85 rue Dalhousie, Lower Town* ☎ *418/643–2158, 866/710–8031* ⊕ *www.mcq. org* ✉ *C$15* ⊙ *June 24–early Sept., daily 9–6; early Sept.–June 23, Tues.–Sun. 10–5.*

Old Port (*Vieux Port*). On warm summer nights, the Old Port harbors an interesting and varied nightlife scene. But daytime is no less fun. Stroll along the riverside promenade, where merchant and cruise ships dock. The old harbor dates from the 17th century, when ships brought supplies and settlers to the new colony. It was restored for the city's 400th anniversary, in 2008. At one time this port was among the busiest on the continent: between 1797 and 1897, Québec shipyards turned out more than 2,500 ships, many of which passed the 1,000-ton mark. At the port's northern end, where the St. Charles meets the St. Lawrence, a lock protects the marina in the Louise Basin from the powerful Atlantic tides that reach this far up the St. Lawrence. ⊠ *Lower Town.*

Marché du Vieux-Port (*Old Port Market*). At the port's northwestern tip, farmers sell fresh produce and cheese and artisans sell their handicrafts. The market, at quai St-André, is open weekdays 9–6 and weekends 9–5 from spring to fall. Some stalls stay open daily in winter, and the market is all dressed up for the Christmas season. Take a stroll through and taste some refreshing local produce, such as apples, berries and charcuterie, or try local wines and ciders. ⊠ *160 Quai St-André, Lower Town.* ⊕ *www.marchevieuxport.com*

WORD OF MOUTH

"If you like art, Le Musée des Beaux-Arts is well worth a visit. It doesn't limit itself to 'dead white guys'–type art but is quite all encompassing. It includes First Nations and Inuit art as well as contemporary commercial pieces."
—knickerbocker

Fodor's Choice ★ **Place Royale.** The houses that encircle this cobblestone square, with steep Normandy-style roofs, dormer windows, and chimneys, were once the homes of wealthy merchants. Until 1686 the area was called Place du Marché, but its name changed when a bust of Louis XIV was placed at its center. During the late 1600s and early 1700s, when Place Royale was continually under threat of British attack, the colonists moved progressively higher to safer quarters atop the cliff in Upper Town. After the French colony fell to British rule in 1759, Place Royale flourished again with shipbuilding, logging, fishing, and fur trading. The *Fresque des Québécois*, a 4,665-square-foot trompe-l'oeil mural depicting 400 years of Québec's history is to the east of the square, at the corner of rue Notre-Dame and côte de la Montagne. ⊠ *Lower Town.*

Musée de la Place Royale. This modern information center, set cleverly within the historic Place-Royale, includes exhibits and a replica of a 19th-century house, where children can try on period costumes. A clever multimedia presentation, good for kids, offers a brief history of Québec. ⊠ *27 rue Notre-Dame, Lower Town* ☎ *418/646–3167* ⊕ *www.mcq. org* 🎟 *C$7; free Tues. Nov.–May* ☉ *June 24–early Sept., daily 9:30–5; mid-Sept.–June 23, Tues.–Sun. 10–5.*

OFF THE BEATEN PATH

Québec–Lévis Ferry. Crossing the St. Lawrence River on this ferry will reward you with a striking view of the Québec City skyline, with the Château Frontenac and the Québec Seminary high atop the cliff. The view is even more impressive at night. Ferries generally run every 20 or 30 minutes from 6 am until 7 pm, and then every hour until 2:20 am; there are additional ferries from April through November. From late June to August you can combine a Québec–Lévis ferry ride with a bus tour of Lévis, getting off at such sights as the star-shaped Fort No. 1, one of three built by the British between 1865 and 1872 to defend Québec. ⊠ *10 rue des Traversiers, 1 block south of pl. de Paris, Lower Town* ☎ *418/643–8420, 877/787–7483* ⊕ *www.traversiers.gouv.qc.ca* 🎟 *C$3.35 each way (pedestrians, cyclists, car passengers); C$8 (car, including driver).*

Rue du Petit-Champlain. The oldest street in the city was once the main street of a harbor village, with trading posts and the homes of rich merchants. Today it has pleasant boutiques, art galleries, and cafés, and on summer days the street is packed with tourists. Natural-fiber weaving, Inuit carvings, hand-painted silks, local fashion design, and enameled copper crafts are among local specialties for sale here. ⊠ *Lower Town* ⊕ *www.quartierpetitchamplain.com.*

QUICK BITES

Bistrot Le Pape-Georges. For a respite from the shoppers on rue du Petit-Champlain, take a table outdoors at Le Pape-Georges and cool off with a drink and creamy, tangy local cheeses and fruit. This stone-and-wood wine bar, the first of its kind in Québec City when it opened 30 years ago, is also nice indoors; there's music on Thursday, Friday, and Saturday night. ⊠ *8 rue du Cul-de-Sac, Lower Town* ☎ *418/692–1320* ⊕ *www.papegeorges.ca.*

WORTH NOTING

Antiques district. Antiques shops cluster around rues St-Pierre and St-Paul, the latter once part of a business district packed with warehouses, stores, and businesses. After World War I, shipping and commercial activities plummeted, and the low rents attracted antiques dealers. Today their shops, together with numerous cafés, restaurants, boutique hotels and art galleries, have made this one of the town's more popular areas. ⊠ *Lower Town.*

Boutique des Métiers d'Art du Québec. This boutique, run by the Conseil des métiers d'art, a coordinating body that oversees all kinds of arts and crafts disciplines and organizes annual fairs, features the best from Québec in glass art, porcelain, jewelry, woodworking and much more, most with a stylish, contemporary feel. ⊠ *29 rue Notre-Dame, Lower Town* ☎ *418/694–0267* ⊕ *www.metiersdart.ca* ☉ *Daily 10–5.*

Place de Paris. A much discussed (and sometimes ridiculed) black-and-white geometric sculpture, *Dialogue avec l'Histoire* (Dialogue with History) dominates this square. A 1987 gift from France, the sculpture is on the site where the first French settlers of Québec landed. ⊠ *Rue Dalhousie, Lower Town.*

10

OUTSIDE THE OLD CITY

Venture outside the walls for a glimpse of the real Québec City. Head to the St-Jean-Baptiste quarter for hipster hideouts and trendy shops. Grande-Allée and avenue Cartier buzz with clubs and bars inside Queen Anne–style mansions. Cafés, galleries, and good restaurants are popping up regularly in St-Roch, the city's urban core. If you do have a car, it's a beautiful drive on boulevard Champlain, which runs from Lower Town all around the southern edge of Québec City, following the St. Lawrence River: you might want to take a stroll along the Promenade Samuel-de-Champlain, a stunning, modern linear park created for the city's 400th anniversary, in 2008. Above are the cliffs that lead to the Plains of Abraham, and farther on you'll see the Sillery Coves. Any one of the steep hills will take you back toward the main roads that run east–west or the highways that cross north–south: Duplessis, the farthest west; Henri IV; Robert-Bourassa; and Dufferin-Montmorency.

GETTING HERE AND AROUND

It's a 15-minute walk from the Old City to avenue Cartier, but the bus system is excellent here and easy to use. There are many bus stops throughout Upper Town, and a number of lines run up and down boulevard René-Lévesque and Grande Allée. There are many options available from place d'Youville or on rue Honoré-Mercier. If you do choose to walk, take a detour to avenue Laurier or avenue Georges VI for a tour through leafy green streets with gorgeous homes.

St-Roch, on the other hand, is a little less convenient by bus from the Old City. Plan to catch cabs, which aren't hard to find, to take you there and back.

TIMING

There's no need to dedicate more than half a day (at most) to see the area around Grande-Allée or the St-Roch neighborhood. Both are great destinations for lunch, an afternoon browsing in the shops, or an evening out at a restaurant or bar.

TOP ATTRACTIONS

Avenue Cartier. The mix of reasonably priced restaurants and bars, groceries and specialty food shops, hair salons, and stores, makes Cartier a favorite lunchtime and after-work stop for many downtown office workers. After business hours the street hums with locals running

Avenue
Cartier **4**

Église St-Jean-
Baptiste **1**

Grande-Allée **7**

Hôtel du
Parlement **6**

Maison J. A.
Moisan **2**

Observatoire
de la Capitale ...**5**

Parc Aquarium
du Québec **9**

Promenade
Samuel-de-
Champlain **10**

St. Matthew's
Cemetery **3**

St-Roch **8**

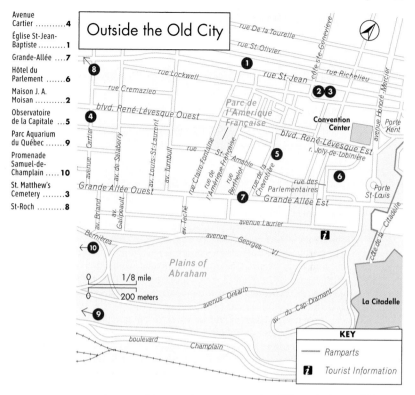

errands or soaking up the sun on patios. When darkness falls, the avenue's patrons get noticeably younger. The attraction? A half dozen nightclubs and pubs that offer everything from wine and quiet conversation to Latin music and earsplitting dance tunes. ⊠ *Montcalm, Outside the Old City.*

Église St-Jean-Baptiste (*St. John the Baptist Church*). Architect Joseph-Ferdinand Peachy's crowning glory in the "Second Empire" style, this church was inspired by the facade of the Église de la Trinité in Paris and rivals the Our Lady of Québec Basilica in beauty and size. The first church on the site, built in 1847, burned in the 1881 fire that destroyed much of the neighborhood. Seven varieties of Italian marble were used in the soaring columns, statues, and pulpit of the present church, which dates from 1884. Its 36 stained-glass windows consist of 30 sections each, and the organ, like the church, is classified as a historic monument. From October to the beginning of June and outside regular opening hours, knock at the **presbytery** at 490 rue St-Jean to see the church. ⊠ *400 rue St-Jean, St-Jean-Baptiste, Outside the Old City* ☏ *418/688–0350* ☉ *June 23–Labor Day, weekdays noon–5, Sun. 9–4.*

Grande-Allée. One of the city's oldest streets, the Grande Allée was the route people took from outlying areas to come sell their furs in town. In the 19th century the wealthy built neo-Gothic and Queen Anne–style mansions here; they now house trendy cafés, clubs, and restaurants. The street actually has four names: inside the city walls it's rue St-Louis; outside the walls, Grande Allée Est; farther west, Grande Allée Ouest; then finally, boulevard Laurier. ⊠ *Outside the Old City.*

**QUICK
BITES** **La Piazzeta.** This colorful, theatrical spot is all about thin-crust square pizza, and a solid stand-by for a good, affordable meal, particularly if you're traveling with children. ⊠ *707 rue St-Jean, Outside the Old City* ☎ *418/529–7489.*

Hôtel du Parlement. The only French-speaking legislature in continental North America, the 125-member Assemblée Nationale du Québec meets behind the stately walls of this Second Empire-style building erected between 1877 and 1886. If the Assemblée is sitting (and your French is up to scratch), see if you can get into the visitor gallery to hear heated exchanges between the federalist-leaning Liberals and the secessionist Parti Québécois. Failing that, the buildings themselves, designed by Québec architect Eugène-Étienne Taché, are worth a visit. The facade is decorated with statues of such important figures of Québec history as Cartier, Champlain, Frontenac, Wolfe, and Montcalm. A 30-minute tour (in English, French, or Spanish) takes in the President's Gallery, the Parlementaire restaurant, the Legislative Council Chamber, and the National Assembly Chamber. Tours may be restricted during legislative sessions. Outdoor tours of the gardens and statues are also available during summer. ⊠ *1045 rue des Parlementaires, Outside the Old City* ☎ *418/643–7239, 866/337–8837* ⊕ *www.assnat.qc.ca* ☞ *Free* ☉ *Guided tours late June–early Sept. weekdays 9–4:15, weekends 10–4:30; early Sept.–late June, weekdays 9–4:15.*

Fodor'sChoice
★ **Maison J. A. Moisan.** Founded in 1871 by Jean-Alfred Moisan, this store claims the title of the oldest continuously operating grocery store in North America. The original display cases, woodwork, and tin ceilings preserve the old-time feel. The store sells hard-to-find products from various regions of Québec, including cheeses, charcuterie, and some outstanding local ales. The original owner's upstairs home has now been turned into a classic B&B with all the trimmings. ⊠ *699 rue St-Jean, Outside the Old City* ☎ *418/522–0685* ⊕ *www.jamoisan.com* ☉ *Daily 8:30 am–9 pm.*

Observatoire de la Capitale. For a bird's-eye view from 31 stories up, check out the Observatoire de la Capitale. Located atop the Édifice Marie-Guyart, the city's tallest building, the observation gallery offers a spectacular panorama of Québec City. The site features an overview of the city's history with 3-D imagery, audiovisual displays in both French and English, and a time-travel theme with a 1960s twist. ⊠ *1037 rue de la Chevrotière, Outside the Old City* ☎ *418/644–9841* ⊕ *www. observatoirecapitale.org* ☞ *C$10.25* ☉ *Feb.–mid-Oct., daily 10–5; mid-Oct.–late Jan., Tues.–Sun. 10–5.*

**QUICK
BITES** **Halles du Petit Quartier.** This small but busy food and shopping mall on avenue Cartier has restaurants and shops that sell jewelry, fish, flowers, cheeses, pastries, breads, vegetables, fresh coffee, and candies. You'll find

some excellent local cheeses, as well as a few Italian and other European specialties—there's no fast food here. If you're looking for picnic snacks for a day trip to the Plains of Abraham, plan to fill your basket here and then head up to the park. ⊠ *1191 av. Cartier, Montcalm, Outside the Old City* ☎ *418/688–1635* ⊕ *www.hallesdupetitquartier.com.*

Fodor's Choice ★ **Promenade Samuel-de-Champlain.** This 2.5-kilometer (1.5-mile) park along the St. Lawrence River is a local favorite, with an amazing view of the river and the two bridges that cross it to the west, as well as some smart, whimsical, and modern landscape design. On a sunny summer day, the place is busy with strollers, bikers, and in-line skaters, as well as kids playing in the fountains and on the lawns. A café and observation tower is at the western end of the park. In summer, special buses will take you from Lower Town to the promenade. ⊠ *Boul. Champlain, Outside the Old City* ☎ *418/528–0773, 418/528–0773* ⊕ *www. capitale.gouv.qc.ca/realisations/promenade-samuel-champlain.*

St-Roch. Hip bars and trendy shops pepper St-Roch, once an industrial area and now a technology hub. There's a fair selection of hotels, most of them catering to business clientele, and new spots popping up constantly. The "main drag" of the neighborhood is boulevard Charest—a mix of office buildings, lunch spots, and after-work hangouts. Jardins Saint-Roch, a large square on this street provides good people-watching opportunities and occasionally, street performances and art events.

Look for Église St-Roch, a massive stone church, and you'll quickly find rue St-Joseph, the district's other major street, known for trendy shops and entertaining buskers. Shop for new duds here and walk west to go dine in one of the neighborhood's sleek new bistros. The popularity of the area has spawned many new restaurants. When it comes time for an after-dinner drink, there's a plethora of pubs and terraces. Korrigane Brasserie Artisanale is a great example, and so is Le Cercle, a restaurant, art gallery, and music venue.

Art abounds in the neighborhood, from the famed street-art-covered viaduct to modern sculptures to outdoor theater and circus acts. Complexe Méduse, on rue de St-Vallier, is an avant-garde arts cooperative that houses multimedia artists, a community radio station, galleries, artists-in-residence, and performance spaces.

10

St-Roch is a long, but downhill jaunt from the Old City and walkable if you have the time. If you're not in the mood for exercise, the best way to reach this neighborhood is by cab. Plan to spend about C$8 each way. There are usually plenty of cabs available for the reverse trip. Taking the bus (800 or 801) is also an option. ⊠ *St-Roch, Outside the Old City.*

St. Matthew's Cemetery. The burial place of many of the earliest English settlers in Canada was established in 1771, and is the oldest cemetery remaining in Québec City. Also buried here is Robert Wood, the disavowed half-brother of Queen Victoria. Closed in 1860, the cemetery has been turned into a park. Next door is **St. Matthew's Anglican Church,** now a public library. It has a book listing most of the original tombstone inscriptions, including those on tombstones removed to make way for the city's modern convention center. ✉ *755 rue St-Jean, Outside the Old City.*

WORTH NOTING

FAMILY **Parc Aquarium du Québec.** Breakfast with the walruses, lunch (carefully) with the polar bears, and spend the afternoon watching the seals do their tricks. When you tire of the mammals, check out the thousands of species of fresh- and saltwater fish in the aquarium's massive, three-level aquatic gallery, or have some hands-on experiences with mollusks, starfish, and stingrays. Don't miss the jellyfish ballet or seahorse tanks in the new pavilion. It is the only aquarium in North America with examples of all five species of cold-water seals. The aquarium is on a cliff top overlooking the St. Lawrence and Québec City's two main bridges. ✉ *1675 av. des Hôtels, Ste-Foy, Outside the Old City* ☎ *866/659–5264, 418/659–5264* ⊕ *www.aquariumduquebec.com* 🎫 *C$17.50* ⊗ *June–Labor Day, daily 10–5; early Sept.–May, daily 10–4.*

WHERE TO EAT

Bistros, sidewalk cafés, and chic, cutting-edge restaurants make up the dining scene in Québec City. "Grab and go" is more the exception than the rule—be prepared to eat at a leisurely pace; dinner can take a few hours. With cuisine ranging from traditional French dishes like foie gras and escargot to distinctly French-Canadian specialties such as *tourtière* (meat pie), as well as many more modern and gastronomical takes on local fare, Québec's thriving culinary community attracts tourists from around the globe. Sample local fare—sip ice cider, indulge in poutine, and dive into sweet maple sugar pie. Crepes—those delectable, paperthin pancakes made of flour, eggs, and milk or cream—can be found on menus everywhere.

With so many options, choosing where to go can be difficult. Many establishments post their *menu du jour* outside, so you can stroll along and let your cravings guide the way. However, bear in mind that reservations are a must at most restaurants during holidays, Winter Carnival, and in the summer months, when the coveted outdoor terraces open. When ordering, remember that in this French-speaking province, an *entrée* is an appetizer and the *plat principal* is the main course. Plan to tip at least 15% of the bill.

Use the coordinate (✛ B2) at the end of each listing to locate a site on the corresponding map.

	WHAT IT COSTS IN CANADIAN DOLLARS			
	$	$$	$$$	$$$$
Restaurants	under C$12	C$12–C$20	C$21–C$30	over C$30

Restaurant prices are the average cost of a main course at dinner or, if dinner is not served, at lunch.

UPPER TOWN

In addition to quick to-go *boulangeries* (bakeries), cafés, and diners, Upper Town also has its share of legendary restaurants known for market-fresh ingredients and legions of creative chefs and sommeliers.

$$$$
CANADIAN

✕ **Aux Anciens Canadiens.** This establishment is named for a 19th-century book by Philippe-Aubert de Gaspé, who once resided here. The house, dating from 1675, has servers in period costume and five dining rooms with different themes. For example, the *vaisselier* (dish room) is bright and cheerful, with colorful antique dishes and a fireplace. There's a more modern menu and a good wine list, but people come for the authentic French-Canadian cooking, like Lac St-Jean *tourtière* (meat pie), and maple-syrup pie with fresh cream. One of the best deals is a three-course meal, starting at C$19.95, available until 5:45 every day. $ *Average main: C$39* ✉ *34 rue St-Louis, Upper Town* ☎ *418/692– 1627* ⊕ *www.auxancienscanadiens.qc.ca* ⌕ *Reservations essential* ⊗ *No lunch Mon.–Wed.* ✛ *F3.*

$
CAFÉ
Fodor's Choice
★

✕ **Café-Boulangerie Paillard.** Owned by Yves Simard and his partner, Rebecca, this bakery, pastry counter, sandwich bar, pizza shop (summer only), and ice-cream parlor is known for its selection of nouvelle French pastries, whole-grain breads, gourmet sandwiches, and artisanal gelato. Long wooden tables, designed to get customers talking to each other, create a convivial atmosphere. There might be a line while the locals buy their lunch, but it's well worth the wait. $ *Average main: C$9* ✉ *1097 rue St-Jean, Upper Town* ☎ *418/692–1221* ⊕ *www.paillard.ca* ✛ *E2.*

$
CAFÉ

✕ **Casse-Crêpe Breton.** Crepes in generous proportions are served in this simple, busy café-style restaurant. From a menu of more than 20 fillings, pick your own chocolate or fruit combinations; design a larger meal with cheese, ham, and vegetables; or sip a bowl of Viennese coffee topped with whipped cream. Tables surround four round griddles at which you watch your creations being made. Crepes made with two to five fillings cost less than C$12. This place is popular, and there can be lines to get in at peak hours and seasons. $ *Average main: C$7* ✉ *1136 rue St-Jean, Upper Town* ☎ *418/692–0438* ⊕ *www.cassecrepebreton. com* ⌕ *Reservations not accepted* ✛ *E2.*

$$$$
SCANDINAVIAN

✕ **Chez Boulay Bistro Boréal.** Chefs Jean-Luc Boulay and Arnaud March- and, who are both revered in this town, delight patrons with elegant interpretations of Nordic cuisine inspired by the boreal (northern) for- ests of the world. A mix of locals celebrating special occasions and tour- ists fresh from shopping rue St-Jean dine on bison tartare, braised beef ravioli with candied red cabbage, and salmon in a flavorful cranberry glaze. Classic desserts have been reinvented in Nordic fashion: Iced nougat with cloudberries is one example. The somber color scheme, rustic-meets-modern graphics, and dark wood trim make this one of the more sophisticated bistros in the neighborhood. $ *Average main: C$35* ✉ *1110 rue Saint-Jean, Upper Town* ☎ *418/380–8166* ⊕ *www. chezboulay.com* ⌕ *Reservations essential* ✛ *E2.*

$
CAFÉ

✕ **Chez Temporel.** At this bustling, veteran café, city dwellers of all sorts—struggling writers, musicians, street-smart bohemians, bureau- crats, businessmen, and busy moms and dads—enjoy Wi-Fi and some of the city's best coffee, croque-monsieurs (open-face French-bread

10

BEST BETS FOR QUÉBEC CITY DINING

With hundreds of restaurants to choose from, how will you decide where to eat? Here are our favorite restaurants by price, cuisine, and experience. In the first column, Fodor's Choice properties represent the "best of the best" in every price category.

Fodor's Choice ★

Café-Boulangerie Paillard, $, p. 265

Laurie Raphaël Restaurant-Atelier-Boutique, $$$$, p. 269

Le Café du Clocher Penché, $$$, p. 273

Le Cercle, $$$, p. 273

L'Initiale, $$$$, p. 270

Panache, $$$, p. 270

Best By Price

$

Café-Boulangerie Paillard, p. 265

Casse-Crêpe Breton, p. 265

Chez Cora, p. 271

Chez Temporel, p. 265

$$

Chez Victor, p. 267

Le Café Krieghoff, p. 273

Le Cochon Dingue, p. 269

Le Parlementaire, p. 274

Le Petite Boîte Vietnamienne, p. 271

Simple Snack Sympathique, p. 270

$$$

Chez Boulay Bistro Boréal, p. 265

Le Café du Clocher Penché, p. 273

Le Hobbit Bistro, p. 274

L'Entrecôte Saint-Jean, p. 267

$$$$

Laurie Raphaël Restaurant-Atelier-Boutique, p. 269

Le Bouchon du Pied Bleu, p. 273

Le Patriarche, p. 268

L'Initiale, p. 270

Panache, p. 270

Restaurant Toast!, p. 270

Best By Cuisine

CAFÉS

Chez Temporel, $, p. 265

Le Cochon Dingue, $$, p. 269

CANADIAN

Chez Boulay Bistro Boréal, $$$, p. 265

Panache, $$$, p. 270

CREPES

Casse-Crêpe Breton, $, p. 265

Chez Cora, $, p. 271

Le Billig, $, p. 273

FRENCH

Le bouchon du Pied Bleu, $$$, p. 273

L'Echaudé, $$$, p. 269

L'Initiale, $$$$, p. 270

Best By Experience

BRUNCH

Casse-Crêpe Breton, $, p. 265

Chez Cora, $, p. 271

Le Café du Clocher Penché, $$$, p. 273

BUSINESS DINING

L'Echaudé, $$$, p. 269

Louis Hébert, $$$, p. 274

GREAT VIEW

Le Café du Monde, $$$, p. 269

HOTEL DINING

Restaurant Toast!, $$$, p. 270

Panache, $$$, p. 270

LATE-NIGHT DINING

Cosmos Café, $$, p. 284

Le Cercle, $$$, p. 273

MOST ROMANTIC

Le Saint-Amour, $$$$, p. 268

L'Initiale, $$$$, p. 270

Panache, $$$, p. 270

sandwiches with ham, tomato, and broiled cheese), gazpacho, chili, tuna sandwiches, and soups. Good, modestly priced beer and wine are also served. Some patrons start their day here with croissants and coffee at 8 am and then return shortly before the place closes at 10 pm. $ *Average main: C$6 ⊠ 25 rue Couillard, Upper Town ☎ 418/694–1813 ☝ Reservations not accepted ⊕ F1.*

$$
MODERN
AMERICAN
✕ **Chez Victor.** This cozy burger joint with brick-and-stone walls attracts an artsy crowd to rue St-Jean. Lettuce, tomatoes, onions, mushrooms, pickles, hot mustard, mayonnaise, and a choice of cheeses (mozzarella, Swiss, blue, goat, and cream) top the hearty burgers. French fries are served with a dollop of homemade mayonnaise (there are five varieties available) and poppy seeds. Salads, sandwiches, and a daily dessert made fresh by the pastry chef are also available. This original location was so successful that spawned several other branches, notably in the Vieux-Port and Sainte-Foy areas. $ *Average main: C$14 ⊠ 145 rue St-Jean, St-Jean-Baptiste ☎ 418/529–7702 ⊕ www.chezvictorburger. com ⊕ A4.*

$
FAST FOOD
FAMILY
✕ **Le Chic Shack.** At this refreshing alternative to the Old City's ubiquitous white-linen bistros, you can get fast food that's also high quality. Burgers made from grass-fed cattle served on soft artisanal brioche buns make this a prime locale for lunch goers. With long tables, red accents, and paper-towel rolls in place of napkin holders, the interior has a touch of retro without feeling overly folksy or forced. Save room for dessert, which includes heavenly dark-chocolate or salted-caramel-maple milk shakes, chocolate ganache, or peanut-butter ice-cream sandwiches. $ *Average main: C$11 ⊠ 15 rue du Fort, Upper Town ☎ 418/692–1485 ⊕ www.chicshack.ca ⊕ G2.*

$$$$
EUROPEAN
✕ **Le Continental.** If Québec City had a dining hall of fame, Le Continental would be there among the best. Since 1956 this historic spot, steps from the Château Frontenac, has been serving solid, traditional, traditionally gourmet dishes. The classic house specialties include orange duckling and filet mignon, which is flambéed in a cognac sauce and then luxuriously covered in a gravy seasoned with mustard and sage. Try the truffled sweetbread ravioli or the foie gras with vegetable confit. $ *Average main: C$60 ⊠ 26 rue St-Louis, Upper Town ☎ 418/694–9995 ⊕ www.restaurantlecontinental.com ⊗ No lunch weekends ⊕ F2.*

10

$$$
FRENCH
✕ **L'Entrecôte Saint-Jean.** Steak frites (steak with fries) is on menus everywhere in Québec City and in lots of other places throughout the world, but this lively establishment has a 30-year reputation as the master of the dish—*L'entrecôte* is a particular sirloin cut, usually long and relatively thin. At this restaurant, it's all about the sauce. Guests choose between three steak sizes, and each comes smothered in the restaurant's signature peppery sauce with a heaping pile of crispy fries. Other French fare graces the menu, such as tender duck confit and smoked salmon salads. For C$28 and up, depending on the size of the steak, the table d'hôte (prix fixe) is a good value. It ends with decadent chocolate profiteroles, proving that this restaurant is more than just beef. This red-and-blue-trimmed house is packed on weekends, and it's wise to call ahead. $ *Average main: C$25 ⊠ 1080 rue St-Jean, Upper Town*

☎ 418/694–0234 🌐 *www.entrecotesaintjean.com* 🕒 *No lunch weekends, Sept.–May* ✥ *E2.*

$$$$ MODERN CANADIAN 🍴 **Le Patriarche.** A hit with connoisseurs, Le Patriarche serves its entire menu in triplicate. Chef Stephen Roth likes to play with food; he takes one ingredient and presents it in three very different styles, leading guests on an adventure in texture and taste. Whether it's the "symphony of foie gras" or the Québec lamb and caribou, each morsel strives for perfection. Set in a converted 1827 house, the spacious upstairs dining room, intimate main level with comfy chairs and windowside tables, and wine cellar with over 200 bottles are all romantic and contemporary without feeling forced. Note that dessert is even sweeter when served as a trio. Guests can create their own five-course prix fixe by adding C$28 to their main course selection. [$] *Average main: C$40* ✉ *17 rue Saint-Stanislas, Upper Town* ☎ *418/692–5488* 🌐 *www.lepatriarche.com* ✍ *Reservations essential* 🕒 *Closed Mon., except in July and Aug. Lunch by appointment only.* ✥ *E2.*

$$$$ FRENCH 🍴 **Le Saint-Amour.** At one of the city's most romantic restaurants, chef Jean-Luc Boulay entices diners with such creations as red-deer steak grilled with a wild-berry and peppercorn sauce, and filet mignon with port wine and local blue cheese. Paul McCartney and Sting have both eaten here. Foie gras is an in-house specialty. Sauces are generally light, with no flour or butter. Desserts are inspired; try the tasting plate of seven different kinds of Valrhona chocolate, served with a glass of vanilla-infused milk. The C$125 discovery menu has nine courses; the C$63 prix-fixe menu has five. More than 1,000 wines are available. [$] *Average main: C$65* ✉ *48 rue Ste-Ursule, Upper Town* ☎ *418/694–0667* 🌐 *www.saint-amour.com* ✍ *Reservations essential* 🕒 *No lunch weekends* ✥ *E3.*

$$$ ITALIAN 🍴 **Portofino Bistro Italiano.** Inside two joined-together 18th-century houses, owners Francois Petit and Yves Moreau helm an Italian restaurant with a bistro flavor. The room is distinctive: burnt-sienna walls, a wood pizza oven set behind a semicircular bar, and caramel tablecloths and chairs. Don't miss the thin-crust pizza and its accompaniment of oils flavored with pepper and oregano. Chef Moreau's *pennini all'arrabbiata*—tubular pasta with a spicy tomato sauce—is also good, as is the homemade tiramisu for dessert. The kitchen closes at 11:30, and a musician performs nightly from 8 to 10:30. [$] *Average main: C$22* ✉ *54 rue Couillard, Upper Town* ☎ *418/692–8888* 🌐 *www.portofino.qc.ca* ✥ *F1.*

$$ ITALIAN 🍴 **Sapristi.** The owners of Les Trois Garçons, a neat burger shop across the street, recently opened this Italian-leaning restaurant in what was a longtime favorite bar, le Chantauteuil. They kept the stone walls and simple wood inlays, and added steel chairs and a bit of a hipster vibe. The menu is satisfying, with a number of imaginative pizzas and pastas, salads and such. Try the fried mozzarella or the chef's risotto, which changes daily. It's also open late for drinks and snacks. [$] *Average main: C$16* ✉ *1001 rue Saint-Jean, Upper Town* ☎ *418/692-2030* 🌐 *sapristi.ca* 🕒 *Daily 11 am–3 am* ✥ *E2.*

LOWER TOWN

Lower Town has its fair share of renowned eateries, and you'll find some of the best terraces in town. Dine after the sun goes down under twinkling lights at L'Echaudé, or satisfy late-night cravings at SSS, which has a special after-hours snack menu. For impeccable upscale fare, go to L'Initiale.

$$$$ FRENCH Fodor's Choice ★ 🍴 **Laurie Raphaël Restaurant-Atelier-Boutique.** Local and regional products are emphasized here—among local celebrity chef Daniel Vézina's creations are crystallized foie gras with truffle snow, and venison tartare. There's a C$100 eight-course tasting menu, and for an additional C$60 each course is paired with a glass of a different wine. If you're seeking adventure, opt for the Chef Chef menu—for C$60 a surprise meal will be delivered to your table. Lunch is C$29. If that's not enough, your sign up for a private cooking class. Don't miss the exclusive food and product lines available at the shop here. [$] *Average main: C$60* ✉ *117 rue Dalhousie, Lower Town* ☎ *418/692–4555* 🌐 *www.laurieraphael.com* ⏲ *Closed Sun., Mon., and Jan. 1–15* ✣ *G1.*

$$$ CAFÉ 🍴 **Le Café du Monde.** Next to the cruise terminal in the Old Port, this massive restaurant has a spectacular view to equal its food. The outdoor terrace in front overlooks the St. Lawrence River, while the side *verrière* (glass atrium) looks onto l'Agora amphitheater and the old stone Customs House. Etched-glass dividers, wicker chairs and palm trees set the scene for the Parisian-bistro-style menu, which includes such classics as steak frites, rotisserie chicken, calamari, and duck liver pâté with raisin jam. [$] *Average main: C$30* ✉ *84 rue Dalhousie, Suite 140, Lower Town* ☎ *418/692–4455* 🌐 *www.lecafedumonde.com* ✍ *Reservations essential* ✣ *H1.*

$$$ FRENCH 🍴 **L'Echaudé.** A mix of businesspeople and tourists frequent L'Echaudé because of its location between the financial and antiques districts. The mahogany lobby and green-and-beige interior is full of warmth, and service is courteous and professional. For lunch, try the duck confit with fries and fresh salad. Every day there's a meat dish, a fish plate, a steak, and pasta on the menu. Highlights of the three-course brunch are eggs Benedict and tantalizing desserts. The interior is modern, with hardwood floors, a mirrored wall, and a stainless-steel bar with backlit river stones underneath. [$] *Average main: C$25* ✉ *73 rue Sault-au-Matelot, Lower Town* ☎ *418/692–1299* 🌐 *www.echaude.com* ✣ *G1.*

$$ CAFÉ 🍴 **Le Cochon Dingue.** The café dishes at this cheerful chain, whose name translates into the Crazy Pig, include delicious mussels, steak with fries, thick soups, and apple pie with vanilla cream. At the boulevard Champlain restaurant location, sidewalk tables and indoor dining rooms artfully blend the chic and the antique; black-and-white checkerboard floors contrast with ancient stone walls. The best-kept secret in Québec City is the full breakfast, served here all week. Meanwhile, a few doors away, you'll find a fresh pastry, sandwich, and pizza shop: Le Petit Cochon Dingue. [$] *Average main: C$14* ✉ *46 boul. Champlain, Lower Town* ☎ *418/692–2013* 🌐 *www.cochondingue.com* ⏲ *No dinner.* ✣ *G3.*

$$$ MODERN CANADIAN 🍴 **Légende.** Set on the ground floor of the Hôtel des Coutellier, in the Old Port area, Légende is set in a large wood and stone room with plush banquettes and an elegant bar. There are a lot of sharing plates—the

10

smartly prepared fish and seafood board (including things like salmon rillettes and welk salad) is particularly delightful. The menu is highly seasonal, and ingredients are exclusively from Québec, with local meats garnished with foraged wild mushrooms and fish with seaside herbs from the Gulf of St Lawrence. Desserts showcase bright and intense flavors of local fruit, among other things. More than 30 wines are offered by the glass, with a strong emphasis on food pairings. [$] *Average main: C$28* ✉ *255 rue Saint-Paul, Lower Town* ☎ *418/614–2555* 🌐 *restaurantlataniere.com* ✥ *D1.*

$$$$ FRENCH Fodor's Choice ★ 🍴 **L'Initiale.** A contemporary setting and gracious service place L'Initiale in the upper echelon of restaurants in this city, in cost as well as quality. Widely spaced tables favor intimate dining, and the warm brown-and-cream interior is cozy. But don't rush to your table. Begin your night in the lounge, where you can peruse the menu at your leisure. Chef Yvan Lebrun, considered unanimously as one of the top chefs in Québec, demonstrates remarkable precision and balance in all his dishes. The constantly changing menu follows the whims of the chef and the season. Try the foie gras or the lamb. There's also a C$129 eight-course tasting menu. For dessert, many small treats are arranged attractively on a single plate. After dinner, you can return to the lounge for your coffee. [$] *Average main: C$65* ✉ *54 rue St-Pierre, Lower Town* ☎ *418/694–1818* 🌐 *www.restaurantinitiale.com* ⏲ *Closed Sun., Mon., and early Jan.* ✥ *G2.*

$$$ CANADIAN Fodor's Choice ★ 🍴 **Panache.** This restaurant, inside the museum-like Auberge Saint-Antoine, has attractive wooden floors and exposed beams from the building's warehouse days. Young chef Louis Pacquelin learned his chops working alongside the world-famous Alain Ducasse, among others. The menus change with the seasons, but fresh, locally sourced ingredients are at the core of the classic, elegant menu. For a true feast, your table can order the Signature Menu, a six-course meal for C$105 per person with a classic wine pairing for an additional C$95. The wine list draws from a 12,000-bottle cellar, with well-chosen cuvées coming from all over the world. [$] *Average main: C$35* ✉ *10 rue St-Antoine, Lower Town* ☎ *418/692–1022* 🌐 *www.saint-antoine.com* ✥ *G2.*

$$$$ MODERN CANADIAN 🍴 **Restaurant Toast!.** At this very chic, very intimate restaurant in Le Priori hotel, mod light fixtures are set against stone-and-brick walls, and a secret garden terrace removes all street noise out back, making it perfect for meeting friends for cocktails or relaxing. You can dine on lobster risotto, a scrumptious pork cassoulet, or fried duck with adobo spice and squash gnocchi. [$] *Average main: C$35* ✉ *17 rue Sault-au-Matelot, Lower Town* ☎ *418/692–1334* 🌐 *www.restauranttoast.com* ✍ *Reservations essential* ✥ *G2.*

$$ ECLECTIC 🍴 **Simple Snack Sympathique** (*SSS*). Throngs of professionals and young urbanites pack restaurant Simple Snack Sympathique (SSS) to dine on artfully prepared dishes, from angel hair pasta with succulent duck confit to tender ribs served alongside crispy fries. It's a chic place to be on Saturday night. Two distinct dining areas let patrons choose between sass and sophistication; one features high tables, "mouthy" wallpaper, and techno music. Just through the curtain is a more relaxed space with a flickering fireplace and exposed brick wall. Come for lunch (weekdays

only), or stop by for late-night grub—SSS is one of the few restaurants open daily until midnight in this part of town—and they have a special snack menu for night owls. [$] *Average main: C$20* ✉ *71 rue St-Paul, Lower Town* ☎ *418/692–1991* 🌐 *www.restaurantsss.com* 🕓 *No lunch weekends.* ✥ *G1.*

OUTSIDE THE OLD CITY

There are many cute cafés and fine eateries within the walls of the Old City, but don't miss the thriving culinary scene beyond them. Le Café du Clocher Penché is arguably the bistro with the best brunch, and it gives you an excuse to visit trendy St-Roch. Or if you're looking for a little more luxury, head to Louis Hébert to nibble on trendy dishes while playing "spot the politico."

Work up a good appetite by wandering through the streets. No visit to Québec is complete without a picnic in the park; pop into one of the city's little out-of-the-way patisseries for buttery croissants and heavenly brioches.

$$$$ MODERN CANADIAN 🍴 **Bistro B.** Chef François Blais, who first made Panache into one of the city's hot spots, decided on a more casual approach when he opened his own restaurant on avenue Cartier. In true "market cuisine" spirit, the whole menu fits on a blackboard, with a handful of appetizers, main courses, and desserts that change daily. The atmosphere is upbeat, the interior is simple, and the cuisine straight to the point and well executed. Weekend brunch is out of the ordinary and well worth it. [$] *Average main: C$35* ✉ *1144 av. Cartier, Montcalm* ☎ *418/614–5444* 🌐 *www.bistrob.ca* ✥ *A6.*

$ ECLECTIC FAMILY 🍴 **Chez Cora.** Substantial breakfasts with mounds of fresh fruit are the specialty at this sunny chain restaurant, which is open from 6 am until 3 pm. Whimsy is everywhere, from the plastic chicken decorations to the inventive dishes, often named after the customers or family members who inspired them. Try the Eggs Ben et Dictine, which has smoked salmon, or the Gargantua—two eggs, sausage, ham, fruit, pancakes, *cretons* (pâtés), and baked beans. Kids love the Banana Surprise, a banana wrapped in a pancake with chocolate or peanut butter and honey. The restaurant also serves light lunch fare, such as salmon bagels, salads, and club sandwiches. [$] *Average main: C$9* ✉ *545 rue du Parvis, St-Roch, Outside the Old City* ☎ *418/524–3232* 🌐 *www.chezcora.com* 🕓 *No dinner* ✥ *B2.*

$$ VIETNAMESE 🍴 **La Petite Boîte Vietnamienne.** Red walls, dark furnishings, and flickering tea lights make this little hideaway a favorite for date night, but the magic doesn't end with the romantic setting—the "Little Vietnamese Box" has made big waves for its food, too. Owner and chef Thi Cam Nhung Le swirls influences from both "here" and "home"—smoked salmon tucked in a spring roll; duck breast with Hanoi flavor; even a spicy Asian fondue. For traditionalists, it's one of the better places hereabouts to try *pho*—a hearty soup made with rice noodles and served with basil, bean sprouts, and lime. Save room to sample the Eastern-inspired desserts, such as fruit fritters with maple syrup or green tapioca pudding. [$] *Average main: C$16* ✉ *281 rue de la Couronne, St-Roch,*

DID YOU KNOW?

Many of the chairs found at cafés along the rue du Petit-Champlain are styled after those of famous cafés found in Paris.

Outside the Old City ☎ *418/204–6323* 🌐 *www.chefle.com* 🕑 *Closed Sun. and Mon.* ✥ *A1.*

$ CANADIAN 🍴 **Le Billig.** This crepe shop specializes in authentic buckwheat-flour crepes. Duck confit with onion marmalade or salted caramel with sweet Chantilly cream are two of the most popular options, but you can't go wrong with simple ham and cheese, either. [$] *Average main: C$12* ✉ *526 rue St-Jean, St-Jean-Baptiste, Outside the Old City* ☎ *418/524–8341* 🕑 *Closed Mon.* ✥ *B3.*

$$$$ BISTRO 🍴 **Le Bouchon du Pied Bleu.** It's worth heading to the outskirts of the Saint-Roch downtown district for this unique dining experience inspired by the French *bouchons*, as bistros are called in the city of Lyon. Big salad bowls appear at your table, for starters, and you can help yourself to your fancy. Don't overdo it, though, as delicious as they are, because the appetizers and entrées that follow come in rich and generous servings, featuring lots of pork and charcuterie and cream. Wash it all down with wines sourced exclusively from the regions near Lyon, served by a jolly mustachioed sommelier. [$] *Average main: C$35* ✉ *179 Saint-Vallier Ouest, St-Roch* ☎ *418/914–3554* 🌐 *piedbleu.com* ✍ *Reservations essential* 🕑 *Closed Mon. and Tues.* ✥ *A2.*

$$$ FRENCH Fodor's Choice ★ 🍴 **Le Café du Clocher Penché.** An amiable staff and inventive bistro cuisine (without pretentious fluff) make this establishment a local favorite. The high ceilings and imposing vault-door give away the fact that this was once a bank. The popular C$16 weekend brunch menu is one of the most original in town, filled with surprising, lovely dishes with fun names. During lunch, the restaurant is packed with suits and skirts who munch on well-prepared salads and pasta and daily-changing specials. Dinner draws the date-night crowd and groups of friends out for a fun, casual meal. The menu changes often, but the ingredients are always fresh and from Québec. [$] *Average main: C$22* ✉ *203 rue St-Joseph Est, St-Roch, Outside the Old City* ☎ *418/640–0597* 🌐 *www.clocherpenche.ca* 🕑 *Closed Mon. No dinner Sun.* ✥ *A2.*

$$ BISTRO 🍴 **Le Café Krieghoff.** Modeled after a typical Paris bistro and named for a Canadian painter who lived up the street (and whose prints hang on the walls), this busy, noisy restaurant with patios in front and back is a popular place with the locals. Open every day from 7 am to midnight, Krieghoff serves specialties that include salmon, quiche, "la Toulouse" (a big French sausage with sauerkraut), steak with french fries, boudin (pig-blood sausage), and "la Bavette" (a French-style minute steak). This place is a big local literary hangout, with great coffee, tea, and desserts. There's a seven-room auberge upstairs catering to upscale families. [$] *Average main: C$15* ✉ *1089 rue Cartier, Outside the Old City* ☎ *418/522–3711* 🌐 *www.cafekrieghoff.qc.ca* ✥ *A6.*

$$$ MODERN EUROPEAN Fodor's Choice ★ 🍴 **Le Cercle.** As a combination bar, restaurant, art gallery, and concert venue, Le Cercle is the hub of Saint-Roch's culinary and cultural life. Movie clips are projected onto the walls, and a garage door lets in city sounds, creating a lively setting, especially during summer. Open every day from mid-morning to late-night, the restaurant and wine bar offers everything from delicious tartars and pasta to unique snacks (try the marinated sturgeon gizzards—really!) and great charcuterie. Even a simple grilled cheese tastes exceptional here. [$] *Average main: C$22*

✉ *226–28 St-Joseph Est, St-Roch, Outside the Old City* ☎ *418/948–8648* 🌐 *www.le-cercle.ca* ✣ *A2.*

$$$ BISTRO 🍴 **Le Hobbit Bistro.** Inspired by Tolkien, Le Hobbit Bistro is also legendary in its own way—albeit on a much smaller scale. Tucked into a converted house that was built in 1846 and open since the 1970s, this little restaurant serves fresh, colorful salads, juicy burgers, and delectable tartares. Highlights include duck confit with a cranberry and orange compote or apple-and-beet salad in a light vinaigrette. Order à la carte or from three different prix-fixe options, aptly named Hunger, Greed, and Decadence. Breakfast is just as good as dinner, with tasty egg sandwiches and flaky croissants. Black-and-white prints of St-Jean-Baptiste create a true neighborhood-bistro vibe. [$] *Average main: C$25* ✉ *700 rue St-Jean, St-Jean-Baptiste* ☎ *418/647–2677* 🌐 *www.hobbitbistro.com* ✍ *Reservations essential* ✣ *C3.*

$$ MODERN CANADIAN 🍴 **Le Parlementaire.** Despite its magnificent beaux arts interior and its reasonable prices, the National Assembly's restaurant remains one of the best-kept secrets in town. Chef Yves Légaré prepares contemporary cuisine with products from Québec's various regions. In summer, for example, the three-course lunch menu typically includes everything from mini-fondues made with Charlevoix cheese to ravioli made from lobster caught in the Gaspé. Other dishes might include pork from the Beauce region, trout from the Magdalen Islands, and candied-duck salad. Opening hours vary, but it routinely serves lunch weekdays from 11:30–2. Depending on the time of year, the restaurant also opens for breakfast and sometimes for Sunday brunch. [$] *Average main: C$17* ✉ *1045 rue des Parlementaires, Montcalm, Outside the Walls* ☎ *418/643–6640* 🌐 *www.assnat.qc.ca* 🕒 *Closed weekends July–Labor Day; closed Sat.–Mon., Labor Day–June. No dinner.* ✣ *D4.*

$$$ FRENCH 🍴 **Louis Hébert.** With its fine French cuisine and convenient location in a 95-year-old house on the bustling Grande Allée, this restaurant has long been popular with many of Québec's élite. Dining areas range from the very public summer terrace to discreet second-floor meeting rooms, a solarium with bamboo chairs, and a cozy dining room with exposed stone walls and warm wood accents. Chef Hervé Toussaint's top dishes include seafood dishes such as shelled lobster, as well as fresh pasta and a rack of lamb. With more than 5,000 bottles of wine on hand, nobody goes thirsty, and the owner checks in on diners in person. [$] *Average main: C$30* ✉ *668 Grande Allée Est, Montcalm, Outside the Old City* ☎ *418/525–7812* 🌐 *www.louishebert.com* 🕒 *Oct.–Apr., no lunch on weekends* ✣ *D4.*

$$$ ECLECTIC 🍴 **Patente et Machin.** This fun, delicious, friendly place has a menu with terrific meats, grilled cheese, and whimsical ideas, like the use of guinea fowl wings in lieu of chicken wings. The food here has personality, humor, and . . . lots of butter. Sit at the varnished plywood counter, have a glass of tasty organic wine, and watch the kitchen run in a way that seems a tad chaotic, but that always delivers. Its twin restaurant, L'Affaire est Ketchup, is a little farther down rue St-Joseph. [$] *Average main: C$25* ✉ *82 rue St-Joseph Ouest, St-Roch, Outside the Old City* ☎ *581/981–3999* ✣ *A2.*

$ DELI 🍴 **Phil Smoked Meat.** There are plenty of smoked meat places in Québec, but Phil Smoked Meat manages to stand out. Frequented by lunching locals and families seeking a budget-friendly meal, the restaurant is on a quiet street behind a cluster of offices in St-Roch. The bright, casual interior seems slightly out of place in this trendy neighborhood, but the fast, friendly service makes patrons feel right at home. In addition to the smoked meat sandwiches, salads, pizzas (try the one with pulled pork), and spaghetti are also on the menu. [$] *Average main: C$12* ✉ *275 rue St-Vallier Est, St-Roch, Outside the Old City* ☎ *418/523–4545* 🌐 *www.philsmokedmeat.com* 🕒 *Closed Sun.* ✣ *A2.*

WHERE TO STAY

More than 35 hotels are located in Old Québec, and there's also an abundance of family-run bed-and-breakfasts. Landmark hotels are as prominent as the city's most historic sights, while modern high-rises outside the ramparts have spectacular views of the Old City. Another option is to immerse yourself in the city's historic charm by staying in an old-fashioned inn, where no two rooms are alike.

Be sure to make a reservation if you visit during peak season (May through September) or during the Winter Carnival, in January and/or February.

During especially busy times, hotel rates usually rise 30%. From November through April, many lodgings offer weekend discounts and other promotions.

Hotel reviews have been shortened. For full information, visit Fodors.com. Use the coordinate (✣ B2) at the end of each listing to locate a site on the corresponding map.

WHAT IT COSTS IN CANADIAN DOLLARS

	$	$$	$$$	$$$$
Hotels	under C$160	C$160–C$200	C$201–C$250	over C$250

Hotel prices are the lowest cost of a standard double room in high season.

UPPER TOWN

Upper Town, inside the Old City's walls, is famous for its accommodations in historic buildings, decorated with antique furnishings and heavy fabrics. Some have restaurants on the premises, though most don't. But with lots of restaurants nearby, finding a good place to dine is easy.

$$$ HOTEL 🏨 **Auberge Place d'Armes.** Old Québec charm meets modern convenience at this property, which attracts a mix of couples and businesspeople staying on expense accounts. **Pros:** central location; romantic. **Cons:** no elevator means working off breakfast on the stairs; no on-site parking. [$] *Rooms from: C$229* ✉ *24 rue St-Anne, Upper Town* ☎ *418/694–9485* 🌐 *www.aubergeplacedarmes.com* 🛏 *21 rooms* 🍽 *Breakfast* ✣ *F2.*

$$ HOTEL 🏨 **Courtyard Marriott Québec.** This former bank building exudes a quiet elegance, with stained-glass windows, two fireplaces, and a tiny

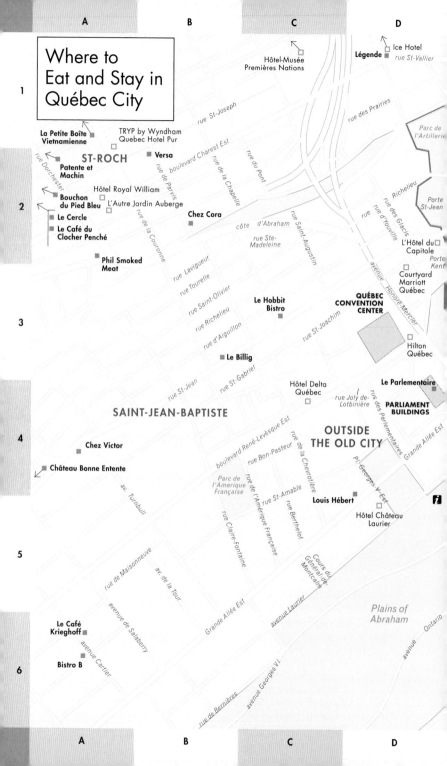

Where to Eat and Stay in Québec City

A **B** **C** **D**

1

Hôtel-Musée
Premières Nations

Légende □ Ice Hotel
rue St-Vallier

rue St-Joseph

rue des Prairies

Parc de
l'Artillerie

La Petite Boîte
Vietnamienne

TRYP by Wyndham
Quebec Hotel Pur

ST-ROCH ■ Versa

boulevard Charest Est

rue de Parvis

rue du Pont

rue de la Chapelle

Richelieu

Patente et
Machin

rue Dorchester

Hôtel Royal William

Porte
St-Jean

2

Bouchon
du Pied Bleu

L'Autre Jardin Auberge

rue de la Couronne

Chez Cora

côte d'Abraham

rue Saint-Augustin

rue des Glacis

rue d'Youville

rue

Porte
St-Jean

L'Hôtel du
Capitole

Porte
Kent

Le Cercle

Le Café du
Clocher Penché

rue Ste-
Madeleine

avenue Honoré-Mercier

Courtyard
Marriott
Québec

Phil Smoked
Meat

rue Lavigueur

rue Tourelle

rue Saint-Olivier

Le Hobbit
Bistro

**QUÉBEC
CONVENTION
CENTER**

3

rue Richelieu

rue d'Aiguillon

rue St-Joachim

Hilton
Québec

Le Billig

rue St-Jean

rue St-Gabriel

Hôtel Delta
Québec

rue Joly de-
Lotbinière

rue des Parlementaires

Le Parlementaire

**PARLIAMENT
BUILDINGS**

SAINT-JEAN-BAPTISTE

4

Chez Victor

Château Bonne Entente

boulevard René-Lévesque Est

rue Bon-Pasteur

rue de la Chevrotière

**OUTSIDE
THE OLD CITY**

Pl.-Georges-V-Est

Grande Allée Est

av. Turnbull

Parc de
l'Amérique
Française

rue de l'Amérique Française

rue St-Amable

rue Berthelot

Louis Hébert

Hôtel Château
Laurier

🅵

5

rue de Maisonneuve

av. de la Tour

rue Claire-Fontaine

Grande Allée Est

Cours du
Général-de-
Montcalm

avenue Laurier

Plains of
Abraham

avenue Ontario

6

Le Café
Krieghoff

avenue Cartier

avenue de Salaberry

Bistro B

rue de Bernières

avenue Georges VI

A **B** **C** **D**

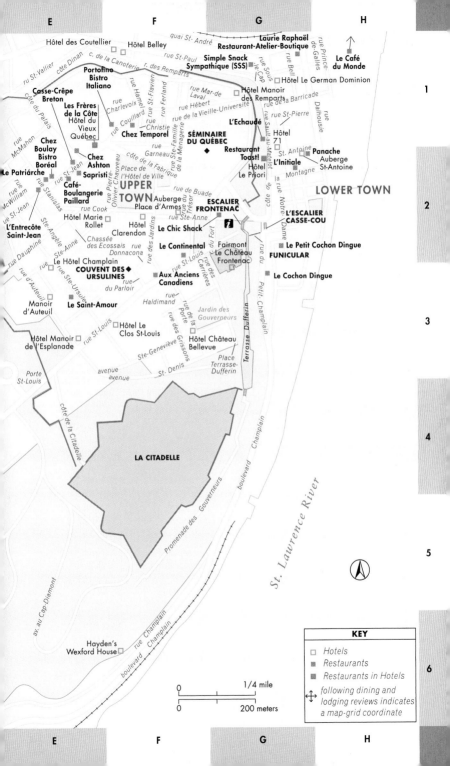

BEST BETS FOR QUÉBEC CITY LODGING

Fodor's offers a selective listing of quality lodging experiences in every price range, from the city's best budget beds to its most sophisticated luxury hotels. Here, we've compiled our top recommendations by price and experience. The very best properties—in other words, those that provide a particularly remarkable experience in their price range—are designated in the listings with the Fodor's Choice logo.

Fodor's Choice ★

Auberge St-Antoine, $$$$, p. 281

Fairmont Le Château Frontenac Hotel, $$$$, p. 279

Hôtel des Coutellier, $$$, p. 282

Hôtel du Vieux-Québec, $, p. 279

Hôtel Le Germain Dominion, $$$$, p. 282

Best by Price

$

Hôtel Belley, p. 282

Hôtel du Vieux Québec, p. 279

Hôtel Manoir de l'Esplanade, p. 280

Hôtel Manoir des Remparts, p. 280

Hôtel Royal William, p. 283

L'Autre Jardin Auberge, p. 283

Manoir d'Auteuil, p. 281

$$

Hôtel Château Bellevue, p. 279

Hôtel Le Priori, p. 282

$$$

Hilton Québec, p. 279

Hôtel 71, p. 282

Hôtel des Coutellier, p. 282

TRYP by Wyndham Quebec Hotel Pur, p. 284

$$$$

Auberge St-Antoine, p. 281

Fairmont Le Château Frontenac Hotel, p. 279

Hôtel Le Germain Dominion, p. 282

Best by Experience

BEST HOTEL BARS

Hôtel Belley, $, p. 282

Hôtel Clarendon, $$, p. 279

BEST FOR ROMANCE

Auberge St-Antoine, $$$$, p. 281

Hôtel Marie Rollet, $, p. 280

GRANDEST GRANDES DAMES

Fairmont Le Château Frontenac Hotel, $$$$, p. 279

Hôtel Château Laurier, $$, p. 283

BEST BUSINESS TRAVEL

Hôtel Delta Québec, $$, p. 283

Hôtel Royal William, $, p. 283

BEST VIEWS

Fairmont Le Château Frontenac Hotel, $$$$, p. 279

Hilton Québec, $$$, p. 279

Hôtel Le Germain Dominion, $$$$, p. 282

BEST PET FRIENDLY

Fairmont Le Château Frontenac Hotel, $$$$, p. 279

Hilton Québec, $$$, p. 279

Hôtel Le Germain Dominion, $$$$, p. 282

TRYP by Wyndham Quebec Hotel Pur, $$, p. 284

BEST HIPSTER HOTELS

Hôtel 71, $$$, p. 282

TRYP by Wyndham Quebec Hotel Pur, $$, p. 284

BEST INTERIOR DESIGN

Auberge St-Antoine, $$$$, p. 281

Hôtel Le Priori, $$, p. 282

BEST SINGLES SCENE

Hôtel 71, $$$, p. 282

L'Hôtel du Capitole, $$, p. 280

wood-lined corner bar in the lobby. **Pros:** the French food from Que Sera Sera restaurant's open kitchen; thoughtful facilities like coffeemakers and baby cribs; laundry machines are a bonus. **Cons:** a bit starchy. $ *Rooms from: C$199* ⊠ *850 pl. d'Youville, Upper Town* ☎ *418/694–4004, 866/694–4004* ⊕ *www.marriott-quebec.com* ⥂ *103 rooms, 8 suites* ⦿*No meals* ✛ *D3.*

$$$$
HOTEL
FAMILY
Fodor's Choice
★
🔳 **Fairmont Le Château Frontenac Hotel.** In this landmark building, the public rooms—from the intimate piano bar to the 700-seat ballroom reminiscent of the Hall of Mirrors at Versailles—are all opulent; guest rooms are just as elegantly furnished, like mini châteaux, with gold and green touches. **Pros:** historic aura adds romance to great river views; pets are treated like royalty. **Cons:** it gets busy in the public spaces; some rooms are small for the price. $ *Rooms from: C$259* ⊠ *1 rue des Carrières, Upper Town* ☎ *418/692–3861, 800/441–1414* ⊕ *www.fairmont.com/frontenac* ⥂ *618 rooms, 30 suites* ⦿*No meals* ✛ *G3.*

$$$
HOTEL
🔳 **Hilton Québec.** Just opposite the National Assembly, the Hilton rises from the shadow of Parliament Hill; rooms on the upper floors have fine views of Vieux-Québec. **Pros:** direct access to the convention center; amazing executive lounge. **Cons:** blocky exterior lacks pizzazz. $ *Rooms from: C$239* ⊠ *1100 blvd. René-Lévesque Est, Upper Town* ☎ *418/647–2411, 800/447–2411 in Canada* ⊕ *www.hiltonquebec.com* ⥂ *538 rooms, 33 suites* ⦿*No meals* ✛ *D3.*

$$
HOTEL
🔳 **Hôtel Champlain.** Tucked away on a quiet street in the Old City, this three-star hotel is a good fit for those after attentive service, boutique charm, and a central location. **Pros:** within walking distance to main attractions; on-site parking—a rare find in this part of town. **Cons:** small bathrooms; no in-room coffee pots means waiting for the communal espresso machine. $ *Rooms from: C$179* ⊠ *115 rue Ste-Anne, Upper Town* ☎ *418/694–0106* ⊕ *www.champlainhotel.com* ⥂ *47 rooms, 5 suites* ⦿*Breakfast* ✛ *E3.*

$$
HOTEL
🔳 **Hôtel Château Bellevue.** Behind the Château Frontenac, this 1898 hotel occupies four heritage houses with the same green roofing, and offers comfortable accommodations in a good location. **Pros:** fun package deals offered with museums, aquariums, restaurants. **Cons:** smallish rooms lack pizzazz. $ *Rooms from: C$199* ⊠ *16 rue de la Porte, Upper Town* ☎ *418/692–2573, 800/463–2617* ⊕ *www.hotelchateaubellevue.com* ⥂ *48 rooms, 1 suite* ⦿*Breakfast* ✛ *F3.*

10

$$
HOTEL
🔳 **Hôtel Clarendon.** Built in 1870, this is the oldest operating hotel in Québec City; half of its rooms have excellent views over Old Québec, and the others overlook a courtyard. **Pros:** the piano in the lounge attracts merrymakers; interesting historic features. **Cons:** brassy acoustics on the reception level. $ *Rooms from: C$164* ⊠ *57 rue Ste-Anne, Upper Town* ☎ *418/692–2480, 888/554–6001* ⊕ *www.hotelclarendon.com* ⥂ *143 rooms* ⦿*No meals* ✛ *F2.*

$
HOTEL
Fodor's Choice
★
🔳 **Hôtel du Vieux Québec.** Visiting students make tracks to this award-winning hotel, with its signature red roof and stone walls. **Pros:** lively location; breakfast delivered to your door with a weather report. **Cons:** with student guests come occasional shenanigans. $ *Rooms from: C$158* ⊠ *1190 rue St-Jean, Upper Town* ☎ *418/692–1850, 800/361–7787* ⊕ *www.hvq.com* ⥂ *45 rooms* ⦿*Breakfast* ✛ *E1.*

$$ HOTEL 🏨 **Hôtel Le Clos St-Louis.** Winding staircases and crystal chandeliers add to the Victorian elegance of this central, four-star inn made up of two updated 1845-era houses. **Pros:** period interiors; cheery breakfast room; great location near wonderful eateries and shops. **Cons:** the Victorian ruffles around the beds won't appeal to everyone; no elevator to whisk guests up to their rooms. [$] *Rooms from: C$199* ✉ *69 rue St-Louis, Upper Town* ☎ *418/694–1311, 800/461–1311* 🌐 *www.clossaintlouis.com* 🛏 *16 rooms, 2 suites* 🍴 *Breakfast* ✥ *F3.*

$ HOTEL 🏨 **Hôtel Manoir de l'Esplanade.** The four 1845 stone houses at the corner of rues d'Auteuil and St-Louis conceal one of the city's good deals: a charming hotel with well-appointed rooms and a continental breakfast with fruit, cheese, and yogurt is included. **Pros:** ancestral fireplaces and dormer windows add to the charm; elevator is a luxury in this part of town; all rooms come with full private bathrooms. **Cons:** central location means some nighttime noise. [$] *Rooms from: C$150* ✉ *83 rue d'Auteuil, Upper Town* ☎ *418/694–0834* 🌐 *www.manoiresplanade.ca* 🛏 *34 rooms, 2 suites* 🍴 *Breakfast* ✥ *E3.*

$ HOTEL 🏨 **Hôtel Manoir des Remparts.** With its homey furnishings, basic cheery rooms, and reasonable rates, this serviceable central hotel attracts many teachers and travelers who can't bring themselves to stay in a hostel. **Pros:** good for people who want to avoid antiques-filled B&Bs. **Cons:** no "wow" factor; no elevator. [$] *Rooms from: C$110* ✉ *3½ rue des Remparts, Upper Town* ☎ *418/692–2056* 🌐 *www.manoirdesremparts.com* 🛏 *34 rooms, 24 with bath* 🍴 *Breakfast* ✥ *G1.*

$ B&B/INN 🏨 **Hôtel Marie Rollet.** In the heart of Vieux-Québec, this intimate inn was built in 1876 by the Ursuline Order; it's got warm woodwork and antiques to match its surroundings. **Pros:** central location; remote-controlled air-conditioning; private bathroom in every room. **Cons:** no elevator; steep stairs. [$] *Rooms from: C$119* ✉ *81 rue Ste-Anne, Upper Town* ☎ *418/694–9271, 800/275–0338* 🌐 *www.hotelmarierollet.com* 🛏 *11 rooms* 🍴 *No meals* ✥ *F2.*

$$$$ HOTEL 🏨 **Ice Hotel** (*Hôtel de Glace*). The first of its kind in North America, this hotel is entirely built from ice and snow each year, and open from the first week in January to the end of March. You can tour the art galleries of ice sculptures, get married in the chapel, lounge in the hot tub, have a drink in a glass made of ice at the bar made of ice, dance in the ice club, then nestle into a bed, made of ice but lined with deerskin (a warm sleeping bag is also provided). It's an interesting mix between boutique (rooms have special themes and designs) and roughing it (toilets are outside) that makes for a unique experience. The standard overnight stay packages start at around C$199 per person and include a welcome cocktail served in an ice glass, access to the Nordic area's hot tubs and sauna, and a hot breakfast. If you'd rather not brave the frigid temperatures for a whole night, you can take a tour of the facilities for C$17.50. [$] *Rooms from: C$398* ✉ *9530 rue de la Faune, about 10 min from downtown Québec City* ☎ *418/623–2888, 877/505–0423* 🌐 *www.hoteldeglace-canada.com* 🛏 *44 rooms* 🍴 *Breakfast* ✥ *D1.*

$$ HOTEL 🏨 **L'Hôtel du Capitole.** This turn-of-the-20th-century structure just outside the St-Jean Gate is a fancy hotel, an Italian bistro, and a 1920s cabaret-style dinner theater (the Théâtre Capitole) all rolled into one;

North America's first ice hotel, rebuilt each winter, is only 15 minutes from Québec City by car, and worth a tour even if you don't spend the night.

art deco furnishings fill the small, simple rooms. **Pros:** whirlpool tubs and fluffy white towels. **Cons:** a theater/hotel complex isn't ideal for romance or getting away from it all. $ *Rooms from: C$195* ✉ *972 rue St-Jean, Upper Town* ☎ *418/694–4040, 800/363–4040* ⊕ *www. lecapitole.com* ↩ *39 rooms, 1 suite* ❑ *No meals* ✛ *D2.*

$
HOTEL
🏠 **Manoir d'Auteuil.** Art deco and art nouveau combine in this hotel, where an ornate sculpted iron banister wraps up through four floors, and the guest rooms, all different, blend modern design with the art deco structure. **Pros:** direct view of the Parliament building; close to the convention center; deco charm. **Cons:** midweek business guests do not invite much chitchat in the lobby; no elevator. $ *Rooms from: C$159* ✉ *49 rue d'Auteuil, Upper Town* ☎ *418/694–1173, 866/662–6647* ⊕ *www.manoirdauteuil.com* ↩ *22 rooms, 5 suites* ❑ *Breakfast* ✛ *E3.*

LOWER TOWN

Many visitors insist on staying near the water, among the quays, warehouses, and cobblestone squares—as well as many boutique hotels, inspired eateries, and impressive entertainment venues.

$$$$
HOTEL
Fodor's Choice
★
🏠 **Auberge St-Antoine.** This charming hotel incorporates the historic stone walls of a 19th-century warehouse along with artifacts dating to the 1600s, many of which were found during an expansion, and are now encased in glass displays in the public areas and guest rooms. **Pros:** unique architectural accents and exhibits. **Cons:** low vacancy rate means guests must plan well in advance. $ *Rooms from: C$269* ✉ *8 rue St-Antoine, Lower Town* ☎ *418/692–2211, 888/692–2211* ⊕ *www. saint-antoine.com* ↩ *84 rooms, 11 suites* ❑ *No meals* ✛ *G2.*

$ B&B/INN 🏨 **Hayden's Wexford House.** The attentive hosts make budget travelers and young couples feel right at home at this charming B&B, which is comfortably removed from the torrent of tourists but only a scenic 15-minute walk from all the Lower Town sites. **Pros:** big breakfast; quiet location near the river with ample street parking. **Cons:** no TVs or telephones means you're truly getting away from it all; books up fast in the summer months. [$] *Rooms from: C$140* ✉ *450 rue Champlain, Lower Town* ☎ *418/524–0524* 🌐 *www.haydenwexfordhouse.com* 🛏 *3 rooms* 🍴 *Breakfast* ✥ *F6.*

$$$ HOTEL 🏨 **Hôtel 71.** This four-star luxury hotel, inside the city's first National Bank of Canada office, has guest rooms with 12-foot-high ceilings and stunning views of Old Québec. **Pros:** fabulous concierge service; luxurious packages. **Cons:** chic interiors might make parents of active kids nervous; valet service is steep. [$] *Rooms from: C$225* ✉ *71 rue St-Pierre, Lower Town* ☎ *418/692–1171, 888/692–1171* 🌐 *www.hotel71.ca* 🛏 *60 rooms, 9 suites* 🍴 *Breakfast* ✥ *G1.*

$ HOTEL 🏨 **Hôtel Belley.** Modern artwork by local artists is everywhere in this modest hotel up the stairs above Belley Tavern, and a stone's throw from the train station, Marché du Vieux-Port, and the antiques district. **Pros:** unique; close to antiques district; hip tourists meet at the tavern downstairs. **Cons:** small capacity means high occupancy; no elevator. [$] *Rooms from: C$125* ✉ *249 rue St-Paul, Lower Town* ☎ *418/692–1694, 888/692–1694* 🌐 *www.hotelbelley.com* 🛏 *8 rooms* 🍴 *No meals* ✥ *F1.*

$$$ HOTEL Fodor'sChoice ★ 🏨 **Hôtel des Coutellier.** Charming details like buttery croissants delivered to the room each morning, exposed brick walls, and lush linens make this boutique hotel a popular roosting spot for lovebirds. **Pros:** elevator, a rarity in this historic part of town; breakfast delivered to the door each morning. **Cons:** small bathrooms; in-room temperature controls aren't intuitive. [$] *Rooms from: C$205* ✉ *253 rue St. Paul, Lower Town* ☎ *418/692–9696, 888/523–9696* 🌐 *www.hoteldescoutellier.com* 🛏 *21 rooms, 3 suites* 🍴 *Breakfast* ✥ *F1.*

$$$$ HOTEL Fodor'sChoice ★ 🏨 **Hôtel Le Germain Dominion.** Sophistication and attention to the smallest detail prevail in the modern rooms of this chic boutique hotel—from the custom-designed swing-out night tables to the white goose-down duvets and custom umbrellas. **Pros:** impressive design; great concierge service; pets welcome. **Cons:** minimal interior is probably not well suited to families with small children. [$] *Rooms from: C$255* ✉ *126 rue St-Pierre, Lower Town* ☎ *418/692–2224, 888/833–5253* 🌐 *www.germaindominion.com* 🛏 *60 rooms* 🍴 *Breakfast* ✥ *G1.*

$$ HOTEL 🏨 **Hôtel Le Priori.** Housed in a 300-year-old building with stone-and-brick walls, this dazzling four-star boutique hotel keeps to a rigorously modern style inside, with custom leather beds, stainless steel sinks, slate floors, and three-head shower jets. **Pros:** both hot and cold food at the buffet breakfast; new desks and mirrors update the rooms. **Cons:** high occupancy rates mean that you'll need to reserve some time ahead. [$] *Rooms from: C$199* ✉ *15 rue Sault-au-Matelot, Lower Town* ☎ *418/692–3992, 800/351–3992* 🌐 *www.hotellepriori.com* 🛏 *20 rooms, 8 suites* 🍴 *Breakfast* ✥ *G2.*

OUTSIDE THE OLD CITY

Booking a room outside the walled city puts you in a mixed area of student housing, convention hotels, and chains, although there are still numerous inns, hotels, and B&Bs to choose from here. Many of the options are within easy proximity to the Plains of Abraham, Hôtel du Parlement, and museums like the Musée des Beaux-Arts du Québec.

$$ **Château Bonne Entente.** Twenty minutes from downtown, the Châ-
HOTEL teau Bonne Entente offers modern simplicity at its finest, with clas-sic rooms featuring white duvets, marble bathrooms, and refinished wood furniture and design-magazine-ready rooms. **Pros:** cutting-edge design; heated bathroom floors in Espace Terzo. **Cons:** chic interiors not practical for kids without attentive nannies. $ *Rooms from: C$179* ⊠ *3400 chemin Ste-Foy, Ste-Foy, Outside the Old City* 🕾 *418/653–5221, 800/463–4390* ⊕ *www.chateaubonneentente.com* ⟿ *120 rooms, 45 suites* ⦿ *No meals* ✛ *A4.*

$$ **Hôtel Château Laurier.** Brown leather sofas and wrought-iron chan-
HOTEL deliers fill the spacious lobby of this former private house. **Pros:** some rooms for budget travelers; Saint-Hubert BBQ serves a great breakfast. **Cons:** some ambient noise, hotel a bit of a maze. $ *Rooms from: C$199* ⊠ *1220 pl. George V Ouest, Outside the Old City* 🕾 *418/522–8108, 877/522–8108* ⊕ *www.hotelchateaulaurier.com* ⟿ *287 rooms, 2 suites* ⦿ *No meals* ✛ *D5.*

$$$ **Hôtel Delta Québec.** Opposite the Parliament Buildings, this hotel,
HOTEL part of a Canadian chain, has standard and business-class rooms, and the latter come with continental breakfast and nightly appetizers and drinks on executive floors. **Pros:** kid-friendly environment. **Cons:** feels like a chain hotel. $ *Rooms from: C$209* ⊠ *690 blvd. René-Lévesque Est, Montcalm, Outside the Old City* 🕾 *418/647–1717, 800/268–1133* ⊕ *www.deltahotels.com* ⟿ *371 rooms, 6 suites* ⦿ *No meals* ✛ *C4.*

$$ **Hôtel-Musée Premières Nations.** A warm welcome, spacious rooms
HOTEL outfitted with real pelts, and river views await at this lodging, restau-
FAMILY rant, and museum complex in Wendake, a 15-minute drive north of the city. **Pros:** ample free parking; trails and nature activities nearby. **Cons:** rustic-meets-contemporary style might not appeal to squeamish animal lovers. $ *Rooms from: C$179* ⊠ *5 pl. de la Rencontre, Wen-dake* 🕾 *418/847–2222* ⊕ *www.maisondespremieresnations.com* ⟿ *53 rooms, 2 suites* ✛ *C1.*

$ **Hôtel Royal William.** Like its namesake, the first Canadian steamship
HOTEL to cross the Atlantic (in 1833), the Royal William brings the spirit of technology and innovation to its task, with spacious rooms designed for business travelers; most rooms are decorated in boutique style, with bamboo wood floors and sleek kitchenettes. **Pros:** friendly staff; con-venient location in a hip area. **Cons:** the public areas are uninspired; business travelers aren't usually big minglers. $ *Rooms from: C$160* ⊠ *360 blvd. Charest Est, St-Roch, Outside the Old City* 🕾 *418/521–4488, 888/541–0405* ⊕ *www.royalwilliam.com* ⟿ *36 rooms, 8 suites* ⦿ *Breakfast* ✛ *A2.*

$ **L'Autre Jardin Auberge.** In the heart of the burgeoning St-Roch district
B&B/INN downtown, this modern, pleasant inn is geared toward the academics,

10

high-tech entrepreneurs, and others who want to be close to the office buildings surrounding it. **Pros:** one of the best buffet breakfasts in town; sustainable business practices. **Cons:** rooms are a bit spartan; no elevator. $ *Rooms from: C$104* ✉ *365 blvd. Charest Est, St-Roch, Outside the Old City* ☎ *418/523–1790, 877/747–0447* ⊕ *www.autrejardin.com* ➮ *25 rooms, 3 suites* ⏐◎⏐ *Breakfast* ✛ *A2.*

$$$ 🖵 **TRYP by Wyndham Quebec Hotel Pur.** For choosy travelers with an image
HOTEL   to maintain, this ultrachic boutique hotel is worthy of your designer luggage. **Pros:** aesthetic perfection; fabulous dining room doubles as a bar late evenings. **Cons:** minimal design doesn't work for everyone. $ *Rooms from: C$219* ✉ *395 rue de la Couronne, St-Roch, Outside the Old City* ☎ *418/647–2611* ⊕ *www.hotelpur.com* ➮ *235 rooms, 7 suites* ⏐◎⏐ *No meals* ✛ *A1.*

NIGHTLIFE AND PERFORMING ARTS

Québec City has a good variety of cultural institutions for a town of its size, from its renowned symphony orchestra to several small theater companies. To sample its nightlife, you'll probably find yourself heading to the clubs and cafés of rue St-Jean, avenue Cartier, and Grande-Allée, and to a lesser extent Lower Town.

Billetech. Tickets for most shows in town are sold through this company. There are outlets around town. ✉ *Colisée Pepsi, Parc de l'Expocité, 250 blvd. Wilfrid-Hamel, Limoilou* ☎ *418/691–7211* ⊕ *www.billetech.com.*

NIGHTLIFE

In winter, nightlife activity grows livelier as the week nears its end, beginning on Wednesday. As warmer temperatures set in, the café-terrace crowd emerges, and bars are active just about every night. Most bars and clubs stay open until 3 am.

UPPER TOWN
BARS AND LOUNGES

Bar 1608. One of the city's most romantic spots is the Château Frontenac's bar, recently renovated and renamed (it used to be Le Saint-Laurent). Have some wine, a bit of charcuterie and cheese, and relax while looking at the St. Lawrence River or the two fireplaces. ✉ *1 rue des Carrières, Upper Town* ☎ *418/266–3906.*

Bar Les Voûtes Napoléon. The brick walls and wine cellar–like atmosphere help make Les Voûtes a popular place to listen to Quebecois music. Much of the beer here's from local microbreweries. ✉ *680 rue Grande-Allée Est, Upper Town* ☎ *418/640–9388* ⊕ *www.voutesde napoleon.com.*

Cosmos Café. This trendy restaurant and club is on the ground floor under Chez Maurice. Great chandeliers, art, and loud music are all part of the show. ✉ *575 rue Grande-Allée Est, Upper Town* ☎ *418/640–0606* ⊕ *www.lecosmos.com.*

La Ninkasi. Just outside the walls, La Ninkasi has an art-exhibition space, plasma screen TVs often tuned to hockey, a stage for local bands, and several gaming tables. Sample from an expansive collection of local brews and find out what's going on in the area's thriving art scene. ✉ *811 rue St-Jean, Upper Town* ☎ *418/529–8538* ⊕ *www.ninkasi.ca.*

Le Pub Saint-Alexandre. This popular English-style pub serves 45 kinds of single-malt scotch and more than 200 kinds of beer, 30 of which are on tap. ✉ *1087 rue St-Jean, Upper Town* ☎ *418/694–0015* ⊕ *www. pubstalexandre.com.*

L'Inox. A popular Upper Town brewpub, L'Inox serves beers that have been brewed on-site, like Montagnais and Coulée-Douce. Some, like Transat and Viking, were developed to mark special events. Inside are billiard tables and excellent European-style hot dogs (featuring long, tasty sausages served on a baguette); outside there's a summer terrace. ✉ *655 rue Grande-Allée Est, Upper Town* ☎ *418/692–2877* ⊕ *www. inox.qc.ca.*

Maurice. This is a bar complex named after the former premier of Qué-bec, Maurice Duplessis. The crowd is young, and the recently revamped atmosphere is racy and provocative. ✉ *575 rue Grande-Allée Est, 2nd fl., Upper Town* ☎ *418/647–2000* ⊕ *www.mauricenightclub.com.*

FOLK, JAZZ, AND BLUES

Bar Le Sacrilège. Across the street from Église St-Jean-Baptiste, this place bears its name well, with a couple of church pews and religious icons. Le Sacrilège has local McAuslan and Boréale microbrews in bottles and on tap, and the special changes daily. It also has the best terrace in the city, an enclosed garden that's constantly full in summer. Live music or DJs play on a regular basis. ✉ *447, rue St-Jean, Upper Town* ☎ *418/649–1985* ⊕ *www.lesacrilege.net.*

Bar Ste-Angèle. This cozy hipster hideaway features live jazz some nights, a variety of delicious cocktails, and a vintage Hollywood theme. There are drink specials on Tuesday. ✉ *26 rue Ste-Angèle, Upper Town* ☎ *418/692–2171.*

OUTSIDE THE OLD CITY
BARS AND LOUNGES

Korrigane Brasserie Artisanale. A popular after-work spot with the locals, this brewery crafts high-quality beer and tapas-inspired pub fare. A friendly vibe and ample seating make Korrigane the ideal spot for a *cinq à sept* or a low-key night out. In addition to the house brews, there's also a good selection of other local brews. ✉ *380 rue Dorchester, St-Roch* ☎ *418/614–0932* ⊕ *www.korrigane.ca.*

Les Salons d'Edgar. Set on the southern edge of the St-Roch neighbor-hood, this bar and eatery attracts a crowd of friendly regulars, mostly in their thirties and forties, but also students from the Université Laval visual arts pavilion, across the street. You can listen to an eclectic selec-tion of music while chatting the night away or having simple, tasty food with a beer or glass of wine from the inexpensive list. ✉ *263 rue St-Vallier Est, St-Roch* ☎ *418/523–7811* ⊗ *Closed July and Aug.*

The rue du Trésor in Upper Town is an alleyway lined with local artists selling paintings and sketches.

CLUBS
Le Boudoir. Some say this is Québec's best and classiest bar for singles and younger couples. The large lower-level dance floor is DJ-powered from Thursday to Sunday, and you'll hear all the latest beats. Le Boudoir's martinis are popular, and a menu of comfort food and side dishes rounds out the supper club's offerings. ⊠ *441 rue du Parvis, St-Roch* ☎ *418/524–2777.*

PERFORMING ARTS

Art is everywhere in Québec City—from theater to chic galleries to accordion street performers and statue mimes in the parks. From September through May a steady stream of concerts, plays, and performances is presented in theaters and halls. In summer, many indoor theaters close, and outdoor shows of all kinds abound, most of them free.

ARTS CENTERS
Fodor's Choice
★
Grand Théâtre de Québec. Québec City's main theater has two stages for symphonic concerts, opera, plays, and touring companies of all sorts. The Grand Théâtre also presents a dance series with Canadian and international companies. Inside, a three-wall mural by the Québec sculptor Jordi Bonet depicts Death, Life, and Liberty. Bonet wrote "La Liberté" on one wall to bring attention to the Quebecois struggle for freedom and cultural distinction. ⊠ *269 blvd. René-Lévesque Est, Upper Town* ☎ *418/643–8131* ⊕ *www.grandtheatre.qc.ca.*

MUSIC

Fodor's Choice ★ **Orchestre Symphonique de Québec** (*Québec Symphony Orchestra*). Canada's oldest symphony orchestra, directed by the dynamic French conductor Fabien Gabel, performs at Louis-Fréchette Hall in the Grand Théâtre de Québec. ✉ *269 blvd. René-Lévesque Est, Upper Town* ☎ *418/643–8486* ⊕ *www.osq.org.*

Théâtre Petit-Champlain. The charming and intimate Théâtre Petit-Champlain is a fine spot to hear contemporary francophone music during the year and take in a play in summer. ✉ *68 rue du Petit-Champlain, Lower Town* ☎ *418/692–2631* ⊕ *www.theatrepetitchamplain.com.*

THEATER

Most theater productions are in French. In summer, open-air concerts are presented at place d'Youville (just outside St-Jean Gate) and on the Plains of Abraham. *The theaters listed below schedule shows from September to May.*

Carrefour international de théâtre de Québec. This international theatrical festival takes over several spaces in late May and early June: the Salle Albert-Rousseau, the Grand Théâtre de Québec, the Théâtre Périscope (near avenue Cartier), and Complexe Méduse. There are usually at least one or two productions in English or with English subtitles, and an outdoor show that takes over different parts of the Saint-Roch district. ☎ *418/692–3131* ⊕ *www.carrefourtheatre.qc.ca.*

Coopérative Méduse. This multidisciplinary arts center, built in a row of historic houses mixed with new structures, is a hub for local artists, and presents edgy installations and live shows. ✉ *541 rue de St-Vallier Est, St-Roch* ☎ *418/640–9218* ⊕ *www.meduse.org.*

École de Cirque. For three weeks every May, students of this circus school and others take to the trapeze to promote their art form through the Circus Days festival. Throughout the year, students and teachers put on various shows, training camps, and workshops in the former church that now houses their school. ✉ *750 av. 2e, Limoilou* ☎ *418/425–0101* ⊕ *www.ecoledecirque.com.*

Grand Théâtre de Québec. Classic and contemporary plays are staged here by city's leading company, le Théâtre du Trident. ✉ *269 blvd. René-Lévesque Est, Montcalm* ☎ *418/643–8131* ⊕ *www.grandtheatre.qc.ca.*

Théâtre Périscope. This multipurpose theater hosts about a dozen different productions a year, staged by several different theater companies. New creations and experimental productions are always part of the mix. ✉ *2 rue Crémazie Est, Montcalm* ☎ *418/529–2183* ⊕ *www.theatre periscope.qc.ca.*

10

SPORTS AND OUTDOOR ACTIVITIES

Scenic rivers and nearby mountains (no more than 30 minutes away by car) make Québec City a great place for exploring the Great Outdoors.

Québec City Tourist Information. Contact the tourist board for information about sports and fitness activities around the city. ✉ *399 rue St-Joseph*

QUÉBEC SUMMER FESTIVAL

Festival d'Été International de Québec (*Québec City Summer Festival*). An annual highlight in the first half of July is this exuberant Summer Festival, 11 days of rock, folk, hip-hop, and world music. It's a great event for hearing unfamiliar performers and expanding your musical horizons. The main concerts take place each evening on three outdoor stages in or near the Old City, including one holding more than 60,000 people on the Plains of Abraham. A pass (C$75) admits you to all events throughout the festival and single-night passes, for around C$30, are also available. Some concerts at indoor theaters cost extra, but free music and activities, such as family concerts and street performers during the day, are also plentiful. At night rue St-Jean near the city gate turns into a free street theater, with drummers, dancers, and skits. Book a room several months in advance if you plan to attend. ☎ *418/523–4540, 888/992–5200* ⊕ *www.infofestival.com.*

Est, St-Roch ☎ *418/641–6654, 877/783–1608* ⊕ *www.quebecregion.com.*

BIKING

There are 64 km (40 miles) of fairly flat, well-maintained bike paths on Québec City's side of the St. Lawrence River and an equal amount on the south shore. Detailed route maps are available through tourism offices. The best and most scenic of the bike paths is the one that follows the old railway bed in Lévis. Take the Québec–Lévis ferry to reach the marvelous views along this 10-km-long (6-mile-long) trail. It's now part of the province-wide Route Verte, a government-funded, 4,000-km-long (2,500-mile-long) circuit of long-distance bicycle paths and road routes.

Corridor des Cheminots. Ambitious cyclists can embark on the 22-km-long (14-mile-long) trail that runs from Québec City near Old Québec to the town of Shannon. It's a slow uphill on the way out—with the reward of an easier ride back.

Côte-de-Beaupré. Paths along the beginning of the Beaupré coast, at the confluence of the St. Charles and St. Lawrence rivers, are especially scenic. They begin northeast of the city at rue de la Vérendrye and boulevard Montmorency or rue Abraham-Martin and Pont Samson (Samson Bridge) and continue 10 km (6 miles) along the coast to Montmorency Falls.

DOG SLEDDING

For centuries dog sledding has been a part of the Canadian winter experience. Outfitters around Québec City generally offer excursions from January through March.

FAMILY **Aventures Nord-Bec Stoneham.** This outfitter will teach you how to mush in the forest. A half-day expedition, which includes initiation, dog sledding, a guided tour of kennels, and a snack, costs C$120 per person.

Overnight camping trips, snowshoeing, and ice fishing are also available. In summer this location offers mountain biking and kennel tours. Transportation between Stoneham (a 30-minute drive from the Old City) and your hotel costs extra. ⊠ *4 chemin des Anémones, Stoneham* ☎ *418/848–3732* ⊕ *www.traineaux-chiens.com.*

GOLF

The Québec City region has 18 golf courses, and most are open to the public. Reservations are essential in summer.

Club de Golf de Cap-Rouge. Established in 1959—well away from the city, at the time—this is one of the closest courses to the city center, just 25 minutes by car from Vieux-Québec, in a pleasant suburban area. Its 18-hole course is set up with variations for women, men, and advanced players. You're close to the St Lawrence River, so be careful that the wind doesn't play tricks on you. ⊠ *4600 rue St-Felix, Cap-Rouge* ☎ *418/653–9381* ⊕ *www.golfcap-rouge.qc.ca* ⊠ *Nonmembers: C$30–C$35 for 9 holes, C$50–C$85 for 18 holes. Members: C$25–C$30 for 9 holes, C$45–C$68 for 18 holes.* 🏌 *18 holes, 6756 yds, par 72, slope 125. .*

Club de Golf de Mont Tourbillon. The cooler air of the Laurentian mountains is quite welcome on a hot summer day, as you play golf and enjoy views of the rolling hillside and Lac Beauport. Mont Tourbillon features three courses and an elegant bistro with a pleasant terrace. It's 25 minutes from the city by car via Route 73 North (take the Lac Beauport exit). In winter, golfing yields the way to long, fun slides. ⊠ *55 montée du Golf, Lac Beauport* ☎ *418/849–4418* ⊕ *www.monttourbillon.com* 🏌 *Blue Course: 18 holes, 6090 yards, par 70, slope 121. White Course: 18 holes, 5590 yards, par 70, slope 117. Red Course: 18 holes, 4625 yards, par 70, slope 113. Greens fee: C$49 weekends, C$41 weekdays .*

Le Saint-Ferréol. Located within sight of the Mont Sainte-Anne ski slopes, this club has one of the best and best-priced courses in the region—it's been fine-tuned by pro Denis Gagné. The course is a half-hour drive northeast of Québec City, and features 18 holes with a 72 par, as well as a large driving range for practice. ⊠ *1700 blvd. les Neiges, St-Ferréol* ☎ *418/827–3778* ⊕ *www.golfstferreol.com* 🏌 *18 holes, 6445 yards, par 72, slope 115. Greens fee: C$44 .*

ICE-SKATING

Ice-skating in Québec City is a popular pastime for locals and visitors alike. In addition to rinks in town, Village Vacances Valcartier (see Snow Slides) just outside Québec City offers skating trails with lighting and sound systems.

Place d'Youville. This well-known outdoor rink just outside St-Jean Gate is open daily October through the end of March, from noon to 10 pm. Skate rental is about C$5, and skating itself is free. A locker will run you C$1. ☎ *418/641–6256.*

RAFTING

Just outside the city, the Jacques-Cartier River (to the west) and Riviére Malbaie (to the east) both make for an easy white-water rafting daytrip. Village Vacances Valcartier (see Snow Slides) also runs 3-hour rafting excursions on the river from May through September.

Excursions Jacques-Cartier. This outfitter runs rafting trips on the Jacques-Cartier River, about 48 km (30 miles) northwest of Québec City, from May through October. Tours originate from Tewkesbury, a half-hour drive from Québec City. A half-day trip ranges from C$55 per person on weekdays to C$76 on weekends, wet suits included. Horseback riding is also available. ⊠ *860 av. Jacques-Cartier Nord, Tewkesbury* ☎ *418/848–7238* ⊕ *www.excursionsj-cartier.com.*

SKIING

Skiing is very popular here, whether it's downhill on one of the mountains surrounding the city or cross-country in an urban park. A dynamic landscape, top-notch ski resorts, and lots of fresh powder have helped make this a major training area for some of Canada's top athletes.

⇨ *For more cross-country and downhill skiing options near Québec City, see the Side Trips from Québec City chapter.*

Québec City Tourism. General information about ski centers in Québec is available from Québec City Tourism. ☎ *877/783–1608, 418/641–6290* ⊕ *www.quebecregion.com.*

Ski Express. In winter, this shuttle runs between major hotels in Old City and major ski centers. It leaves hotels in Old City at 8 and 10 am for the ski hills and leaves the ski hills at 2:30 and 4:30 pm. The cost is C$53–C$140; reserve and pay in advance at hotels. ☎ *418/525–5191* ⊕ *www.taxicoop-quebec.com.*

CROSS-COUNTRY

Regroupement des Stations de Ski de Fond. Thirty-seven cross-country ski centers in the Québec area have 2,000 km (1,240 miles) of groomed trails and heated shelters between them; contact this group for more information. ⊕ *www.skidefondraquette.com.*

SKI CENTERS

Les Sentiers du Moulin. This center is 19 km (12 miles) north of the city, and it has more than 20 marked trails covering 12 km (7 miles) singletrack, and 15 km (9 miles) multitrack. ⊠ *99 chemin du Moulin, Lac Beauport* ☎ *418/849–9652.*

Parc des Champs-de-Bataille (*Battlefields Park*). You can reach this park from Place Montcalm. It has more than 10 km (6 miles) of scenic, marked, cross-country skiing trails. Skis and snowshoes can be rented at the Maison de la Découverte. ⊠ *835 av. Wilfrid-Laurier, Montcalm.*

DOWNHILL

Multiple downhill ski resorts are nearby, and some are barely 30 minutes away from downtown Québec City. Most have night skiing. ⇨ *For information on Le Massif and Mont-Ste-Anne, see the Côte-de-Beaupré section in Chapter 11, Side Trips from Québec City.*

Le Relais. There are 25 trails and a vertical drop of 734 feet at this relatively small, family-friendly ski center, where you can buy lift tickets by the hour. Le Relais is about 20 minutes from downtown Québec City. ⊠ *1084 blvd. du Lac, Lac Beauport* ☎ *418/849–1851* ⊕ *www. skirelais.com.*

Station Touristique Stoneham. Stoneham is 20 minutes north of Old Québec. The hill has a vertical drop of 1,380 feet, with a number of long, easy slopes and a some more challenging runs. It has 42 downhill runs and seven lifts, plus three terrain parks and one super-half-pipe. ⊠ *1420 av. du Hibou, Stoneham* ☎ *418/848–2411, 800/463–6888* ⊕ *www.ski-stoneham.com.*

SNOW SLIDES

The snow slide from Dufferin Terrace is easily one of the most exciting winter activities in Québec.

FAMILY **Glissades de la Terrasse.** A wooden toboggan takes you down a 270-feet-high snow slide that's adjacent to the Château Frontenac. Three rides cost C$10. ☎ *418/829–9898.*

FAMILY **Village Vacances Valcartier.** Hop on an inner tube or carpet and shoot down one of more than 35 snow slides here. Or join six to 12 others for a snow-raft ride on one of three groomed trails. You can also take a dizzying ride on the Tornado, a giant inner tube that seats eight and spins down the slopes. Rafting and sliding cost C$34 per day, C$36 with skating and the Tornado. Trails open daily at 10 am; closing times vary. ⊠ *1860 blvd. Valcartier, Valcartier* ☎ *418/844–2200, 888/384–5524* ⊕ *www.valcartier.com.*

SNOWMOBILING

Québec is the birthplace of the snowmobile, and with 32,000 km (19,840 miles) of trails, it's one of the best places in the world for the sport. Two major trails, the 2,000-km (1,250-mile) Trans-Québec Snowmobile Trail and the 1,300-km (806-mile) Fur Traders Tour, run just north of Québec City. Trail maps are available at tourist offices.

10

SM Sport. Snowmobile rentals with this company begin at C$45 per hour, or C$118 per day, plus tax and the cost of gas. These folks will also pick up from several downtown hotels for an additional price, starting at C$20 per person. ⊠ *11337 blvd. Valcartier, Loretteville* ☎ *418/842–2703* ⊕ *www.smsport.ca.*

WATER PARKS

FAMILY **Village Vacances Valcartier.** The largest water park in Canada has a wave pool, a 1-km (½-mile) tropical-river adventure called the Amazon, more than 35 waterslides, and a 100-foot accelerating slide on which bathers reach a speed of up to 80 kph (50 mph). Mirage features a heated pool and a huge number of water games. There's also a winding indoor river in a medieval setting. Admission is C$35 a day for those at least

DID YOU KNOW?

If you visit Québec City during the Carnaval de Québec you'll have the opportunity to tour Bonhomme's Ice Palace.

52 inches tall, C$28 for those under 52 inches. ✉ *1860 blvd. Valcartier, Valcartier* ☎ *418/844–2200, 888/384–5524* ⊕ *www.valcartier.com.*

WINTER CARNIVAL

For three weekends in January or February, Québec City throws one of the biggest winter parties in the world. Each year, an Ice Palace is built as the center of the festivities, which include dog sled races, two parades, and events on several city streets. Ice bars are plentiful on the Grande Allée and the streets fill with families and visitors singing songs and blowing into trumpets.

FAMILY

Fodor'sChoice

★

Carnaval de Québec. A flurry of activity, mainly on the Plains of Abraham but also on several of the city's main drags, surrounds Carnaval de Québec, which occurs over three weekends every January and February. Snow and ice sculpture contests, dog sled relays, and canoe races in the St. Lawrence chase away winter doldrums. Visitors brave the cold to get a glimpse of Bonhomme, the friendly Carnival Master, and tour his Ice Palace, which is rebuilt each year. Caribou, a strong mixture of red wine, hard liquor, and maple syrup, is a popular libation during the festivities. ⊕ *www.carnaval.qc.ca.*

SHOPPING

On the fashionable streets of Vieux-Québec, shopping has a European tinge. The boutiques and specialty shops clustered along narrow streets such as rue du Petit-Champlain and rues de Buade and St-Jean are especially traditional.

Stores are generally open Monday–Wednesday 9:30–5:30, Thursday and Friday until 9, Saturday until 5, and Sunday noon–5. In summer most shops have later evening hours.

SPAS

Sibéria Spa. A 20-minute drive from Vieux-Québec, Siberia Spa offers everything from thermal and cold baths and a eucalyptus steam room to a yurt tent for relaxing to a quiet pavilion where you can sit by a fire in comfortable chairs, looking out to the Jacques Cartier River. Admission is C$42 (C$29, evenings) for use of the spa, with massages and packages running from C$80 to C$254. It's normally adults only, but families are welcome on Sunday mornings, between 9 am and noon, and on regular hours during the holidays and spring break. ✉ *339 blvd. du Lac, Lac Beauport* ☎ *418/841–1325* ⊕ *www.siberiastationspa.com* ⊗ *Mon.–Thurs. 11–8, Fri.–Sun. 9–8.*

UPPER TOWN

ART GALLERIES

Galerie Brousseau et Brousseau. Inuit art is the specialty of this large, well-known gallery. The gallery director, Jean-Francois Brousseau, selects works by artists represented by the North Canadian Inuit cooperatives,

10

and the gallery receives much praise for improving life in the Canadian Arctic. ⊠ *35 rue St-Louis, Upper Town* ☎ *418/694–1828* ⊕ *www.sculpture.artinuit.ca.*

CLOTHING

Bedo. Head to this popular chain for trendy, well-priced items to round out your work wardrobe. Bedo also has great sales racks to sort through at the end of seasons. ⊠ *1161 rue St-Jean, Upper Town* ☎ *418/692–0761* ⊕ *www.bedo.ca.*

CRAFTS

Les Trois Colombes. Handmade items, including native and Inuit carvings, furs, ceramics, and clothing made from handwoven fabric, are available at this interesting shop. ⊠ *46 rue St-Louis, Upper Town* ☎ *418/694–1114.*

DEPARTMENT STORES

La Maison Simons. This large Canadian chain store started here in Québec City in the 19th century, and is still owned by its founding family. The store carries designer clothing, linens, and other household items. ⊠ *20 côte de la Fabrique, Upper Town* ☎ *418/692–3630* ⊕ *www.simons.ca.*

FOOD

Les Délices de l'Érable. Find a sweet souvenir at this maple syrup shop, which has everything from maple cookies to muffins and serves the best gelato in town. An exhibit space upstairs explains the process behind maple syrup and showcases artifacts from this Québec tradition. ⊠ *1044 rue St-Jean, Upper Town* ☎ *418/692–3245* ⊕ *www.mapledelights.com.*

GIFTS

Point d'Exclamation!. Handcrafted bags, jewelry, hair accessories, paper, notebooks, cards, and paintings by 140 Quebecois artisans fill Diane Bergeron's shop. ⊠ *762 rue St-Jean, Upper Town* ☎ *418/525–8053.*

JEWELRY

Zimmermann. Exclusive handmade jewelry can be found at this Upper Town shop, a city landmark. ⊠ *46 côte de la Fabrique, Upper Town* ☎ *418/692–2672* ⊕ *www.zimmermann-quebec.com.*

LOWER TOWN

ANTIQUES

French-Canadian, Victorian, and art deco furniture, clocks, silverware, and porcelain are some of the rare collectibles found here. Authentic Québec pine furniture, characterized by simple forms and lines, is rare—and pricey.

Antiquités Bolduc. The largest antiques store on rue St-Paul sells furniture, household items, old paintings, and knickknacks from the 19th and 20th centuries. ⊠ *89 rue St-Paul, Lower Town* ☎ *418/694–9558* ⊕ *www.lesantiquitesbolduc.com.*

Gérard Bourguet Antiquaire. You're not likely to find any bargains here, but this shop has a very good selection of authentic 18th- and 19th-century Québec pine furniture. ⊠ *97 rue St-Paul, Lower Town* ☎ *418/694–0896* ⊕ *www.gerardbourguet.com.*

L'Héritage Antiquité. This is probably the best place in the antiques district to find good Quebecois furniture, clocks, oil lamps, porcelain, and ceramics. It's a very welcoming store as well. ⊠ *109 rue St-Paul, Lower Town* 🕾 *418/692–1681.*

ART GALLERIES

Lacerte Art Contemporain. Head to this well-established gallery in an old car-repair garage for contemporary art and sculpture. ⊠ *1 côte Dinan, Lower Town* 🕾 *418/692–1566* ⊕ *www.galerielacerte.com.*

CLOTHING

Le Blanc Mouton. Locally designed creations for women, including accessories and jewelry, fill this boutique in Quartier Petit-Champlain. ⊠ *51 Sous le Fort, Lower Town* 🕾 *418/692–2880.*

SHOPPING MALLS

Fodor'sChoice ★ **Quartier Petit-Champlain.** A pedestrian mall in Lower Town, surrounded by rues Champlain and du Marché-Champlain, Quartier Petit-Champlain has some 50 boutiques, local businesses, and restaurants. This popular district is the best area for Québec wood sculptures, weavings, ceramics, and jewelry. ⊠ *Lower Town* 🕾 *418/692–2613* ⊕ *www. quartierpetitchamplain.com.*

OUTSIDE THE OLD CITY

CLOTHING

Boutique Flirt. This brightly colored boutique carries some underwear for men as well as its main specialty, women's lingerie (including many pieces in hard-to-find sizes). They carry Aubade, Freya, Parah, Simone Perèle, Prima Donna, Marie Jo, and Empreinte, among others. ⊠ *525 rue St-Joseph Est, St-Roch, Outside the Old City* 🕾 *418/529–5221* ⊕ *www.lingerieflirt.com.*

Signatures Québécoises. The belly of the immense, Gothic-style Église St-Roch holds a large collection of wardrobe items and accessories from burgeoning Québec designers. ⊠ *560 rue St-Joseph Est, St-Roch, Outside the Old City* 🕾 *418/648–9976* ⊕ *www.signaturesquebecoises.com.*

DEPARTMENT STORES

Large department stores can be found in the malls of suburban Ste-Foy.

La Baie. Part of the historic Hudson's Bay Company chain, La Baie carries clothing for the entire family, as well as household wares and cosmetics. ⊠ *Pl. Laurier, Outside the Old City* 🕾 *418/627–5959.*

FOOD

Camellia Sinensis Maison de Thé. This modest space stocks 150 different teas from China, Japan, Africa, and beyond, most of them imported by the owners themselves. You can sign up for a number of tea-tasting sessions and workshops. ⊠ *624 St-Joseph Est, St-Roch, Outside the Old City* 🕾 *418/525–0247* ⊕ *www.camellia-sinensis.com.*

La Boîte à Pain. Baker Patrick Nisot offers a selection of baguettes, multigrain breads (pumpernickel, rye), special flavors (olive, tomato and pesto, Sicilian), and dessert breads. Sandwiches and salads are also

10

available for lunch. No credit cards are accepted. ⊠ *289 St-Joseph Est, St-Roch, Outside the Old City* ☎ *418/647–3666.*

FURS

J.B. Laliberté. In business since 1867, the well-established Laliberté carries men's and women's furs and accessories. ⊠ *595 rue St-Joseph Est, St-Roch, Outside the Old City* ☎ *418/525–4841.*

GIFTS

Baltazar. Neon soap dishes, vases, and utensils, unique cookbooks, wall decorations, and gifts in a range of prices make this local favorite for hip urban housewares a good place to find your next conversation piece. ⊠ *835 rue St-Joseph, St-Roch, Outside the Old City* ☎ *418/524–1991* ⊕ *www.baltazar.ca.*

SHOPPING MALLS

FAMILY **Galeries de la Capitale.** Thirty-five restaurants, some 280 shops, an IMAX theater, and an adjacent indoor amusement park make this the ideal mall for a whole day of family retail therapy. ⊠ *5401 blvd. des Galeries, Lebourgneuf, Outside the Old City* ☎ *418/627–5800* ⊕ *www.galeries delacapitale.com.*

TOYS/GAMES

FAMILY **Benjo.** Whimsy runs wild at Benjo. This store features games and toys, kids' clothes, a large café with thrones for little princes and princesses, an ample bookstore filled with French storybooks (and some English), and even an electric train you can ride around the store. ⊠ *550 blvd. Charest Est, St-Roch, Outside the Old City* ☎ *418/640–0001* ⊕ *www. benjo.ca.*

EXCURSIONS

Huron-Wendat Village. A 25-minute drive outside city limits takes you into another world, that of the Huron-Wendat Nation, one group of Canada's First Nations peoples. The Huron-Wendat are famous for their handcrafted clothing, decorations, and hunting tools, which are on display at the village. This "traditional site" offers a fascinating traditional village exhibition, complete with longhouse, dances, and storytelling. Visitors can take guided tours and discover some stunning crafts in the huge gift shop. Traditional meals are served in an on-site restaurant. ⊠ *575 rue Stanislas-Kosca, Wendake* ☎ *418/842–4308* ⊕ *www.huron-wendat.qc.ca* ▣ *Guided tour C$12.75* ☉ *Daily 9–5.*

SIDE TRIPS FROM QUÉBEC CITY

WELCOME TO SIDE TRIPS FROM QUÉBEC CITY

TOP REASONS TO GO

★ **Ski at Le Massif:** This three-peak ski resort has the largest vertical drop in Eastern Canada, at more than 2,500 feet.

★ **Farm-hop on Île d'Orléans:** The "Garden of Québec" is covered with farmland and bed-and-breakfasts, and makes for the perfect day or overnight trip from Québec City.

★ **Whale-watch in Tadoussac:** About 220 km (137 miles) east of Québec City, you can see small white beluga whales—an endangered species—year-round in the Saguenay River.

★ **See Basilique Ste-Anne-de-Beaupré:** More than a million people a year make pilgrimages to this church, named after the patron saint of Québec.

★ **Take the footbridge across Montmorency Falls:** These waterfalls on the Côte-de-Beaupré are double the height of Niagara Falls. The bridge and stairs, which go over and around them, make for a spectacular stroll.

1 Côte-de-Beaupré. Driving along this coast offers views of Île d'Orléans, as well as Montmorency Falls and the famous pilgrimage site, Ste-Anne-de-Beaupré.

2 Île d'Orléans. This island is called the "Garden of Québec" for all the produce, flowers, and prepared goods that stock restaurants and homes throughout the province. Spend the day here farm-hopping and sampling everything from ice wine to foie gras as you go.

3 Charlevoix. People refer to Charlevoix as the "Switzerland of Québec" due to its terrain of mountains, valleys, streams, and waterfalls. Charlevoix's charming villages line the shore of the St. Lawrence River for about 200 km (125 miles).

Laurentides Park

Laurentides Park

175

Mont-Ste-Anne Park

138

Basilique St-Anne-de-Beaupré

Château-Richer

Montmorency Falls

Beauport

ÎLE d'ORLÉANS

CÔTE DE BEAUPRÉ

1

2

QUÉBEC CITY

Charny

279

11

GETTING ORIENTED

Île d'Orléans and the Côte-de-Beaupré are about 25 km (15 miles) east of Québec City. The Charlevoix region is about 110 km (70 miles) northeast of Québec City, so consider spending the night.

Updated by
Rémy Charest

Experience a deeper understanding of this region's history and culture by venturing outside the city. In addition to the beauty of Montmorency Falls and Côte-de-Beaupré, get acquainted with rural life and the region's French heritage on the charming Île d'Orléans. There's also much to see and do in the Charlevoix area—a diverse landscape of mountains and rolling valleys with stunning views of the St. Lawrence River. Baie-St-Paul is a hub for art and food lovers, and Tadoussac is known for its rustic excursions, such as whale-watching and fjord tours.

Montmorency Falls is an excellent first stop in any adventure outside the city. From there, you can cruise up Québec's Côte-de-Beaupré and eventually make your way to Ste-Anne-de-Beaupré, where there's an immense neo-Roman basilica. Or take the bridge to Île d'Orléans, where you can pick fresh berries, sample ice cider (also known as ice apple wine), fermented from frozen apples, and shop for antiques. A leisurely drive around the island can be done in a day.

Charlevoix, a couple of hours from Québec City, takes more planning and probably an overnight stay, but is well worth the drive. There are plenty of gorgeous villages and picnic spots along the way. Artists of all disciplines draw inspiration from this region, which is steeped in natural beauty and Algonquin history. Approaching Tadoussac, at the eastern edge of Charlevoix, the St. Lawrence River begins to seem like the open sea—it's more than 20 km (12 miles) wide at this point. Slicing into the land is the dramatic Saguenay Fjord, one of the largest fjords in the world.

QUÉBEC CITY SIDE TRIPS PLANNER

11

WHEN TO GO

Côte-de-Beaupré, Île d'Orléans, and Charlevoix are spectacular in the fall, when you can leaf-peep and go apple picking. Summer means roadside stands featuring fresh-from-the-farm produce on Île d'Orléans or Côte-de-Beaupré. Artists flock to Baie-St-Paul in Charlevoix for festivals and gallery openings. It's also the perfect time to see beluga whales in Tadoussac. In winter, in all regions, there are plenty of cold-weather activities, including cross-country skiing, snowshoeing, and ice fishing. The area's best downhill skiing can be found in Charlevoix, but if you don't want to tackle driving on mountain roads, consider taking a shuttle. Spring has its own magic, when the snow melts and the maple syrup starts to flow.

GETTING HERE AND AROUND

The best, and in some cases the only way to explore these regions is by car, and this makes it easy to spend as much or as little time in any given area as desired. Start by heading northeast out of Québec city on Route 440 (Autoroute Dufferin–Montmorency) and then Route 138 (Boulevard Sainte-Anne).

Another way to explore the exceptional beauty of the region is to hop aboard Le Massif Charlevoix, a train that runs mid-June through mid-October along the shoreline from Parc de la Chute-Montmorency station to Baie-St.-Paul or La Malbaie, with several excursion options. ⇨ *For further details see under Baie-St.-Paul and La Malbaie.*

Train Information Le Massif de Charlevoix train ☎ *418/632–5876, 877/536–2774* ⊕ *www.lemassif.com/train.*

That said, most people traveling to this region do so by car, making it easy to spend as much or as little time in any given area as desired. Québec continues to expand its Route Verte (Green Route), a 5,000-km (3,100-mile) network of bike trails in the southern part of the province.

⇨ *For more information on getting here and around, refer to Travel Smart.*

RESTAURANTS

Some of the restaurants on the Côte-de-Beaupré and Île d'Orléans are open only during high season, May to October, so check ahead. But visitors who do arrive in season won't be disappointed by the dining options available. Fast-food or chain outlets are essentially absent from the island, and your best—and most widely available—option is to sample some of the regional cuisine on offer. And while fine dining is the order of the day on Île d'Orléans, those traveling on a budget won't go hungry, as there are some good pubs and family-style restaurants with fairly reasonable prices.

In Charlevoix, the same rules apply—call ahead if you're visiting from June to September or during the Christmas holidays. During summer, Charlevoix is a food lover's haven, with fresh berries and cheeses sold roadside and plenty of bistros in the towns. Pick up a map of *La Route des Saveurs*, a route through the region dotted with restaurants and farms, and taste your way to Tadoussac.

HOTELS

Reservations at hotels are highly recommended, although off-season it's possible to book a room the same day. B&Bs are the most common lodging options on Île d'Orléans, although there are a handful of inns and one motel as well. Côte-de-Beaupré, on the other hand, not only has plenty of inns and B&Bs, but several hotels and motels as well.

Given its status as one of Québec's premier summer vacation destinations, the Charlevoix region has lots to offer travelers on almost any budget. Nevertheless, it's wise to book ahead in high season, especially if you're looking for one of the less expensive rooms here, which tend to fill up pretty quickly during the summer months.

Hotel reviews have been shortened. For full information, visit Fodors. com.

WHAT IT COSTS IN CANADIAN DOLLARS				
	$	$$	$$$	$$$$
Restaurants	under C$12	C$12–C$20	C$21–C$30	over C$30
Hotels	under C$160	C$160–C$200	C$201–C$250	over C$250

Restaurant prices are the average cost of a main course at dinner or, if dinner is not served, at lunch. Hotel prices are the lowest cost of a standard double room in high season.

VISITOR INFORMATION

Association Touristique Régionale de Charlevoix ⊠ *495 blvd. de Comporté, C.P. 275, La Malbaie* ☎ *418/665–4454, 800/667–2276* ⊕ *www. tourisme-charlevoix.com.*

Centre d'Interpretation de la Côte-de-Beaupré (*Beaupré Coast Interpretation Center*). ⊠ *7976 av. Royale, C.P. 40, Château-Richer* ☎ *418/824–3677* ⊕ *www.histoire-cotedebeaupre.org.*

CÔTE-DE-BEAUPRÉ

As legend has it, when explorer Jacques Cartier first caught sight of the north shore of the St. Lawrence River in 1535, he exclaimed, "*Quel beau pré!*" ("What a lovely meadow!"), because the area was the first inviting piece of land he had spotted since leaving France. Today the Côte-de-Beaupré (Beaupré Coast), first settled by French farmers, stretches 40 km (25 miles) east from Québec City to the famous pilgrimage site of Ste-Anne-de-Beaupré. Historic Route 360, or avenue Royale, winds its way from Beauport to St-Joachim, east of Ste-Anne-de-Beaupré. The impressive Chute Montmorency (Montmorency Falls) lie between Québec City and Ste-Anne-de-Beaupré.

GETTING HERE AND AROUND

Route 440 (Autoroute Dufferin–Montmorency) heads northeast from Québec City along the Côte-e-Beaupré. It's approximately 9.5 km (6 miles) to the exit for the Chutes Montmorency and about 35 km (21 miles) to Ste-Anne-de-Beaupré.

TOP ATTRACTIONS

Fodor's Choice ★ **Basilique Ste-Anne-de-Beaupré.** On Route 138, east of Québec City, this small town is named for Québec's patron saint, and each year more than a million pilgrims visit the region's most famous religious site here, dedicated to the mother of the Virgin Mary.

The French brought their devotion to St. Anne (also the patron saint of shipwrecked sailors) when they sailed across the Atlantic to New France. According to local legend, St. Anne was responsible over the years for saving voyagers from shipwrecks in the harsh waters of the St. Lawrence. In 1650 Breton sailors caught in a storm vowed to erect a chapel in honor of this patron saint at the exact spot where they landed.

The present neo-Roman basilica, constructed in 1923, is the fifth to be built on the site where the sailors first touched ground. The original 17th-century wood chapel was built too close to the St. Lawrence and was swept away by river flooding.

The gigantic structure is in the shape of a Latin cross, and has two imposing granite steeples. The interior has 22 chapels and 18 altars, as well as rounded arches and numerous ornaments in the Romanesque style. The 214 stained-glass windows, completed in 1949, are by Frenchmen Auguste Labouret and Pierre Chaudière.

Tributes to St. Anne can be seen in the shrine's mosaics, murals, altars, and ceilings. A bas-relief at the entrance depicts St. Anne welcoming her pilgrims, and ceiling mosaics represent her life. Numerous crutches and braces posted on the back pillars have been left by those who have felt the saint's healing powers. ⊠ *10018 av. Royale, Ste-Anne-de-Beaupré* ☎ *418/827–3781* ⊕ *www.ssadb.qc.ca* ⊠ *C$2* ☉ *Daily 8–5 (to 8 pm June–Sept.). Guided tours June–Sept. 4.*

Musée de Sainte Anne. In the parking lot of the Basilique Ste-Anne-de-Beaupré, this museum exhibits church treasures, including an impressive collection of votive offerings, many works of art, and donations made by pilgrims. ⊠ *10018 av. Royale, Ste-Anne-de-Beaupré* ☎ *418/827–6873* ⊕ *www.sanctuairesainteanne.org* ⊠ *C$2* ☉ *Daily 9:30–4:30.*

Chute Montmorency. The river cascading over a cliff into the St. Lawrence is one of the most beautiful sights in the province—and at 27 stories high, the falls are almost double the height of Niagara's. The Montmorency River was named for Charles de Montmorency, viceroy of New France in the 1620s and explorer Samuel de Champlain's immediate commander. A cable car runs to the top of the falls in **Parc de la Chute-Montmorency** (Montmorency Falls Park) from late April to late October. During very cold weather the falls' heavy spray freezes and forms a giant loaf-shape ice cone known to the Quebecois as the Pain du Sucre (Sugarloaf); this phenomenon attracts sledders and sliders from Québec City. Summer activities include three via ferrata trails built onto the cliff.

The park also has a historic side. The British general James Wolfe, on his way to conquer New France, camped here in 1759. In 1780 Sir Frederick Haldimand, then the governor of Canada, built a summer home atop the cliff. The structure burned down in 1993, however, and what stands today, Manoir Montmorency, is a re-creation.

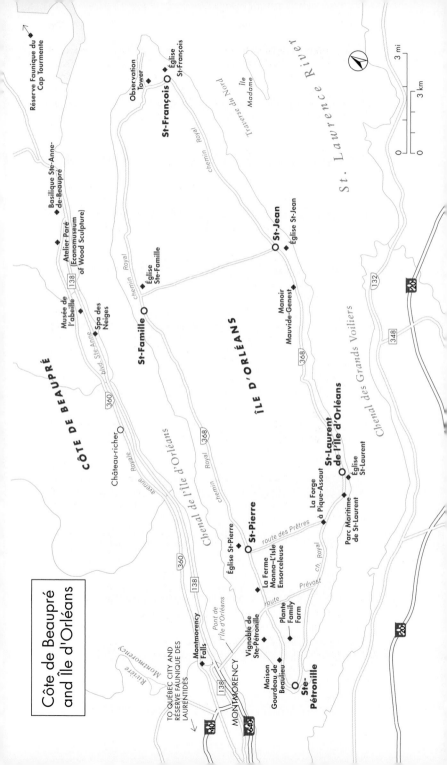

Côte de Beaupré and Île d'Orléans

CÔTE DE BEAUPRÉ

Réserve Faunique du Cap Tourmente

Basilique Ste-Anne-de-Beaupré

Atelier Paré (Economuseum of Wood Sculpture)

138

Musée de l'abeille

Spa des Neiges

blvd. Ste-Anne

360

avenue Royale

Château-richer

138

360

TO QUÉBEC CITY AND RÉSERVE FAUNIQUE DES LAURENTIDES

Montmorency Falls

Rivière Montmorency

MONTMORENCY

138

40

440

Pont de l'île d'Orléans

Maison Gourdeau de Beaulieu

Vignoble de Ste-Pétronille

Ste-Pétronille

Plante Family Farm

route

ch. Royal

Prévost

La Ferme Monna—L'Isle Ensorceleuse

Église St-Pierre

St-Pierre

chemin Royal

368

Chenal de l'île d'Orléans

ÎLE D'ORLÉANS

route des Prêtres

La Forge à Pique-Assaut

St-Laurent de l'Île d'Orléans

Église St-Laurent

Parc Maritime de St-Laurent

368

Manoir Mauvide-Genest

St-Jean

Église St-Jean

Église Ste-Famille

St-Famille

chemin Royal

Observation Tower

St-François

Église St-François

Chenal des Grands Voiliers

Île Madame

Traverse du Nord

chemin Royal

St. Lawrence River

132

20

348

20

3 mi

3 km

0   0

Offering a stunning view of the falls and river below, it's open year-round, with a restaurant and terrace open in summertime. ✉ *2490 av. Royale, Beauport* ☎ *418/663–3330* ⊕ *www.sepaq.com* 🖾 *Free. Cable car from C$9.25 one-way or C$11.25 round-trip; parking C$10 ($6.52 late Dec.–Mar. 31)* ⊙ *Site open year-round. Cable car Apr. 6–June 23 and Aug. 27–Oct., daily 9–6; June 24–Aug. 26, daily 8:30–7:30, Dec. 26–Apr. 5, weekends 10–4.*

WORTH NOTING

Atelier Paré (Economuseum of Wood Sculpture). Two centuries of wood sculpture tradition are showcased at this "economuseum," a combination workshop and store. Visitors can watch artisans at work, tour an outdoor museum, see a 13-minute video presentation (in English and French), and learn about key characters in Québec's history and culture through the Legend Theatre Workshop. ✉ *9269 av. Royale, Ste-Anne-de-Beaupré* ☎ *418/827–3992* ⊕ *www.atelierpare.com* 🖾 *Free; guided tour C$4* ⊙ *Mid-May–mid-Oct., daily 9–5; mid-Oct.–mid-May, Wed.–Sun. 1–4.*

Chapelle Commémorative (*Memorial Chapel*). Across from Basilique Ste-Anne-de-Beaupré, this chapel was designed by Claude Bailiff and built in 1878. It was constructed on the transept of a church built in 1676, and Bailiff made use of the old stones and foundation. Among the remnants is a white-and-gold-trimmed pulpit designed by François Baillargé in 1807 and adorned with a sculpture depicting Moses and the Ten Commandments.

Scala Santa, a smaller chapel next to this one, resembles a wedding cake. On bended knees, pilgrims climb its replica of the Holy Stairs, representing the steps Jesus climbed to meet Pontius Pilate. ✉ *10018 av. Royale, Ste-Anne-de-Beaupré* ⊕ *www.shrinesaintanne.org* ⊙ *Early May–mid-Oct., daily 8–5.*

FAMILY **Musée de l'abeille.** Things are buzzing at this workshop and store devoted to bees and honey, which is one of a group of "economuseums" focusing on traditional trades. A giant glassed-in hive with a tube leading outdoors allows you to take a close look at life inside a beehive. You can taste honey and honey wine made by bees that have fed on different kinds of flowers, including clover and blueberry. It's a 10-minute drive east of Montmorency Falls. ✉ *8862 blvd. Ste-Anne, Château-Richer* ☎ *418/824–4411* ⊕ *www.musee-abeille.com* 🖾 *Free* ⊙ *Daily 9–5.*

Réserve Faunique du Cap Tourmente (*Cap Tourmente Wildlife Reserve*). Recognized as a Wetland of International Significance, this nature reserve protects a vital habitat for migrating greater snow geese, and sees gatherings of more than 800,000 every October and May, with tens of thousands of birds present every day. The park harbors hundreds of other kinds of birds and mammals, and more than 700 plant species. This enclave also has 18 km (11 miles) of hiking trails; naturalists give guided tours. It's on the north shore of the St. Lawrence River, about 8 km (5 miles) east of Ste-Anne-de-Beaupré. ✉ *570 chemin du Cap Tourmente, St-Joachim* ☎ *418/827–4591* ⊕ *ec.gc.ca* 🖾 *C$6* ⊙ *Mid-Apr.–Oct., daily 8:30–5.*

11

OFF THE BEATEN PATH

Réserve Faunique des Laurentides. The wildlife reserve, incorporating the Parc national de la Jacques-Cartier, is approximately 80 km (49 miles) north of Québec City via Route 175, which leads to the Saguenay region. It has great hiking trails and camping spots, and good lakes for fishing, for which it's advisable to reserve a time slot 48 hours ahead by phone. ☎ 418/528–6868, 418/890–6527 *fishing reservations* ⊕ *www. sepaq.com/rf/lau/.*

WHERE TO EAT

$$$$

CANADIAN

✕ **Auberge Baker.** The best of old and new blend at this restaurant in an 1840 French-Canadian farmhouse, built by the owners' ancestors, which lies east of Château-Richer toward Sainte-Anne-de-Beaupré. Antiques and old-fashioned woodstoves decorate the dining rooms, where you can sample traditional Québec dishes, from *tourtière* (meat pie) and pork hocks to maple-sugar pie. You can also opt for contemporary dishes such as the excellent herbed-and-breaded grilled lamb loin and pastry-wrapped "Ferme d'Oc" goose leg confit and prosciutto. A lower-priced lunch menu is served until 4. Upstairs is a five-room B&B, also decorated in Canadiana; two exterior buildings hold two additional rooms. $ *Average main: C$35* ⊠ *8790 av. Royale, Château-Richer* ☎ *418/824–4478, 866/824–4478* ⊕ *www.auberge-baker.qc.ca.*

SPORTS AND THE OUTDOORS

Le Massif. This three-peak ski resort has Canada's longest vertical drop east of the Rockies—2,526 feet. Owned by Daniel Gauthier, a cofounder of Cirque du Soleil, the resort has two multiservice chalets at the top and bottom. Six lifts and one gondola service the 53 trails, which are divided into runs for different levels; the longest run is 4.8 km (3 miles). Nonskiers can go snowshoeing at the top of the mountain, and there is also an exciting, 7.5-km (4¾-mile) sled trail. Equipment can be rented on-site, and the resort offers daycare for younger children and shuttles from Québec City, Beaupré, Baie-Saint-Paul, and the Montréal area. ⊠ *1350 rue Principale, Petit-Rivière-St-François* ☎ *418/632–5876, 877/536–2774* ⊕ *www.lemassif.com.*

Mont-Ste-Anne. Part of the World Cup downhill circuit, Mont-Ste-Anne is one of the largest resorts in eastern Canada, with a vertical drop of 2,050 feet, 66 downhill trails, two half-pipes for snowboarders, a terrain park, and 13 lifts, including a gondola. The mountain stays active even after the sun goes down, with 18 lighted downhill trails. Cross-country skiing is also a draw here, with 21 trails totaling 224 km (139 miles). When the weather warms, mountain biking becomes the sport of choice. Enthusiasts can choose from 150 km (93 miles) of mountain-bike trails and 14 downhill runs (and a gondola up to the top). Three bike runs are designated "extreme zones." ⊠ *2000 blvd. du Beau-Pré, Beaupré* ☎ *418/827–4561, 888/827–4579* ⊕ *www.mont-sainte-anne.com.*

SHOPPING

SPAS

Spa des neiges. An *inukshuk* (Inuit stone marker) greets you at the entrance to this spa, set in elegant wood buildings right by the St. Lawrence River. Just the view, looking towards Île d'Orléans, could be enough to relax anyone, but you can also enjoy the thermal baths (starting at C$35) or get one of the many packages that include massages or a whole range of treatments, including body wraps, mani-pedis, exfoliation, and light therapy. ⊠ *9480 blvd. Sainte-Anne, Ste-Anne-de-Beaupré* ☎ *418/702–0631* ⊕ *www.spadesneiges.com* ☉ *Sun.–Wed. 10–7, Thurs. and Fri. 10–10, Sat. 10–9.*

ÎLE D'ORLÉANS

The Algonquins called it Minigo, the "Bewitched Place," and over the years the island's tranquil rural beauty has inspired poets and painters. Île d'Orléans is only 15 minutes by car from downtown Québec City, but a visit here is one of the best ways to get a feel for traditional life in rural Québec. Centuries-old homes and some of the oldest churches in the region dot the road that rings the island.

Île d'Orléans is at its best in summer, when the fields burst with strawberries and raspberries, and, later, lush orchard trees bend under the weight of apples, plums, or pears. Roadside stands sell woven articles, maple syrup, baked goods, jams, fruits, and vegetables. You can also pick your own produce at about two dozen farms. The island, immortalized by one of its most famous residents, the poet and songwriter Félix Leclerc (1914–88), is still fertile ground for artists and artisans.

The island was discovered at about the same time as the future site of Québec City, in 1535. Explorer Jacques Cartier noticed an abundance of vines and called it the Island of Bacchus, after the Greek god of wine. (Today, a couple of vineyards are working hard to earn back that moniker, with increasing success.) In 1536, Cartier renamed the island in honor of the duke of Orléans, son of the French king François I. Its fertile soil and abundant fishing made it so attractive to settlers that in the 17th century, there were more people living here than in Québec City.

About 8 km (5 miles) wide and 35 km (22 miles) long, Île d'Orléans is made up of six small villages that have sought over the years to retain their identities. The bridge to the mainland was built in 1935, and in 1970 the island was declared a historic area to protect it from most sorts of development.

WORD OF MOUTH

"In the summer I just love Île d'Orléans, the island on the St. Lawrence, with its galleries, farms, and cideries … If you wanted to go much farther afield, go east to Baie St. Paul (hometown to the founder of Cirque de Soleil) an hour or so. It's a beautiful little town full of great galleries and restaurants and has fantastic Le Massif skiing next door during the winter." —MsLizzy

11

GETTING HERE AND AROUND

To get to Île d'Orléans, take Route 440 (Autoroute Dufferin–Montmorency) northeast. After a drive of about 10 km (6 miles) take the bridge (Pont de l'Île d'Orléans) to the island. The main road, chemin Royal (Route 368), circles the island, extending 67 km (42 miles) through the island's six villages; the route turns into chemin du Bout de l'Île as it loops around the western tip of the island.

VISITOR INFORMATION

Contact **Tourist Information Center Île d'Orléans** ⊠ *490 Côte du Pont, St-Pierre-de-Île d'Orleans* ☎ *418/828–9411, 866/941–9411.*

STE-PÉTRONILLE

17 km (10½ miles) northeast of Québec City.

The lovely village of Ste-Pétronille, the first to be settled on Île d'Orléans, is west of the bridge to the island. Founded in 1648, the community was chosen in 1759 by British general James Wolfe for his headquarters. With 40,000 soldiers and a hundred ships, the English bombarded French-occupied Québec City and the surrounding shorelines.

In the late 19th century the English population of Québec developed Ste-Pétronille into a resort village. This area is considered to be the island's most beautiful, not only because of its spectacular views of Montmorency Falls and Québec City but also for its Regency-style English villas and exquisitely tended gardens.

GETTING HERE AND AROUND

Once across the bridge from the mainland, the Côte du Pont leads to Route 368. Turn right on chemin Royal and drive 4 km (2½ miles) to Ste-Pétronille.

EXPLORING

Maison Gourdeau de Beaulieu. The island's first home was built in 1648 for Jacques Gourdeau de Beaulieu, who was the first seigneur (a landholder who distributed lots to tenant farmers) of Ste-Pétronille. Remodeled over the years, this white house with blue shutters now incorporates both French and Québec styles. Its thick walls and dormer windows are characteristic of Breton architecture, but its sloping, bell-shape roof, designed to protect buildings from large amounts of snow, is typical Québec style. The house is not open to the public. ⊠ *137 chemin du Bout de l'Île.*

Plante Family Farm. Pick apples and strawberries (in season) or buy fresh fruits, vegetables, and apple cider at this family farm. In March/April, enjoy maple-sugar treats from the roadside sugar shack. ⊠ *20 chemin du Bout de l'Île* ☎ *418/828–9603.*

Vignoble de Ste-Pétronille. Since they bought it in 2003, Louis Denault and Nathalie Lane have turned this vineyard into one of the best wine producers in Québec. Most of the wine is produced from a hybrid variety called vandal-cliché, which was bred by a Laval University biologist to thrive in the area's climate. Here, the grape helps produce fresh, crisp white wines, as well as a delicious ice wine. The winery has also started producing small amounts of Riesling, and does some tasty reds. In the

Montmorency Falls along the Côte-de-Beaupré might not be as wide, but it's nearly twice as tall as Niagara Falls.

summer, Panache Mobile, a food cart managed by Panache, one of Québec City's best restaurants, serves delicious lunches on a terrace with a stunning view of the St Lawrence River and Montmorency Falls. ✉ *1A chemin du Bout de l'Île* ☎ *418/828–9554* 🌐 *www.vignobleorleans.com* 🎫 *Guided tour C$6* 🕒 *Daily May–Nov.; times vary, call for up-to-date schedule.*

WHERE TO STAY

$$ B&B/INN 🏨 **Auberge La Goéliche.** This English-style country manor (rebuilt in 1996–97 following a fire) is steps away from the St. Lawrence River, and the small but elegant rooms, decorated with antiques, all have river views. **Pros:** spectacular location; notably pleasant staff celebrated for their hospitality. **Cons:** riverfront but no access to the water; some rooms only have very small TVs with no remote. [$] *Rooms from: C$188* ✉ *22 chemin du Quai* ☎ *418/828–2248, 888/511–2248* 🌐 *www.goeliche.ca* 🛏 *16 rooms, 3 suites* 🍴 *Breakfast.*

SHOPPING

FOOD

Chocolaterie de l'Île d'Orléans. Belgian chocolate is combined with local ingredients to produce the handmade confections here: with a maple butter filling, for example, or *framboisette,* made from raspberries. In summer try the ice creams and sherbets. They've also opened a smaller counter in the presbytery of Saint-François, at the other end of the island. ✉ *150 chemin du Bout de l'Île* ☎ *418/828–2250* 🌐 *www.chocolaterieorleans.com.*

ST-LAURENT DE L'ÎLE D'ORLÉANS

9 km (5½ miles) east of Ste-Pétronille.

Founded in 1679, St-Laurent is one of the island's maritime villages. Until as late as 1935, residents here used boats as their main means of transportation. St-Laurent has a rich history in farming and fishing. Work is underway to help bring back to the island some of the species of fish that were once abundant here.

GETTING HERE AND AROUND

Continue along chemin Royal from Ste-Pétronille, looping around the western end of the island and driving east along the southern shore.

EXPLORING

Église St-Laurent. The tall, inspiring church that stands next to the village marina on chemin Royal was built in 1860 on the site of an 18th-century church that had to be torn down. One of the church's procession chapels is a miniature stone reproduction of the original. ✉ *1532 chemin Royal* ☎ *418/828–2551* 🎟 *Free* 🕒 *Mid-June–Oct., daily 10–5.*

La Forge à Pique-Assaut. This working forge belongs to the talented local artisan Guy Bel, who has done ironwork restoration for Québec City. He was born in Lyon, France, and studied there at the École des Beaux-Arts. You can watch him and his team at work; his stylish candlesticks, chandeliers, fireplace tools, and other ironwork are for sale. ✉ *2200 chemin Royal* ☎ *418/828–9300* 🌐 *www.forge-pique-assaut.com* 🕒 *Late June–early Sept., daily 10–5; call for reservations rest of yr.*

Parc Maritime de St-Laurent. This former boatyard includes the Chalouperie Godbout (Godbout Longboat), which holds a collection of tools used by specialist craftsmen during the golden era of boatbuilding. You can picnic here and watch fishermen at work, trapping eels in tall nets at low tide. ✉ *120 chemin de la Chalouperie* ☎ *418/828–9672* 🌐 *www.parcmaritime.ca* 🎟 *C$5* 🕒 *June 14–Oct. 13, daily 10–5.*

WHERE TO EAT AND STAY

$$ CAFÉ 🍴 **Moulin de St-Laurent.** You can dine inside amid old stone walls or outside on the patios at the foot of a tiny, peaceful waterfall at this restaurant, which was converted from an early-18th-century stone mill. Scrumptious snacks, such as quiche and salads, are available on the terrace, and evening dishes include regional salmon and sweetbreads. You can stay overnight at one of the Moulin de St-Laurent's chalets—nine available in summer; six in winter—on the edge of the St. Lawrence. Lodging packages, which include some meals, are also available. [$] *Average main: C$20* ✉ *754 chemin Royal* ☎ *418/829–3888, 888/629–3888* 🌐 *www.moulinstlaurent.qc.ca* 🕒 *Restaurant closed mid-Oct.–May.*

$ B&B/INN 🏨 **Le Canard Huppé.** The food here is among the best the island has to offer, and the inn features large, unique, and comfortable rooms in a beautiful location between the St. Lawrence River and the island's lush, verdant fields. **Pros:** inventive

> **WORD OF MOUTH**
>
> "Ile d'Orleans is a must and you need a car to appreciate it. Combine it with a trip to Montmorency Falls. Both are very close to Québec City…" —QuebecFan

cuisine; many sights and areas of interest very nearby; good for cyclists. **Cons:** interiors are getting a bit old. $ *Rooms from: C$105* ✉ *2198 chemin Royal* ☎ *418/828–2292, 800/838–2292* ⊕ *www.canardhuppe. com* ↪ *9 rooms, 1 suite* ⊙ *Restaurant by reservation only Nov.–May* ⊙| *Breakfast.*

ST-JEAN

12 km (7 miles) northeast of St-Laurent.

The village of St-Jean used to be occupied by river pilots and navigators. At sea most of the time, the sailors didn't need the large homes and plots of land that the farmers did. Often richer than farmers, they displayed their affluence by building their houses with bricks brought back from Scotland as ballast. Most of St-Jean's small, homogeneous row houses were built between 1840 and 1860.

GETTING HERE AND AROUND

From St-Laurent, continue northeast along chemin Royal.

EXPLORING

Église St-Jean. At the eastern end of the village sits a massive granite structure built in 1749, with large red doors and a towering steeple. The church resembles a ship; it's big and round and appears to be sitting right on the river. Paintings of the patron saints of seamen line the interior walls. The church's cemetery is also intriguing, especially if you can read French. Back in the 1700s, piloting the St. Lawrence was a dangerous profession; the cemetery tombstones recall the many lives lost in these harsh waters. ✉ *2001 chemin Royal* ☎ *418/828–2551* ☎ *Free* ⊙ *Late May–early Oct., daily 10–5.*

Manoir Mauvide-Genest. St-Jean's beautiful Normandy-style manor was built in 1734 for Jean Mauvide, the surgeon to Louis XV, and his wife, Marie-Anne Genest. The most notable thing about this house, which still has its original thick walls, ceiling beams, and fireplaces, is the degree to which it has held up over the years. The house serves as an interpretation center of New France's seigneurial regime, with 18th-century furniture, a historic vegetable garden, a multimedia presentation, and tours with guides dressed in 18th-century costumes. ✉ *1451 chemin Royal* ☎ *418/829–2630* ⊕ *www.manoirmauvidegenest.com* ☎ *C$6, C$9 with guided tour* ⊙ *Mid-May–mid-Oct., daily 10–5.*

WHERE TO EAT

$

BAKERY

✕ **La Boulange.** This excellent, friendly bakery is located in the village of St-Jean's historic rectory, across the street from the church and a promenade along the river. In addition to delicious fresh croissants, pastries, and breads, La Boulange also offers pizzas and other light lunches that you can enjoy on the large covered porch in the summer. $ *Average main: C$12* ✉ *2001 chemin Royal* ☎ *418/829–3162* ⊕ *laboulange.ca* ⚠ *Reservations not accepted* ⊙ *No dinner. Closed Jan.–May; Mon. and Tues. early June and early Sept.–early Oct.; Mon.–Wed. early Oct.–Dec.*

ST-FRANÇOIS

11

12 km (7 miles) northeast of St-Jean.

Sprawling open fields separate 17th-century farmhouses in St-François, the island's least-toured and most rustic village. At the eastern tip of the island, this community was settled mainly by farmers. St-François is the perfect place to visit one of the island's *cabanes à sucre* (maple-sugaring shacks), found along chemin Royal. Stop at a hut for a tasting tour; sap is gathered from the maple groves and boiled until it's reduced to syrup (it takes 40 gallons of sap to produce one gallon of syrup). Boiled a little more and poured over snow, it becomes a delicious toffee. Maple-syrup season is from mid-March through April.

GETTING HERE AND AROUND
From St-Jean, continue northeast along chemin Royal.

EXPLORING
Église St-François. Built in 1734, St-François is one of eight extant provincial churches dating from the French regime. At the time the English seized Québec City in 1759, General James Wolfe knew St-François to be a strategic point along the St. Lawrence. Consequently, he stationed British troops here and used the church as a military hospital. In 1988 a car crash set the church on fire, and most of the interior treasures were lost. A separate children's cemetery stands as a silent witness to the difficult life of early residents. ⊠ *341 chemin Royal* ☎ *418/828–2551* 🖱 *Free* ☉ *Mid-June–mid-Oct., daily 10–5.*

Observation Tower. This wooden tower within a picnic area is well sited for viewing the majestic St. Lawrence and the many small islands in the estuary. In spring and fall wild Canada geese can be seen here. The area is about 2 km (1 mile) north of Eglise St-François on chemin Royal.

STE-FAMILLE

14 km (9 miles) west of St-François.

The village of Ste-Famille, founded in 1661, has exquisite scenery, including abundant apple orchards and strawberry fields with views of Côte-de-Beaupré and Mont-Ste-Anne in the distance. But it also has historic charm, with the area's highest concentration of stone houses dating from the French regime.

GETTING HERE AND AROUND
From St-François, chemin Royal cuts north across the eastern tip of the island and continues west along the northern shore.

EXPLORING
Église Ste-Famille. This impressive church, constructed in 1749, is the only one in Québec province to have three bell towers at its front. The ceiling was redone in the mid-19th century with elaborate designs in wood and gold. The church also holds a famous painting, *L'Enfant Jésus Voyant la Croix* (Baby Jesus Looking at the Cross). It was done in 1670 by Frère Luc (Father Luc), who had been sent from France to decorate churches in the area. ⊠ *3915 chemin Royal* ☎ *418/828–2656* 🖱 *Free* ☉ *Late June–mid-Oct., daily 10–5.*

WHERE TO EAT

$$ CANADIAN 🍴 **Microbrasserie de l'île d'Orléans.** This is one of the most interesting microbreweries in the Québec City region, producing a colorful range of beers named after historical characters from Île d'Orléans. You can taste them all at the adjoining pub, along with standard pub fare, like burgers, pizzas, fries, and such. The pub's terrace is particularly pleasant, and there's a beautiful view towards the St. Lawrence River. It's a great place to take a break from a tour of the island. [$] *Average main: C$14* ✉ *3885 chemin Royal* ☎ *418/203–0588* 🌐 *www.microorleans.com* 🕒 *Closed Mon.–Thurs. mid-Oct.–May.*

ST-PIERRE

14 km (9 miles) southwest of Ste-Famille.

Established in 1679, this town is set on a plateau that has the island's most fertile land and has long been the center of traditional farming industries. The best products grown here are potatoes, asparagus, and corn. The Espace Félix-Leclerc—an exhibit by day and a *boîte à chansons* (combination coffeehouse and bar with live performances) by night—works to honor the late singer and songwriter, who made St-Pierre his home. If you continue west on chemin Royal, just ahead is the bridge to the mainland and Route 440.

GETTING HERE AND AROUND

From Ste-Famille, continue southwest along chemin Royal. After visiting St-Pierre, the same road will take you back to the bridge to return to the mainland.

EXPLORING

Église St-Pierre. The oldest church on the island dates from 1717. It's no longer used for worship, but it was restored during the 1960s and is open to visitors. Many original components are still intact, such as benches with compartments below where hot bricks and stones were placed to keep people warm in winter. Félix Leclerc, the first Quebecois singer to make a mark in Europe, is buried in the cemetery nearby. ✉ *1249 chemin Royal* ☎ *418/828–9824* 🎟 *Free* 🕒 *May, daily 10–4; June, Sept., and Oct., daily 10–5; July and Aug., daily 9:30–5.*

La Ferme Monna–L'Isle Ensorceleuse. This family farm has won international awards for its crème de cassis, a liqueur made from blackcurrants. The farm offers free samples of the strong, sweet cassis or one of its blackcurrant wines; the tour explains how they are made. In summer you can sample foods made with cassis at La Monnaguette, the house bistro featuring a terrace overlooking the river. ✉ *726 chemin Royal* ☎ *418/828–1057* 🌐 *www.cassismonna.com* 🎟 *Free; guided tour C$5* 🕒 *May–Oct., daily 10–7; by reservation rest of yr.*

SHOPPING

FOOD

Poissonnerie Joseph Paquet. The only remaining commercial fisherman on the island smokes his catch and sells it from a tiny shack. You can sample some very tasty smoked eel as well as smoked trout and salmon. Also available are fresh and smoked walleye pike and sturgeon, all from the St. Lawrence River. Other products include a sturgeon mousse and the rare sturgeon *méchoui*: the fish is marinated in salt the traditional way, and then roasted on a spit. You can organize fishing trips here, too. ✉ *2705 chemin Royal* ☎ *418/828–2670* ⊕ *www.poissonneriejospaquet. com* ☉ *June 24–Oct. 8, daily 10–6; Oct. 9–Dec. and Mar.–June 23, daily 9–6. Jan. and Feb. on request.*

CHARLEVOIX

Bordered by the Laurentian Mountains to the north, the Saguenay River to the east, and the St. Lawrence River to the south, the Charlevoix region is famous for awe-inspiring vistas and kaleidoscopes of color that change throughout the day. The region also has rich historical significance for both French Canadians and English Canadians.

Jacques Cartier, is believed to have explored the area in 1535. More certain is a visit 73 years later by Samuel de Champlain.

New France's first historian, the Jesuit priest François-Xavier de Charlevoix (pronounced shar-le-*vwah*), is the region's namesake. The area's first nonindigenous inhabitants arrived as early as the mid-1600s. Among other things, they developed a small shipbuilding industry that eventually specialized in sturdy schooners called *goélettes*, which were used to haul everything from logs to lobsters up and down the coast in the days before rail and paved roads. In the 19th century, as steamships plied the St. Lawrence, Charlevoix became a popular summer destination for well-to-do English Canadians and British colonial administrators from Montréal and Québec City. Since then, tourism—and hospitality—has become Charlevoix's trademark.

The region has attracted and inspired generations of painters, poets, writers, and musicians from across Québec and Canada, and became a UNESCO World Biosphere Reserve in 1989. In summer, hiking, fishing, picnicking, sightseeing, and whale-watching are the area's main attractions. Winter activities include downhill and cross-country skiing, snowmobiling, ice fishing, dog sledding, and snowshoeing. Charlevoix's many great local food products and restaurants are also a big draw for tourists.

GETTING HERE AND AROUND

To get to Charlevoix from Québec City, take Route 440 (Autoroute Dufferin–Montmorency) northeast and then continue on Route 138 past Côte-de-Beaupré. From there you'll be able to branch out for destinations such as Petite-Rivière-St-François or Baie-St-Paul.

BAIE-ST-PAUL

120 km (72 miles) northeast of Québec City.

Baie-St-Paul, one of the oldest towns in the province, is popular with craftspeople and artists. With its centuries-old mansard-roof houses, the village is on the banks of a winding river, on a wide plain encircled by high hills–the crater of a large meteor that crashed to earth 350 million years ago. Boutiques and a handful of commercial galleries line the

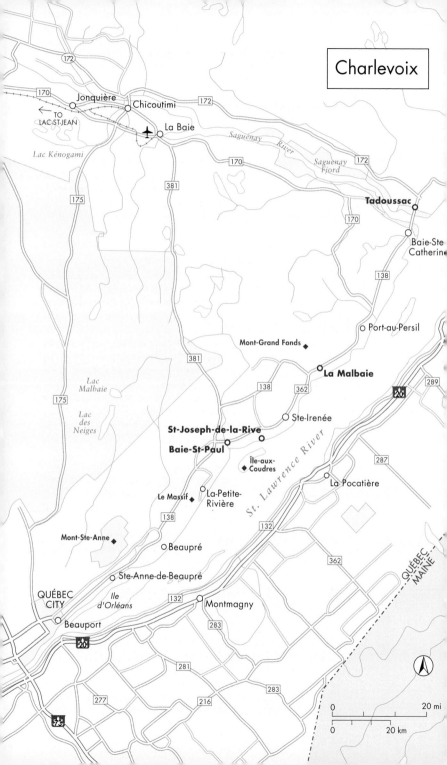

historic narrow streets in the town center; most have original artwork and crafts for sale. In addition, each August more than a dozen artists from across Canada take part in the "Symposium of Modern Art."

GETTING HERE AND AROUND

By road, Baie-St-Paul is approximately 95 km (59 miles) northeast of Québec City via Route 440 and Route 138. Le Massif de Charlevoix train runs day trips from the Chutes Montmorency station mid-June–early July Thursday through Sunday, then Wednesday through Sunday until mid-October. Departing at 9:10 am and including breakfast en route, it arrives in Baie-St-Paul at 11:45 am; the return journey, including dinner, leaves at 3 pm and arrives back at Chutes Montmorency station at 4:45 pm. The fare is C$229 round trip, plus C$60 for guaranteed river side seat.

EXPLORING

Maison René Richard. Many of Québec's greatest landscape artists, including Jean-Paul Lemieux and Clarence Gagnon, have depicted the area, and a selection of these works are on show here (some are also for sale). The gallery was Gagnon's former studio and also the home of painter René Richard's for the last 43 years of his life. Guided tours of the studio are available for groups. ✉ *58 rue St-Jean-Baptiste* ☎ *418/435–5571* 🎫 *Free; call for group tour rates* ⏱ *Daily 10–6.*

Musée d'Art Contemporain de Baie-St-Paul. This museum highlights modern and contemporary art created by Charlevoix artists from 1920 to 1970. It also has a robust collection from the province in general, with works from Georges D. Pepper, Kathleen Daly, René Richard, the Bolduc sisters, and others. For more than 30 years, the museum has been organizing a yearly modern art symposium, held in late July and early August. ✉ *23 rue Ambroise-Fafard* ☎ *418/435–3681* ⊕ *www. macbsp.com* 🎫 *C$7* ⏱ *June 24–Sept. 1, daily 10–5; Sept. 3–June 23, Tues.–Sun. 11–5.*

WHERE TO STAY

$

B&B/INN

🏨 **Auberge la Maison Otis.** Three buildings in the village center make up this calm and romantic inn that's in a good location for exploring the shops and galleries. **Pros:** lots of activities available for all age groups on-site or very nearby; reasonable spa packages; opportunity to see original local art works for free. **Cons:** the lodging in separate buildings can be a little awkward, though there are covered, heated walkways; may close during winter if business is slow. 💲 *Rooms from: C$125* ✉ *23 rue St-Jean-Baptiste* ☎ *418/435–2255, 800/267–2254* ⊕ *www.maison otis.com* 🛏 *29 rooms, 4 suites, 3 apartments* 🍴 *Some meals.*

$$

HOTEL

🏨 **Hôtel La Ferme.** More luxurious than the standard sleepy inns of Baie-St-Paul, this hotel, owned by the group behind Le Massif ski resort, has a great location and a good range of room options. **Pros:** location on public square, with on-site train station; in-room espresso makers. **Cons:** layout with multiple pavilions is a bit complicated. 💲 *Rooms from: C$175* ✉ *50 rue de la Ferme* ☎ *418/240–4100, 877/536–2774* ⊕ *www.lemassif.com* 🛏 *145 rooms, 7 suites* 🍴 *No meals.*

EN ROUTE

Route 362. From Baie-St-Paul, instead of the faster Route 138 to La Malbaie, drivers can choose the open, scenic coastal drive on Route 362. This section of road has memorable views of charming villages and rolling hills—green, white, or ablaze with fiery hues, depending on the season—meeting the broad expanse of the "sea," as the locals like to call the St. Lawrence estuary.

ST-JOSEPH-DE-LA-RIVE

20 km (12½ miles) northeast of Baie-St-Paul.

A secondary road descends sharply into St-Joseph-de-la-Rive, with its line of old houses hugging the mountain base on a narrow shore route. Enjoyed for its warm microclimate, the town has a number of peaceful inns and inviting restaurants. Drive through and see the traces of early town life and the beginning of local industry: an old firehouse and a hydroelectric building that houses a generator dating back to 1928.

GETTING HERE AND AROUND

From Baie-St-Paul, drive northeast on rue Leclerc (Route 362).

EXPLORING

Île-aux-Coudres. A free, government-run ferry from the wharf in St-Joseph-de-la-Rive takes you on the 15-minute trip to the island where Jacques Cartier's men gathered *coudres* (hazelnuts) in 1535. Since then, the island has produced many a *goélette* (a type of sailing ship), and the families of former captains now run several small inns. You can bike around the island and see windmills and water mills, or stop at the stores selling paintings and crafts, such as traditional handwoven household linens. ☎ *877/787–7483 ferry schedules.*

Musée Maritime de Charlevoix (*Maritime Museum*). This museum, housed in an old, still-active shipyard, commemorates the days of the St. Lawrence *goélettes*, the feisty little wooden freighters that were the chief means of transporting goods along the north shore of the St. Lawrence River well into the 1960s. Very large families lived in cramped conditions aboard the boats, some of which are part of the exhibits. To modern eyes, it doesn't look like a comfortable existence, but the folklore of the goélettes, celebrated in poetry, paintings, and song, is part of the region's strong cultural identity. ✉ *305 rue de l'Église* ☎ *418/635–1131* 🌐 *www.musee-maritime-charlevoix.com* 🎟 *C$5* 🕒 *Mid-May–mid-Oct., daily 9–5; mid-Oct.–Nov., by group reservation only.*

WHERE TO STAY

$ HOTEL 🏨 **Hôtel Cap-aux-Pierres.** About a third of the rooms here have views of the river, and there's the option of comfortable motel accommodations, too. **Pros:** indoor and outdoor pools; beautiful environment; good food. **Cons:** rooms are relatively unspectacular. [$] *Rooms from: C$109* ✉ *444 chemin la Baleine, Île-aux-Coudres* ☎ *888/554–6003, 418/438–2711* 🌐 *www.hotelcapauxpierres.com* 🛏 *98 rooms* 🕒 *Closed mid-Oct.–Apr.* 🍴 *Multiple meal plans.*

Baie-St-Paul is a charming small town popular with writers and artists. Each August it hosts a modern art show.

SHOPPING
BOOKS

Papeterie Saint-Gilles. This paper factory produces handcrafted stationery using a 17th-century process. There's also a small museum, which explains through photographs and demonstrations how paper is manufactured the old-fashioned way. Slivers of wood and flower petals are pressed into the paper sheets, which are as thick as the covers of a paperback book. The finished products—made into writing paper, greeting cards, and one-page poems or quotations—make beautiful, if pricey, gifts. Visitors can wander through the museum for free and guided tours can be arranged for groups. ⊠ *354 rue F.A. Savard* ☎ *418/635–2430, 866/635–2430* ⊕ *www.papeteriesaintgilles.com.*

LA MALBAIE

35 km (22 miles) northeast of St-Joseph-de-la-Rive.

La Malbaie, one of the province's most elegant and historically interesting resort towns, was known as Murray Bay when wealthy Anglophones summered here. The area became popular with American and Canadian politicians in the late 1800s, when Ottawa Liberals and Washington Republicans partied decorously all summer with members of the Québec bourgeoisie. William Howard Taft built the "summer White House," the first of three summer residences, in 1894, when he was the American civil governor of the Philippines. He became the 27th president of the United States in 1908.

A hiker takes in the view of an ancient glacial valley.

Many Taft-era homes now serve as handsome inns, offering old-fashioned coddling with such extras as breakfast in bed, whirlpool baths, and free shuttles to the ski areas in winter. Many serve lunch and dinner to nonresidents, so you can tour the area going from one great French or Quebecois meal to the next.

GETTING HERE AND AROUND
Even if you don't want to visit St-Joseph-de-la-Rive, Route 362 between Baie-St-Paul and La Malbaie is much more scenic and well worth the extra half hour it adds to the trip from Québec City. Le Massif de Charlevoix train offers a day trip to La Malbaie Thursday through Sunday from mid-June to early July and Wednesday through Sunday until mid-October. It departs Chute Montmorency station at 9:10 am, with a stop en route at Baie-St-Paul; the round-trip takes 11 hours including time to get off and explore, and the fare, including breakfast and a four-course dinner, is C$369 (plus C$60 for a guaranteed river side seat).

EXPLORING
Casino de Charlevoix. The casino is one of three gaming halls in Québec (the others are in Montréal and Gatineau) owned and operated by Loto-Québec. Charlevoix's, the smallest of the three, still draws around 1 million visitors a year—some of whom stay at the Fairmont Le Manoir Richelieu, which is connected to the casino by a tunnel. There are 21 gaming tables and more than 900 slot machines. The minimum gambling age is 18, and a photo ID is required to enter the casino. ⊠ 183 rue Richelieu, Pointe-au-Pic ☎ 418/665–5300, 800/665–2274 ⊕ www. casino-de-charlevoix.com ♥ Apr. 26–Sept. 1, Sun.–Thurs. 10 am–1 am,

Fri. and Sat. 10 am–3 am; Sept. 2–late Apr., Sun.–Thurs. 11 am–midnight, Fri. and Sat. 10 am–3 am.

Musée de Charlevoix. The museum traces the region's history through a major permanent exhibit. Folk art, paintings, and artifacts help reveal the past, starting with the French, then the Scottish settlers, and the area's evolution into a vacation spot and artists' haven. Temporary exhibits change every season. ✉ *10 chemin du Havre* ☎ *418/665–4411* 🌐 *www.museedecharlevoix.qc.ca* 🎟 *C$7* 🕒 *June–mid-Oct., daily 9–5; mid-Oct.–May, weekdays 10–5, weekends 1–5.*

OFF THE BEATEN PATH

Poterie de Port-au-Persil. Visiting potters, many from France, study Canadian ceramic techniques at this pottery studio, about 25 km (15½ miles) east of La Malbaie. Classes for amateurs are available from late June through August (by the hour or longer, starting at C$12). Half of the bright yellow barn housing the studio is a store, with ceramics and other crafts made by Québec artists. ✉ *1001 rue St-Laurent (Rte. 138), St-Siméon* ☎ *418/638–2349* 🌐 *www.poteriedeportaupersil.com* 🕒 *May–late June, daily 10–4:30; late June–Labor Day, daily 9–6; Labor Day–mid-Oct., Wed.–Sun. 10–4.*

WHERE TO STAY

$ B&B/INN

🏨 **Auberge des Peupliers.** About half the guest rooms at this hilltop inn overlook the St. Lawrence River, and the country-style accommodations are spread among three buildings, including a farmhouse more than two centuries old. **Pros:** lounge with fireplace and bar perfect for relaxing; excellent food and service. **Cons:** need to drive to downtown La Malbaie. [$] *Rooms from: C$129* ✉ *381 rue St-Raphaël, Cap-à-l'Aigle* ☎ *418/665–4423, 888/282–3743* 🌐 *www.aubergedespeupliers.com* 🛏 *22 rooms* 🍴 *Breakfast.*

$$$$ B&B/INN

🏨 **Auberge la Pinsonnière.** An atmosphere of country luxury prevails at this Relais & Châteaux inn, which has an impressive art collection and an excellent restaurant with one of the largest wine cellars in North America. **Pros:** friendly staff; fireplaces in every room; views of Murray Bay; 12,000 bottles in the wine cellar; a wonderful, albeit very steep, trail leading down to the river. **Cons:** restaurant is not good for vegetarians; expensive. [$] *Rooms from: C$295* ✉ *124 rue St-Raphaël, Cap-à-l'Aigle* ☎ *418/665–4431, 800/387–4431* 🌐 *www.lapinsonniere.com* 🛏 *18 rooms* 🍴 *No meals.*

$$$ RESORT FAMILY

🏨 **Fairmont Le Manoir Richelieu.** Linked to the Casino de Charlevoix by tunnel, this castlelike building and its sweeping grounds come with stunning views has great sports and leisure facilities. **Pros:** good for families, with kids' club, kids' menu, and babysitting; scenic location; variety of dining options on-site. **Cons:** some rooms could use updating. [$] *Rooms from: C$229* ✉ *181 rue Richelieu, Pointe-au-Pic* ☎ *418/665–3703, 800/463–2613* 🌐 *www.fairmont.com* 🛏 *405 rooms, 17 suites* 🍴 *Breakfast.*

PERFORMING ARTS

Domaine Forget. This music and dance academy has a 604-seat hall in Ste-Irenée, 15 km (9 miles) south of La Malbaie. Musicians from around the world, many of whom teach or study at the school, perform during its International Festival. The festival, which runs from mid-June to late

August, includes Sunday musical brunches with a variety of music, a buffet lunch, and a view of the St. Lawrence. Some weekend concerts are also held in the fall and spring. ✉ *5 rang St-Antoine, Ste-Irenée* ☎ *418/452–3535, 888/336–7438* ⊕ *www.domaineforget.com.*

SPORTS AND THE OUTDOORS

GOLF

Club de Golf Fairmont Le Manoir Richelieu. Be warned: If you come and play this course, you'll have to work extra hard on your focus, just to keep your eyes off the gorgeous scenery overlooking the St Lawrence River. Originally established in 1925 and recently restored and expanded, this is a links-style course with three nine-hole courses that offers quite a bit of challenge, thanks to the design (the fairways are relatively wide, but feature a number of strategically-placed bunkers, trees, and mounds) and to the course's hilltop undulations. ✉ *181 rue Richelieu, Pointe-au-Pic* ☎ *418/665–2526, 800/665–8082* ⊕ *www.fairmont.com* ✉ *C$65–C$114 for all courses* ⅃. *St-Laurent Course: 9 holes, 3128 yards, par 36; Richelieu Course: 9 holes, 3148 yards, par 36; Tadoussac Course: 9 holes, 2918 yards, par 35 .*

SKIING

Mont-Grand Fonds. This winter-sports center 12 km (7 miles) north of La Malbaie has 14 downhill slopes, a 1,105-foot vertical drop, and three lifts. It also has 160 km (99 miles) of cross-country trails. Two trails meet International Ski Federation standards, and the ski center occasionally hosts major competitions. You can also go dog sledding, sleigh riding, ice-skating, and tobogganing here. ✉ *1000 chemin des Loisirs* ☎ *418/665–0095, 877/665–0095* ⊕ *www.montgrandfonds.com.*

TADOUSSAC

71 km (44 miles) north of La Malbaie.

Most people come to Tadoussac for the whale-watching excursions and cruises along the magnificent Saguenay Fjord. Beluga whales, highly recognizable because of their all-white color, small size, and high-pitch call, live here year-round, and breed in the lower portion of the Saguenay in summer. The many marine species that live at the confluence of the fjord and the seaway attract other whales, too, such as pilots, finbacks, and humpbacks.

Sadly, the beluga is endangered; the whales, together with 35 other species of mammals and birds and 21 species of fish, are threatened by pollution in the St. Lawrence River. This has spurred a C$100-million project (funded by the federal and provincial governments) aimed at removing or capping sediment in the most polluted areas, stopping industrial and residential emissions into the river, and restoring natural habitat. There's still much work to be done, but greater attention is being given to this unique ecosystem, now a National Marine Conservation Area.

The short drive here from La Malbaie leads past lovely villages and views along the St. Lawrence. Jacques Cartier made a stop at this point in 1535, and from 1600 to the mid-19th century it was an important

In Tadoussac from May to October, you can see whales living in the Saguenay River.

meeting site for fur traders. As the Saguenay River flows south from Lac St-Jean, it has a dual character: between Alma and Chicoutimi, the once rapidly flowing river has been harnessed for hydroelectric power; in its lower section, it becomes wider and deeper and flows by steep mountains and cliffs en route to the St. Lawrence.

GETTING HERE AND AROUND

From La Malbaie, drive northeast on Route 138. You must take a free 10-minute ferry ride from Baie-Ste-Catherine to get to Tadoussac. The ferries leave every 20 minutes, from 4 am to midnight, then every half hour until 4 am. For more information on ferry schedules call ☎ *418/643–2019.*

VISITOR INFORMATION

Contact **Tourist Information Center Tadoussac** ✉ *197 rue des Pionniers* ☎ *418/235–4744, 866/235–4744.*

EXPLORING

Centre d'Interprétation des Mammifères Marins. You can learn more about the whales and their habitat at this interpretation center run by members of a locally based research team. They're only too glad to answer questions. In addition, explanatory videos and exhibits (including a collection of whale skeletons) serve as a good introduction to the mighty cetaceans. ✉ *108 rue de la Cale-Sèche* ☎ *418/235–4701* ⊕ *www.gremm. org* 🎟 *C$12* ⏱ *Mid-May–mid-June, daily noon–5; mid-June–mid-Sept., daily 9–8; mid-Sept.–late Oct., daily 11–6.*

Parc Marin du Saguenay–St-Laurent. The 800-square-km (309-square-mile) marine park, at the confluence of the Saguenay and St. Lawrence rivers, has been created to protect this marine area's three fragile ecosystems. ✉ *Park office: 182 rue de l'Église* ☎ *418/235–4703, 888/773–8888* 🌐 *www.parcmarin.qc.ca.*

> **WORD OF MOUTH**
>
> "The Charlevoix region was a delightful surprise to us when we were there in July. La Malbaie was an amazing spot with great accommodations and restaurants, and we enjoyed the local cheese makers and bakeries in the area." —irecommend

WHERE TO STAY

$$$ HOTEL FAMILY 🏨 **Hôtel Tadoussac.** In a stunning natural environment, this rambling white Victorian-style hotel with a red mansard roof is as much a symbol of Tadoussac as the Château Frontenac is of Québec City, and it's a great choice for an active or a romantic stay. **Pros:** views over the bay; summer kids' club with day care; spa; ongoing sustainability program; restaurants suit different tastes and budgets. **Cons:** no air-conditioning in rooms. [$] *Rooms from: C$209* ✉ *165 rue du Bord de l'Eau* ☎ *418/235–4421, 800/561–0718* 🌐 *www.hoteltadoussac.com* 🛏 *149 rooms* 🕒 *Closed mid-Oct.–early May* 🍴 *Multiple meal plans.*

SPORTS AND THE OUTDOORS

WHALE-WATCHING

The best months for seeing whales are August and September, although some operators extend the season at either end if whales are around. Fjord tours are also available.

Croisières AML. This outfitter offers two- and three-hour whale-watching tours starting at C$59. The tours, in Zodiacs or larger boats, depart from Tadoussac pier. Tours of the Saguenay Fjord are also available and there are also tours departing from Baie-Ste-Catherine. ☎ *418/692–1159, 800/463–1292* 🌐 *www.croisieresaml.com.*

Croisières Dufour. This company offers 2¼- and 3-hour whale-watching cruises (starting at C$69) from Tadoussac and Baie-Ste-Catherine. The tours, some of which cruise up the Saguenay Fjord, use Zodiacs or larger boats. You can also get a daylong excursion combined with whale-watching from Québec City. ☎ *800/463–5250, 418/692–0222* 🌐 *www.dufour.ca.*

FRENCH VOCABULARY

One of the trickiest French sounds to pronounce is the nasal final *n* sound (whether or not the n is actually the last letter of the word). You should try to pronounce it as a sort of nasal grunt—as in "huh." The vowel that precedes the *n* will govern the vowel sound of the word, and in this list we precede the final *n* with an *h* to remind you to be nasal.

Another problem sound is the ubiquitous but untransliterable *eu*, as in *bleu* (blue) or *deux* (two), and the very similar sound in *je* (I), *ce* (this), and *de* (of). The closest equivalent might be the vowel sound in "put," but rounded. The famous rolled *r* is a glottal sound. Consonants at the ends of words are usually silent; when the following word begins with a vowel, however, the two are run together by sounding the consonant. There are two forms of "you" in French: *vous* (formal and plural) and *tu* (a singular, personal form). When addressing an adult you don't know, *vous* is always best.

ENGLISH	FRENCH	PRONUNCIATION

BASICS

ENGLISH	FRENCH	PRONUNCIATION
Yes/no	Oui/non	wee/nohn
Please	S'il vous plaît	seel voo play
Thank you	Merci	mair-**see**
You're welcome	De rien	deh ree-**ehn**
Excuse me, sorry	Pardon	pahr-**don**
Good morning/ afternoon	Bonjour	bohn-**zhoor**
Good evening	Bonsoir	bohn-**swahr**
Good-bye	Au revoir	o ruh-**vwahr**
Mr. (Sir)	Monsieur	muh-**syuh**
Mrs. (Ma'am)	Madame	ma-**dam**
Miss	Mademoiselle	mad-mwa-**zel**
Pleased to meet you	Enchanté(e)	ohn-shahn-**tay**
How are you?	Comment allez-vous?	kuh-mahn- tahl-ay **voo**
Very well, thanks	Très bien, merci	tray bee-ehn, mair-**see**
And you?	Et vous?	ay voo?

NUMBERS

English	French	Pronunciation
one	un	uhn
two	deux	deuh
three	trois	twah

ENGLISH	FRENCH	PRONUNCIATION
four	quatre	**kaht**-ruh
five	cinq	sank
six	six	seess
seven	sept	set
eight	huit	wheat
nine	neuf	nuf
ten	dix	deess
eleven	onze	ohnz
twelve	douze	dooz
thirteen	treize	trehz
fourteen	quatorze	kah-torz
fifteen	quinze	kanz
sixteen	seize	sez
seventeen	dix-sept	deez-**set**
eighteen	dix-huit	deez-**wheat**
nineteen	dix-neuf	deez-**nuf**
twenty	vingt	vehn
twenty-one	vingt-et-un	vehnt-ay-**uhn**
thirty	trente	trahnt
forty	quarante	ka-**rahnt**
fifty	cinquante	sang-**kahnt**
sixty	soixante	swa-**sahnt**
seventy	soixante-dix	swa-sahnt-**deess**
eighty	quatre-vingts	kaht-ruh-**vehn**
ninety	quatre-vingt-dix	kaht-ruh-vehn-**deess**
one hundred	cent	sahn
one thousand	mille	meel

COLORS

black	noir	nwahr
blue	bleu	bleuh

ENGLISH	FRENCH	PRONUNCIATION
brown	brun/marron	bruhn/mar-**rohn**
green	vert	vair
orange	orange	o-**rahnj**
pink	rose	rose
red	rouge	rouge
violet	violette	vee-o-**let**
white	blanc	blahnk
yellow	jaune	zhone

DAYS OF THE WEEK

Sunday	dimanche	dee-**mahnsh**
Monday	lundi	luhn-**dee**
Tuesday	mardi	mahr-**dee**
Wednesday	mercredi	mair-kruh-**dee**
Thursday	jeudi	zhuh-**dee**
Friday	vendredi	vawn-druh-**dee**
Saturday	samedi	sahm-**dee**

MONTHS

January	janvier	zhahn-vee-**ay**
February	février	feh-vree-**ay**
March	mars	marce
April	avril	a-**vreel**
May	mai	meh
June	juin	zhwehn
July	juillet	zhwee-**ay**
August	août	ah-**oo**
September	septembre	sep-**tahm**-bruh
October	octobre	awk-**to**-bruh
November	novembre	no-**vahm**-bruh
December	décembre	day-**sahm**-bruh

ENGLISH	FRENCH	PRONUNCIATION

USEFUL PHRASES

ENGLISH	FRENCH	PRONUNCIATION
Do you speak English?	Parlez-vous anglais?	par-lay **voo ahn**-glay
I don't speak . . .	Je ne parle pas . . .	zhuh nuh parl pah
French	français	frahn-**say**
I don't understand.	Je ne comprends pas.	zhuh nuh kohm-**prahn** pah
I understand.	Je comprends.	zhuh kohm-**prahn**
I don't know.	Je ne sais pas.	zhuh nuh say **pah**
I'm American/British.	Je suis américain/ anglais.	a-may-ree-**kehn**/ ahn-**glay**
What's your name?	Comment vous appelez-vous?	ko-mahn voo za-pell-ay-**voo**
My name is . . .	Je m'appelle . . .	zhuh ma-**pell** . . .
What time is it?	Quelle heure est-il?	kel air eh-**teel**
How?	Comment?	ko-**mahn**
When?	Quand?	kahn
Yesterday	Hier	yair
Today	Aujourd'hui	o-zhoor-**dwee**
Tomorrow	Demain	duh-**mehn**
Tonight	Ce soir	suh **swahr**
What?	Quoi?	kwah
What is it?	Qu'est-ce que c'est?	kess-kuh-**say**
Why?	Pourquoi?	**poor**-kwa
Who?	Qui?	kee
Where is . . .	Où est . . .	oo ay
the train station?	la gare?	la gar
the subway station?	la station de métro?	la sta-**syon** duh may-**tro**
the bus stop?	l'arrêt de bus?	la-**ray** duh **booss**
the post office?	la poste?	la post
the bank?	la banque?	la bahnk

ENGLISH	FRENCH	PRONUNCIATION
the . . . hotel?	l'hôtel . . .?	lo-**tel**
the store?	le magasin?	luh ma-ga-**zehn**
the cashier?	la caisse?	la **kess**
the . . . museum?	le musée . . .?	luh mew-**zay**
the hospital?	l'hôpital?	lo-pee-**tahl**
the elevator?	l'ascenseur?	la-sahn-**seuhr**
the telephone?	le téléphone?	luh tay-lay-**phone**
Where are the restrooms?	Où sont les toilettes?	oo sohn lay twah-**let**
(men/women)	(hommes/femmes)	(**oh**-mm/**fah**-mm)
Here/there	Ici/là	ee-**see**/la
Left/right	A gauche/à droite	a goash/a draht
Straight ahead	Tout droit	too drwah
Is it near/far?	C'est près/loin?	say pray/lwehn
I'd like . . .	Je voudrais . . .	zhuh voo-**dray**
a room	une chambre	ewn **shahm**-bruh
the key	la clé	la clay
a newspaper	un journal	uhn zhoor-**nahl**
a stamp	un timbre	uhn **tam**-bruh
I'd like to buy . . .	Je voudrais acheter . . .	zhuh voo-**dray** **ahsh**-tay
cigarettes	des cigarettes	day see-ga-**ret**
matches	des allumettes	days a-loo-**met**
soap	du savon	dew sah-**vohn**
city map	un plan de ville	uhn plahn de **veel**
road map	une carte routière	ewn cart roo-tee-**air**
magazine	une revue	ewn reh-**vu**
envelopes	des enveloppes	dayz ahn-veh-**lope**
writing paper	du papier à lettres	dew pa-pee-**ay** a **let**-ruh
postcard	une carte postale	ewn cart pos-**tal**
How much is it?	C'est combien?	say comb-bee-**ehn**

ENGLISH	FRENCH	PRONUNCIATION
A little/a lot	Un peu/beaucoup	uhn peuh/bo-**koo**
More/less	Plus/moins	plu/mwehn
Enough/too (much)	Assez/trop	a-say/tro
I am ill/sick.	Je suis malade.	zhuh swee ma-**lahd**
Call a . . .	Appelez un . . .	a-play uhn
doctor	Docteur	dohk-**tehr**
Help!	Au secours!	o suh-**koor**
Stop!	Arrêtez!	a-reh-**tay**
Fire!	Au feu!	o fuh
Caution!/Look out!	Attention!	a-tahn-see-**ohn**

DINING OUT

A bottle of . . .	une bouteille de . . .	ewn boo-**tay** duh
A cup of . . .	une tasse de . . .	ewn tass duh
A glass of . . .	un verre de . . .	uhn vair duh
Bill/check	l'addition	la-dee-see-**ohn**
Bread	du pain	dew pan
Breakfast	le petit-déjeuner	luh puh-**tee** day-zhuh-**nay**
Butter	du beurre	dew burr
Cheers!	A votre santé!	ah vo-truh sahn-**tay**
Cocktail/aperitif	un apéritif	uhn ah-pay-ree-**teef**
Dinner	le dîner	luh dee-**nay**
Dish of the day	le plat du jour	luh plah dew **zhoor**
Enjoy!	Bon appétit!	bohn a-pay-**tee**
Fixed-price menu	le menu	luh may-**new**
Fork	une fourchette	ewn four-**shet**
I am diabetic.	Je suis diabétique.	zhuh swee dee-ah- bay-**teek**
I am vegetarian.	Je suis végétarien(ne).	zhuh swee vay-zhay-ta-ree-**en**
I cannot eat . . .	Je ne peux pas manger de . . .	zhuh nuh **puh** pah mahn-**jay** deh

ENGLISH	FRENCH	PRONUNCIATION
I'd like to order.	Je voudrais commander.	zhuh voo-**dray** ko-mahn-**day**
Is service/the tip included?	Est-ce que le service est compris?	ess kuh luh sair-**veess** ay comb-**pree**
It's good/bad.	C'est bon/mauvais.	say bohn/mo-**vay**
It's hot/cold.	C'est chaud/froid.	Say sho/frwah
Knife	un couteau	uhn koo-**toe**
Lunch	le déjeuner	luh day-zhuh-**nay**
Menu	la carte	la cart
Napkin	une serviette	ewn sair-vee-**et**
Pepper	du poivre	dew **pwah**-vruh
Plate	une assiette	ewn a-see-**et**
Please give me . . .	Donnez-moi . . .	doe-nay-**mwah**
Salt	du sel	dew sell
Spoon	une cuillère	ewn kwee-air
Sugar	du sucre	dew **sook**-ruh
Waiter!/Waitress!	Monsieur!/ Mademoiselle!	muh-**syuh**/ mad-mwa-**zel**
Wine list	la carte des vins	la cart day vehn

MENU GUIDE

FRENCH	ENGLISH

GENERAL DINING

Entrée	Appetizer/Starter
Garniture au choix	Choice of vegetable side
Plat du jour	Dish of the day
Selon arrivage	When available
Supplément/En sus	Extra charge
Sur commande	Made to order

PETIT DÉJEUNER (BREAKFAST)

Confiture	Jam
Miel	Honey

FRENCH	ENGLISH
Oeuf à la coque	Boiled egg
Oeufs sur le plat	Fried eggs
Oeufs brouillés	Scrambled eggs
Tartine	Bread with butter

POISSONS/FRUITS DE MER (FISH/SEAFOOD)

Anchois	Anchovies
Bar	Bass
Brandade de morue	Creamed salt cod
Brochet	Pike
Cabillaud/Morue	Fresh cod
Calmar	Squid
Coquilles St-Jacques	Scallops
Crevettes	Shrimp
Daurade	Sea bream
Ecrevisses	Prawns/Crayfish
Harengs	Herring
Homard	Lobster
Huîtres	Oysters
Langoustine	Prawn/Lobster
Lotte	Monkfish
Moules	Mussels
Palourdes	Clams
Saumon	Salmon
Thon	Tuna
Truite	Trout

VIANDE (MEAT)

Agneau	Lamb
Boeuf	Beef
Boudin	Sausage
Boulettes de viande	Meatballs

FRENCH	ENGLISH
Brochettes	Kebabs
Cassoulet	Casserole of white beans, meat
Cervelle	Brains
Chateaubriand	Double fillet steak
Choucroute garnie	Sausages with sauerkraut
Côtelettes	Chops
Côte/Côte de boeuf	Rib/T-bone steak
Cuisses de grenouilles	Frogs' legs
Entrecôte	Rib or rib-eye steak
Épaule	Shoulder
Escalope	Cutlet
Foie	Liver
Gigot	Leg
Porc	Pork
Ris de veau	Veal sweetbreads
Rognons	Kidneys
Saucisses	Sausages
Selle	Saddle
Tournedos	Tenderloin of T-bone steak
Veau	Veal

METHODS OF PREPARATION

A point	Medium
A l'étouffée	Stewed
Au four	Baked
Ballotine	Boned, stuffed, and rolled
Bien cuit	Well-done
Bleu	Very rare
Frit	Fried
Grillé	Grilled
Rôti	Roast

FRENCH	ENGLISH
Saignant	Rare

VOLAILLES/GIBIER (POULTRY/GAME)

Blanc de volaille	Chicken breast
Canard/Caneton	Duck/Duckling
Cerf/Chevreuil	Venison (red/roe)
Coq au vin	Chicken stewed in red wine
Dinde/Dindonneau	Turkey/Young turkey
Faisan	Pheasant
Lapin/Lièvre	Rabbit/Wild hare
Oie	Goose
Pintade/Pintadeau	Guinea fowl/Young guinea fowl
Poulet/Poussin	Chicken/Spring chicken

LÉGUMES (VEGETABLES)

Artichaut	Artichoke
Asperge	Asparagus
Aubergine	Eggplant
Carottes	Carrots
Champignons	Mushrooms
Chou-fleur	Cauliflower
Chou (rouge)	Cabbage (red)
Laitue	Lettuce
Oignons	Onions
Petits pois	Peas
Pomme de terre	Potato
Tomates	Tomatoes

TRAVEL SMART
MONTRÉAL AND
QUÉBEC CITY

GETTING HERE AND AROUND

■ AIR TRAVEL

Flying time (gate-to-gate) to Montréal is about 1½ hours from New York, 2½ hours from Chicago, 4 hours from Dallas, and 6 hours from Los Angeles. Flying time to Québec City is about 2 hours from New York, 3 hours from Chicago, 5 hours from Dallas, and 7 hours from Los Angeles.

Trudeau Airport offers self-serve check-in and boarding passes at electronic kiosks throughout the airport. Make sure you arrive at the airport two hours before your flight's scheduled departure.

Security measures at Canadian airports are similar to those in the United States.

Airport Security Issues Transportation Security Administration ⊕ *www.tsa.gov.*

AIRPORTS

For service to Montréal, Montréal–Pierre Elliott Trudeau International Airport, also known by its previous name, Dorval International Airport, is 20 km (12.5 miles) west of the city. Québec City's Jean Lesage International Airport is about 13 km (9 miles) northwest of Downtown. Both airports handle domestic and international flights.

Airport Information Aéroports de Montréal ✉ *800 pl. Leigh-Capreol, Suite 1000, Dorval* ☎ *514/394-7200* ⊕ *www.admtl.com.* **Jean Lesage International Airport** *(YQB).* ☎ *418/640-3300, 877/769-2700* ⊕ *www.aeroportdequebec.com.* **Montréal–Pierre Elliott Trudeau International Airport** *(YUL).* ☎ *800/465-1213, 514/394-7377* ⊕ *www.admtl.com.*

GROUND TRANSPORTATION

In Montréal, a taxi from Trudeau International to Downtown costs C$40. All taxi companies must charge the same rate for travel between the airport and Downtown.

The least expensive way to get from Trudeau International Airport into the city is to take the 747 Express Bus, operated by Société de transport de Montréal. Shuttles leave from Montréal Central Bus Station, which is connected to Berri–UQAM métro station. They run approximately every 15 minutes all day long, except during the rush hours of 4 pm–6 pm, when they leave every 10 minutes. The cost is C$10 one-way, payable in coins only (no bills). Also available from automated dispensers in the airport are C$10 day bus passes, which not only buy you a ticket for the airport shuttle but also unlimited travel on the entire Montréal bus and métro system for a 24-hour period.

In Québec City, taxis are available immediately outside the airport exit near the baggage-claim area. A ride into the city costs a flat rate of C$34.25. Two local taxi firms are Taxi Coop de Québec, the largest company in the city, and Taxi Québec. Private limo service is expensive, starting at C$65 for the ride from the airport into the city. Try Groupe Limousine A-1.

Montréal Contacts Société de transport de Montréal ☎ *514/786-4636* ⊕ *www.stm.info.*

Québec City Contacts Groupe Limousine A-1 ☎ *418/523-5059, 866/523-5059* ⊕ *www.limousinequebec.com.* **Taxi Coop de Québec** ☎ *418/525-5191* ⊕ *www.taxicoop-quebec.com.* **Taxi Québec** ☎ *418/525-8123* ⊕ *taxiquebec.com.*

FLIGHTS

Of the major U.S. airlines, American, Delta, United, and US Airways serve Montréal; Delta also flies to Québec City.

Regularly scheduled flights from the United States to Montréal and Québec City as well as flights within Canada are available on Air Canada and the regional airlines associated with it, including Air Canada Jazz (reservations are made through Air Canada). Porter Airlines also has connecting service to Montréal and

Québec City from select U.S. cities, via Toronto's Billy Bishop Airport.

Airline Contacts Air Canada ☎ *888/247–2262* ⊕ *www.aircanada.com.* **American Airlines** ☎ *800/433–7300* ⊕ *www.aa.com.* **Delta Airlines** ☎ *800/221–1212 for U.S. reservations, 800/241–4141 for international reservations* ⊕ *www.delta.com.* **Porter Airlines** ☎ *888/619–8622* ⊕ *www.flyporter.com.* **US Airways** ☎ *800/428–4322 for U.S. and Canada reservations, 800/622–1015 for international reservations* ⊕ *www.usairways.com.*

▌ BIKE TRAVEL

Québec continues to expand its Route Verte (Green Route), a network of bike trails covering the southern half of the province, which will eventually link with trails in New England and New York. More than 90% of the marked trails are already open, and when the project is completed, there will be 5,000 km (more than 3,100 miles) of bikeways. For information and a map, head to Vélo Québec's website.

Contact Vélo Québec ☎ *514/521–8356, 800/567–8356* ⊕ *www.velo.qc.ca.*

▌ BOAT AND FERRY TRAVEL

The Québec–Lévis ferry, which crosses the St. Lawrence River, gives you a magnificent panorama of Old Québec on its trips to and from Lévis. Although the crossing takes 15 minutes, the waiting time can increase the trip to an hour. The cost is C$3.25. The first ferry from Québec City leaves weekdays at 6:20 am from the pier at rue Dalhousie, opposite Place Royale. Crossings run every 20 minutes during weekday rush hours, from 6:20 am to 9 am and 3 pm to 6 pm. At other times it runs every 30 minutes until 2:20 am. On weekends and holidays, the ferry leaves every 30 minutes from 6:30 am to 2:20 am. Schedules can change, so be sure to check the ferry website or call ahead.

Boat and Ferry Information Québec–Lévis ferry ☎ *877/787–7483* ⊕ *www.traversiers.gouv.qc.ca.*

▌ BUS TRAVEL

Several private bus lines serve the province. Orléans Express is probably the most convenient, as it offers regular service between Montréal and Québec City and its buses are clean and comfortable. The trip takes three hours. Limocar, another bus line, serves the Eastern Townships. Greyhound Lines offers interprovincial service and is timely and comfortable, if not exactly plush. Megabus offers somewhat more luxurious service to the province of Ontario and the city of Buffalo. Smoking isn't permitted on any buses.

Bus terminals in Montréal and Québec City are usually efficient operations, with service all week and plenty of agents on hand to handle ticket sales. In villages and some small towns the bus station is simply a counter in a local convenience store, gas station, or snack bar. Getting information on schedules beyond the local ones is sometimes difficult in these places. In rural Québec it's a good idea to bring along a French–English dictionary, although most merchants and clerks can handle a simple ticket sale in English.

On a daily basis, buses from Montréal to Québec City depart 20 times per day between 6 am and 11 pm. A one-way ticket costs C$56.80, taxes included; round-trip costs C$90.89. Tickets can be purchased only at terminals. All intercity bus lines servicing Montréal arrive and depart from the city's Downtown bus terminal, the Station Centrale d'Autobus Montréal, which is conveniently next to the Berri-UQÀM métro station. The staff has schedule and fare information for all bus companies at the station.

Many bus companies offer discounts if you book in advance, usually either 7 or 14 days ahead. Discounts are also often available for kids (children ages 15 and under can travel for free on most bus lines if tickets are booked three days in advance).

In major bus terminals, most bus lines accept at least some of the major credit cards. Some smaller lines require cash or take only Visa or MasterCard. All accept traveler's checks in U.S. or Canadian currency with suitable identification, but it's advisable to exchange foreign currency (including U.S. currency) at a bank or exchange office. Be prepared to use cash to buy a ticket in really small towns.

Most bus lines don't accept reservations for specific seats. You should plan on picking up your tickets at least 45 minutes before the bus's scheduled departure time.

Bus Information Central Bus Station
✉ *1717 rue Berri, Montréal* ☎ *514/842–2281*
⊕ *www.gamtl.com.* **Gare du Palais Bus Station** ✉ *320 rue Abraham-Martin, Québec City* ☎ *418/525–3000.* **Greyhound Lines**
☎ *800/231–2222, 800/661–8747 in Canada*
⊕ *www.greyhound.com.* **Limocar** ☎ *866/692–8899* ⊕ *limocar.ca.* **Orléans Express**
☎ *888/999–3977, 514/395–4000* ⊕ *www.orleansexpress.com.* **Voyageur/Greyhound Canada** ☎ *800/661–8747* ⊕ *www.greyhound.ca.*

▌ CAR TRAVEL

Montréal is accessible from the rest of Canada via the Trans-Canada Highway, which crosses the southern part of the island as Autoroute 20, with Autoroute 720 leading into Downtown. Autoroute 40 parallels Route 20 to the north; exits to Downtown include St-Laurent and St-Denis. From New York, take I–87 north until it becomes Autoroute 15 at the Canadian border; continue for another 47 km (29 miles) to the outskirts of Montréal. You can also follow U.S. I–89 north until it becomes the two-lane Route 133, which eventually joins Autoroute 10, an east–west highway that leads west across the Champlain Bridge and into Downtown. From I–91 through Massachusetts via New Hampshire and Vermont,

you can take Route 55 to Autoroute 10. Again, turn west to reach Montréal.

At the border you must clear Canadian Customs, so be prepared with your passport and car registration. On holidays and during the peak summer season, expect to wait a half hour or more at the major crossings.

Montréal and Québec City are linked by Autoroute 20 on the south shore of the St. Lawrence River and by Autoroute 40 on the north shore. On both highways, the ride between the two cities is about 240 km (149 miles) and takes about three hours. U.S. I–87 in New York, U.S. I–89 in Vermont, and U.S. I–91 in New Hampshire connect with Route 20, as does Highway 401 from Toronto.

Driving northeast from Montréal on Route 20, follow signs for Pont Pierre-Laporte (Pierre Laporte Bridge) as you approach Québec City. After you've crossed the bridge, turn right onto boulevard Laurier (Route 175), which becomes the Grande Allée.

The speed limit is posted in kilometers; on highways the limit is 100 kph (about 62 mph), and the use of radar-detection devices is prohibited.

In Québec the road signs are in French, but the important ones have pictograms. Signs with a red circle and a slash indicate that something, such as a left or right turn, is prohibited. Those with a green circle show what's permitted. Parking signs display a green-circled "P" with either the number of hours you can park or a clock showing the hours parking is permitted. It's not unusual to have two or three road signs all together to indicate several different strictures. Keep in mind the following terms: *centre-ville* (Downtown), *arrêt* (stop), *détenteurs de permis* (permit holders only), *gauche* (left), *droit* (right), *ouest* (west), and *est* (east).

Drivers must carry vehicle registration and proof of insurance coverage, which is compulsory in Canada. Québec drivers are covered by the Québec government no-fault insurance plan. Drivers from outside Québec can obtain a Canadian Non-Resident Inter-Provincial Motor Vehicle Liability Insurance Card, available from any U.S. insurance company. The card is accepted as evidence of financial responsibility in Canada, but you're not required to have one. The minimum liability in Québec is C$50,000. If you are driving a car that isn't registered in your name, carry a letter from the owner that authorizes your use of the vehicle.

GASOLINE

Gasoline is always sold in liters; 3.8 liters make a gallon. As of this writing, gas prices in Québec fluctuate considerably, ranging from C$1.25 to C$1.40 per liter (this works out to about $4.25 to $4.76 per gallon U.S.). Fuel comes in several grades, denoted as *regulière, supérieure,* and *prémium.*

PARKING

Expect on-street parking in Montréal to be hard to find; your best bet is to leave the car at your hotel garage and take public transportation or a cab. If you must drive, ask your concierge to recommend a garage near your destination. Be extra careful where you park if it snows, to avoid getting towed. Parking in Québec City is much less stressful, although it's also advisable to leave the car at the hotel and walk—especially if you're heading to Vieux-Québec.

ROAD CONDITIONS

In Montréal and Québec City the jumble of bicycle riders, delivery vehicles, taxis, and municipal buses can be chaotic. In the countryside at night, roads are lighted at exit points from major highways but are otherwise dark. Roads in the province aren't very good, especially during the spring pothole season—be prepared for some spine-jolting bumps and potholes, and check tire pressure once in a while.

In winter, Montréal streets are kept mostly clear of snow and ice, but outside the city the situation can deteriorate. Locals are notorious for exceeding the speed limit, so keep an eye on your mirrors. For up-to-date reports on road conditions throughout the province, go to Transport Québec's website.

Contact Transport Quebec ⊕ *www. quebec511.gouv.qc.ca.*

ROADSIDE EMERGENCIES

Dial 911 in an emergency. Contact CAA, the Canadian Automobile Association, in the event of a flat tire, dead battery, empty gas tank, or other car-related mishap. Automobile Association of America membership includes CAA service.

Emergency Services CAA ☎ *800/222–4357, 514/861–1313* ⊕ *www.caaquebec.com.*

Insurance Information Insurance Bureau of Canada ☎ *514/288–4321, 866/422–4331 in Québec* ⊕ *www.ibc.ca.* **Société de l'assurance automobile du Québec** ☎ *800/361–7620, 514/873–7620, 418/643–7620* ⊕ *www.saaq.gouv.qc.ca.*

RULES OF THE ROAD

By law, you're required to wear seat belts even in the backseat. Infant seats also are required. Radar-detection devices are illegal in Québec; just having one in your car is illegal. Speed limits, given in kilometers, are usually within the 90 kph–100 kph (50 mph–60 mph) range outside the cities.

Right turns on a red light are allowed in most of the province, the island of Montréal being the notable exception, where they're prohibited. Driving with a blood-alcohol content of 0.08% or higher is illegal and can earn you a stiff fine and jail time. Headlights are compulsory in inclement weather. Drivers aren't permitted to use handheld cell phones. The laws here are similar to the rest of North America; to consult Québec's Highway Code go to the Société de l'assurance automobile du Québec's website.

Contact Ministère des Transports du Québec ☎ *888/355–0511* ⊕ *www.mtq.gouv. qc.ca.* **Société de l'assurance automobile du Québec** ☎ *800/361–7620, 514/873–7620, 418/643–7620* ⊕ *www.saaq.gouv.qc.ca.*

CAR RENTAL

Rates in Montréal run from about C$30 to C$60 a day for an economy car with air-conditioning and unlimited kilometers. If you prefer a manual-transmission car, check whether the rental agency of your choice offers stick shifts; many agencies in Canada don't.

You must be at least 21 years old to rent a car in Québec, and some car-rental agencies don't rent to drivers under 25. Most rental companies don't allow you to drive on gravel roads. Child seats are compulsory for children ages five and under.

Rentals at the airports near Québec City and Montréal are usually more expensive than neighborhood rentals.

Major Rental Agencies Alamo
☎ 877/222–9075 ⊕ www.alamo.com. **Avis**
☎ 800/331–1084 ⊕ www.avis.com. **Budget**
☎ 800/472–3325 from Canada, 800/218–7792 from the U.S. ⊕ www.budget.com. **Hertz**
☎ 800/654–3001 ⊕ www.hertz.com. **National Car Rental** ☎ 877/222–9058 ⊕ www.nationalcar.com.

▌ TRAIN TRAVEL

Amtrak offers its daily Adirondak service from New York City's Penn Station to Montréal, although the train sometimes arrives too late to make any connecting trains that evening. Connections are available, often the next day, to Canadian rail line VIA Rail's Canadian routes. The ride takes up to 11 hours, and one-way tickets start at C$67.

VIA Rail trains run from Montréal to Québec City often and take three hours. The train arrives at the 19th-century Gare du Palais in Lower Town. Trains on the Montréal—Québec City route run five times daily on weekdays, three times daily on weekends, with a stop in Ste-Foy. Tickets can be purchased in advance at VIA Rail offices, at the station prior to departure, through a travel agent, or online. VIA's supersaver (escape) fare ranges from C$45 to $66, and is usually

nonrefundable. If you're lucky you can sometimes find Web-only fares for as little as C$29. Keep in mind such discounted fares are usually nonrefundable.

Business class tickets start at C$90 each way, and includes early boarding, seat selection, and a three-course meal with wine.

To save money, look into rail passes. But be aware that if you don't plan to cover many miles, you may come out ahead by buying individual tickets. VIA Rail offers a Canrail pass (for travel within Canada) and a Corridor Pass (for travel anywhere between Windsor, Ontario, and Québec City). Senior citizens (60 and older), children (11 and under), and students are often entitled to discounts.

The Massif de Charlevoix train system takes you from Québec City to La Malbaie, Charlevoix for a one-day excursion. The small villages and the natural beauty along the route are impressive. There are different packages available based on the seasons. Prices start at C$189 per person.

Information Amtrak ☎ 800/872–7245
⊕ www.amtrak.com. **Le Massif de Charlevoix** ☎ 877/536–2774, 418/632–5876 ⊕ www.lemassif.com. **VIA Rail Canada** ☎ 888/842–7245 from U.S., 514/989–2626 Montreal ⊕ www.viarail.ca.

ESSENTIALS

■ ACCOMMODATIONS

In Montréal and Québec City you have a choice of luxury hotels, moderately priced modern properties, and small older hotels with fewer conveniences but sometimes more charm. Options in small towns and in the country include large, full-service resorts; small, privately owned hotels; roadside motels; and bed-and-breakfasts. Even outside the cities it's a good idea to make reservations before you plan to pull into town.

Expect accommodations to cost more in summer than in the colder months (except for places such as ski resorts, where winter is high season). When making reservations, ask about special deals and packages. Big-city hotels that cater to business travelers often offer weekend packages, and many city hotels offer rooms at up to 50% off in winter. If you're planning to visit Montréal or Québec City or a resort area in high season, book well in advance. Also be aware of any special events or festivals that may coincide with your visit and fill every room for miles around. For resorts and lodges, remember that winter ski season is a period of high demand, and plan accordingly.

⇨ *For more information on apartment rentals, student housing options, and B&Bs, see the Lodging Alternatives box in Chapter 8.*

APARTMENT AND HOUSE RENTALS

The *Gazette* (⊕ *www.montrealgazette. com*), Montréal's English-language daily, has a wide selection of rental listings.

BED-AND-BREAKFASTS

B&Bs, which are also known as *gîtes* in Québec, can be found in both the country and the cities. For assistance in booking these, be sure to check out B&B websites (⊕ *www.gitesetaubergesdupassant. com* and ⊕ *www.bedsandbreakfasts.ca* are good resources for B&Bs throughout

the province). Room quality varies from house to house as well, so ask to see a few rooms before making a choice.

The nonprofit organization Agricotours has extensive listings of B&Bs, both urban and rural, as well as farms that take paying guests.

Reservation Services BB Canada ⊕ *www. bbcanada.com*. **Bed and Breakfast Quebec** ⊕ *www.bedbreakfastsquebec.com*. **Bed & Breakfast.com** ☎ *512/322–2710, 800/462–2632* ⊕ *www.bedandbreakfast.com*. **Montréal Reservation** ⊕ *www.montrealreservation.com*.

HOTELS

Canada doesn't have a national rating system for hotels, but Québec's tourism ministry rates the province's hotels and bed-and-breakfasts; the stars are more a reflection of the number of facilities and amenities than of the hotel's performance. Hotels are rated zero to three stars (B&Bs, zero to four suns), with zero stars or suns representing minimal comfort and few services and three stars or four suns being the very best. All hotels listed have private baths unless otherwise noted.

■ COMMUNICATIONS

INTERNET

Most hotels—even several B&Bs—now have Wi-Fi either in-room or in-hotel. If you're looking for a cybercafé, head to the area around McGill or Concordia universities.

Contacts Cybercafes. More than 4,000 Internet cafés worldwide are listed. ⊕ *www. cybercafes.com*.

LANGUAGE

Although Canada as a whole has two official languages—English and French—the province of Québec has only one. French is the language you hear most often on the streets here; it's also the language of government, businesses, and schools. Only in Montréal, the Gatineau (the area around Hull), and the Eastern Townships is English more widely spoken. Most French Canadians speak English as well, but learning a few phrases before you go is useful. Canadian French has many distinctive words and expressions, and it's as different from the language of France as North American English is from British English.

PHONES
CALLING WITHIN CANADA
As you'd expect, pay phones are scarce these days. Phone numbers appear just as they do in the United States, with a three-digit area code followed by a seven-digit number. The area codes for Montréal are 514 and 438; in Québec City, it's 418.

CALLING OUTSIDE CANADA
The country code for the United States is 1.

MOBILE PHONES
If you have a multiband phone and your service provider uses the world-standard GSM network, you can probably use your phone abroad. Roaming fees can be steep, however: 99¢ a minute is considered reasonable. It's almost always cheaper to send a text message than to make a call, since text messages are often free or have a very low set fee (usually less than 5¢).

If you just want to make local calls, consider buying a new SIM card (note that your provider may have to unlock your phone for you to use a different SIM card) and a prepaid service plan in the destination. You'll then have a local number and can make local calls at local rates. If your trip is extensive, you could also simply buy a new cell phone in your destination, as the initial cost will be offset over time.

Contacts Cellular Abroad ☎ *800/287–5072* ⊕ *www.cellularabroad.com.* **Mobal** ☎ *888/888–9162* ⊕ *www.mobalrental.com.*

▌CUSTOMS AND DUTIES

U.S. Customs and Immigration has pre-clearance services at **Pierre Elliott Trudeau International Airport**, which serves Montréal. This allows U.S.-bound air passengers to depart their airplane directly on arrival at their U.S. destination without further inspection and delays.

American visitors may bring in, duty-free, for personal consumption, 200 cigarettes; 50 cigars; 7 ounces of tobacco; and 1 bottle (1.5 liters or 40 imperial ounces) of liquor or wine or 24,355-milliliter (12-ounce) bottles or cans of beer. Any alcohol and tobacco products in excess of these amounts are subject to duty, provincial fees, and taxes. You can also bring in gifts up to a total value of C$750.

Cats and dogs must have a certificate issued by a licensed veterinarian that clearly identifies the animal and vouches that it has been vaccinated against rabies during the preceding 36 months. Certificates aren't necessary for Seeing Eye dogs. Plant material must be declared and inspected. There may be restrictions on some live plants, bulbs, and seeds. You may bring food for your own use, as long as the quantity is consistent with the duration of your visit and restrictions or prohibitions on some fruits and vegetables are observed.

Canada's firearms laws are significantly stricter than those in much of the United States. All handguns and semiautomatic and fully automatic weapons are prohibited and cannot be brought into the country. Sporting rifles and shotguns may be imported provided they are to be used for sporting, hunting, or competing while in Canada. All firearms must be declared to Canada Customs at the first point of entry. Failure to declare firearms will result in their seizure, and criminal charges may be made. Regulations require visitors to have a confirmed Firearms Declaration to bring any guns into Canada; a fee of C$25 applies, valid for 60 days but good for one year if renewed before it expires. For more information, contact the Canadian Firearms Centre.

Information in Montréal and Québec City Canada Border Services Agency ⊠ *2265*

blvd. St-Laurent, Ottawa, Ontario ☎ 800/461–9999 in Canada ⊕ www.cbsa-asfc.gc.ca.
Canadian Firearms Centre ☎ 800/731–4000 ⊕ www.cfc-cafc.gc.ca.

U.S. Information U.S. Customs and Border Protection ⊕ www.cbp.gov.

▌ EATING OUT

French-Canadian fast food follows the same concept as American fast food, though barbecue chicken is also popular. Local chains to watch for include St-Hubert, which serves rotisserie chicken; Chez Cora, which specializes in breakfasts; and La Belle Province, Lafleur, and Valentine, all of which serve hamburgers, hot dogs, and fries. For a vegetarian option, try the excellent Montréal chain Le Commensal.

MEALS AND MEALTIMES
Unless otherwise noted, the restaurants listed in this guide are open daily for lunch and dinner.

PAYING
Major credit cards are widely accepted in both Montréal and Québec City.

⇨ For guidelines on tipping, see Tipping below.

RESERVATIONS AND DRESS
Regardless of where you are, it's a good idea to make a reservation if you can. We only mention them specifically when reservations are essential or when they aren't accepted. We mention dress only when men are required to wear a jacket or a jacket and tie.

WINES, BEER, AND SPIRITS
Some of the best local microbreweries include Unibroue (Fin du Monde, U, U2), Brasseurs du Nord (Boréale), and McAuslan (Griffon, St. Ambroise). The local hard cider P.O.M. is also excellent. Caribou, a traditional concoction made from red wine, vodka (or some other liquor), spices, and, usually, maple syrup, is available at many winter events and festivals throughout the province, such as Québec City's winter carnival. Small bars may also offer the drink in season.

The province's liquor purveyor, SAQ, stocks a wide choice of wines (with a heavy emphasis on those from France) and is also the only place you can buy hard liquor; most SAQ stores are open regular business hours. Supermarkets and convenience stores carry lower-end wines, but they can sell wine and beer until 11 pm all week (long after SAQ stores have closed). The minimum legal age for alcohol consumption is 18.

▌ EMERGENCIES

All embassies are in Ottawa. The U.S. consulate in Montréal is open weekdays 8:30–noon; additionally it's open Wednesday 2–3:30 pm. The U.S. Consulate maintains a list of medical specialists in the Montréal area.

In Montréal, the main English-language hospital is Montréal General Hospital (McGill University Health Centre). Many pharmacies in Montréal stay open until midnight, including Jean Coutu and Pharmaprix stores. Some are open around the clock, including the Pharmaprix on chemin de la Côte-des-Neiges.

In Québec City, the Centre Hospitalier Universitaire de Québec is the city's largest institution and incorporates the teaching hospitals Pavillon CHUL in Ste-Foy and Pavillon Hôtel-Dieu, the main hospital in Vieux-Québec. Most outlets of the big pharmacy chains in the region (including Jean Coutu, Racine, Brunet, and Uniprix) are open every day and offer free delivery.

Foreign Embassies and Consulates U.S. Consulate General ⊠ 1155 rue St-Alexandre, Montréal ☎ 514/398–9695 ⊕ montreal.usconsulate.gov ⊠ 2 pl. Terrasse Dufferin, Québec City ☎ 418/692–2095 ⊕ quebec.usconsulate.gov. **U.S. Embassy** ⊠ 490 Sussex Dr., Ottawa, Ontario ☎ 613/688–5335 ⊕ canada.usembassy.gov.

Hospitals Centre Hospitalier Universitaire de Québec, Pavillon CHUL ✉ *2705 blvd. Laurier, Ste-Foy* ☎ *418/525–4444, 418/654–2114 emergencies* ⊕ *www.chuq.qc.ca*. **Centre Hospitalier Universitaire de Québec, Pavillon Hôtel-Dieu** ✉ *11 côte du Palais, Upper Town* ☎ *418/525–4444, 418/691–5042 emergencies* ⊕ *www.chuq.qc.ca/fr/le_chuq/ nos_etablissements/hdq*. **Montréal General Hospital (McGill University Health Centre)** ✉ *1650 av. Cedar, Downtown* ☎ *514/934–1934* ⊕ *muhc.ca/mgh* Ⓜ *Guy-Concordia*.

▌HOLIDAYS

Canadian national holidays are as follows: New Year's Day (January 1), Good Friday (late March or early April), Easter Monday (the Monday following Good Friday), Victoria Day (called Fête des Patriotes in Québec; late May), Canada Day (July 1), Labor Day (early September), Thanksgiving (mid-October), Remembrance Day (November 11), Christmas, and Boxing Day (December 26). St. Jean Baptiste Day (June 24) is a provincial holiday.

▌MONEY

Throughout this book, prices are given in Canadian dollars, which at this writing are worth roughly the same as American dollars. The price of a cup of coffee ranges from less than C$1 to C$2.50 or more, depending on how upscale or downscale the place is; beer costs C$3 to C$7 in a bar; a smoked-meat sandwich costs about C$5 to C$6; and museum admission can cost anywhere from nothing to C$15.

Prices throughout this guide are given for adults. Substantially reduced fees are almost always available for children, students, and senior citizens.

ATMS AND BANKS

Your own bank will probably charge a fee for using ATMs abroad; the foreign bank you use may also charge a fee. Nevertheless, you'll usually get a better rate of exchange at an ATM than you will at a currency-exchange office or even when changing money in a bank. And extracting funds as you need them is a safer option than carrying around a large amount of cash.

ATMs are available in most bank, trust-company, and credit-union branches across the province, as well as in most convenience stores, malls, and self-serve gas stations.

CREDIT CARDS

It's a good idea to inform your credit-card company before you travel, especially if you're going abroad and don't travel internationally very often. Otherwise, the credit-card company might put a hold on your card owing to unusual activity—not a good thing halfway through your trip. Record all your credit-card numbers—as well as the phone numbers to call if your cards are lost or stolen—in a safe place, so you're prepared should something go wrong. Both MasterCard and Visa have general numbers you can call (collect if you're abroad) if your card is lost, but you're better off calling the number of your issuing bank, since Master-Card and Visa usually just transfer you to your bank; your bank's number is usually printed on your card.

If you plan to use your credit card for cash advances, you'll need to apply for a PIN at least two weeks before your trip. Although it's usually cheaper (and safer) to use a credit card abroad for large purchases (so you can cancel payments or be reimbursed if there's a problem), note that some credit-card companies *and* the banks that issue them add substantial percentages to all foreign transactions, whether they're in a foreign currency or not. Check on these fees before leaving home, so there won't be any surprises when you get the bill.

Reporting Lost Cards American Express ☎ *800/528–4800 in U.S., 800/668–2639 in Canada* ⊕ *www.americanexpress.com*. **Diners Club** ☎ *800/234–6377 in U.S., 800/363–3333 in Canada* ⊕ *www.dinersclub.com*. **MasterCard** ☎ *800/627–8372 in U.S., 800/307–7309* *in Canada* ⊕ *www.mastercard.com.* **Visa** ☏ *800/847–2911 in U.S. and Canada* ⊕ *www. visa.com.*

CURRENCY AND EXCHANGE

U.S. dollars are accepted in much of Canada, especially in communities near the border. Traveler's checks (some are available in Canadian dollars) and major U.S. credit cards are accepted in most areas.

The units of currency in Canada are the Canadian dollar (C$) and the cent, in almost the same denominations as U.S. currency ($5, $10, $20, 5¢, 10¢, 25¢, etc.). The $1 and $2 bill are no longer used in Canada; they have been replaced by $1 and $2 coins (known as "loonies," because of the loon that appears on the coin, and "toonies," respectively).

At this writing, the exchange rate is US$1 to C$1.05, nearly at par.

Bank cards are widely accepted in Québec and throughout Canada. There are many branches of Québec's financial cooperative, La Caisse populaire Desjardins (a "Caisse Pop" as it's locally referred to), as well as bank machines (ATMs), throughout the region.

Currency Conversion Google ⊕ *www. google.com.* **Oanda.com** ⊕ *www.oanda.com.* **XE.com** ⊕ *www.xe.com.*

▌PACKING

If you're visiting Montréal anytime between November and May be sure to bring some warm clothes, or be prepared to purchase some while you're here. Come winter Montréal gets cold—very cold—with temperatures almost always dipping below the freezing mark from December until late March. A good winter coat, scarf, hat (locally called a "tuque"), gloves, and warm winter boots are pretty much a necessity in Québec if you want to be comfortable going outside in the winter months. In summer, however, temperatures regularly rise above 86°F (30°C) and Downtown Montréal in particular can get very humid, so bring a few pairs of shorts, sandals, and warm weather clothes. While it seems unbelievable, tales abound here of hapless tourists arriving at the airport in June with their skis and snowshoes in tow, wondering where all the snow is. Also, while a large Anglophone community resides in Montréal and many of its immediate surroundings, the official language here is French, and all road signs are in this language, so having a good French/English dictionary with you is always helpful.

▌PASSPORTS AND VISAS

All travelers will need a passport or other accepted secure documents to enter or reenter the United States. Naturalized U.S. residents should carry their naturalization certificate. Permanent residents who aren't citizens should carry their "green card." U.S. residents entering Canada from a third country must have a valid passport, naturalization certificate, or "green card."

▌RESTROOMS

Aside from the ones in municipal parks there's a noticeable lack of public restrooms in Downtown Montréal. That said, there's almost always a shopping mall or commercial establishment within striking distance should you find yourself in urgent need of relief. Most establishments won't give you much grief about coming in off the street to use their restroom, although generally the more discreet you are about it, the better.

Find a Loo The Bathroom Diaries ⊕ *www. thebathroomdiaries.com.*

▌TAXES

A goods and services tax (GST or TPS in Québec) of 5% applies on virtually every transaction in Canada except for the purchase of basic groceries. In addition to imposing the GST, Québec levies a provincial sales tax of 9.975% on most goods and services as well.

Departing passengers in Montréal pay a C\$25, plus GST, airport-improvement fee that's included in the cost of an airline ticket.

Information Canada Customs and Revenue Agency ✉ *Summerside Tax Centre, 275 Pope Rd., Suite 104, Summerside, Prince Edward Island* ☎ *800/668–4748 in Canada, 902/432–5608* ⊕ *www.ccra-adrc.gc.ca.*

∎ TIME

Montréal and Québec City are both in the Eastern Standard Time zone. Los Angeles is three hours behind local time and Chicago is one hour behind.

∎ TIPPING

Tips and service charges aren't usually added to a bill in Canada. In general, tip 15% of the total bill. This goes for waiters and waitresses, barbers and hairdressers, and taxi drivers. Porters and doormen should get about C\$2 a bag. For maid service, leave at least C\$2 per person a day (C\$3 to C\$5 in luxury hotels).

∎ TOURS

DAY TOURS AND GUIDES

In Montréal, from May through October, Amphi Tour sells a unique one-hour tour of Vieux-Montréal and the Vieux-Port on both land and water in an amphibious bus. Bateau-Mouche runs four harbor excursions and an evening supper cruise daily from May through October. The boats are reminiscent of the ones that cruise the canals of the Netherlands—wide-beamed and low-slung, with a glassed-in passenger deck. Boats leave from the Jacques Cartier Pier at the foot of Place Jacques-Cartier in the Vieux-Port.

Gray Line has nine different types of tours of Montréal from June through October and one tour the rest of the year. There are also day trips to Ottawa and Québec City. The company offers pickup service

at the major hotels and at Info-Touriste (✉ *1001 sq. Dorchester*).

In Québec City, Autocar Dupont/Old Québec Tours runs bus tours of the city, departing across the square from the Hôtel Château Laurier (✉ *1230 pl. Georges V*); you can buy tickets at most major hotels. The company runs guided tours in a minibus as well as tours of Côte-de-Beaupré and Île d'Orléans, and whale-watching excursions to Charlevoix. Tours run year-round and cost C\$34–C\$123. Call for a reservation and the company will pick you up at your hotel.

Croisières AML has day and evening cruises, some of which include dinner, on the St. Lawrence River aboard the MV *Louis-Jolliet*. The 1½- to 3-hour cruises run from May through mid-October and start at C\$35 plus tax.

Contacts Amphi Tour. In Montréal, from May through October, Amphi Tour sells a unique one-hour tour of Vieux-Montréal and the Vieux-Port on both land and water in an amphibious bus. ☎ *514/849–5181* ⊕ *www.montreal-amphibus-tour.com* ✉ *C\$10–C\$35.* **Bateau-Mouche.** Four harbor excursions and an evening supper cruise are run daily from May through October. The company has also introduced a weekend brunch cruise into the mix. ☎ *514/849–9952, 800/361–9952* ⊕ *www.bateaumouche.ca* ✉ *From C\$24.* **Croisières AML.** Day and evening cruises on the St. Lawrence River, some of which include gourmet dinner, set out from Pier Chouinard, beside the Québec–Lévis ferry terminal. The 1½- to 4-hour cruises run from May through mid-October. Full day and overnight excursions will take you farther along the river toward Charlevoix for whale watching. ✉ *10 rue Dalhousie, Lower Town, Québec City* ☎ *866/856–6668* ⊕ *www.croisieresaml.com*

From C$35.**Fitz and Follwell Co.** For bike tours, food tours, snow tours, underground city tours, and more, check out this Montréal-based company. Excursions may include hot chocolate, fresh bagels, a lunch of poutine, or dinner with wine. ⊠ *115 av. du Mont-Royal Ouest, The Plateau, Montréal* 514/840–0739 *www.fitzandfollwell.com Bike tours from C$75; walking tours from C$69.* **Gray Line.** Gray Line has five different types of tours of Montréal from June through October and one tour the rest of the year. There are also day trips to Québec City and The Laurentians. The company offers pickup service at the major hotels and at Info-Touriste (E1001 sq. Dorchester). ⊠ *Montréal* 800/472-9546 *www.grayline.com From $26.* **Old Québec Tours.** Hop-on, hop-off double-decker bus tours of the city are run by this company; you can buy tickets at most major hotels. They also run guided bus tours, and can take you along the Côte-de-Beaupré and to Île d'Orléans, plus whale-watching excursions to Charlevoix. 418/664-0460, 800/267-8687 *www. oldquebectours.com C$34–C$120.*

⬛ TRIP INSURANCE

Comprehensive trip insurance is valuable if you're booking a very expensive or complicated trip (particularly to an isolated region) or if you're booking far in advance. Comprehensive policies typically cover trip cancellation and interruption, letting you cancel or cut your trip short because of illness, or, in some cases, acts of terrorism in your destination. Such policies might also cover evacuation and medical care. Some also cover you for trip delays because of bad weather or mechanical problems as well as for lost or delayed luggage.

Another type of coverage to consider is financial default—that is, when your trip is disrupted because a tour operator, airline, or cruise line goes out of business. Generally you must buy this when you book your trip or shortly thereafter, and it's available to you only if your operator isn't on a list of excluded companies.

Always read the fine print of your policy to make sure that you're covered for the risks that most concern you. Compare several policies to be sure you're getting the best price and range of coverage available.

Insurance Comparison Info Insure My Trip 800/551–1337 *www.insuremytrip.com.* **Square Mouth** 800/240–0369 *www. squaremouth.com.*

Comprehensive Insurers Allianz Global Assistance 866/884–3556 *www. allianztravelinsurance.com.* **AIG Travel Guard** 800/826–4919 *www.travelguard.com.* **CSA Travel Protection** 800/711–1197 *www.csatravelprotection.com.* **Travelex Insurance** 888/228–9792 *www.travelex-insurance.com.* **Travel Insured International** 800/243-3174 *www.travelinsured.com.*

⬛ VISITOR INFORMATION

In Montréal, Centre Info-Touriste, on Square Dorchester, has extensive tourist information on Montréal and the rest of the province of Québec, as well as a currency-exchange service and Internet café. It's open June 21 through August, daily 9–7; September through October, daily 9–6; November through March, daily 9–5; and April through June 20, daily 9–6. The Vieux-Montréal branch is open May 27 through September 5, from 9 to 7, September 6 to October 10, from 9 to 6, and October 11 to November 13, from 9 to 5.

Tourisme-Montréal, the city tourist office, doesn't operate an information service for the public, but its website has a wealth of well-organized information.

In Québec City, the Québec City Region Tourism and Convention Bureau's visitor information centers in Montcalm and Ste-Foy are open June 24–early September, daily 8:30–7:30; early September–mid-October, daily 8:30–6:30; and mid-October–June 23, Monday–Saturday 9–5, Sunday 10–4. A mobile information service operates between mid-June and

September 7 (look for the mopeds marked with a big question mark).

The Québec government tourism department, Tourisme Québec, has a center open September–June 20, daily 9–5; and June 22–August, daily 8:30–7. Tourisme Québec can provide information on specific towns' tourist bureaus.

In the Laurentians, the major tourist office is the Association Touristique des Laurentides, just off Route des Laurentides 15 Nord at Exit 51 in Les Portes des Nord service center. The office is open mid-June–September, daily 8:30–8; October–mid-June, Saturday–Thursday 8:30–5 and Friday 8:30–6. Mont-Tremblant, Piedmont/St-Sauveur, Ste-Adèle, St-Adolphe-d'Howard, Ste-Agathe-des-Monts, St-Eustache, St-Jovite, and Val-David have regional tourist offices that are open year-round. Seasonal tourist offices (open mid-June–early September) are in Ferme Neuve, Grenville, Labelle, Lac-du-Cerf, Lachute, Nominique, Notre-Dame-du-Laus, Oka, St-Jérôme, Ste-Marguerite-Estérel, and St-Sauveur.

In the Eastern Townships, year-round regional provincial tourist offices are in Bromont, Coaticook, Granby, Lac-Mégantic, Magog-Orford, Sherbrooke, and Sutton. Seasonal tourist offices (open June–early September) are in Birchton, Danville, Dudswell, Dunham, Eastman, Frelighsburg, Lac-Brome (Foster), Lambton, Masonsville, Pike River, Ulverton, and Waterloo. The schedules of seasonal bureaus are irregular, so it's a good idea to contact the Association Touristique des Cantons de l'Est before visiting. This association also provides lodging information.

At the Beaupré Coast Interpretation Center, in a former convent, guides in costume explain displays on the history of the region. Admission is C$6. The center is open daily 9:30–4:30. For information about Canadian national parks in Québec, contact Parks Canada. Contact Sépaq for information about camping and lodgings in Québec province's network of 22

"Parcs Nationaux" and 15 game reserves (*réserves fauniques*). For information on camping in the province's private trailer parks and campgrounds, request the free publication "Québec Camping," from Tourisme Québec.

Agricotours, the Québec farm-vacation association, can provide lists of guest farms in the province.

Contacts Association Touristique des Cantons de l'Est ✉ *20 rue Don Bosco Sud, Sherbrooke* ☎ *819/820–2020, 800/355–5755* ⊕ *www.cantonsdelest.com.* **Association Touristique des Laurentides** ✉ *La Porte-du-Nord rest area, Autoroute des Laurentides, Exit 51* ☎ *450/224–7007, 800/561–6673* ⊕ *www.laurentides.com.* **Association Touristique Régionale de Charlevoix** ✉ *495 blvd. de Comporté, C.P. 275, La Malbaie* ☎ *418/665–4454, 800/667–2276* ⊕ *www.tourisme-charlevoix.com.* **Canadian Tourism Commission** ☎ *604/638–8300* ⊕ *www.travelcanada.ca.* **Centre d'Interpretation de la Côte-de-Beaupré** (*Beaupré Coast Interpretation Center*). ✉ *7976 av. Royale, C.P. 40, Château-Richer* ☎ *418/824–3677* ⊕ *www.histoire-cotedebeaupre.org.* **Centre Info-Touriste** ✉ *1255 rue Peel, Suite 100, Downtown, Montréal* ☎ *514/873–2015, 877/266–5687* ⊕ *www.bonjourquebec.com* Ⓜ *Peel or Bonaventure* ✉ *174 rue Notre-Dame Est, at pl. Jacques-Cartier, Vieux-Montréal, Montréal* Ⓜ *Champ-de-Mars.* **Parks Canada** ☎ *613/860–1251, 888/773–8888* ⊕ *www.pc.gc.ca.* **Québec City Tourist Information** ✉ *835 av. Laurier, Montcalm, Québec City* ☎ *418/641–6290, 877/783–1608* ⊕ *www.quebecregion.com.***Sépaq** ☎ *800/665–6527* ⊕ *www.sepaq.com.* **Terroir & Saveurs** ✉ *Montréal* ☎ *514/252–3138* ⊕ *www.terroiretsaveurs.com.* **Tourisme-Montréal** ☎ *877/266–5687* ⊕ *www.tourisme-montreal.org.* **Tourisme Québec** ✉ *1001 rue du Sq. Dorchester, No. 100, C.P. 979, Downtown, Montréal* ☎ *877/266–5687, 514/873–2015* ⊕ *www.bonjourquebec.com* ✉ *12 rue Ste-Anne, Place-d'Armes, Upper Town, Québec City* ☎ *877/266–5687* ⊕ *www.bonjourquebec.com.*

INDEX

A

À Table Tout Le Monde (shop), 116
Abbaye St-Benoît-du-Lac, 222–223
Accommodations. ⇨ See Hotels
Air travel, 34, 237, 336–337
ALT Montreal Griffintown ⏃, 184
Ancien Palais de Justice, 247
Antiques district (Québec City), 259
Antiques shops, 117–118, 123, 128, 222
Apartment rentals, 187, 341
Aquarium de Québec, 20, 264
Art galleries, 21
Montréal, 114, 118, 128–129
Québec City, 293–295
side trips from Québec City, 317
Arts. ⇨ See Nightlife and the arts
Astrolab du Mont-Mégantic, 230
Atelier Paré (Economuseum of Wood Sculpture), 305
ATMs, 344
Au Pays des Merveilles, 20, 204
Au Petit Poucet ✕, 205
Au Pied de Cochon ✕, 161
Auberge Baker ✕, 307
Auberge Bonaparte ⏃, 184
Auberge Château Bromont ⏃, 218
Auberge de la Fontaine ⏃, 191
Auberge des Peupliers ⏃, 321
Auberge du Coq de Montagne ✕, 207–208
Auberge du Vieux-Port ⏃, 184
Auberge Knowlton ⏃, 220, 222
Auberge La Goéliche ⏃, 310
Auberge la Maison Otis ⏃, 317
Auberge la Pinsonnière ⏃, 321
Auberge le Jardin d'Antoine ⏃, 191
Auberge l'Étoile Sur-le-Lac ⏃, 224
Auberge Place d'Armes ⏃, 275

Auberge Restaurant Clos Joli ✕, 203
Auberge St-Antoine ⏃, 281
Auberge Watel ⏃, 206
Auguste ✕, 229
Aux Anciens Canadiens ✕, 265
Aux Berges de l'Aurore ✕, 230
Avenue Bernard, 63
Avenue Laurier Ouest, 115

B

Baie-St-Paul, 315, 317–318
Baldwin Barmacie (bar), 99
Ballet, 107
Ballooning, 25
Balnea Réserve Thermale, 219
Banks, 344
BarBounya ✕, 168
Bars and lounges
Montréal, 87–81, 96, 98, 99–100
Québec City, 284–285
Basilique Cathédrale Notre-Dame-de-Québec, 239, 241
Basilique Notre-Dame-de-Montréal, 14, 38
Basilique Ste-Anne-de-Beaupré, 303
Beautys Luncheonette ✕, 162
Bed-and-breakfasts, 187, 341
Beer, 19
Big in Japan Bar, 98
Biking, 18–19, 337
Montréal, 11, 20, 34, 46, 132, 134
Québec City, 288
Bily Kun (bar), 98
Binerie Mont-Royal ✕, 162
Biodôme, 76, 78
Biosphère, 80, 83
Bistro B. ✕, 271
Bistrot Le Pape-Georges ✕, 259
Bixi (bicycle rentals), 20
Black and Blue Festival, 25
Blackstrap ✕, 176
Bleu Comme Le Ciel (shop), 122
Blues clubs, 285
Boat and ferry travel, 21, 250, 257, 318, 337
Boat tours, 135, 206
Boating, 134–135, 206
Bookstores, 118–119, 319
Boris Bistro ✕, 147

Bottega Pizzeria ✕, 26, 171–172
Bouillon Bilk ✕, 154
Boulevard St-Laurent, 60–61, 115
Boutique des Metiers d'Arts du Québec, 259
Boutique 1861 (shop), 124
Brasserie Les Enfants Terribles ✕, 166
Brasserie T ✕, 154
Brit & Chips ✕, 147
Bromont, 216–220
Bromont Five-Star Flea Market, 219
Browns (shop), 122
Burgundy Lion ✕, 154–155
Bus travel, 237, 337–338
Business hours, 87, 112, 146

C

Café-Boulangerie Paillard ✕, 265
Café Ferreira ✕, 155
Café Italia ✕, 26
Café Myriade ✕, 26, 155
Café Olympico ✕, 168
Café Souvenir ✕, 166–167
Caffé San Simeon ✕, 172
Canadian Museum of History, 214–215
Car racing, 137
Car rentals, 340
Car travel, 34, 237, 301, 338–340
Carnaval de Québec, 24, 293
Casa Biance Bed & Breakfast ⏃, 191–192
Casino de Charlevoix, 320
Casino de Montréal, 83
Casinos, 83, 100, 320–321
Casse-Crêpe Breton ✕, 265
Cathedral of the Holy Trinity, 248
Cathédrale Marie-Reine-du-Monde, 47, 49
Cavalli ✕, 155
Centre Bell, 53
Centre des Sciences de Montréal, 43
Centre d'Interprétation des Mammifères Marin, 323
Ceramics shops, 259
Chalet du Mont-Royal, 69
Chapelle Commémorative, 305
Chapelle des Ursulines, 241

Chapelle Notre-Dame-de-Bon-Secours, *40*

Chapelle Notre-Dame-de-Lourdes, *57*

Chapelle Notre-Dame-du-Sacré-Coeur, *38*

Charlevoix, *12, 315–324*

Château Bonne Entente ⊡, *283*

Château Dufresne, *78–79*

Cheese, *145*

Chez Ashton ✕, *246–247*

Chez Boulay Bistro Boréal ✕, *265*

Chez Cora ✕, *271*

Chez Doval ✕, *162*

Chez l'Epicier ✕, *147*

Chez Roger ✕, *172*

Chez Temporel ✕, *265, 267*

Chez Victoire ✕, *162*

Chez Victor ✕, *267*

Chiesa della Madonna della Difesa, *64–65*

Children, activities for, *20*

   dining, *146*

   lodging, *180*

Chinatown, *56, 160*

Christ Church Cathedral, *49*

Church of St. Andrew and St. Paul, *53*

Chute Montmorency, *20, 303, 305*

Cimetière de Notre-Dame-des-Neiges, *72*

Cimetière Mont-Royal, *72–73*

Cinq-á-Sept, *18*

Circuit Gilles Villeneuve, *84*

Circus, *42, 103–104*

Cirque du Soleil, *42, 103*

Classical music

   Montréal, *105–106*

   Québec City, *287*

Climate

   Montréal, *35*

   Québec City, *237*

   side trips from Montréal, *198, 212, 216*

   side trips from Québec City, *301*

Clock Tower, *42*

Clothing stores

   Montréal, *114, 116, 119–121, 124–125, 126, 127–128, 129–130*

   Québec City, *294, 295*

   side trips from Montréal, *222*

Club Chasse et Pêche ✕, *147, 150*

Club Unity (gay club), *96*

Comedy clubs, *92*

Communications, *341–342*

Consulates, *343*

Côte de Beaupré, *12, 302–308*

Côte-des-Neiges, *70–73, 192*

Courtyard Marriott Québec ⊡, *275, 279*

Craft shops, *17, 229, 294*

Credit cards, *7, 344–345*

Creperie Catherine ✕, *208*

Croix sur la Montagne, *69*

Cuisine, *16–17, 18, 26–27, 144–145*

Currency and exchange, *345*

Customs and duties, *342–343*

D

Da Emma ✕, *150*

Damas ✕, *168*

Dance, *106–107*

Dance clubs, *92, 98, 286*

De farine & d'eau fraîche ✕, *160–161*

Delta Montréal ⊡, *188*

Department stores, *121–122, 294, 295*

Dinette Triple Crown ✕, *172*

Dining, *7, 343.* ⇨ *See also* Restaurants

Discovery Pavilion of the Plains of Abraham, *247*

Dogsledding, *288–289*

Dominion Square Tavern ✕, *90–91, 155–156*

Downtown Montréal

   dining, *154–160*

   lodging, *188–190*

   nightlife and the arts, *90–93*

   shopping, *117–123*

   sightseeing, *47–56*

   tours, *26*

Dress code, *102, 146, 343*

Duc de Lorraine ✕, *72*

Duo (shop), *124–125*

Duties, *342–343*

E

E.R.A. Vintage Wear (shop), *119–120*

Eastern Townships, *12, 215–230*

Economuseum of Wood Sculpture (Atelier Paré), *305*

Edgar ✕, *215*

Édifice Price (skyscraper), *248*

Éditions de Robes (shop), *127*

Église de la Visitation de la Bienheureuse Vierge Marie, *65*

Église Notre-Dame-des-Victoires, *254*

Église Ste-Famille, *313*

Église St-François, *313*

Église St-Jean, *312*

Église St-Jean Baptiste, *261*

Église St-Laurent, *311*

Église St-Pierre, *314*

Église Très-Saint-Nom-de-Jésus, *76*

Embassies, *343*

Emergencies, *339, 343–344*

Épik Montreal ⊡, *184*

Equestrian events, *220*

Espace Pepin (shop), *114, 116*

Espace pour la Vie Jardin Botanique, *20, 75–76*

Estrimont Suites & Spa ⊡, *223*

Exporail (museum), *64*

F

Factoreries St-Sauver (mall), *201*

Fairmont Le Château Frontenac Hotel ⊡, *15, 241, 279*

Fairmont Le Château Montebello ⊡, *214*

Fairmont Le Manoir Richelieu ⊡, *321*

Fairmont Le Reine Elizabeth ⊡, *188*

Fairmont Tremblant ⊡, *208*

FCO di Fiumicino ✕, *150–151*

Féria de Vélo de Montréal, *134*

Ferries, *21, 250, 257, 318, 337*

Festival d'Été de Québec, *24, 288*

Festival International de Jazz de Montréal, *24–25, 103*

Festival International de Films du Monde, *25*

Festival of Colors, *25*

Festival OFF, *25*

Festival Orford, *223*

Festivals and seasonal events, *21, 24–25*

   Montréal, *84, 103, 134*

   Québec City, *24, 288, 293*

   side trips from Montréal, *209, 220, 223*

   side trips from Québec City, *321–322*

Fête de la Nouvelle France, *25*

Fête des Neiges de Montréal, *24*

Film, *107–109*

Fire Station No. *1, 76*
Fireworks, *21*
Fodor, Eugene, *7*
Folk music, *285*
Food shops
Montréal, *122, 125, 127, 128*
Québec City, *294, 295–296*
side trips from Québec City,
310, 314–315
Fortifications of Québec
National Historic Site,
241–243
Free and discount activities, *21*
French culture, *16*
French language, *28, 325–334,
341–342*
Fringe Festivals, *24*
Furco (bar), *91*
Fur Trade at Lachine National
Historic Site, *46*
Furriers, *17, 128, 296*

G

Garde Manger ✕ , *151*
Gardens. ⇨ *See* Parks and
gardens
Gatineau, *214–215*
Gatineau Park, *215*
Gay and lesbian nightlife,
96, 100
Gay Village, *58–59*
Gibbys ✕ , *151*
Gift shops, *294, 296*
Golden Square Mile, *47*
Golf
Montréal, *135–136*
Québec City, *289*
side trips from Montréal, *204,
209, 219, 226–227*
side trips from Québec City,
322
Grand Séminaire de
Montréal, *53*
Grande-Allée, *261–262*
Grosse Île National Park, *248,
250*
Gus ✕ , *172–173*

H

Halles du Petit-Cartier (food
mall), *262–263*
Hambar ✕ , *151*
Hayden's Wexford House 🏨 ,
282
Henri Henri (shop), *121*
Henry Stuart House, *250*
Hilton Montréal Bonaventure
🏨 , *188*
Hilton Québec 🏨 , *279*

History, *33, 242*
Hochelaga-Maisonneuve,
74–79
Hockey, *18, 136–137*
Holidays, *344*
Holt Renfrew (department
store), *121*
Hôpital Géneral des Soeurs-
Grises, *43*
Horse racing, *220*
Hospitals, *344*
Hôtel Belley 🏨 , *282*
Hôtel Cap-aux-Pierres 🏨 , *318*
Hôtel Champlain 🏨 , *279*
Hôtel Château Bellevue 🏨 ,
279
Hôtel Château Bromont 🏨 ,
218–219
Hôtel Château Laurier 🏨 , *283*
Hôtel Chez Swann 🏨 , *188*
Hôtel Clarendon 🏨 , *279*
Hôtel de Ville, *43–44*
Hôtel Delta Québec 🏨 , *283*
Hôtel des Coutellier 🏨 , *282*
Hotel Domaine Monté-Bello
🏨 , *214*
Hôtel du Lac 🏨 , *208*
Hôtel du Parlement, *262*
Hôtel du Vieux Québec 🏨 ,
279
Hôtel Gault 🏨 , *184*
Hotel Herman ✕ , *169*
Hôtel La Ferme 🏨 , *317*
Hôtel Le Clos St-Louis 🏨 , *280*
Hôtel Le Crystal 🏨 , *188–189*
Hôtel le Germain 🏨 , *189*
Hôtel Le Germain Dominion
🏨 , *282*
Hôtel Le Priori 🏨 , *282*
Hôtel Le St-James 🏨 , *185*
Hôtel Manoir de L'Esplanade
🏨 , *280*
Hôtel Manoir des Remparts
🏨 , *280*
Hôtel Marie Rollet 🏨 , *280*
Hôtel Musée Premieres Nations
🏨 , *283*
Hôtel Nelligan 🏨 , *185*
Hôtel Royal William 🏨 , *283*
Hôtel St. Paul 🏨 , *185*
Hôtel 71 🏨 , *282*
Hôtel Tadoussac 🏨 , *324*
Hôtel 10 🏨 , *191*
Hôtel Terrasse Royale 🏨 , *192*
Hotels, *7, 341*
best bets, *181, 278*
children, *180*
facilities, *179*
lodging alternatives, *187, 212*

Montréal, *178–192*
neighborhoods, *179*
parking, *180*
price categories, *7, 180, 197,
275, 302*
Québec City, *275–284*
reservations, *178–179*
side trips from Montréal,
*196, 201, 203, 204, 206,
208, 214, 215, 218–219,
220, 222, 223, 224, 226,
227–228, 230*
side trips from Québec City,
*302, 310, 311–312, 317,
318, 321, 324*
House rentals, *341*
Houseware shops, *116, 125,
206*
Hudson, *200*
Huron-Wedat Village, *296*
Hyatt Regency Montréal 🏨 ,
189

I

Ice Hotel 🏨 , *280*
Ice-skating, *17*
Montréal, *137*
Québec City, *289*
Ice wine, *145*
Île-aux-Coudres, *318*
Île d'Orléans, *12, 308–315*
Île Ste-Hélène, *42*
Inferno ✕ , *26, 173*
Insectarium, *20, 75–76*
Insurance, *347*
InterContinental Montréal 🏨 ,
185
International Fireworks Com-
petition, *84*
Internet, *341*
Islands, The, *80–84, 100*
Itineraries, *22–23*
Izakaya Iwashi ✕ , *169*

J

Jardin Botanique, *20, 75–76*
Jardin des Gouverneurs, *243*
Jazz clubs, *285*
Jewelry stores, *122, 130, 294*
Joe Beef ✕ , *156*
Jogging, *137*
Juste pour Rire, *25*

K

Kazu ✕ , *156*
Kem CoBa ✕ , *169*
King Edward Pier, *42*
Kitchen Galerie ✕ , *173*
Knowlton, *220, 222*

L

La Banquise ✕ , 162–163
La Belle Bédaine Casse-Croûte ✕ , 213–214
La Boulange ✕ , 312
La Chronique ✕ , 169
La Citadelle (fortress), 15, 20, 243, 245
La Clef des Champs ✕ , 204
La Cornetteria ✕ , 173
La Croissanterie Figaro ✕ , 167
La Ferme Monna L'Isle Ensorceleuse, 314
La Forge à Pique-Assaut (ironworks), 311
La Malbaie, 319–322
La Petite Boîte Vietnamienne ✕ , 271, 273
La Piazzeta ✕ , 262
La Roches des Brises (vineyard), 199
La Ronde (amusement park), 84
La Vielle Europe (shop), 125
Labo Culinaire Foodlab ✕ , 156
Lac aux Castors, 69
Lac Brome, 220, 222
Lachine Canal Historic Site, 45–46
Lachine Canal Nautical Centre, 46
Lachine Canal Visitor Services Centre, 46
Laloux ✕ , 163
Language, 28, 325–334, 341–342
Latin Quarter
 lodging, 190–191
 nightlife and the arts, 93, 96
 sightseeing, 57–58
Laurentians, 12, 197–209
Laurie Raphaël Restaurant-Atelier-Boutique ✕ , 269
L'Autre Jardin Auberge 🛏 , 283–284
Lawrence ✕ , 170
Le Billig ✕ , 273
Le Bouchon du Pied Bleu ✕ , 273
Le Café du Clocher Penché ✕ , 273
Le Café du Monde ✕ , 269
Le Café Krieghoff ✕ , 273
Le Canard Huppé 🛏 , 311–312
Le Carré Des Saveurs ✕ , 201
Le Centre Sheraton 🛏 , 189
Le Cep d 'Argent (winery), 224
Le Cercle ✕ , 273–274
Le Chantecler 🛏 , 204

Le Chic Shack ✕ , 267
Le Cochon Dingue ✕ , 269
Le Comptoir Charcuteries et Vins ✕ , 163
Le Continental ✕ , 267
Le Drugstore (gay club), 96
Le Glacier Bilboquet ✕ , 26
Le Grand Lodge 🛏 , 208
Le Hobbit Bistro ✕ , 274
Le Lab (bar), 98
Le Loft Hotel 🛏 , 191
Le Marriott Château Champlain 🛏 , 189
Le Mas des Oliviers ✕ , 156–157
Le Napolean ✕ , 214
Le Parlementaire ✕ , 274
Le Patriarche ✕ , 268
Le Petit Alep ✕ , 174
Le Petit Hôtel 🛏 , 185
Le Petit Italien ✕ , 167
Le Place d'Armes Hôtel & Suites 🛏 , 185–186
Le Saint-Amour ✕ , 268
Le St-Martin Hôtel Particulier 🛏 , 190
Le Saint-Sulpice 🛏 , 186
Le Taj ✕ , 157
Le Vin Papillon ✕ , 157–158
L'Echaudé ✕ , 269
Légende ✕ , 269–270
Leméac ✕ , 167
L'Entrecôte Saint-Jean ✕ , 267–268
L'Escalier du Casse-Cou, 254
Les 400 Coups ✕ , 151–152
Les FrancoFolies de Montréal, 24
Les Grands Ballets Canadiens de Montréal, 107
L'Express ✕ , 163
LHOTEL 🛏 , 186
L'Hôtel du Capitole 🛏 , 280–281
Lingerie shops, 122, 125
L'Initiale ✕ , 270
L'International des Feux Loto-Québec, 25
Little Italy, 26, 64–65, 128, 171–175
Lodging, 7, 187, 212, 341. ⇨ See also Hotels
Loews Hôtel Vogue 🛏 , 190
Loft rentals, 187
Louis Hébert ✕ , 274
Lower Town (Québec City)
 dining, 269–271
 lodging, 281–284
 shopping, 294–295

 sightseeing, 253–259
Lyla (shop), 126

M

M sur Masson ✕ , 176
Maestro S.V.P. ✕ , 164
Magnan ✕ , 158
Magog, 224–227
Maison Chevalier, 254
Maison Christian Faure ✕ , 152
Maison de Mere d'Youville, 43
Maison Gourdeau de Beaulieu, 309
Maison J.A. Moisan (shop), 262
Maison Kam Fung ✕ , 26, 160
Maison Louis-Jolliet, 254, 256
Maison Pierre du Calvet, 44
Maison Publique ✕ , 164
Maison René Richard (gallery), 317
Maison St-Gabriel, 40
Maison Smith, 69
Maisonneuve, 76
Manoir d'Auteuil 🛏 , 281
Manoir Hovey 🛏 , 227–228
Manoir Mauvide-Genest, 312
Maple syrup, 145
Marché Bonsecours, 44
Marché du Vieux-Port, 257
Marché Jean-Talon, 26, 65, 128
Marché Maisonneuve, 76
Marie Saint Pierre (shop), 120
M:brgr ✕ , 158
McGill University, 53, 55
Méchant Boeuf ✕ , 152
Melina Phyllo Bar ✕ , 170
Memorial Chapel, 305
Mezcla ✕ , 161
Microbrasserie d l'île de Orléans ✕ , 314
Mile End neighborhood
 dining, 168–171
 nightlife and the arts, 99–100
 shopping, 127
 sightseeing, 63–64
Milos ✕ , 170
Mister Steer ✕ , 158
MO851 (shop), 124
Moishe's ✕ , 164
Mondiale de la Bière, 24
Money matters, 7, 344–345
Money-saving tips, 35
Mont-St-Sauveur Water Park, 200
Mont-Tremblant, 14, 207–209
Montcalm Monument, 245
Montebello, 213–214

Montmorency Falls, *20, 303, 305*
Montréal, *12, 30–192*
Montréal Canadiens Hall of Fame, *55*
Montréal en Lumière, *24*
Montréal International Jazz Festival, *24–25, 103*
Morin Heights, *202–203*
Morrin Cultural Centre, *250*
Mortimer Snodgrass (shop), *117*
Moulin de St-Laurent ✕ , *311*
Moulin Wakefield Mill Hotel and Spa 🛏 , *215*
Musée d'Archéologie et d'Histoire Pointe-à-Callière, *41*
Musée d'Art Contemporain, *49–50*
Musée d'Art Contemporain de Baie-St-Paul, *317*
Musée de Charlevoix, *321*
Musée de la Civilisation, *20, 256*
Musée de la Nature et des Sciences, *228–229*
Musée de la Place Royale, *257*
Musée de L'Abeille, *305*
Musée de l'Amérique Francophone, *250–251, 252*
Musée de Québec, *20*
Musée de Sainte Anne, *303*
Musée des Beaux-Arts de Montréal, *14, 50–51*
Musée des Beaux-Arts de Sherbrooke, *229*
Musée des Hospitalières de l'Hôtel-Dieu, *61–62*
Musée des Ursulines, *245*
Musée du Château Ramezay, *42*
Musée du Fort, *251*
Musée du Ski des Laurentides, *201*
Musée Historique du Comté de Brome, *220*
Musée Maritime de Charlevoix, *318*
Musée McCord de l'Histoire Canadienne, *51*
Musée National des Beaux-Arts du Québec, *245–246*
Musée Royal 22e Régiment, *243, 245*
Museums, *21, 35*
Montréal, *14, 20, 40, 41–42, 43, 46, 49–51, 55, 61–62, 64, 75–76, 78, 80, 83*

Québec City, *243, 245–246, 247, 250–251, 252, 256, 257*
side trips from Montréal, *201, 214–215, 220, 228–229*
side trips from Québec City, *303, 305, 309, 312, 317, 318, 321*
Music, live
Montréal, *10, 21, 93, 99, 100, 105–106*
Québec City, *285, 287*

N

Nightlife and the arts, *11*
Montréal, *86–110*
Québec City, *284–287*
side trips from Montréal, *209, 222, 228, 229*
side trips from Québec City, *321–322*
Nora Gray ✕ , *158–159*
North Hatley, *227–228*
Notre-Dame-des-Bois, *229–230*
Nouveau Palais ✕ , *170–171*

O

Observation Tower (St-François), *313*
Observatoire de la Capitale, *262*
Observatoire de l'Est, *69*
Officer's Quarters, *246*
Ogilvy (department store), *122*
Oka, *198–200*
Old Montréal
dining, *147–154*
lodging, *180, 184–186*
nightlife and the arts, *87–90*
shopping, *114–117*
sightseeing, *36–45*
Old Port (Montréal), *14–15, 20, 42*
Old Port (Québec), *256–257*
Olive + Gourmando ✕ , *152–153*
Opera, *105*
Orange Rouge ✕ , *160*
Oratoire St-Joseph, *71–72*
Orchestre Symphonique de Montréal, *105*
Orchestre Symphonique de Québec, *287*
Osteria Venti ✕ , *153*
Outaouais, *12, 209–215*
Outdoor activities. ⇨ *See* Sports and outdoor activities
Outremont neighborhood
dining, *166–168*
nightlife and the arts, *100*

shopping, *126–127*
sightseeing, *63*
Outside the Old City (Québec City)
dining, *271, 273–275*
lodging, *283–284*
nightlife and the arts, *285–286*
shopping, *295–296*
sightseeing, *260–264*

P

Packing, *345*
Panache ✕ , *270*
Parc Aquarium du Québec, *20, 264*
Parc de la Chute-Montmorency, *20, 303, 305*
Parc de l'Artillerie, *246*
Parc des Champs-de-Bataille, *246*
Parc d'Oka, *199–200*
Parc du Mont-Mégantic, *230*
Parc du Mont-Orford, *223*
Parc du Mont-Royal, *14, 66–69, 72*
Parc Jean-Drapeau, *83*
Parc Jeanne d'Arc, *246*
Parc Lafontaine, *20, 62*
Parc Maisonneuve, *76*
Parc Marin du Saguenay-St-Laurent, *323–324*
Parc Maritime de St-Laurent, *311*
Parc National du Mont-Tremblant, *207*
Parc Omega, *213*
Park ✕ , *175*
Parks and gardens
Montréal, *14, 20, 45–46, 62, 66–69, 72, 75–76, 83*
Québec City, *243, 246, 248, 250*
side trips from Montréal, *199–200, 207, 213, 215, 223, 230*
side trips from Québec City, *303, 305, 311, 323–324*
Passports, *345*
Pastaga ✕ , *174*
Patente et Machin ✕ , *274*
Patisserie Au Kouign Amann ✕ , *164–165*
Patisserie Rhubarbe ✕ , *165*
Patrice Pâtissier ✕ , *159*
Performing arts. ⇨ *See* Nightlife and the arts
Phil Smoked Meat ✕ , *275*
Piggery (theater), *228*
Pilsen Pub ✕ , *227*

Pintxo ✕ , *165*
Pizzeria Magpie ✕ , *171*
Place d'Armes (square; Mon-
tréal), *45*
Place d'Armes (square; Québec
City), *247*
Place de la Grande-Paix, *45*
Place de Paris (square), *259*
Place des Arts, *55*
Place du Canada, *55–56*
Place Jacques-Cartier, *43*
Place Royale (square; Mon-
tréal), *20, 45*
Place Royale (square; Québec
City), *257*
Place Ville-Marie, *55*
Plage de l'Île Notre-Dame, *84*
Plains of Abraham (battle site),
15, 20, 247
Plante Family Farm, *309*
Planetariums, *79*
Plateau Mont-Royal
dining, 26, 161–166
lodging, 191–192
nightlife and the arts, 98–99
shopping, 124–126
sightseeing, 60–62
Pôle des Rapides, *46*
Politics, *10, 21*
Portofino Bistro Italiano ✕ ,
268
Portus Calle ✕ , *165*
Poterie de Port-au-Persil, *321*
Poutine, *18, 144*
Pretty Ballerinas (shop),
129–130
Prices, *7*
hotels, 180, 197, 275, 302
restaurants, 146, 197, 264, 302
Promenade des Gouverneurs,
247
Promenade Samuel-de-Cham-
plain, *263*
Public transportation, *34, 87*
Pullman (bar), *91*

Q

Qing Hua Dumplings ✕ , *159*
Quartier Latin
lodging, 190–191
nightlife and the arts, 93, 96
sightseeing, 57–58
Quartier Petit-Champlain
(mall), *295*
Québec City, *12, 232–296*
Québec City Summer Festival,
24, 288
Québec-Lévis Ferry, *257*

R

Racines ✕ , *153*
Rafting, *290*
Redpath Museum of Natural
History, *21, 55*
Refuge Morin Heights 🏨 , *203*
Relais St-Denis 🏨 , *201*
Réserve Faunique des Lauren-
tides (wildlife reserve), *307*
Rèserve Faunique du Cap Tourmente (wildlife reserve), *305*
Reservoir (bar), *98*
Restaurant Helena ✕ , *153*
Restaurant Le Cheval de Jade
✕ , *208*
Restaurant le H4C ✕ , *175*
Restaurant Toast! ✕ , *270*
Restaurants, *7, 26, 343*
best bets, 143, 266
business hours, 146
cafés, 19
children, 146
dress, 146, 343
late-night, 106
menu guide, 331–334
Montréal, 142–176
prices, 7, 146, 197, 264, 302
*Québec City, 262–263,
264–275*
reservations, 146, 343
*side trips from Montréal,
196, 201, 203, 204, 205,
207–208, 213–214, 215,
227, 229*
*side trips from Québec City,
301, 307, 311, 312, 314*
*wines, beer, and spirits, 145,
343*
Restrooms, *345*
Rio Tinto Alcan
Planétarium, *79*
Ristorante Lucca ✕ , *174*
Ritz-Carlton Montréal 🏨 , *190*
Rosalie ✕ , *159–160*
Rosemont, *176*
Rotisserie Panama ✕ , *171*
Route des Vins, *218*
Route 362, *318*
Route Verte, *135*
Royal Phoenix (gay bar), *100*
Rue Amherst, *115*
Rue Bernard, *115*
Rue Chabanel, *115*
Rue du Petit-Champlain, *259*
Rue Notre-Dame Ouest, *115*
Rue Prince-Arthur, *62*
Rumi ✕ , *165–166*

S

Ste-Adèle, *203–204*
Ste-Agathe-des-Monts, *206*
Ste-Famille, *313–314*
St-François, *313*
St. George's Anglican
Church, *56*
St-Jean, *312*
St-Jean-sur-Richelieu's Hot-Air
Balloon Festival, *25*
St-Joseph-de-la-Rive, *318–319*
St-Laurent de l'Ille d'Orléans,
311–312
St-Louis Forts and Châteaux
National Historic Site,
247–248
St. Matthew's Cemetery,
263–264
St. Patrick's Basilica, *51*
Ste-Pétronille, *309–310*
St-Pierre, *314–315*
St-Roch, *263*
St-Sauveur-des-Monts,
200–202
St-Viateur Bagel & Café ✕ ,
26, 166
Sapristi ✕ , *268*
Scala Santa, *305*
Schwartz's Delicatessen ✕ ,
26, 166
Shed 16's Labyrinthe, *42*
Séminaire du Québec, *251–252*
Sherbrooke, *228–229*
Shoe stores, *123, 125–126,
130*
Shopping, *17, 26*
*centers and malls, 117, 123,
201, 262–263, 295, 296*
hours, 112
markets, 125, 128, 219, 257
Montréal, 112–130
*Québec City, 259, 262–263,
293–296*
sales tax, 112, 114
shopping districts, 115
*side trips from Montréal, 201,
203, 205–206, 219, 222, 229*
*side trips from Québec City,
308, 314–315, 319*
Side trips
from Montréal, 194–230
from Québec City, 298–324
Simple Snack Sympathique ✕ ,
270–271
Ski chalets, lodging in, *212*
Skiing, *17*
Montréal, 137, 140
Québec City, 290–291

side trips from Montréal,
   201–202, 204, 206, 209,
   219, 227
side trips from Québec City,
   307, 322
Snow slides, *291*
Snowboarding, *137, 140*
Snowmobiling, *291*
Sofitel Montréal ⊤, *190*
Spa Eastman ⊤, *224, 226*
Sparrow ✕, *171*
Spas, *19, 203, 219, 293, 308*
Sports and outdoor activities,
   11, 17, 18–19, 20
Montréal, 46, 132–140
Québec City, 287–293
side trips from Montréal,
   201–202, 204, 206, 209,
   219–220, 226–227
side trips from Québec City,
   307, 322, 323, 324
Springhill Suites by Marriott
   ⊤, *186*
Square Dorchester, *55–56*
Square St-Louis, *58*
Square Victoria, *45*
Stade Olympique, *79*
Stationery shops, *118–119*
Steamies, *145*
Stewart Museum, *83*
Student housing, *187*
Su ✕, *176*
Subway (Métro), *62*
Supper clubs, *93, 99*
Swimming, *140*
Symbols, *7*

T

Tadoussac, *15, 20, 322–324*
Tapeo ✕, *174*
Tarte au Sucre, *144*
Taxes, *112, 114, 345–346*
Taxis, *35*
Telephones, *342*
Terrasse Dufferin (boardwalk),
   20, 247
Theater
Montréal, 24, 55, 76, 109–110
Québec City, 286, 287
side trips from Montréal, 222,
   228, 229
Théâtre Denise Pelletier, *76*
Théâtre du Nouveau Monde,
   110
Théâtre Lac Brome, *222*
Tickets, *87, 103*
Time zones, *346*
Timing the trip
Montréal, 35

Québec City, 237
side trips from Montréal, 198
side trips from Québec City,
   301
Tipping, *346*
TNT (shop), *130*
Toqué! ✕, *153–154*
Tour Olympique, *79*
Tourist passes, *35*
Tours, *346–347*
Montréal, 26–27, 44, 135
Québec City, 234–235, 251
side trips from Montréal, 206
Tours Martello, *252*
Tourtière, *144*
Town of Mount Royal (TMR),
   73, 130
Toy shops, *117, 296*
Train travel, *64, 237, 301, 340*
Transportation, *336–340*
Montréal, 34–35, 87
Québec City, 237
side trips from Montréal, 198,
   212, 216
side trips from Québec City,
   301, 309, 315
Très Chic Styling (shop), *126*
TRYP by Wyndham Québec
   Hotel Pur ⊤, *284*

U

Underground City, *47, 51, 53*
Upper Town (Québec City)
dining, 265, 267–268
lodging, 275, 279–281
nightlife and the arts, 284–285
shopping, 293–294
sightseeing, 238–254
Upstairs Jazz Bar & Grill, *93*

V

Val-David, *205–206*
Van Horne ✕, *167–168*
Verdun, *176*
Vestibule (shop), *127–128*
Victoria Village, *115*
Vieux-Montréal (Old Montréal)
dining, 147–154
lodging, 180, 184–186
nightlife and the arts, 87–90
shopping, 114–117
sightseeing, 36–45
Vieux Port (Montréal), *14–15,*
   20, 42
Vieux Port (Québec), *256–257*
Vignoble de l'Orpailleur (vine-
   yard), *218*
Vignoble de Ste-Pétronille
   (vineyard), *309–310*

Vignoble Domaine Côtes
   d'Ardoise (vineyard), *218*
Vignoble Les Trois Clochers
   (vineyard), *218*
Village, The, *57, 58–59, 96,*
   123, 160–161
Village du Père Noël, *20, 205*
Vinizza ✕, *175*
Visas, *345*
Visitor information, *87, 103,*
   198, 207, 213, 216, 237,
   302, 309, 347–348
Vocabulary, *325–334*

W

W Montréal ⊤, *186*
Walking tours
Montréal, 44
Québec City, 234–235, 251
Water parks, *20, 200, 291, 293*
Weather
Montréal, 35
Québec City, 237
side trips from Montréal, 198,
   212, 216
side trips from Québec City,
   301
Web sites, *347–348*
Westmount neighborhood,
   128–130, 175
Whale-watching, *323, 324*
Wineries, *199, 218, 224,*
   309–310, 314
Winter Carnival, *293*
Winter sports, *17*
Wolfe-Montcalm Monument,
   243
Wolfe Monument, *248*
Word, The (shop), *119*

PHOTO CREDITS

NOTES

NOTES

NOTES

NOTES

NOTES

NOTES

NOTES

NOTES

NOTES

NOTES

ABOUT OUR WRITERS

 Chris Barry is a native Montrealer and freelance journalist who has contributed to scores of publications over the years and has been writing for the *Fodor's Montréal and Québec City* guide since 2002. He's currently finishing a book documenting his years as a professional rock-and-roll musician in the 1970s, '80s, and '90s. Chris updated the Montréal Nightlife, Performing Arts, and Sports and the Outdoors chapters of this book.

 Rémy Charest is a Québec City–based writer and translator. He has been writing about wine and food since 1997 for *Le Devoir, Coup de Pouce, EnRoute, Wine Access, Châtelaine, Palate Press,* and the Quebecor/Sun Media chain of newspapers. Time permitting, he posts on two wine blogs (*www.winecase.ca* in English, and *www.achacunsabouteille.wordpress. com* in French) as well as two food blogs (*www.foodcase.ca* in English, and *www. achacunsafourchette.wordpress.com* in French). He updated the Québec City and Side Trips from Québec City chapters.

 Marcella DeVincenzo is a freelance writer from Montréal who adores her city: she is particularly fond of finding Montréal's hidden gems and sharing them with the world. Marcella has two websites, *www. cucinachronicles.ca* and *www.foodnoise. co,* and is currently coauthoring a cookbook called *Respecting the Vegetable.* For this edition, Marcella updated the Exploring, Experience, and Side Trips from Montréal chapters.

 Joanne Latimer doesn't expect any sympathy, since she's tasked with grading the linens at boutique hotels. As a freelance writer and Canadian National Magazine Award winner, her work appears in *Maclean's,* the *New York Times,* the *Montreal Gazette,* and the *Ottawa Citizen.* Her blog, www. sinussister.com, is a comedy sensation, with endorsement from comics Rob Corddry, Colin Quinn, Jimmy Carr, Russell Howard, and Alonzo Bodden. Joanne is based in Montréal and updated the Where to Stay chapter.

 Vanessa Muri is a lifestyle writer and editor from Montréal, working regularly for fashion and beauty magazine *The Kit, Tourism Montréal,* and is the former Montréal editor of *sweetspot.ca.* She loves fashion, food, wine, and travel, though not necessarily in that order. Having lived in London and Tokyo, the lures of her hometown ultimately proved difficult to resist. For this edition, Vanessa updated the Montréal Shopping and Travel Smart chapters.

 Mayssam Samaha is a food and travel writer and blogger. Born and raised in Lebanon, she lived in New York City before settling in Montréal and starting her blog, www.willtravelfor-food.com. From Michelin-starred restaurants across the planet to the latest hole-in-the-wall down the street, Mayssam roams the planet in search of culinary discoveries. She updated the Where to Eat chapter for this edition.

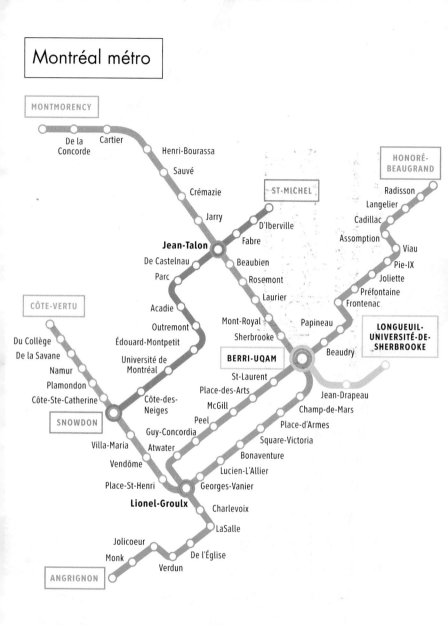

Montréal métro

MONTMORENCY

De la Concorde · Cartier
Henri-Bourassa
Sauvé
Crémazie
Jarry

ST-MICHEL

D'Iberville
Jean-Talon · Fabre
De Castelnau · Beaubien
Parc · Rosemont
Laurier
Acadie
Outremont · Mont-Royal · Papineau
Édouard-Montpetit · Sherbrooke

HONORÉ-BEAUGRAND

Radisson
Langelier
Cadillac
Assomption
Viau
Pie-IX
Joliette
Préfontaine
Frontenac
Beaudry

CÔTE-VERTU

Du Collège
De la Savane
Namur
Plamondon
Côte-Ste-Catherine

Université de Montréal

BERRI-UQAM

LONGUEUIL-UNIVERSITÉ-DE-SHERBROOKE

SNOWDON

Côte-des-Neiges
St-Laurent
Place-des-Arts
McGill
Peel
Guy-Concordia
Atwater
Jean-Drapeau
Champ-de-Mars
Place-d'Armes
Square-Victoria
Bonaventure
Lucien-L'Allier
Georges-Vanier

Villa-Maria
Vendôme
Place-St-Henri
Lionel-Groulx
Charlevoix
LaSalle

Jolicoeur
Monk
De l'Église
Verdun

ANGRIGNON